AMERICA:
THE STORY OF A FREE PEOPLE

BY

ALLAN NEVINS AND
HENRY STEELE COMMAGER

THE HERITAGE OF AMERICA

AMERICA: THE STORY OF A FREE PEOPLE

L. C. Handy Studios

ABRAHAM LINCOLN

From a photograph made by Brady in 1864

AMERICA
THE STORY OF A
FREE PEOPLE

by

ALLAN NEVINS *and*
HENRY STEELE COMMAGER

ILLUSTRATED

LITTLE, BROWN AND COMPANY · BOSTON
1942

Out of the flesh, out of the minds and hearts
Of thousand upon thousand common men,
Cranks, martyrs, starry-eyed enthusiasts,
Slow-spoken neighbors, hard to push around,
Women whose hands were gentle with their kids
And men with a cold passion for mere justice.
We made this thing, this dream.
This land unsatisfied by little ways,
Open to every man who brought good will,
This peaceless vision, groping for the stars,
Not as a huge devouring machine
Rolling and clanking with remorseless force
Over submitted bodies and the dead
But as live earth where anything could grow,
Your crankiness, my notions and his dream,
Grow and be looked at, grow and live or die,
But get their chance of growing and the sun.
We made it and we make it and it's ours.
We shall maintain it. It shall be sustained.
            —STEPHEN VINCENT BENÉT, *Listen to the People*

ACKNOWLEDGMENTS

For arrangements made with various publishing houses, authors, and literary agents whereby certain copyrighted material was permitted to be reprinted, and for the courtesy extended by them, the following acknowledgments are gratefully made: —

To BRANDT AND BRANDT for the quotation from "Listen to the People," from *Selected Works of Stephen Vincent Benét,* published by Farrar & Rinehart, Inc., copyright, 1941, by Stephen Vincent Benét.

To THE MACMILLAN COMPANY for Vachel Lindsay's "Bryan, Bryan, Bryan."

To EVERETT DICK and D. APPLETON-CENTURY COMPANY, INC. for the quotation from *The Sod-House Frontier.*

To THE BOBBS-MERRILL COMPANY for the quotation from Herbert Quick's *The Hawkeye.*

CONTENTS

ILLUSTRATIONS

MAPS

Chapter One

THE PLANTING OF THE COLONIES

Natural Features of North America

THE history of English settlement in America began on a beautiful April morning in 1607, when three storm-beaten ships of Captain Christopher Newport anchored near the mouth of Chesapeake Bay, sending ashore men who found "fair meadows, and goodly tall trees, with such fresh waters as almost ravished" them to see. With these ships were George Percy, the active, handsome son of the Earl of Northumberland, and Captain John Smith. Percy records how they found noble forests, the ground carpeted with flowers; fine strawberries, "four times bigger and better than ours in England"; oysters "very large and delicate in taste"; much small game; "stores of turkey nests and many eggs"; and an Indian town, where the savages brought them corn bread and tobacco smoked in clay pipes with copper bowls. For a time these first experiences in Virginia seemed enchanting. Percy's *Observations* describes the delight of the newcomers in the richly colored birds, the fruits and berries, the fine sturgeon, and the pleasant scenery. But his brave narrative, full of a wild poetry, ends in something like a shriek. For he tells how the Indians attacked the settlers, "creeping on all fours from the hills, like bears, with their bows in their mouths"; how the men were seized by "cruel diseases, such as swellings, fluxes, burning fevers"; and how many died

I

of sheer famine, "their bodies trailed out of their cabins like dogs to be buried."

The planting of a new nation in America was no holiday undertaking. It meant grim, dirty, toilsome, dangerous work. Here was a great shaggy continent, its Eastern third covered with pathless forests; its mountains, rivers, lakes, and rolling plains all upon a grandiose scale; its Northern stretches fiercely cold in winter, its Southern areas burning hot in summer; filled with wild beasts, and peopled by a warlike, cruel, and treacherous people still in the Stone Age of culture. In many respects it was a forbidding land. It could be reached only by a voyage so perilous that some ships buried as many as they landed. But despite all its drawbacks, it was admirably fitted to become the home of an energetic, thriving people.

North America is a roughly triangular continent, of which the widest part—a rich, variegated, and, in general, well-watered area—lies between the twenty-sixth and fifty-fifth parallels. Here the climate is healthful, with a warm summer which permits of fine crops and a cold winter that stimulates men to activity. Europeans could establish themselves in this area without any painful process of adjustment. They could bring their chief food crops: wheat, rye, oats, beans, carrots, and onions. They found in the new land two novel foods of remarkable value—maize and potatoes. The "Indian corn," if planted in May, would yield roasting ears in July and later furnished fodder for cattle, husk beds for the settlers, and an unequaled yield of grain. Everywhere game abounded, the deer and bison roaming in millions, the passenger pigeons darkening the sky with their flocks. The coastal waters were rich in fish. A search in due time revealed that North America contained more iron, coal, copper, and petroleum than any other continent. It had almost boundless forests. Bays and harbors gave many shelters along the Eastern shore, which in general was low, while broad rivers—the St. Lawrence, Connecticut, Hudson, Delaware, Susquehanna, Potomac, James, Pedee, Savannah—made it easy to penetrate a considerable distance into the interior. A foothold could be gained and enlarged without excessive hardship.

Certain natural features of the continent were destined to have a marked effect upon the future course of the American nation. The many bays and inlets on the Atlantic Coast made for numerous small colonies rather than a few large ones. Fifteen in all were soon established, counting Nova Scotia and Quebec, and they gave America in its early history a rich variety of institutions. Each clung tenaciously to its own character. When independence came, the nation built out of thirteen of these units simply had to be a federation. Behind the coastal plain rose a wide, wild mountain barrier, the Appalachian range. It was so hard to cross that the coastal settlements grew fairly thick and sturdy, with well-rooted ways, before the people expended any great strength upon trans-Appalachian expansion. When they did push west, they traversed the mountains to find before them a huge central plain, the Mississippi basin. This, comprising nearly half the area of the United States and more than half of its cultivated land, was so flat that communication was easy; particularly as it was seamed east and west by many navigable streams—the Wisconsin, Iowa, Illinois, Ohio, Cumberland, Tennessee, Arkansas, and Red—and north and south by the great Mississippi-Missouri river system. Settlers covered this fertile basin with rapid ease. Men from all parts of the seaboard and all countries of western Europe intermingled in it on equal terms. It became a great pool in which a new democracy and a new American sentiment developed.

Farther west were high plains with so dry a climate that

they, with the high Rocky Mountains just beyond, long delayed the onward sweep of settlement. The gold and other minerals of the distant Pacific slope attracted a host of adventurous pioneers several decades before these half-arid plains were wrested from the Indians. California was a populous and powerful state at a time when a wide un-settled belt still separated it and Oregon from the older parts of the United States. But this belt did not long remain a solitude. Following the buffalo hunters, the cattle ranchers rapidly covered the plains, while population gradually thickened as the railroads brought the materials needed for the conquest of the treeless country: barbed wire, wind-mills, lumber, and agricultural implements. Irrigated farms, too, gained in number. By 1890 the frontier had substan-tially disappeared, and the wild West was no more.

It was inevitable from the beginning that the movement of settlement in America should in general follow east-to-west lines. From the Atlantic seaboard the St. Lawrence and Great Lakes waterway, which offered the readiest access to the interior, ran roughly in an east-and-west di-rection. The Mohawk Valley break in the northern Appa-lachians, which in due time furnished a site for the Erie Canal, afforded another east-west route. The Ohio Valley, a third great artery for settlement, roughly follows an east-west line. To a striking degree, emigration all the way from the Atlantic to the Rockies tended to pursue parallels of latitude. It was also inevitable that the French sovereignty over Louisiana, and the Mexican sovereignty over Califor-nia and the Southwest, should melt away before the ad-vance of English-speaking Americans. Even in colonial days keen-sighted observers pointed out that the people who controlled the Ohio Valley must in time control the Missis-sippi. It was equally true that the people who controlled the Mississippi basin must eventually control the whole area west of it. With superior numbers and energy, the Americans made the most of their geographical advantages.

It was fortunate for the white settlers that the Indians of North America were too few and too backward to be a grave impediment to colonization. They harassed and at times delayed it; they never really stopped it. When the first Europeans arrived, the Indians east of the Mississippi probably numbered not more than two hundred thousand. Those of the whole continent north of Mexico certainly did not exceed five hundred thousand. Armed only with the bow and arrow, the tomahawk, and the war club, and ignorant of any military art save the ambush, they were ordinarily no match for well-accoutered and vigilant bodies of whites. For that matter, they had shown little capacity to subdue nature, and, as they lived mainly by hunting and fishing, their resources were precarious. Most of the hundreds of tribes in the fifty-nine recognized "families" north of Mexico were small and could muster no formidable war bands. The most powerful Indian organization was the Five (later Six) Nations of the Iroquois family, whose stronghold was western New York, who had a general council, and who pursued an aggressive policy which made them dreaded by the neighboring Algonquin tribes. In the Southeast the Creeks had set up another strong confederacy of the Muskogean family. Far in the Northwest, on the upper plains, the Sioux had established a somewhat looser organization.

The struggle between the settlers and the Indians in the colonial period passed through several well-marked stages. No sooner were the first colonies planted than most of them came into sharp local conflict with small neighboring tribes. A good illustration is afforded by the fierce, brief Pequot War in New England, which in 1637 ended in the complete destruction of the Pequot tribe inhabiting the Connecticut Valley; another illustration is furnished by the war between the Virginia settlers and Powhatan's tribes, which began in 1622 and also ended in utter Indian defeat. But as the white newcomers advanced, seizing larger tracts of land, the Indians formed extensive tribal alliances for resistance. King Philip, for example, rallied several important New England tribes who fought heroically for two years before they were crushed; while the North Carolina settlers faced a similar combination in the Tuscarora War, and the South Carolina settlers in the Yamassee War. These struggles were stern and extensive and caused the whites severe losses in life and property. Finally came the phase of warfare in which the Indians found European allies. Some of the Northern tribes combined with the French; some of the Southern tribes received arms and encouragement from the Spaniards. Fortunately for the English-speaking settlers, the powerful Iroquois Confederacy took a friendly attitude and lent active aid in operations against the French. In the end, the hostile Indians were as decisively defeated in this third phase of warfare as in the preceding two.

The Early Settlers

To the raw new continent the first British settlers came in bold groups. The ships that under Christopher Newport sailed into Hampton Roads on the 13th of May, 1607, carried men alone. They laid out Jamestown, with a fort, a church, a storehouse, and a row of little huts. When calamity fell upon them, Captain John Smith showed a nerve, resourcefulness, and energy that in the second year made him president and practical dictator of the colony. Agriculture was slowly developed; in 1612 John Rolfe began to grow tobacco, and as it brought high prices in the London market everyone took it up, till even the market place was planted with it; hogs and cattle increased.

Yet growth was slow. By 1619 Virginia had no more than two thousand people. That year was notable for three events. One was the arrival of a ship from England with ninety "young maidens" who were to be given as wives to those settlers who would pay a hundred and twenty pounds of tobacco for their transportation. This cargo was so joyously welcomed that others like it were soon sent over. Equally important was the initiation of representative government in America. On July 30, in that Jamestown church where John Rolfe several years earlier had cemented a temporary peace with the Indians by marrying Pocahontas, met the first legislative assembly on the continent: a governor, six councilors, and two burgesses each from ten plantations. The third significant event of the year was the arrival in August of a Dutch ship with Negro slaves, of whom it sold twenty to the settlers.

While Virginia was thus shooting into vigor, a congregation of English Calvinists who had settled in Holland were making plans to remove to the New World. These "Pilgrims," who had been persecuted because they denied the ecclesiastical supremacy of the king and wished to set up a separate Church of their own, had originally come from the village of Scrooby, in Nottinghamshire. In every way they were a remarkable body. They had three leaders of conspicuous ability: the teacher John Robinson, a learned, broad-minded, generous-hearted graduate of Cambridge; their sage elder, William Brewster, also a Cambridge man; and William Bradford, shrewd, forcible, and idealistic. The rank and file possessed integrity, industry, and sobriety, as well as courage and fortitude. They had endured popular hostility in England; they had withstood loneliness and harsh toil in Holland. Now, securing a patent to settle in America, a ship called the *Mayflower*, and a store of provisions, they prepared to face the rigors of the wilderness.

Sailing from Plymouth one hundred and two in number, the Pilgrims on December 11 (Old Style), 1620, landed on the Massachusetts coast. That winter more than half of them died of cold and scurvy. But the next summer they raised good crops, and in the fall a ship brought new settlers. Their resolution never faltered. When the Narraganset chief, Canonicus, sent them a bundle of arrows in a snake-skin as a challenge to war, Bradford stuffed the skin with bullets and returned it with a defiant message.

Then in rapid succession emerged other English colonies. The parent hive was ready to send forth its swarms. A May day in 1629 saw the London wharves a scene of bustle and cheery excitement; five ships carrying four hundred settlers and nearly two hundred head of livestock, the largest body thus far sent across the Atlantic at one time, were sailing for Massachusetts Bay. Before the end of June they arrived at Salem, where John Endecott and a small group of asso-ciates had planted a town the previous autumn. These people were Puritans—that is, members of the Church of England who at first wished to reform or purify its doc-trines and who finally withdrew from it—and they opened a great Puritan exodus. In the spring of 1630 John Win-throp reached Salem with eleven ships carrying nine hun-dred settlers, enough to found eight new towns, including Boston. The Massachusetts Bay colony grew so rapidly that it was soon throwing off branches to the south and west. Roger Williams, a minister of Salem who courageously taught the separation of Church and state, with other rad-ical views, was driven into the Rhode Island wilderness. Here in 1636 he founded Providence as a place of perfect religious toleration. In that year, too, the first migration to Connecticut began under the resolute Reverend Thomas Hooker, who moved a great part of his congregation from Cambridge westward in a body. Another notable colony sprang into existence in 1634, when the first settlement was made in Maryland under the guidance of the liberal-minded Cecilius Calvert, second Lord Baltimore. Most of the gentlemen who first went thither were, like the founder, English Catholics, while most of the common folk were Protestants. Toleration was therefore essential, and Maryland was a home of religious freedom, attracting people of varied faiths. Before long, settlers from Virginia were venturing into what is now North Carolina, a number taking up land along Albemarle Sound about 1650.

The seat of one rich colony was gained by conquest. The Dutch had sent Henry Hudson, an English mariner, to explore the river which bears his name—a task executed in 1609. Dutch fur traders had followed him, and in 1624 a small settlement was effected on Manhattan Island. The province of New Netherland grew but slowly and failed to develop institutions of self-government. Meanwhile, the English never gave up their claim to the entire coast, and the Connecticut settlements were anxious for the seizure of their troublesome neighbor. Why permit this alien element in the very center of British America? Charles II granted the area to his brother, the Duke of York, who took vigorous action. In the summer of 1664 three warships arrived before New Amsterdam. They carried a body of soldiers who were reinforced by Connecticut troops, while forces were promised from Massachusetts and Long Island. Most of the Dutch settlers, sick of despotic rule, made no objection to a change of sovereignty. Although old Peter Stuyvesant declared he would rather be "carried out dead" than surrender, he had no choice. The British flag went up over the town renamed New York and, save for a brief intermission during a subsequent Anglo-Dutch war (1672–1674), it stayed there. Indeed, the British flag now waved from the Kennebec to Florida.

Yet one of the most interesting colonies did not take on firm outlines till late in the century. A number of settlers, British, Dutch, and Swedish, had found their way into the area which later became Pennsylvania and Delaware. When the kindly, farsighted William Penn came into control of the region in 1681, he prepared to erect a model common-wealth on the principles of the Quakers—that sect which Voltaire later called the most truly Christian of peoples. In his benevolent fashion, he quieted the Indian title by friendly treaties of purchase. To attract colonists he offered liberal terms, assuring all that they could obtain land, estab-lish thrifty homes, and live in justice and equality with their neighbors. No Christian would suffer from religious discrimination. In civil affairs the laws would rule, and the people would be a party to the laws. He directed the estab-lishment of Philadelphia, his "city of brotherly love," with gardens surrounding each house, so that it would be "a green country town . . . and always be wholesome." In 1682 he came over himself, bringing about a hundred col-onists. Pennsylvania throve wonderfully, attracting a great variety of settlers from Britain and the Continent, but keeping its Quaker lineaments.

Roughly speaking, two main instruments were used in this work of transferring Britons and others across the seas and founding new states. It was the chartered trading com-pany, organized primarily for profit, which planted Vir-ginia and Massachusetts. The London Company, so-called because organized by stockholders resident in London, had been granted its charter in 1606 to plant a colony between the thirty-fourth and forty-first degrees of latitude. The Plymouth Company, whose stockholders lived in Plymouth, Bristol, and other towns, was chartered that same year to establish a colony between the thirty-eighth and forty-fifth degrees. These companies could distribute lands, operate

mines, coin money, and organize the defense of their colonies. The king, who granted the charters, kept ultimate
jurisdiction over the colonial governments. After heavy
financial losses, the London Company in 1624 saw its charter revoked, the king making Virginia a royal colony. The
Plymouth Company promoted various small Northern settlements and fishing stations, but made no money, and
after reorganization asked in 1635 for annulment of its
charter, calling itself "only a breathless carcass."

Yet if neither the London nor Plymouth Company was
profitable financially, both did an effective work in colonization. The London Company was in a very real sense the
parent of Virginia; the Plymouth Company and its successor, the Council for New England, founded town after
town in Maine, New Hampshire, and Massachusetts.
And a third corporation, the Massachusetts Bay Company,
had a peculiar character and a special destiny. It originated
as a body of stockholders, most of them Puritans, who had
commercial and patriotic motives. Undaunted by the failure
of the earlier companies to pay dividends, they believed that
better management would yield profits. Charles I granted a
charter early in 1629. Then a strange development took
place. When the king and High Church party under Arch-
bishop Laud became masters of the Church of England,
many Puritan leaders wished to emigrate. They had property, social position, and an independent spirit. They did
not wish to go out to Massachusetts Bay as mere vassals of
a company in London. Moreover, they hoped to secure liberty to set up the kind of Church government they liked.
Therefore, the principal Puritans of the company simply
bought up all its stock, took the charter, and sailed with it
to America. A commercial company was thus converted
into a self-governing colony—the colony of Massachusetts
Bay.

The other principal instrument of colonization was the proprietary grant. The proprietor was a man belonging to the British gentry or nobility, with money at his command, to whom the Crown gave a tract in America as it might have given him an estate at home. The old rule of English law was that all land not otherwise held belonged to the king, and America fell under this rule. Lord Baltimore received Maryland; William Penn, the son of an admiral to whom the king owed money, received Pennsylvania; and a group of royal favorites under Charles II received the Carolinas. All these proprietors were given large powers to devise a government. Lord Baltimore, who had some of the absolutist ideas of the Stuarts, was averse to giving his colonists any lawmaking power, but finally yielded to a popularly created assembly. Penn was wiser. In 1682 he called together an assembly, all of whom were elected by the settlers, and allowed them to enact a constitution, or "Great Charter." This vested many of the powers of government in representatives of the people—and Penn accepted the scheme.

As soon as it was proved that life in America might be prosperous and hopeful, a great spontaneous migration from Europe began. It came by uneven spurts and drew its strength from a variety of impulses. The first two great waves went to Massachusetts and Virginia. From 1628 to 1640 the Puritans in England were in a state of depression and apprehension, suffering much actual persecution. The royal authorities were committed to a revival of old forms in the Church and determined to make it completely dependent on the Crown and the archbishops. Political as well as ecclesiastical turmoil racked the land. The king dissolved Parliament and for ten years got on without it. He imprisoned his chief opponents. As his party seemed bent on subverting English liberty, many Puritans believed that the best course was to quit the island and build in America a new state. In the great emigration of 1628–1640, some twenty thousand of the sturdiest people of England left home. No fewer than twelve hundred ship voyages were made across the Atlantic with settlers, livestock, and furniture. Boston became one of the important seaports of the world, ministering to an area full of bustle and vitality. Harvard College was founded. Among the settlers were the ancestors of Franklin, the Adamses, Emerson, Hawthorne, and Abraham Lincoln. One striking characteristic of this movement was the migration of many Puritans not as individuals or families but in whole communities. Certain English towns were half depopulated. The new settlements consisted not of traders and farmers alone, but of doctors, lawyers, schoolteachers, businessmen, craftsmen, and ministers. New England became a microcosm of old England, carrying in extraordinary degree the seeds of future growth.

When the Civil War began in England in 1642 the Puritan exodus slackened; but what may be loosely called the Cavalier exodus began soon afterward. It gained volume in 1649, when Charles was beheaded, and continued vigorously until the Restoration in 1660. As the Puritan migration had lifted the population of New England above thirty thousand, so the Cavalier migration was the main factor in increasing Virginia's population by 1670 to almost forty thousand. And the influx brought a remarkable amount of wealth, for though few of the newcomers were Cavaliers, many were from the prosperous classes. Having capital, they bought and cultivated large estates. Virginia, at first predominantly a poor man's colony, became full of the well-to-do. This immigration brought over some of the greatest names in American history. Washington's great-grandfather, John Washington, came to Virginia in 1657. The family traditions of the Marshalls state that their American progenitor had been a captain in the royal forces during the English war and came to Virginia when the royalists were worsted. After the influx we meet in Virginia history such notable families as the Harrisons, the Carys, the Masons, the Carters, and the Tylers.

But no real social distinction can be drawn between the settlers of Massachusetts and those of Virginia. The people who made both commonwealths great were drawn from the same large middle-class stratum. In England the Washingtons had been simply country squires, who had a tiny manor called Sulgrave in Northamptonshire; one had been mayor of Northampton. John Marshall's great-grandfather seems to have been a carpenter. The first Randolph in Virginia sprang from a family of Warwickshire squires of no great consequence. None of these Cavaliers was of better birth or more gentility than the Puritan John Winthrop, who came of a well-to-do family which owned the manor of Groton in Suffolk. None was of better origin than Sir Richard Saltonstall, who left many notable descendants in New England, or William Brewster, who as an undersecretary of state had been a man of influence at court. The great majority of the emigrants to both Massachusetts and Virginia before 1660 were yeomen, mechanics, shopkeepers, and clerks of modest means; while many in all parts of America were indentured servants, who paid for their passage by a stated term of labor. Their real wealth lay in their sturdy integrity, self-reliance, and energy.

The Rise of Self-Government

Wherever the colonists went, they carried with them in theory the rights of freeborn Britons, inheriting the traditions of the English struggle for liberty. This was specifically asserted in Virginia's first charter, which declared that the settlers were to have all the liberties, franchises, and immunities "as if they had been abiding and born within this our Realm of England." They were to have the protection of Magna Charta and the common law. This was a foundation principle of great significance. But to make it effective the colonists had to display constant vigilance and at times to wage a grim struggle. From almost the beginnings of their history, they began to rear their own fabric of constitutional government, contending for a stronger representative system, a control of the purse, and fuller guarantees of personal liberty.

The Virginia legislature, born in 1619, began at once to make a variety of laws. When the Crown revoked the charter of the Virginia Company, the House of Burgesses continued to show undiminished vigor. Indeed, within a few years it laid down certain fundamental rules upon its own rights. It declared that the governor was not to levy any taxes without legislative authority, that the money raised was to be employed as the legislature directed, and that the Burgesses were to be exempt from arrest. A little later the House declared that nothing might contravene a legislative act, while it took steps to safeguard trial by jury. So long as the Commonwealth endured in England, the Virginia legislature was a powerful body. Unfortunately, after the Restoration of the Stuarts it fell into weakness. But against its subserviency to the royal governor there was presently a fierce reaction.

In Massachusetts Bay also a representative system soon evolved. The terms of the charter seemed to give John Winthrop and his twelve assistants power to govern all the settlers. In the fall of 1630 a large body of colonists applied to this governing group to be made freemen of the corporation. It was decided the next year to grant the request; but "to the end that the body of the commons shall be preserved of good and honest men," thereafter nobody should "be admitted to the freedom of this body politic but such as are members of some of the churches within the limits of the same." A theocracy, or church-state, was thus erected. At the same time the twelve assistants resolved that they should keep their seats year after year unless removed by a special vote of the freemen. As they held practically all judicial and legislative powers, this security of tenure created a little oligarchy. The governor, the assistants, and the ministers held the colony in the hollow of their hands.

But, fortunately, a revolt was not long delayed. When a tax for defense was laid on Watertown in 1632, the unrepresented citizens grumbled and refused to pay it for fear of "bringing themselves and posterity into bondage." To pacify such complainants, it was soon decided that the governor and assistants should be guided in laying taxes by a board consisting of two delegates from every town. The foundation of a true legislature was thus laid. This body of town delegates, in fact, meeting with the governor and assistants, made up a one-chambered legislature. When it sat in 1634 it took full legislative authority into its hands, passing laws, admitting new freemen, and administering oaths of allegiance. Thus the second popular body of representatives on the continent had sprung into life. As the unicameral system worked badly, a decade later it divided into two bodies, the assistants making the upper house, the town delegates the lower. For half a century the colony of Massachusetts Bay continued to be a Puritan republic, governed by its own legislators. And when it was made a royal province in 1691 under a new charter, the legislature remained a strong body. The Crown thereafter chose the governor, but the people chose the house, and the house kept a tight grip upon the purse.

Meanwhile, two permanent little republics sprang up on American soil—Rhode Island and Connecticut. The first overflow from Massachusetts Bay had established several towns in the lower Connecticut Valley. In 1639 their freemen met in Hartford and drew up the Fundamental Orders of Connecticut, the first written constitution framed by an American commonwealth for itself, the first, indeed, in the Western world. It provided for a governor, a body of assistants, and a lower house consisting of four deputies from each town, all to be popularly elected. After the Stuart Restoration, Connecticut obtained a charter from the Crown (1662), but it was drawn in amazingly liberal terms; the freemen were to have power to govern themselves just as they liked, subject only to the vague restriction that no laws should be contrary to those of England. Rhode Island fared equally well. When its towns first drew together, Roger Williams had obtained for them a charter granting the fullest possible powers of self-government. The Restoration made a fresh application necessary. But the new charter of 1663 made Rhode Island, like Connecticut, a little republic within the British Empire, and it remained so until the Revolution. Electing all its own officers, making all its own laws, it was probably the freest community on the face of the earth.

By the year 1700 a general system of colonial government had taken form. Connecticut and Rhode Island held a special status as completely self-governing commonwealths, choosing all their own officers. The other colonies were either proprietary or royal, but no matter which they had much the same political framework. A governor was appointed by either the king or proprietor. About him and to some extent supporting him was a council, which outside Massachusetts was also appointed by the Crown or proprietor. But whereas the governor was nearly always a Briton, the councilors were usually Americans; and though they generally represented the wealthier class, they often had

views very different from those of the governor. At first
their functions were chiefly administrative and judicial, but
they developed more and more into an upper legislative
chamber. Every colony had its representative assembly,
chosen by those adult males who could meet certain property or other qualifications. This popular house initiated
legislation, fixed appropriations, and levied taxes. Its
strength lay in its power to represent public opinion and in
its control of the purse—the same elements which made
Parliament so powerful in Britain after 1689.

The colonists had done much for themselves and posterity in winning and holding representative institutions.
Three fundamental facts distinguished their political system. The first was the exalted valuation they placed upon
written charters as guaranties of their liberties. England had
no written constitution. But from the earliest years the colonists had learned to hold sacred the rights written into the
charters granted to trading companies, proprietaries, or the
people themselves. This regard for a written system of
fundamental law was to have a profound effect on American history. The second important fact was the almost
constant conflict between the governors and the assemblies.
They represented two antagonistic elements: the governor
standing for vested right and imperial interests, the assembly for popular rights and local interests. Finally, a marked
feature of colonial politics was the insistence of the assemblies upon control over appropriations. They contended for
a variety of objects—frequent elections, the exclusion of
royal officeholders from their ranks, the right to choose
their own speakers; above all, they asserted that they alone
should grant or withhold appropriations. They met much
opposition, but usually they made this demand good.

It was not true that the British colonies suffered from
tyranny. By and large, they enjoyed a political freedom that

in the seventeenth and eighteenth centuries was unequaled in any other part of the globe. But they did experience much class government. Theocratic New England had its ruling few whose power had to be broken. In the South, patrician landholders and merchants tried to set up a political monopoly.

Now and then, class tyranny raised an especially ugly head—and the colonists struck at it. The first such blow came in Virginia in Bacon's Rebellion of 1676. Indentured servants who had worked out their terms, immigrants tilling frontier farms, the lesser planters, and numerous laborers and slave overseers felt themselves maltreated. After 1670 no landless man had a vote. In various other ways they were deprived of a voice in political affairs. Assemblies sat practically unchanged for long periods—one, 1661–1675, for fourteen years; offices were parceled out to favorites of the royal governor and the richest planters. Education was above the reach of the poor. They were ill-guarded against Indian attacks, for the governor and his associates, with an eye to the fur trade, befriended the savages. Taxes were heavy. Markets were distant from the outer farms, and when the price of tobacco fell, the farmers were left in sore straits.

Finally an Indian attack upon the exposed settlements led to a dramatic revolt. The settlers clamored for protection, and when Governor Berkeley and the coastal planters gave them procrastinating answers, they became outraged. Nathaniel Bacon, putting himself at the head of angry men from the upper reaches of the James and York rivers, delivered a blow which destroyed the principal Indian stronghold and slew one hundred fifty savages. When later he went to sit in the assembly at Williamsburg, the haughty governor seized him; but an instant uprising along the heads of the rivers forced his release, and he fled. When he returned it was with four hundred armed men clanking behind him. Berkeley and the council hurried out of the capitol to meet the determined young planter. Tearing open his clothing to expose his chest, the governor exclaimed: "Here! Shoot me! 'Fore God, a fair mark, shoot!" But Bacon answered: "No, may it please your honor, we will not hurt a hair of your head, nor any man's. We are come for a commission to save our lives from the Indians, which you have so often promised, and now we will have it before we go." His followers, shaking their cocked fusils at the assembly windows, shouted in chorus: "We will have it!" Addressing the assembly in a stormy harangue of half an hour, Bacon demanded protection for the settlers, proper auditing of the public accounts, reduction of taxes, and other reforms.

The revolt quickly whirled itself out like a summer storm rushing across the dusty fields of Virginia. Governor Berkeley and his associates made promises, which shrewd observers did not believe they would keep. Presently the governor summoned the Gloucester and Middlesex militia to the number of twelve hundred, demanding that they help him put down the rebel Bacon. Thereupon a deep, indignant murmur arose of "Bacon, Bacon, Bacon," and the militiamen disgustedly walked out of the field still muttering "Bacon, Bacon, Bacon." Open warfare followed. Bacon stormed Jamestown and on a fine summer day burned it entire; he took possession of a twenty-gun ship in the James River. Then, at the crisis of his operations, he died of malaria, and his rebellion collapsed. It had begun as a thoroughly justified assertion of the rights of small farmers, laborers, and frontiersmen to protection against the savages and to fair political and financial treatment; it had led to open insurrection against the royal government. The vengeful Berkeley was presently bowing ironically to one of Bacon's lieutenants as a prisoner: "Mr. Drummond! You are very welcome. I am more glad to see you than any man in Virginia. Mr. Drummond, you shall be hanged in half an hour." But abortive as the rebellion seemed, it had exemplified the frontier spirit of independence and sturdy self-assertion—the American spirit—in a memorable fashion. It was not forgotten.

Church and State in the Colonies

As the thirst for political freedom grew in America, so did the spirit of religious toleration. From early times the British colonies were the homes of many sects which learned to live together harmoniously.

The Church of England was transplanted to Virginia with the first settlers. One of the first buildings erected in Jamestown was that plain church which, now beautifully restored, still looks out over the river. When Lord Delaware came as governor in 1616, he had it repaired and enlarged, so that it became a structure of dignity, with cedar pews, walnut altar, a tall pulpit and lectern, and a baptismal font. Here the planters married the girls who came over by shiploads; here their children were christened. As Virginia grew, new parishes were created and churches erected, to be supported by public taxation as the Established Church was supported in England. For some years every settler was taxed a bushel of corn and ten pounds of tobacco for the clergy. This was not sufficient; and in 1632 the legislature passed an act compelling every settler, in addition to the former contribution, to set aside for the minister his twentieth calf, twentieth goat, and twentieth pig. After the Stuart Restoration the annual stipend in tobacco was made larger and more certain. In addition, the clergy were supposed to have free grants of land, called glebes, and other perquisites. The Anglican estab-

PHYSIOGRAPHIC MAP OF EASTERN NORTH AMERICA
SHOWING POINTS TOUCHED BY EARLY EXPLORERS··

lishment was very much a reality in Virginia, as it became in other parts of the South, notably Maryland and South Carolina.

Nevertheless, the Virginia Church was neither a flourishing body materially nor one which impressed itself spiritually or intellectually upon the settlers. Social and economic conditions were unfavorable to its growth. Most parishes were spread out over huge tracts of sparsely settled territory. The boundaries of many, following the riverbanks closely, were from thirty to sixty miles in length. Those who went to church had to travel long distances over execrable roads, or to paddle laboriously for hours up or down the streams. Naturally, attendance was irregular; even George Washington, a devout vestryman, was open to the charge of capricious churchgoing. In bad winter weather the minister would find most of the pews empty. One man complained that he sometimes traveled fifty miles to hold service and found only a handful present. In these sparsely settled parishes, too, the minister's support was often meager. As prices fell, the local taxes, unevenly collected in tobacco and livestock, were inadequate, and when the legislature raised them, the poorer parishes made bitter complaints.

With salaries low, tenure insecure, and many hardships to meet, it was difficult to obtain ministers of ability, piety, and zeal. The best clergymen would not emigrate from England to the colonies; they could find better careers at home. Those who came were often dull of mind, lazy of body, or dubious in morals. We soon find governors and others complaining that the Virginia clergy were "a pack of scandalous fellows," given to "many vices not agreeable to their coats," and addicted to "swearing, drunkenness, and fighting." They were like Fielding's Parson Trulliber. Reform movements were undertaken, one of which led to the founding in 1693 of the second colonial college, William and Mary, primarily as a training school for young ministers. But the establishment remained unsatisfactory down to the Revolution.

In Virginia and other parts of the South the Anglican Church accepted public support, but had no control whatever over the state. In Massachusetts and Connecticut, the Puritan Church was for decades largely identified with the state, exercised a marked control over the government, and, in fact, long maintained a rigid ecclesiastical despotism.

The fundamental reason for the Puritan migration to Massachusetts was to establish a church-state and not to find religious freedom. The Puritans were not religious radicals; they were religious conservatives. In England they had believed in the Church of England, but had wished to modify the absolutism of its hierarchy and to alter it by abolishing Catholic forms, observing the Sabbath strictly, and keeping a close watch upon morals. Failing in their hope to capture the establishment, they sought the American wilderness to set up their "particular Church," supported by public taxation, interwoven with the state, and tolerating no opposition. When Endicott founded the first Puritan church in Salem, two men in his company hauled an Anglican prayerbook out of their luggage and wished to read the services. He promptly put them and their obnoxious prayerbook on board ship and hustled them back to England. The Puritan leaders at once created a close-knit church-state, its authority vested in an aristocracy of iron-willed, able, and despotic Church rulers.

The triumph of this Calvinist church-state, with its harsh discipline, meant that the Pilgrim or Separatist ideal of self-governing congregations was submerged. At Plymouth the Pilgrims had established a little Church democracy, the people managing their religious affairs without deference to bishops or synods. But the Puritans found this anarchical and demoralizing, for they believed in a firmly centralized control.

There were four steps in the erection of this church-state in Massachusetts. The first was a basic provision that unless a man was a member of the Puritan Church in good standing, he could not vote or hold office. The second made attendance at church compulsory or everyone, thus guarding the Church and colony against unbelievers. The third required that the Church and state both approve the incorporation of any new church. No nest of dissenters or unbelievers could set up shop for themselves in any part of Massachusetts; those who wanted a church which did not strictly conform to the Puritan type must emigrate to some other part of America. Finally, a provision for state support made it possible for the state to act with the Church heads in punishing any rebellion or infraction of discipline. The synod of the Puritan churches promulgated, in 1646, what is called the Cambridge Platform, providing that if any church congregation rebelled against the synod, or the Church rules, the civil government stopped the minister's pay, discharged him, and put in his place a man who would conform.

This church-state in Massachusetts, this rule by a combination of priests and magistrates, lasted with gradually declining vigor till 1691, when an improved charter was granted by William and Mary and Massachusetts was made a royal province. The theocracy had just one great achievement to its credit. The grim Puritan organization resisted the encroachments of Charles II with a dogged determination which counted powerfully in the development of political freedom in the New World. This resistance did much to pave the way for the task of achieving political independence late in the next century. But the theocracy had a number of things to its discredit. It was an oppressive tyranny; it committed some shameful acts of persecution against Quakers and others; it was hostile to freedom of thought and speech; and its fanatical temper helped to account for the Salem witchcraft delusion, during which nineteen men and women were hanged. As population thickened and new ideas took root, a strong liberal party had arisen to combat the conservatives under Increase Mather and his pedantic son, Cotton, both Boston ministers of renown. It was a happy moment for America when the theocracy declined.

In Roger Williams and Anne Hutchinson, Massachusetts sent forth two great apostles of religious liberty. Williams, a highly educated man who had been graduated from Cambridge in England, and a most devout Christian, was a radical opponent of the whole Puritan idea of theocracy. He believed that Church and state should be entirely separated; that it was folly to try to compel men to attend church; and that dissenters should be calmly tolerated. The government, according to his view, should protect all well-behaved sects alike. Williams, ordered by the Massachusetts authorities to return to England, instead escaped through the snows to make Rhode Island a land in which his principles could be applied. Anne Hutchinson was not quite so distinguished a figure. She preached doctrines akin to what later, in Emerson's day, was called transcendentalism. It was the duty of every individual, she said, to follow the promptings of an inner supernatural light; and it was the presence of the Holy Ghost within, and not any amount of good works or sanctification, which really saved an individual. Living for a time in the Rhode Island country, she finally perished in an Indian massacre in New York.

Throughout the middle colonies, toleration early became the rule. In New York alone was any serious effort made to establish the Anglican Church, and even there it almost completely failed. The great majority of the people belonged to other sects. As the contemporary historian William Smith wrote, the people were for "an equal, universal toleration of Protestants." The Jews supported a synagogue. In the Quaker colonies of Pennsylvania and Delaware, sects of all kinds were welcomed, and many small and peculiar denominations, chiefly German, found root there. Catholics were not molested, and in Philadelphia the Mass was publicly celebrated. Maryland also was a land where faiths long hostile lived in general concord. In 1649 an assembly which was partly Catholic, partly Protestant, passed a Toleration Act which is one of the great landmarks of religious freedom. It dealt harshly with non-Christians and with unitarians, but it placed Protestants and Catholics on precisely the same plane. A pregnant phrase was written into Maryland's Toleration Act. Its authors declared that toleration was wisdom because "the inforceing of the conscience in matters of Religion hath frequently fallen out to be of dangerous Consequence." As the decades passed, most colonists became convinced that it was just and prudent to let men worship as they pleased.

Chapter Two

THE COLONIAL HERITAGE

A Developing Americanism

Two main factors may be distinguished in the development of a distinctive American nationality during the colonial period, a national character that was fairly well fixed when the Revolution began. One factor was a new people —an amalgamation of different national stocks. The other factor was a new land—a country rich, empty, and demanding as the price of its bounty only that the newcomers should bring it industry and courage. By 1775 a distinctively American society, with its own social, economic, and political traits, was emerging. At some points it approached closely to the European pattern: the merchants, professional men, and mechanics of Boston and New York were not easily distinguishable from similar groups in London and Bristol. But the great mass of Americans were growing quite distinct from the European type in the old homeland.

The emigration to America had fortunately taken place in a way which made the English language and English institutions everywhere dominant, so that the country possessed a general unity. Neither the Germans nor the French Huguenots set up a separate colony, as they might have done; they mingled with the first British comers, adopting their language and outlook. The English migration soon swamped the Dutch in the Hudson Valley. Yet this happy unity of tongue and basic institutions coexisted with a remarkable diversity in national origins.

It is important that we neither exaggerate nor underestimate the amalgamation of peoples in colonial days. At the time of the Revolution probably three fourths to nine tenths of the white colonists were still of British blood; but the infusion of Dutch, German, French, and other Continental stocks was significant. The first great waves of settlement had been English waves, and New England and the lowland parts of the South remained almost purely English. But while the original flow continued, in the eighteenth century two other heavy waves of emigration came from Europe—the German and the Scotch-Irish. Each was represented, at the outbreak of the Revolution, by hundreds of thousands of settlers.

It was the German immigration which first became important. Western German areas, and the Rhineland in especial, were filled with misery and discontent. The ravages of the French armies under Louis XIV had been of the most cruel character. They were followed by a systematic religious persecution of the Lutherans and other sects, reinforced by the political tyranny of the small German princes. When the government of Queen Anne and her successors offered safety and religious freedom under the English flag, by tens of thousands the Germans poured into England and her colonies. An advance guard from Crefeld had come to William Penn's domains as early as 1683, making Germantown a seat of thriving handicrafts. The first paper mill in the colonies was set up there by the Rittenhouse family; beer was brewed and cloth woven. But the real tide began to flow after 1700. Some went to the Mohawk Valley in New York, some to New Brunswick in

New Jersey, but most of them to Pennsylvania. As time passed, several thousand Germans and Swiss came in a single year.

So great was this influx that Benjamin Franklin estimated that just before the Revolution one third of the Pennsylvania population was German. In considerable areas little English was used, and in 1739 a German newspaper was set up at Germantown. Lutheran, Moravian, Mennonite and United Brethren settlements dotted the province. Baron Stiegel's iron foundry and glass factory became famous, as did Sauer's printing establishment. But most of the Germans were thrifty farmers whose hard work made the limestone region of Pennsylvania a huge wheat granary. They did not take readily to pioneering, but preferred to buy in a region already settled, protected, and partly improved. They cleared the land thoroughly; they built big barns before they spent much energy on houses; they kept their stock fat and sleek, their fences high and strong. Living frugally, they sold as much as possible of their produce. The women worked in the fields, but they nevertheless reared large families.

The Scotch-Irish, a more aggressive stock, furnished the chief pioneering element in Pennsylvania, the Shenandoah Valley, and the upland parts of Carolina. They also fled from oppression at home, for they suffered under the Anglican establishment in Ireland, while the English laws against Irish manufactures were disastrous to their weaving industry. Coming over in shiploads, they brought with them a bitter anti-English feeling. They were more Scotch than Irish, most of them being Presbyterians who had migrated to Ulster within the past century; and the Presbyterian Church organization had given them a natural understanding and love of democratic institutions. Some of them settled in New Hampshire, some in Ulster and

Orange counties in New York; but their principal refuge was Pennsylvania and the valleys stretching southward into Virginia and Carolina. Plunging into the wilderness, they lived by hunting, cleared the land, erected log cabins, and hewed the first rough farms out of the forests. These "bold and indigent strangers," as a Pennsylvania official called them, were impatient of legal restraints and of quitrents charged by the Penns and other landowners. They hated the Indians and were quick to quarrel with them. Their acquisitiveness gave point to the old remark: "They kept the Sabbath and everything else they could lay their hands on." They made wonderfully efficient pioneer settlers. Spreading south and west, reaching upland Georgia and penetrating Kentucky before the Revolution, rearing large families, showing marked gifts for politics and Indian fighting, the Scotch-Irish began to lay a strong impress on American life. Among them were names later famous—Calhoun, Jackson, Polk, Houston, McKinley.

In the Shenandoah and other interior valleys the Scotch-Irish, English, Germans, Dutch, and others soon mingled their bloods in a rich melting pot of the new American people. The last colony to be founded, Georgia, also represented a mixture of peoples. General James Oglethorpe, supported by other philanthropic Englishmen, obtained a royal charter for it in 1732 as a refuge for poor debtors and other unfortunates and as an outpost against Spanish and Indian aggression. To Georgia the paternal trustees brought carefully selected English people, a large body of German Protestants, and a number of Scotch Highlanders. At first salvery was prohibited. All non-Catholic faiths were encouraged, and Anglicans, Moravians, Presbyterians, Anabaptists, Lutherans, and Jews worshiped side by side. The Anglican Church at Savannah was distinguished by two famous ministers, John Wesley and George Whitefield.

Other non-English groups were smaller but not unimportant. The revocation of the Edict of Nantes brought hundreds—possibly thousands—of French Huguenots to the English colonies, and names like Laurens and Legaré in South Carolina, Maury in Virginia, Deano and Jay in New York, Revere and Faneuil in Massachusetts, suggest how widely they scattered. A sprinkling of Swiss came with the Germans; there were substantial numbers of Swedes and Finns along the Delaware, and, chiefly in the towns, small groups of Italians and Portuguese Jews. Town names like Radnor and Bryn Mawr in Pennsylvania and Welsh Neck in South Carolina remind us that the Welsh too made their contribution. It is clear that even in the colonial era America was something of a melting pot.

The second great factor in shaping a distinct American nationality was the land, and especially the frontier. At the outset the coastal strip itself, impinging on the dark forest, was the frontier. The early settlers were unbelievably inexperienced. The Pilgrims searched the Plymouth thickets for spices and thought the wild beasts they heard might be "lions"; some of the dandies at Jamestown thought they could live there much as in London streets. But the newcomers had to adjust themselves to the cruel, primitive wilderness, or die. At the very beginning we meet in Captain John Smith and Miles Standish men whose daring and endurance remind us of such later heroes as Robert Rogers, Daniel Boone, and Kit Carson. From the Indians the settlers learned how to plant and fertilize corn, to cook succotash, to make canoes and snowshoes, to stalk game, to tan deerskins, to grow expert in woodcraft. By hard experience the pioneer became hunter, farmer, and fighter all in one. A new agriculture, a new architecture, a new domestic economy, arose. Within a decade there were men in the New World who had little in common with the old neighbors they had left in England—and their children had still less. They possessed a more rugged, practical, homespun outlook upon life. The frontier was pushed back to the highest navigation point on the rivers by 1700 or thereabouts, back to the Alleghenies by 1765, and on across the mountains just before the Revolution. Successive generations were subjected to its influence and emerged from the experience reshaped as by a gigantic, irresistible mold.

On the frontier a rough equality of social condition was the rule—and, indeed, such equality prevailed outside the few large towns. There was no icing on the cake of American society. The English redemptioners working out their passage costs by five years of labor, the poor debtors freed from prison, the Germans fleeing from the ravaged Palatinate, the Scotch-Irish driven out by English mercantile laws—all had nothing. They had to struggle hard for property. As plebeians, they disliked the aristocrats who had obtained large land grants, or who made fortunes from trade and speculation. But no matter how poor, the average settler felt in America a sense of opportunity and independence that he had not known in Europe. This feeling was born of the wide spaces and abundant natural wealth of the country. St. John Crèvecoeur, a French gentleman who came to the American colonies about 1759, wrote that "the rich stay in Europe, it is only the middling and poor that emigrate." He added: "Everything tends to regenerate them; new laws, a new mode of living, a new social system; here they are become men." And in an eloquent passage he described the emergent Americanism, based on unfettered activity in a land of vast natural resources:

> A European, when he first arrives, seems limited in his intentions as well as in his views; but he very suddenly alters his scale. He no sooner breathes our air

than he forms new schemes, and embarks on designs he never would have thought of in his own country. There the plenitude of society confines many useful ideas, and often extinguishes the most laudable schemes which here ripen into maturity. . . . He begins to feel the effects of a sort of resurrection; hitherto he had not lived, but simply vegetated; he now feels himself a man, because he is treated as such; the laws of his own country had overlooked him in his insignificancy; the laws of this cover him with their mantle. Judge what an alteration there must arise in the mind and thoughts of this man! He begins to forget his former servitude and dependence, his heart involuntarily dilates and glows, and his first swell inspires him with those new thoughts which mark an American.

But while an American character was developing, down to at least 1750 few of the colonists had any real consciousness of the fact. They thought of themselves primarily as loyal British subjects, secondarily as Virginians, New Yorkers, or Rhode Islanders. By that year the thirteen colonies had taken firm root and contained almost 1,500,000 people. They ran the whole length of the coast from the spruce of the Androscoggin Valley to the palmettos of the St. Johns. Each had characteristics of its own, while they fell into four fairly well-defined sections.

One section was New England, a country of small, rocky, well-tilled farms, of lumbering, and of a wide variety of maritime employments: construction of the kind Longfellow described in *The Building of the Ship,* codfishing like that described by Kipling in *Captains Courageous,* and overseas trade similar to that described by R. H. Dana in *Two Years Before the Mast.* Another section was the middle colonies, made up partly of small farms and partly of great estates, with a good deal of small-scale manufacturing, and with lively shipping interests in New York and Philadelphia. A third was composed of the Southern colonies, where large· plantations, worked by gangs of black slaves, producing indigo, rice, and tobacco, were the most prominent, though by no means the most common, feature. Finally, there was the most American section of all: the great border strip or back country, stretching from Maine to Georgia, where pioneer hunters, hardy log-cabin settlers, and a sprinkling of more solid farmers pushed toward the interior. This border country was much the same north and south. In western Massachusetts, western Pennsylvania, and western Carolina alike it produced hard-hitting, resourceful men, indifferent to book learning, impatient of restraint, and invincibly optimistic.

The New England Colonies

The coastal settlements of New England possessed great expansive power. We have already seen that one migration of Massachusetts people founded Rhode Island and another migration founded the twin colonies of Connecticut and New Haven, later combined into one. A third body of Puritans scattered northward into Maine and New Hampshire, areas originally claimed by non-Puritan promoters, and there quickly became dominant. Massachusetts by 1650 asserted political control over both the New Hampshire and the Maine settlements, but toward the end of the century the former were made into a distinct royal province. This marked expansive quality of New England was to continue generation after generation and was to send wave after wave of the descendants of the Puritans westward until they reached the Pacific.

Throughout the colonial period New England kept a remarkably homogeneous population, its 700,000 people at the time of the Revolution being almost purely English in blood. They were generally alike in language, manners, piety, and ways of thought; little Rhode Island alone standing somewhat apart, for its political radicals and dissenting church groups gave it a peculiar stamp. The Yankees had sprung in the main from a remarkably sturdy, independent, and intelligent English stock and took a stern pride in their ancestry—the choice grain sieved out, as one leader put it, to plant the wilderness. Those who tilled the land or fished the seas made a comfortable living, while merchants, shipowners, and small manufacturers often accumulated considerable wealth. The foreign commerce of Boston alone employed six hundred vessels by 1770; the fisheries of Massachusetts, furnishing large exports to Europe and the West Indies, were estimated to be worth $1,250,000 annually. With good reason the codfish was made the emblem of the commonwealth. Most New England households were self-supporting, weaving their own cloth, growing their own food, making their own furniture and shoes. Industry, thrift, hardheaded enterprise, and a narrow piety were Yankee characteristics; and if the people were not much liked in other sections, they were universally respected.

In New England both Church and school held a place of special dignity. All Puritan communities looked to their minister as an intellectual as well as a religious mentor and to the meetinghouse for the greater part of their social intercourse. The clergy were vigorous, aggressive men, strong not only in learning but in community leadership, and regarded with awe by their followers. They taught damnatory doctrines with gusto, and Jonathan Edwards' word pictures of sinners writhing in the torments of hell were famous. John Cotton declared that he loved to "sweeten his mouth" with a passage of the stern Calvin every night before he slept. But the clergy had to be men

PILGRIMS GOING TO CHURCH

From a painting by Boughton

of power, rectitude, and erudition. They were deeply versed in theology and the ancient languages. President Chauncy of Harvard, who had the Old Testament read to him in Hebrew in the morning and the New in Greek in the afternoon, commented upon them in Latin; many another minister could have done the same. As for public education, it received early provision. Harvard was founded in 1636, and in that same decade elementary schools were set up in various places. While Massachusetts was still in her infancy, the legislature required every town of fifty householders to support a school.

As time passed, the early rigidity of New England life was pleasantly modified. The carrying trade and mercantile interests brought in not only wealth but new ideas. Lawyers, physicians, and other professional men grew numerous. In Massachusetts and Connecticut the Sabbath, which lasted from six o'clock Saturday till sunset on Sunday, was stringently kept; no travel was allowed, no tavern might entertain a guest, games were forbidden, and even a knot of men talking in the streets might be arrested. But new fashions like periwigs came in, the Anglicans introduced a merry observance of Christmas, and politics, money getting, love-making, and feasting began to play a more frankly recognized part in life.

A document which gives an unrivaled picture of the great transition from the old order to the new in Massachusetts is the diary of Samuel Sewall, who was graduated from Harvard in 1671 and began three years later a record which he kept up till 1729. This grimly old-fashioned Puritan, who became Chief Justice, liked a glass of Madeira and a ride in his chariot, but detested all innovation. As we read his three volumes, a many-colored vision rises before us. We see the little city of Boston, solidly built on its neck of land, with the three hills, the spires the fortress, and the harbor crowded with shipping. We hear the watchman call the hours and the public crier make his rounds. We feel the shudder that runs through the town when news comes of pirates on the coast, or of the Comte de Frontenac ready to descend upon New England with his French and Indian forces. We see the citizens hunting after stray cows, as Sewall himself did, "from one end and side of the Town to t'other"; gathering in groups to discuss the nominations for council; and streaming to that favorite amusement, a funeral. When the harbor is solid ice up to the island Castle, we shiver with the poor churchgoers as we hear the hard-frozen sacramental bread "rattling sadly as broken into the plates." Smallpox runs over the town. Childbirths are numerous, for every goodwife is a fruitful branch, but child deaths almost keep them pace. We see training day celebrated on the Common, with the Ancient and Honorable Artillery and other companies brave in uniforms, great firing and excitement, and gentlemen and ladies dining in tents on the grass. We look at the redcoats with disfavor and hear with horror that the royal governor has given a ball at his palace that lasted till three in the morning. We join the concourse that goes out to Broughton's Hill to see malefactors hanged. We see the constables breaking up ninepin games on Beacon Hill, or as censorious Puritans called it, Mount Whoredom, and watch Sewall as a magistrate riding through Charlestown or Boston on Saturday at sundown ordering the shop shutters put up. But little by little we see the old Puritan strictness giving way to the modern age.

Crime and pauperism were rarer in thrifty, orderly New England than in other colonies. Indentured servants, at first unknown, became common in the eighteenth century, but they and other laborers found it easy to attain independence, and slavery declined. The town system of government, with all the public business transacted at a town meeting of qualified voters, fostered self-reliance. Boston, New Haven, and other large centers came to have numerous aristocrats with fine houses, coats of arms, and plate, while class lines were real and distinct. But in no part of the world did the common people show a sturdier self-respect.

The Middle Colonies

The middle colonies had a far more varied, cosmopolitan, and tolerant society, less elevated but also less austere. Pennsylvania, with its sister province Delaware, counted by the Revolution about 350,000 people; New York and New Jersey together possessed not far from that number. As elsewhere in America, the great mass of the people depended upon the soil for subsistence. In the better parts of these provinces the landowners rapidly grew prosperous. Quaker farms in Pennsylvania, for example, boasted of substantial brick houses, rooms wainscoted or papered, heavy furniture, and good china and glassware. The tables, where farmers and their servants ate together, groaned with simple but varied fare. Meat, rare in many parts of Europe, was eaten thrice daily. So rapidly did farm appliances increase that by 1765 Pennsylvania boasted nine thousand wagons. Agriculture was more varied than in other sections; a variety of grains were grown, fine orchards were numerous, all kinds of livestock were raised, and many landowners had their own honey and fish ponds. The Hudson Valley was marked by the manorial estates of the Van Rensselaers, Cortlandts, Livingstons, and other aristocrats, who had huge houses with retinues of servants, and whose annual rent days possessed a feudal quality. But Long Island and upper New York were full of small holdings as well.

Besides the tillers of the soil, Pennsylvania and New York had an increasing number of merchants, tradesmen, and mechanics. The carrying trade, devoted chiefly to the export of lumber, furs, grain, and other natural products, and the import of manufactures, sugar, and wines, was extensive and profitable. Just before the Revolution nearly five hundred vessels, with more than seven thousand seamen, plied out of Delaware Bay, while the Hudson and Long Island Sound were full of shipping. Both Philadelphia and New York had become great distributing points for interior trade. One way of making a fortune was to send grain and dried fish to the West Indies, bringing back slaves or molasses; another was to load furs at Albany and exchange them in London for fine textiles, china, or furniture. Small manufactures were gaining a foothold. In Pennsylvania and New Jersey iron furnaces sprang up, and the export of iron products led Parliament to pass an act to suppress rolling mills. In New York glassware and felt hats were made. As wealth increased, professional men grew more common. The lawyers of the principal towns achieved political leadership and did as much as any other group to bring on the Revolution.

A more mixed and polished society could be found in New York and even in staid Philadelphia than in New England. The merchants and shippers, keeping in close touch with Europe, dispensed a gay and fashionable hospitality. When John Adams paused in New York on his way to Philadelphia, he was impressed by the splendid houses, fine silver, and elaborate cuisine. That city boasted of its clubs, its balls, its concerts, its open-air pleasure gardens, its coffeehouses, and its private theatricals. A New York

funeral sometimes cost several thousand dollars. The Dutch
had shown a taste for holidays which the English gradually
acquired; wealthy people dressed in the latest London
mode, with silks and velvets, powdered wigs and small-
swords; and the mixture of sects and races helped ideas
to circulate briskly. Philadelphia, with its broad streets
and well-swept sidewalks, had a quieter elegance. But it
was notable for its public institutions, and it cultivated
those scientific studies in which Franklin, Benjamin Rush,
and the botanist William Bartram gained distinction.
Neat, substantial, and prosperous, it seemed to Thomas
Jefferson a more impressive city than London or Paris—
and Jefferson was no mean judge. Religious doctrines in
New York became so liberal that churchmen complained of
the "freethinking," while politics aroused more passion in
that province than anywhere else in British America. In
Quaker-dominated Pennsylvania, opinion was more conservative; but just before the Revolution the Quaker
ascendancy in politics was violently shaken by the Scotch-
Irish and Germans.

Throughout the middle colonies a large population of
Negroes added to the color of life. The Quakers were
deeply hostile to slavery and in the late colonial period
produced one antislavery leader of international renown—
that "beautiful soul," as Lamb called him, John Woolman.
Nor did slavery flourish among the Scotch-Irish and Germans, who worked hard with their own hands. But it was
common in the cities and on the manorial estates along
the Hudson. In general, life had an ampler quality in the
middle provinces than in New England. The climate, the
soil, and the people were more genial. There was nothing
else in the North quite like New Year's Day in New York,
when salutes were fired at dawn, and gentlemen went
about town paying calls, eating delicacies, and consuming

so much wine and punch that they often had to be taken home in carriages. There was nothing quite like the reception New York gave to a new royal governor, with pomp and ceremony; or like the celebration on one of the manors when an heir was married.

The Southern Colonies

The distinctive features of the Southern colonies, and particularly of Virginia and South Carolina, the richest and most influential, were three. They were the almost exclusively rural character of their life, Charleston and Baltimore being the only towns of even slight importance; the prominent place held by large estates, with troops of slaves, imposing mansions, and ostentatious living; and the sharp stratification of society into classes. Among the whites, the upper class was composed of well-to-do and often aristocratic planters, who furnished a singularly able political leadership; the middle class was made up of small planters, farmers, and a few tradesmen, factors, and mechanics; while the lower class was of "poor whites." Below all three groups were the slaves, who in Virginia by 1770 numbered somewhat less than half the total population of 450,000, in Maryland were fully one third of the population of about 200,000, and in South Carolina outnumbered the whites in the ratio of two to one.

The diffusion of population was partly the result of the plantation system, each estate being to a great degree self-sufficient, and partly of the aversion of Southerners to towns. The great landowners carried on a direct trade with England or with Northern cities, requiring no large mercantile group. Slavery all but crushed the life out of a promising handicraft system. In vain did Virginia pass laws designed to create large towns—one, for example, requiring each county to erect a house in Williamsburg. The largest center in the colony when the Revolution opened was Norfolk, with about seven thousand people, while Williamsburg had only two hundred straggling houses. Colonel Byrd had written of Fredericksburg in 1732 that besides the "top man of the place," it had only "one merchant, a tailor, a smith, an ordinary-keeper, and a lady who acts both as doctress and coffee-house keeper." The situation was much the same elsewhere in the South. Charleston just before the Revolution was a rustic-looking town of fifteen thousand people, half Negroes, with unpaved sandy streets; Baltimore was a rather rude port of about the same size, dependent on its trade in farm products from the "back country." The lack of towns had some unhappy consequences. Boston possessed a newspaper as early as 1690, but it was not until 1736 that the *Virginia Gazette* appeared. No theatrical performance was given by a professional company in Virginia until within twenty-five years of the Revolution; and the dependence of the tidewater section on more enterprising parts of the empire for even brooms, chairs, hoes, and rough crockery aroused complaint among farsighted leaders.

The great plantations of Maryland, Virginia, and South Carolina were scattered through the low country, generally fronting on some river or creek which afforded water transportation. Each had its family mansion, usually of brick or stone, its storehouses, blacksmith shop, cooperage, and other outbuildings, and its straggling huts of the Negro quarters. Many of the large houses, like General Ringgold's Fountain Rock, William Byrd's Westover, George Mason's Gunston Hall, and John Rutledge's estate near Charleston, were beautifully designed and finished. Inside were paneled halls, fine staircases, and large rooms. The best houses contained handsome mahogany furniture, some made in America but most of it imported from England, heavy silver services with London hallmarks, silk or velvet hangings, good family portraits, engravings (Hogarth being a prime favorite), and considerable libraries. Robert Carter of Nomini Hall had more than fifteen hundred volumes, and the third William Byrd more than four thousand. A good many planters had town houses also in Annapolis, Williamsburg, or Charleston, to which they traveled every autumn in their family coach for a season of balls, dinners, cardplaying, racing, and legislative activities. As a class the planters were often charged with indolence. But the proper care of a great plantation required much labor and anxiety; Washington worked hard in his oversight of Mount Vernon, while Robert Carter of Nomini Hall, whose holdings included sixty thousand acres scattered over Virginia, a textile establishment, a share in an ironworks, various mines, and handicraft shops, was incessantly busy. The planters were also charged with lack of intellectual tastes. But they took a passionate interest in politics, held most of the elective offices, and talked and wrote on governmental questions with extraordinary ability, and a surprising number of them interested themselves in science and achieved election to the Royal Society.

The lesser planters and farmers of the South—typified very well by Thomas Jefferson's father Peter, who acquired cheap frontier land by surveying and helped clear it himself—were hard-working, intelligent, thrifty men. They hewed away the wilderness, built modest houses, and acquired property; many tilled broad tracts with the aid of slaves; some, like Peter Jefferson, married into the aristocracy. They were a sturdy race, self-reliant and independent in temper, and determined to maintain their British liberties. If they lacked polish and education, they had plenty of hard sense and produced brilliant political leaders of democratic views, like Jefferson, James Madison, and Patrick Henry. Indeed, differences between the upper and middle classes in the South often grew vague, and inter-marriage tended to knit the two together. In Maryland particularly, the eighteenth century witnessed a strong tendency to break up cumbersome estates into small, efficient farms. Merchants and attorneys stood on a somewhat lower level than landholders, while shopkeeping was regarded for generations with the same condescension which it then met in England. Business communities like Baltimore and Norfolk stood on a plane distinctly inferior to the colonial capitals. But land speculation flourished among the best circles in the South as well as North. The second William Byrd in 1737 founded Richmond by breaking up an estate on the upper James and selling it in town lots.

The lowest white stratum of society in the South was marked off by distinct lines. Some convicts, released debtors, and indentured servants who came over from Europe deteriorated under frontier conditions and made up a body, illiterate, vulgar, and shiftless, which was despised even by the Negroes. Of course, no degradation necessarily attached to an indenture. Many emigrants of high character paid for their passage to America by giving bond service. They included English and Continental craftsmen—cabinet-makers, tailors, silversmiths, jewelers, gunsmiths, and the like—who might have given the South a far greater degree of industrialism but for the rapid spread of slavery. Men of distinction escaped from the Fleet Prison in London by assisted emigration. Convicts were often transported for trivial offenses, and in hard times some Britons would commit small crimes to get sent overseas. When they arrived, their time was sold to the highest bidder. Nevertheless, the South acquired a sizable element of vagabondish, unenterprising, and turbulent folk, who made lazy farmers and poor citizens. In due time science was to show that climate, a defective diet, and the hookworm had far more to do with their slovenliness and waywardness than any innate faults. Slavery, too, brought manual labor into contempt. William Byrd, in the record he kept of a surveying expedition (*History of the Dividing Line*), has described with humorous exaggeration these shiftless countrymen, content with rude comforts, hostile to law, taxes, and the Established Church, and fond of "the felicity of having nothing to do":

> They make their wives rise out of their beds early in the morning, at the same time that they lie and snore, till the sun has run one-third of his course, and dispersed all the unwholesome damps. Then, after stretching and yawning for half an hour, they light their pipes, and, under the protection of a cloud of smoke, venture into the open air; though, if it happens to be ever so little cold, they quickly return shivering to the chimney corner. When the weather is mild they stand leaning with both their arms upon the cornfield fence, and gravely consider whether they had best go and take a small heat at the plough; but generally find reason to put it off till another time. Thus they loiter away their lives, like Solomon's sluggard, with their arms across.

The Negro slaves were brought chiefly from the west coast of Africa, from Senegambia on the north to Angola on the south. After the close of the seventeenth century, when the monopoly of the Royal African Company was ended, the trade was in the hands of a wide variety of firms and individuals, both American and British. Many fortunes in Boston, Newport, New York, and Southern ports were built upon the traffic. The most active market was probably that maintained at Charleston, with numerous firms competing. Henry Laurens, who was prominent in the business for some years after 1750, has told us that planters would come long distances and eagerly bid fine young Negroes up to £40 sterling. Whereas in the North slaves were commonly sold by the importer directly to the purchaser, for cash, in the South they often went in batches to merchants and other middlemen who bartered them for tobacco, rice, or indigo. Field hands were clothed in coarse garments, housed in rude huts, and worked hard in the fields under severe overseers; household servants had kindlier treatment. Both North and South, mulattoes soon became numerous. As slavery increased in the South, few indentured servants or other white laborers could be found working on the great tobacco and rice plantations.

It is clear that New England and the lowland South were very unlike, while the middle colonies had some of the traits of both. New England was adapted to nothing but small farms; lowland Virginia, South Carolina, and Georgia to large plantations. In New England, the people worked in a stimulating climate with their own hands; in Virginia, hard labor under the broiling sun was done by slave gangs driven by overseers. In New England, the small holdings and the great stretches of unoccupied land encouraged parents to divide their estates equally among their children; in the South, the large slave-worked estates could seldom be broken up without economic loss, and men kept them together by laws of primogeniture and entail. In New England, the people associated in compact villages to maintain their church congregations; in most of the South, congregations counted for little and the plantations spread over so wide an area that villages were impossible. While in New England the town was the natural unit of government (though counties were created), in the South the county was all-important. In New England, the general rule was that local officers should be chosen by the people; in the South, some were appointed by the provincial authorities and some selected by an aristocratic clique. Parish vestrymen were not elected by the parishioners, for example, but chose their own successors. The Puritans, though by no means the dour, fanatical, unhappy race they are sometimes painted, were likely to be grimly conscientious and self-disciplined; the Southerners were sunnier, freer, and more pleasure-loving. Between the two, in many respects, stood the middle colonies.

Yet, as the eighteenth century wore on, as population and wealth grew, and as society became more complex, social and economic groupings cut across sectional lines. The merchants of Charleston and Portsmouth, Norfolk and Boston, with their busy offices full of bustling clerks, their handsome houses rich in mahogany, plate, and pier glasses, were much alike. A Laurens and a Hancock would have been at home with each other at once. The mechanics of the seaports—vulgar, boisterous, full of class-conscious radicalism, and ready to sally out of their taverns in a mob on small provocation—were much alike from Carolina to Massachusetts. The small farmers—economical, hard-working, and in countless instances almost self-sustaining—were alike in New Hampshire and Maryland, in Pennsylvania and Virginia. And the pioneers of the border area were everywhere stamped with the same traits.

The Back Country

The fourth great section, the border or back country, had come into clear existence during the eighteenth century. It stretched from the haunts of the hardy Green Mountain Boys and the ragged forest clearings of the Mohawk Valley down along the eastern fringes of the Alleghenies, on through the Shenandoah Valley in Vir-

AREAS OF SETTLEMENT IN AMERICA
SHOWING FRENCH FORTS ON THE ST. LAWRENCE AND MISSISSIPPI
TO 1700   TO 1775

ginia, and into the Piedmont area of the Carolinas. Here lived a rude, simple, and intrepid people, who were purely American in outlook.

Buying cheap land at a shilling or two an acre, or taking it by "tomahawk claim," they cleared tracts in the wilderness, burned the brush, and planted corn and wheat among the stumps. They built rude cabins of hickory, walnut, or persimmon logs, notching the timbers into each other at the four corners, chinking the crevices with clay, laying a puncheon floor, and making windowpanes of paper soaked in lard or bear's grease. The men dressed in homespun hunting shirts and deerskin leggings, the women in fabrics made on the spinning wheel and loom set up in every home. They pegged their chairs and tables together from wooden slabs; they ground their meal in homemade block mortars; they ate with pewter spoons from pine trenchers; they went barefoot or wore skin moccasins. Their food was hog-and-hominy, with roast venison, wild turkeys or partridges, and fish from the nearest stream. For defense against Indians the scattered settlers built a fort at some central spring, with bulletproof blockhouses and stockade. They had their own exuberant amusements —merry barbecues at political rallies, where oxen were roasted whole; the "infare" or housewarming of newly married couples, with dancing and drinking; shooting matches, quilting bees, and balls with the Virginia reel. As in the wilder parts of Scotland and Ireland, feuds and sporadic fighting furnished much excitement. On the Pennsylvania border the Scotch-Irish and Germans waged vindictive combats. In Virginia and the Carolinas personal encounters knew no rules, and "gouging" matches made men who had lost an eye no uncommon sight. All border dwellers regarded the Indians with enmity; some tribes were friendly, but in general the settlers waged constant war with the wilderness and the red man and were thus trained to alertness, hardiness, and clannish solidarity.

The border produced picturesque and energetic traders with the Indians, such as George Croghan in the North and the versatile, cultivated James Adair in the Southwest; both friends of the savages, wide-ranging adventurers, and men with a vision of rapid western development. Croghan in late colonial days was active in keeping the Iroquois peaceful in New York, and in opening up the country at the headwaters of the Ohio River; Adair boasted that he was acquainted with two thousand miles of Indian trail. The border produced land speculators like Richard Henderson of North Carolina, who, shortly before the Revolution, resolved to buy much of present-day Kentucky from the Cherokees and convert it into a sort of proprietary colony. It produced daring fighters like Robert Rogers, a Scotch-Irishman of New Hampshire who made himself the hero of the northeastern frontier in the French and Indian War, and John Sevier, who in the Tennessee country boasted of "thirty-five battles, thirty-five victories." It produced the archetype of restless pioneers in Daniel Boone, a North Carolinian of Devon stock, who in 1769 passed through the magic door that pierced the wild Appalachian wall into Kentucky—the Cumberland Gap. By a series of lonely explorations in this rich Indian hunting ground, Boone did much to make the natural attractions of Kentucky known; and he served Henderson and various colonizing groups well. But, above all, the border produced sturdy pioneer farmers who steadily widened the belt of settlement and civilization.

If a land of hardship and peril, the back country was to many also an area of irresistible novelty and fascination. The pages of William Byrd exhale an impression of its natural enchantments. Telling how he ran the boundary line into the wilderness he describes the sweet grapes, both black and white, twining all over the trees; the wild turkeys, whirring away in flocks on every hand; the multitude of pigeons, clouding the skies as they passed between the Gulf and Canada, and sometimes breaking down the larger limbs of mulberries and oaks. He pictures the fat bears, swimming clumsily across the rivers; the opossums, feeding on wild fruits; the wolves, which "entertain'd" them a great part of the night; and the slow-grazing buffalo, of which Byrd's party killed a powerful two-year-old bull. He mentions the sturgeon, which in summer basked on the surface of the rivers. He tells of the ledges of purple-and-white marble, the clear streams pouring over sandy beds where mica gleamed in the sun like gold, the rich forests of oak, hickory, and locust, the distant peaks glimmering against the western sunset. He notes the soft haziness of the sky where the Catawbas or Tuscaroras had fired the brush to drive out game. He tells of the thrill of coming upon an Indian encampment, and observing the grave, dignified demeanor of the braves, often with "something great and venerable in their countenances," and the comeliness of the copper-colored maidens, neither very clean nor very chaste, but bashful before the white men. Once the joys of the wilderness had been tasted, many pioneers preferred it to any other environment.

Culture

By the latter part of the colonial period, culture was beginning to thrive bravely in favored communities. In New England particularly, great emphasis was placed upon education. While the colonies there were still in their infancy, all except Rhode Island had made some elementary schooling compulsory. A number of grammar schools existed. Two flourishing colleges, Harvard and Yale, had been established, and two more, Dartmouth and the College of Rhode Island (now Brown), were gaining a foothold. At Harvard, which had commodious brick buildings, a library of five thousand volumes, and good scientific apparatus, the instruction in theology, philosophy, and the classics lagged little behind that of the best European universities.

In the middle colonies, Maryland alone had a system of public education, and it was ill-organized and weak. Both the Quakers and the Germans conducted schools which were to some extent under Church supervision, while Pennsylvania had many private schools, particularly in and near Philadelphia. New York had some good town schools on Long Island and some grammar schools in New York City, but no general system of instruction. In the South, education was largely in private hands. Ministers and others kept a good many private schools; the Virginia rector, Jonathan Boucher, for example, took boys at twenty pounds apiece, among them Washington's stepson. Rich planters there and in the Carolinas hired private tutors from Great Britain and the Northern colonies, who taught reading, writing, practical mathematics, and Latin and Greek. Only two free schools each existed in Virginia and South Carolina. A number of colleges were founded in the middle and lower colonies—William and Mary in Virginia, which trained Jefferson and many another public figure; the College of Philadelphia (now University of Pennsylvania), which Franklin did so much to set up; the college at Princeton; and King's College, now Columbia University, in New York, which trained Alexander Hamilton and Gouverneur Morris. Wealthy families in New York and the South often sent their sons to the British universities or to the Inns of Court in London.

Newspapers, magazines, almanacs, and even books of

enduring merit were being published in the colonies. The oldest printing press in America was set up as early as 1639 at Cambridge, and its activity was never interrupted. On the eve of the Revolution Boston had five newspapers, and Philadelphia three. Bookdealers became important colonial figures, and a number of libraries (Boston's was founded in 1656) were established. One Philadelphia publisher in 1771 imported a thousand sets of Blackstone's *Commentaries* and himself issued a thousand more. Two men achieved a lasting European reputation as writers, Jonathan Edwards in theology and philosophy and Benjamin Franklin in science and belles-lettres. Both the wealthy Yankee judge, Samuel Sewall, a conservative, stubborn, industrious administrator, and the cultivated planter, Colonel William Byrd of Virginia, Fellow of the Royal Society and first gentleman of Virginia, kept diaries which, like John Woolman's *Journal,* will not be forgotten. The simple Quaker farmer, John Bartram, a precise scientific observer, was called by Linnaeus the world's greatest "natural botanist"; the indomitably busy Cadwallader Colden of New York gained fame by his *History of the Five Indian Nations;* David Rittenhouse of Pennsylvania became internationally known as an astronomer and mathematician. John Mitchell of Virginia, Fellow of the Royal Society, won eminence in botany, medicine, and agriculture. The learned divine, Cotton Mather, who has been called the "literary behemoth" of New England, published no fewer than 383 books and pamphlets, of which his *Magnalia Christi Americana* (American Wonders of Christ) was almost a library in itself. One historian of the late colonial period, Thomas Hutchinson of Massachusetts, is still read with pleasure and profit. Good artists were at work in the colonies, and the eminent Benjamin West, going to England shortly before the Revolution, succeeded Sir Joshua Reynolds as president of the Royal Academy.

A vivid idea of the way in which cultural appliances increased may be drawn from Franklin's *Autobiography*. Born in Boston (1706) in a family so large that he recalled thirteen children sitting at table at once, Franklin was largely self-educated. His father, who had come from Northamptonshire in England, had a little library containing, besides books of polemic divinity, Defoe's *Essay on Projects,* Cotton Mather's *Essays to Do Good,* and Plutarch's *Lives.* Apprenticed at twelve to a printer, the bright lad got hold of other books—Bunyan, Locke, Shaftesbury, Collins, and some ancient classics in translation. With a few pence he bought a volume of Addison's *Spectator,* which fired him with an ambition to write essays. When he went to Philadelphia to better himself, he found literature just taking root in that city. Keimer, the printer, was equipped with "an old shatter'd press, and one small, worn-out font of English." After a sojourn in England, the indefatigably enterprising Franklin set himself to improve the Quaker city.

He established a Junto or "club of mutual improvement," which began with nine members and threw out influential branches. He set on foot a circulating subscription library, the first in America (1731), which rapidly expanded. He founded an academy which, duly incorporated and enriched by gifts from the Penns and others, grew into the university. He started a journal designed to avoid contention and to print real news—*The Saturday Evening Post.* He founded in 1743 the American Philosophical Society. Franklin tells us of the remarkable effect of George Whitefield's eloquent preaching, which coaxed money from reluctant Quaker pockets. He tells, too, how in homes like his own, such luxuries as china and silver crept in to replace plain crockery and pewter; and how inoculation for smallpox was introduced—he bitterly blamed himself, when he lost a fine son of four, for neglecting it. Science always interested him; and presently, sending up a kite into the thunderclouds, he was performing the famous experiment which led a French epigrammatist to say that he seized the lightning from the skies. The political activities which justified the second half of the epigram—"and the scepter from the tyrant"— began in earnest when in 1754 he represented Pennsylvania at the first intercolonial gathering, the Albany Congress. From 1753 to 1774 he was deputy postmaster general for the colonies, and his improvement of the mails contributed not a little to American culture. Altogether, Franklin's career showed both how much could be made of the cultural resources of the colonies and how much an able leader could do to strengthen them.

Wealth was accumulating faster and faster; finer houses were being built, luxury in food and dress was increasing, fashionable conventions were growing commoner. By 1750 all along the seaboard a well-to-do society, acquainted with the best European thought, could be found. In Boston and New York, Philadelphia and Charleston, as much elegance was visible as in any British or French towns outside of London and Paris. But at the same time the frontier was steadily being pressed westward, and the first rivulets of immigration were pouring through the passes of the Appalachians into the Ohio and Kentucky country. Hardy pioneers of the border, with their long rifles and keen axes, cared nothing for luxury, fashion, or ideas; their mission in life was to tame the wilderness. Between the fashionable planters and merchants on one side, the Indian-slaying frontiersmen on the other, stood the great mass of plain middle-class people who were the typical Americans of 1775. Yeomen farmers and small planters, brawny mechanics and bustling shopkeepers, they had grown up with no real knowledge of any land but America, and no taste for any but American ways of life. They were loyal subjects of the Crown, admiring England and proud of their British birthrights; but at least subconsciously they felt that America had a destiny of her own.

The Colonial Heritage

Part of the heritage that the colonies were to bequeath the young nation is evident at a glance. The fact of a common language, the English tongue, was of immeasurable value. It was one of the great binding elements which made a true nation possible. The long and steadily broadening experience with representative forms of government was another priceless part of the heritage. We may take it rather for granted until we remember that the French and Spanish colonies had nothing to show in representative self-government; the British alone permitted their colonists to erect popular assemblies and to create governments in which both electors and representatives had real political responsibility. The result was that British colonists were politically minded and politically experienced. The respect paid to essential civil rights was another important element in the heritage, for the colonists had as firm a belief in freedom of speech, of the press, and of assembly as did Britons at home. These rights were not completely secure, but they were cherished. The general spirit of religious toleration in the colonies, and the recognition that different sects could and should get on with entire amity, must be included in the roster. Every faith was protected under the British flag; despite the traditional fear of Catholicism in England, Parliament was even charged by some colonials after 1763 with showing excessive favor to that religion. Equally valuable was the spirit of racial toleration, for people of different blood—English, Irish, German, Huguenot, Dutch, Swedish—mingled and intermarried with little thought of any difference.

And we should certainly mention the strong spirit of individual enterprise which manifested itself in the colonies, an individualism always noteworthy in Britain herself, but which was now heightened under the pressure of life in a rich but wild and difficult land. The British never permitted such monopolies within the colonies as had crushed individual effort in the French and Spanish dominions. Enterprise irrepressibly responded to opportunity. Taken together, these parts of the colonial heritage were a treasure worth far more than shiploads of gold or acres of diamonds.

Two basically American ideas had also taken root during the colonial period. One was the idea of democracy, in the sense that all men are entitled to a rough equality of opportunity. It was to gain opportunity for themselves and still more for their children that a host of settlers had come to the New World. They hoped to establish a society in which every man should not only have a chance, but a good chance; in which he might rise from the bottom to the very top of the ladder. This demand for equality of opportunity was to bring about increasing changes in the social structure of America, breaking down all sorts of special privileges. It was to effect marked changes in education and intellectual life, making America the "most common-schooled" nation in the world. It was to produce great political changes, giving the ordinary man a more direct control of government. Altogether, it was to be a mighty engine for the betterment of the masses.

The other basic idea was the sense that a special destiny awaited the American people and that they had before them a career such as no other nation was likely to achieve. This general wealth, the energy of the people, and the atmosphere of freedom which enveloped both. It imparted to Americans a fresh and buoyant optimism and an aggressive self-confidence. The idea of a peculiarly fortunate destiny was to be one of the main forces in the swift expansion of the American people across the continent. It was sometimes to have evil effects; that is, it was to lead Americans to rely all too easily upon Providence when they should have been taking painful thought to meet their difficulties—it was to make them complacent when they should have been self-critical. But, along with the idea of democracy, it was on the whole to give American life a freshness, breadth, and cheerfulness that were matched nowhere else. The new land was a land of promise, of hope, of steadily widening horizons.

Chapter Three

THE CONQUEST OF NEW FRANCE AND THE MOVEMENT FOR INDEPENDENCE

The French Wars

As the British colonies in America grew strong and expanded, they were certain to come into collision with their neighbors north, west, and south, the French and the Spaniards. It was certain, too, that the quarrels of Britain, France, and Spain in the Old World would involve the subjects of these nations in the New, for neither then nor later was America isolated from the rest of the Western world. One of the epic stories of North American history is that of the momentous series of conflicts waged between Latin and Anglo-Saxon, conflicts the more dramatic because they involved not merely peoples but ideas and cultures. They were wars between absolutism and democracy, between a rigidly disciplined despotism and free institutions, between men of one intolerant faith and men of many mutually tolerant sects. With the vast wilderness for background, with the Indians as participants, with soldiers of high ability—Frontenac, Montcalm, Wolfe, Amherst, Washington—as leaders, they were marked by episodes of savage cruelty, heroic gallantry, and masterful strategy. The prize of this conflict was the control of the continent.

The Spaniards had been the first to gain a strong foothold in North America. Following Columbus' discovery of the New World, they soon effectively occupied the principal West Indian islands. In 1519 the indomitable soldier, Hernando Cortez, with a small army hewed his way to the center of Mexico, defeated the forces of the Aztec emperor Montezuma, and seized the country. Twenty years later another iron-willed Spanish gentleman, Hernando de Soto, landed in Florida (already the scene of several abortive Spanish adventures), defeated the Indians, left a garrison behind him, and with some six hundred men set out on four years of restless wandering across what are now the Southern States, going as far west as Oklahoma and Texas. Other Spanish explorers, notably Coronado, using Mexico as a base, made expeditions northward in search of legendary wonders, such as the Seven Cities which, situated on great heights, had jewel-studded doorways and whole streets of busy goldsmiths. The Spaniards founded their first settlement in Florida, St. Augustine, in 1565. Before the sixteenth century ended, Spanish soldiers and priests, after bloody fighting, had established themselves in New Mexico, where from Santa Fé thereafter a long line of military governors ruled over the sleepy province. Meanwhile, a hardy Jesuit missionary of Italian parentage, Eusebio Francisco Kino, had explored Lower California and the Arizona country, building chapels and baptizing the wondering Indians. But not until 1769 was California proper occupied by a force of Spanish soldiers, with whom came Franciscan missionaries under Junípero Serra to help found San Diego and Monterey.

The French had not made good their foothold in Canada until just before the English colonists settled in Virginia. To be sure, a *voyageur* of Brittany, Jacques Cartier, had in 1535 carried the French flag up the St. Lawrence to the site of Montreal and half a dozen years later had made a fruitless attempt to colonize part of the new territory.

Indian hostility and the terrible cold of winter sent the settlers home in discouragement. Not until 1603 did the founder of New France appear—Samuel de Champlain, at thirty-six a veteran soldier and sailor, who had narrated his adventures on the Spanish Main so well that the king had made him royal geographer. In 1608 he laid the foundations of Quebec, the first permanent European settlement in New France. For purposes of exploration the next year he accompanied a party of Hurons and Algonquins against the Iroquois, traversed the lake which now carries his name, and near Ticonderoga emptied his musket at hostile savages. The incident has been credited with causing the long enmity of the Iroquois against the French, but that enmity was produced rather by geography and the fur trade, in which the Five Nations were natural middlemen between the English and the Western tribes. The Company of New France, formed under Richelieu's auspices in 1628, did something to give energy to the colonizing venture. And when Louis XIV came into full control of France in 1658, with the sagacious Colbert his chief minister of state, the royal authorities gave the Canadian settlements generous support.

The colonial undertakings of the Spanish, French, and British were alike in being rather haphazard and unplanned, but they differed sharply in other respects. The Spanish conquests involved the subjugation of a fairly numerous, static, and industrious body of natives by a small number of enterprising soldiers, traders, and adventurers intent on a rapid accumulation of wealth. This meant that Spain transferred many features of the feudal system to America. A few thousand hardheaded, hard-fisted conquistadors, ruthless in their methods, were soon in control of millions of Indians. Humane churchmen like Las Casas tried with scant success to lessen the rigors of their domination. The Spaniards opened rich mines in which they worked tens of thousands of Indians to death; they laid out great ranches on which they raised cattle, with some tropical products—sugar, vanilla, cacao, and indigo. The Spaniards were overlords; the Indians, the Negroes (who were soon imported in great numbers, especially into Caribbean lands and Portuguese Brazil), and the mixed-blood offspring of all three races were serfs or slaves. The system produced a great deal of wealth; but this went into a few grasping hands, while the masses remained in poverty. No definite middle class developed. The Spaniard liked to be a ranch owner, a churchman, or a soldier, but he did not like to be a merchant or industrialist. Foreigners, and especially Protestants, were rigidly excluded. As a consequence, toleration never developed. Representative institutions, at least outside occasional town councils, had no existence, and all rule came from above.

The French came to America only in small numbers; and their civilization was molded chiefly by geographical and economic conditions, the autocracy of the French government, and the Catholic Church. What they sought was not silver, gold, or cattle, but fish and furs. They penetrated a chilly, inhospitable land, with a roving population of Indians, many of them hostile. The deeper they pushed into the interior, the more furs they could procure. Establishing but few and weak agricultural settlements, they therefore thrust their posts farther and farther into the wilderness, following the main watercourses—the St. Lawrence, the Great Lakes, the Wisconsin, Illinois, Wabash, and Mississippi, and finally even the waters of Manitoba. While the English colonists created self-governing communities and exhibited boundless individual initiative, Paris gave the French colonies a government both despotic and paternal; though daring leaders appeared, the people never learned to stand on their own feet and take care of themselves. While England encouraged men of every faith to emigrate, France allowed none but Catholics to set foot in Canada. When the final struggle came the British colonies had nearly twenty men for every Frenchman; they were well planted, while the French had few roots in the soil; and they were energetically resourceful, while the French depended upon a centralized authority.

The history of New France passed through five distinct epochs. The first was the thirty-five-year period of beginnings coterminous with the career of the hardy Champlain. After sailing up the St. Lawrence in 1603, the next year he helped found Port Royal (Annapolis) in what is now Nova Scotia. Until his death in 1635 he labored amain to develop Canada as a French colony; to spur on the work of exploration, he himself reaching Lakes George, Ontario, and Huron; and to make the fur trade profitable. The second era had for its most prominent feature the missionary activity of a band of devoted men, representing the Franciscans, the Recollects, the Ursulines, and above all the Jesuits. Some, like Isaac Jogues and Jean de Brébeuf, both tortured to death by the Iroquois, showed unconquerable heroism. In their own *Relations* they wrote one of the most inspiring pages of Catholic history. But their most fruitful field of endeavor was destroyed when in 1649–1650 the Iroquois practically wiped out the Huron tribesmen among whom the Jesuits had met their greatest success, while in 1654 the Erie tribe was likewise exterminated. Commercially the colony in this period was a failure. The year 1660 found not more than a few thousand French people precariously settled in all Canada.

The third era was more fruitful. New France became a royal province, with a governor, intendant, and other officials modeled on those of the French provinces. Louis

XIV, taking a keen personal interest in its fortunes, furnished generous subsidies as well as orders and advice. Fresh shiploads of colonists were sent out. At Quebec in 1659 arrived the first bishop, François Xavier de Laval-Montmorency, who had resolved that Canada should be ruled by the Church, under a regime as strict and austere as that of the Puritan theocracy in New England. His mark is upon Quebec's life still, for, coming into conflict with governor after governor, he usually had his own way.

Finally, however, ambitious ecclesiastics met more than their match when the iron-willed Comte de Frontenac arrived in 1672 as governor and inaugurated the fourth era. A man of tremendous ability and determination, he asserted the dominance of the civil authorities over the Church, temporarily broke the strength of the Iroquois, and fought off the fleet of thirty-four ships which Sir William Phipps led against Quebec in King William's War (1690). During this period the greatest of the French explorers were busy in the Far West—Radisson and Groseilliers, who penetrated beyond Lake Superior; Joliet and Marquette, who mapped much of the upper Mississippi Valley; and La Salle, who descended the Mississippi to its mouth. Before Frontenac died at the close of the century, he had begun to prepare New France for the desperate struggle which all men of vision saw must be fought out with the British. This struggle, running through the Wars of the Spanish Succession and Austrian Succession (Queen Anne's War and King George's War) into the Seven Years' War, fills the fifth and closing epoch in the history of New France.

In the protracted conflict the French had certain advantages. They had been active in taking posts of strategic power. Steadily, by a line of forts and fur-trading posts, they had marked out a huge crescent-shaped empire, stretching from Quebec in the Northeast through Detroit and St. Louis down to New Orleans in the South. They expected to hold and develop this great hinterland, pinning the British to the narrow belt east of the Appalachians. France was a stronger nation militarily than Britain and could send over powerful armies. The highly centralized government of New France was better fitted for conducting war than was the loose association of ill-co-ordinated colonial governments.

But for three principal reasons an ultimate British victory was certain. First, 1,500,000 people of the British colonies in 1754 were a fast-increasing body, compact, tenacious, and resourceful; while New France had fewer than 100,000 scattered and ill-disciplined people. Second, the British held a better strategic position. Operating on inside lines, they could effectively strike westward at what is now Pittsburgh, northwestward toward Niagara, and northward at Quebec and Montreal. They also had the better navy, could more speedily reinforce and supply their troops, and could lay siege to Quebec by water. Finally, they were capable of producing better captains. In Chatham they eventually found a political leader, and in Wolfe, Amherst, and Lord Howe (to whom Massachusetts raised a monument in Westminster Abbey) generals whom the French did not equal; while colonial officers, like the alert Washington who guided Braddock's army, Phineas Lyman who repulsed the French at Lake George, and Lieutenant Colonel Bradstreet who captured Fort Frontenac, won high distinction. The final British victories coincided with equal triumphs under Clive in India.

The seventy years of conflict that closed in 1763 were full of stirring events. Arresting figures emerged—on the French side Cadillac, who founded Detroit, Iberville, who challenged the British from Hudson Bay to the West Indies, and Bienville, who founded New Orleans and laid claim to the Ohio Valley; on the British side the alert and aggressive Governor William Shirley of Massachusetts, the dashing fighter Sir William Pepperell, and the shrewd Governor Horatio Sharpe of Maryland. The story included stubborn sieges like that of Louisbourg, twice taken by the imperial forces; sanguinary pitched battles like those fought at Ticonderoga, where first the French and then the British won; sickening Indian raids on border towns like Deerfield, Massachusetts; and grueling wilderness marches. The rout of Braddock by the French and Indians in 1755, as his army was nearing the site of Pittsburgh, was a humiliating disaster. But the defeat was shortly wiped out by Forbes's capture of that strategic position. In 1759 Wolfe, trying to come to grips with Montcalm at Quebec, took a desperate chance, scaled the high cliffs at night, and brought the enemy to battle on the Plains of Abraham commanding the city. In the ensuing action both he and Montcalm were killed. Not yet thirty-three, the British commander had said the previous night that he would rather have written Gray's *Elegy* than have the glory of beating the French; his real glory was that he forever linked his name with the predominance of the English-speaking peoples in North America, for the capture of Quebec decided the war.

By the treaty of peace in 1763 England took all of Canada from France, and Florida from Spain, which had entered the war against the British Empire. North America from the Atlantic to the Mississippi, with New Orleans excepted, became British. At the same time Louisiana passed from French to Spanish sovereignty.

Imperial Relations

The triumphant Seven Years' War jarred the American colonies into a totally new position with respect to Great Britain. It removed the sharp menace that had been offered by the well-armed French holdings to the north and west, half encircling the colonies as with a jagged scythe. It removed the lesser pressure of the Spaniards to the south. Its campaigns gave many colonial officers and men valuable training in war, and enhanced their self-confidence. It did something to create sentiment for uniting the provinces; a number of proposals for union were broached, the most notable being that drafted by the Albany Congress in 1754, attended by representatives of seven colonies. This plan, which Franklin bore the principal part in shaping, called for a president general appointed by the king, and a federal council whose members should be chosen by the colonial assemblies. The council was to provide for general defense, control Indian relations, and levy taxes for general purposes, while the president general was to have a veto power. Though the plan failed to gain support, it did much to educate people in the idea of union. So, too, did the spectacle of men from different provinces fighting side by side.

Just as the war lessened the old dependence on Great Britain, so it reduced the respect paid to her. Colonial troops, though badly equipped and ill-disciplined, found on several fields that they could fight as well as the British regulars—and in wilderness fighting could do better. They found many English officers blundering, just as the British found many colonials incompetent; they saw that the brave but inept Braddock would have done well to take young George Washington's advice. The New Englanders, electing their officers on a democratic basis, thought badly of the aristocratic British system of appointing commanders.

Finally, the victorious close of the war and the huge expansion of the empire raised questions which became a subject of practical dissension between the colonists and the British government. Of deliberate "tyranny" there was none. But the administration of the empire had to be tightened and systematized. Its defense against jealous neighbors had to be provided for, and this meant taxation. Its economic organization under the Navigation Acts or "acts of trade" had to be revised and strengthened.

British administrative control over the colonies had hitherto been extremely lax. Under the Crown, the principal imperial agency of government was the Board of Commissioners for Trade and Plantations, which had taken almost complete form by 1696. The principal ministers were ex officio members, but the bulk of the work was generally done by a small body of fairly expert and hard-working officials. It guarded the commercial interests of the mother country and the colonies, supervised colonial finances and systems of justice, gave some guidance to colonial enterprise, and proposed new imperial policies. It had certain powers of investigation; it drafted instructions to the royal governors; it nominated colonial officials when offices fell vacant; and it could demand reports from these officers. Parliament, of course, exercised considerable legislative powers over the colonies. In fact, it was the only body available which could deal in a large way with the commercial and other relations of the British Empire, both externally and internally. The Crown, too, had extensive powers. Not only did it appoint the governors of the eight royal provinces (for by 1760 only Rhode Island and Connecticut were self-governing charter colonies, and only Pennsylvania, Delaware, and Maryland were proprietary colonies); it could disallow any laws passed by the colonial legislatures. Such vetoes were normally interposed by the Privy Council, acting on the careful advice of the Board of Trade and Plantations. The Privy Council could also sit as a court of appeal in colonial cases.

The principal parliamentary enactments down to the close of the Seven Years' War had been the various Navigation Acts, applying certain economic principles on which the well-being of the British Empire was supposed to rest. The mercantilist theory of the times held that the wealth of a nation was proportioned directly to its stock of property, gold, or silver; and that individual or corporate enterprise should be controlled by the state to enhance this power. The empire was regarded not as a federation, but as a unit, a consolidated state. In this unit it was supposed that the colonies could contribute to national wealth and power by giving employment to imperial shipping and by producing articles which Britain would otherwise have to buy from foreign lands—sugar, tobacco, rice, naval stores and other raw materials. In return, the mother country could supply manufactures to the colonies, the two main elements in the empire thus becoming complementary. As early as 1651 Parliament, alarmed by the growth of Dutch shipping, passed a Navigation Act which required all colonial exports to England to be carried in English-owned and English-operated vessels. A series of later enactments enlarged the system. They gave England and the colonies a monopoly of the carrying trade of the empire; required certain colonial exports to the European continent to be transshipped in English ports; and regulated the importation of European goods into the colonies in such a way as to favor English manufactures. London limited colonial enterprise in some directions, but encouraged it in others.

At first these laws were not thoroughly enforced. But when in 1763 Britain undertook a revamping and tightening of the colonial system, the mercantilist statutes were overhauled.

The Problem of Federalism in the Empire

Indeed the whole imperial system was overhauled, and the process, involving as it did a reconsideration of the relations of colonies to mother country, precipitated the Revolution. It is this problem of imperial organization, now first presented in a clear-cut fashion, that gives unity and meaning to much of the complex and confused history of the next generation. How to organize and govern an empire so that the advantages of centralized power and of local autonomy could both be preserved—that was the question, and it was one of the most difficult questions that ever confronted statesmen of any age. Could some system be devised whereby the general government at Westminster would exercise control over all matters of a general imperial nature—war, peace, foreign affairs, Western lands, Indians, trade, and so forth—while the various local governments in Massachusetts, Virginia, South Carolina, and elsewhere were allowed to control all matters of strictly local concern? Could a line be drawn between these general and local concerns, be drawn with such skill that it would leave the central government with adequate powers and yet not infringe upon the liberties of men in their local affairs?

This was, of course, the problem of federalism. The British Empire of the mid-eighteenth century, in operation and in fact, if not in theory or law, was a federal empire. It was an empire in which powers were distributed between central and local governments. Parliament had, for a century and a half, controlled all matters of general concern; the local assemblies had, from the beginning, exercised practical control over all matters of local concern. Had the empire, somehow, been frozen in 1750 this would have been clear.

But in law the empire was not a federal but a centralized one. In law and theory Parliament had all power. And when, after 1763, British statesmen addressed themselves to the task of reorganizing the empire they fell back upon the legal or theoretical supremacy of Parliament. They insisted, in the words of the Declaratory Act of 1766, that the colonies "have been, are, and of right ought to be, subordinate unto and dependent upon the imperial Crown and Parliament of Great Britain," and that Parliament had "full power and authority to make laws and statutes of sufficient force and validity to bind the colonies and people of America . . . in all cases whatsoever."

Faced with the opportunity to create a real federal system British statesmen muffed the chance. But the problem was not solved in 1776, nor did it end with the separation of colonies and mother country. It was simply transferred to the United States. From 1775 on to 1787 Americans were confronted with the same problem—with the problem of achieving a unified government for general purposes and maintaining intact the autonomy of the state governments over local concerns. The first American effort to solve this problem—the Articles of Confederation—was a failure. Taught by bitter experience Americans tried again, and in the Federal Constitution of 1787 did construct an enduring federal system.

One of the great themes of this Revolutionary period, then, one which we must not lose sight of amidst the smoke of battle and the march toward democracy, is the solution of the problem of imperial organization and the emergence of a federal system. That system, as finally elaborated, was built upon the experience of a century in the British Empire, the debates and discussions in Britain and America after

1763, the trials of war and the tribulations of the Confederation. The final achievement of federalism, in the Constitution of 1787, was one of the great constructive achievements of the age.

General Causes of Discontent

It is not easy to say when the Revolution began; but it is certain that it was not in 1775. John Adams tried to emphasize the Revolution proper and the Revolutionary War, declaring that the former really ended before the latter began. "The revolution was in the minds of the people, and the union of the colonies," he wrote, "both of which were accomplished before hostilities commenced. The revolution and union were gradually forming from the years 1760 to 1776." Adams was an observant and ambitious young lawyer, who ought to know. But his statement that the Revolution was "in the minds of the people" confronts us with the necessity for another distinction. After all, only a minority of the American colonists by July, 1776, had been convinced of the wisdom of seceding from the British Empire. Probably half the Americans at that date still wished to avert a political divorce. Throughout the war, by John Adams' own testimony, fully one third of the colonists remained opposed to the rebellion, one third were indifferent. It would, therefore, be more accurate to say that the Revolution prior to 1776 was in the minds of part of the people, and the struggle of 1776–1781 was a struggle to impose it on the rest of the people and to make the British government recognize it.

In dealing with the economic causes of the Revolution we have to discriminate sharply between different sections and interests. The Northern merchant had a wholly different set of grievances from the Southern planter, and the Western land speculator from either.

The Mercantile or Navigation Acts injured the Northern colonies far more than the Southern. These Northern colonies had no valuable staples which they could carry direct to England to exchange for manufactured goods. In general, they had to pay for their imports from England with hard money, and to get it they had to trade with the West Indies. They carried wheat, meat, and lumber to the West Indies and in return got cotton, indigo, or sugar. They also got molasses, which they made into rum and traded in Africa for slaves who were in turn sold in the West Indies or the Southern colonies. When Parliament passed the Molasses Act in 1733, this by prohibitive levies restricted New England's trade with the West Indies to the British islands alone. Had the law been rigidly enforced, the New Englanders would have suffered heavy losses. But the Molasses Act was evaded in the most wholesale manner. For example, Rhode Island imported about 14,000 hogsheads of molasses annually, of which 11,500 came from the French and Spanish West Indies. Smuggling was no crime. The English authorities winked at it, and some of them frankly pointed out that in the end the money derived from this illicit trade went to English merchants and manufacturers. The Livingston family in New York, and John Hancock in Massachusetts, grew wealthy from smuggled goods.

The Sugar Act of 1764 was virtually a re-enactment of the old Molasses Act of 1733 in such terms as to make it enforceable. The old prohibitive and uncollectible rate of sixpence a gallon was reduced to threepence, and provision was made for the seizure of all vessels evading the law. Perhaps a rate of twopence would have been justifiable, but the West Indian lobby in Parliament shoved it up to the higher figure. This meant a heavy blow to the economic interests of New England. Rhode Island protested that the

THOMAS JEFFERSON BY THOMAS SULLY

West Indian business was the whole foundation of that colony's trade with England and that of her 14,000 hogsheads of molasses, the British West Indies could furnish only 2500 at most. One clause provided that cases under the Sugar Act could be tried by any vice-admiralty court in America, which meant that a merchant might find his ship and crew taken all the way to Halifax for trial. He could claim no damages if the jury acquitted him. The colonial leader Jared Ingersoll said that the procedure was like burning a barn to roast an egg—decidedly irritating to the man who owned the barn.

Another annoyance lay in the fact that the export tax on continental goods shipped to the colonies from Great Britain was raised in 1764 from 2.5 per cent to 5 per cent. Customs officials were ordered to show more strictness, and enforcement was strengthened by various steps—for example, the stationing of warships in American waters to seize smugglers, and the issuance of "writs of assistance" to enable Crown officers to search suspected premises.

The South was in a wholly different position. It had little or no trade with the West Indies. It sent its staples—tobacco, indigo, naval stores, lumber, hides—direct to England and took manufactured goods in return. But this trade with England was based on a system favorable to the mother country and unfavorable to the colonists. It was in the hands of British mercantile houses and the factors or agents whom they sent out to the provinces. The factors bought tobacco and other commodities at prices often unfairly low; they sold clothing, furniture, wines, carriages, and other goods at prices often unfairly high. Easygoing planters fell into the habit of ordering what they liked from London, paying by notes, and letting their debts run up to ruinous sums. Many debts became hereditary from father to son; as Jefferson wrote after the Revolution: "These planters were a species of property annexed to certain mercantile houses in London." In fact, he computed the total Virginia debt owed to British merchants at the beginning of the Revolution at over two million pounds, estimating it at twenty or thirty times as much as all the money in circulation in Virginia. The planters naturally disliked their English creditors in the same way that Western farmers, at a later period, disliked Eastern mortgage holders. They were quite aware of the fact that the easiest way to get rid of this crushing burden was to rebel against the English yoke altogether and seek refuge in the moratorium or cancellation provided by war.

In the quarter century after 1750, some Southern legislatures passed liberal bankruptcy acts and stay laws which favored debtors. When these reached England the Privy Council almost always vetoed them. The result was an indignant feeling that the rich in England were grinding the faces of the poor. Parliament also tried to stop the resort of the colonies to paper money. Most provinces issued a good deal of paper after 1730, and some made it legal tender; but they met more and more opposition in London. Finally, in 1764 Parliament flatly forbade the colonies to make paper money legal tender for debts, thus creating a new and important grievance of debtor groups all over British America.

Another large economic interest was concerned with land speculation and the settlement of the West. In the Western country, wealth was attained in two main ways: by trading with the Indians for furs and by organizing land companies to acquire, parcel out, and sell great tracts of the wilderness. The fur trader and land speculator wished a free hand in those years just as the oil prospector and timber cutter wish a free hand in the West today. Besides these two groups, we find after 1760 another, the colonial veterans of the Seven Years' War who had been granted Western lands as bounties. Virginia in especial had rewarded her soldiers in this fashion, while Governor Dinwiddie had promised 200,000 acres to the troops who would be brave enough to drive off the French from their great holdings in the Ohio Valley.

Many of the plain people of Pennsylvania, Virginia, and the Carolinas were land hungry. By the close of the war it was clear that there would shortly be a great stampede for the West. One land company after another was being organized; the greatest men on the continent—Benjamin Franklin, George Washington, Sir William Johnson—were keenly interested; there was a confusion of claims, purchases, and surveys.

But while this host were clutching at Western lands, the British government was determining upon a new policy of strict control and policing in the West. To keep peace with the Indians, to prevent the colonists from spreading too far west and thus outgrowing English control, and to put an end to the chaos of overlapping claims, it proclaimed in 1763 that all settlement must stop at the crest of the Appalachians. Lands beyond this "Proclamation Line" were temporarily barred off as a Crown domain, and no Indian lands anywhere were to be sold except to the Crown. The theory was that a little delay could do no harm, that the restive Indians should be given time to quiet down, and that lands could then gradually be opened to the colonists. The Board of Trade and Plantations was soon supporting a scheme for a new Western colony called Vandalia. But this proclamation gave grave offense to the fur traders, the land companies, the bounty holders, and those generally who were hungry for Western holdings. It seemed to slam shut the door which Americans had just fought the French to force open.

The ecclesiastical grievances of the colonies centered in

the relations with the Anglican Church, which was the state-supported Church in all the colonies south of Delaware and in part of New York as well. Three colonies, to be sure, had a Congregational establishment, but although the Congregational establishment was more rigorous, it was the Anglican Church that excited antagonism.

This antagonism rested upon two principal foundations: the fact that many colonists objected violently to paying taxes for the Church and the fact that they feared an Episcopalian hierarchy of political tendencies. Each Anglican clergyman in the South had his parsonage, his glebe, his fixed salary paid by taxes, and his fees. In all the colonies the Episcopalians were decidedly in a minority. In Virginia nearly all the great families of the lowlands—the Washingtons, Lees, Randolphs, Carters, Masons, Carys—were Episcopalians. But west of Richmond, the dissenters— Quakers, Baptists, Lutherans, Presbyterians—were far more numerous. North Carolina had only a handful of Episcopalians, though the authorities tried to make the people support nine Episcopalian ministers. In South Carolina the Church was stronger, but even there the dissenters, with about eighty congregations, were heavily in the majority. No pious dissenter relished paying for the support of an Episcopalian clergyman as well as for one of his own faith.

Another ground for dispute lay in the question of imperial defense. Some Indian fighting was certain, while the French thirsted for revenge, and the Spaniards beyond the Mississippi could not be trusted. The British government did not believe that the colonies could defend themselves. It complained that they had been slow and stingy in raising troops in the recent war and had failed to act in harmony. The only central agency was the imperial government in London. Under George Grenville, therefore, it was shortly decided to keep ten thousand soldiers in North America, paying one third of the cost of maintenance out of colonial taxation. This meant raising about £360,000 a year in the colonies. Grenville, after giving a year's notice and assuring the colonies that he would take a better plan if they offered it, brought in a bill for a stamp tax on newspapers and legal and other documents. Parliament passed it in 1765 "with less opposition than a turnpike bill," and along with it a measure requiring the colonies to furnish the troops with fuel, light, bedding, cooking utensils, and help in obtaining billets. To England this seemed a trifle, but to the colonists the Stamp Act was a clear instance of taxation without representation.

Finally, America was a fertile soil for doctrines of a republican or quasi-republican character. The population for a century and a half had been living in an atmosphere of democracy or "leveling." Economic differences were few; economic opportunity was equally open to all. What aristocracy did exist simply stimulated the growth of democratic principles. There was a little seaboard class or clique which held most of the wealth, and in some provinces, like Virginia and South Carolina, the political power, and against this the rising democracy of the interior conducted a long struggle. The small farmers of the back country, the Scotch-Irish and German immigrants, the laborers and mechanics of the towns, constantly asserted themselves against the older merchants and planters. They did so in the generation before the Revolution with an energy which shocked their superiors, and the same spirit contributed to their revolutionary zeal against the mother country.

When we list the leaders in the revolt against England, we find that they fall into two main groups. One was a set of educated men, writers and thinkers—such men as Samuel Adams, John Adams, John Jay, James Otis, Alexander Hamilton, John Morin Scott, George Clinton, William Livingston, Benjamin Franklin, John Dickinson, Charles Carroll of Carrollton, Thomas Jefferson, Richard Henry Lee, George Mason, Willie Jones, and John Rutledge. They were abetted by a set of radicals of poor education or none, sprung from the mechanics and the backwoodsmen —men like Alexander McDougall, Isaac Sears, and John Lamb in New York; like Daniel Roberdeau and George Bryan in Pennsylvania; like Patrick Henry in Virginia; like Thomas Person and Timothy Bloodworth in North Carolina; like Christopher Gadsden and Thomas Sumter in South Carolina. The second group was impetuous, fiery-tempered, and inclined to take radical views of government; they liked a pure democracy, or something near it. They derived their inspiration from intellectuals like Jefferson and Sam Adams, but they gave the Revolutionary movement, once it was fairly started, much of its brute energy. The first group, however, was much more important in starting it. The educated men used voice and pen earnestly, sending out flocks of pamphlets, filling the newspapers with essays, and spreading their political views by public meetings.

These colonial writers and pamphleteers harked back to two powerful groups of British thinkers: the group which had written to justify the doctrines of the Puritan Commonwealth and the group which had justified the Whig revolution of 1688. That is, they drew their arguments from Sidney, Harrington, Milton, and, above all, John Locke. The second book of Locke's *Two Treatises of Government* contains the germs of the American Declaration of Independence. Locke maintained that the supreme function of the state is to protect life, liberty, and property, to which every man is entitled. Political authority, he said, is held in trust for the benefit of the people alone. When the natural rights of mankind are violated, the people have the right and duty of abolishing or changing the government. This doctrine is written into the preamble to the Declaration of Independence. "The true remedy of force without authority is to oppose force to it," Locke asserted. He also laid another great foundation stone for the Revolution when he expounded, in his *Letter on Toleration,* the view that Church and state properly occupy separate spheres and should be kept apart. In its healthiest character, he showed, the Church is a voluntary organization, supported freely by its members and not by the taxing power of government.

Locke and the thinkers who stood with him were profoundly admired by all educated Americans interested in politics. The Americans in fact inherited their political philosophy at the very time that the British diverged from it. British constitutional practice after 1688 developed a misshapen and undemocratic system of representation. A ruling oligarchy emerged, resting upon a rotten-borough system, upon the refusal to grant representatives to new manufacturing towns, and upon the systematic disfranchisement of large parts of the population. Disfranchisement and rotten boroughs or their equivalent existed in America, but not to the same extent. In fact, a constant struggle went on in America throughout the eighteenth century to broaden the electorate and to see that new counties and western areas were given their fair representation along with the older settlements. America had a substantial measure of true representative government; England had a system of misrepresentative government. Americans believed in natural rights expressed in a fair democratic system, while many Englishmen believed in absolute parliamentary sovereignty and in a distorted governmental system. When trouble with the mother country began in 1765, Americans found that they had a political philosophy full-fashioned to their needs.

Misunderstanding

Seldom have two contestants more completely misunderstood each other than the American colonists and British Crown managed to do in the ten years preceding the Revolution. We must repeat that none of the early British steps was inspired by a desire to "tyrannize" over America. The effort to solve the Indian problem, to garrison the colonies for their own protection, and to strengthen the customs service seemed to ministers in London fair and moderate. But to multitudes of Americans these measures looked like a closely geared engine of oppression. Hard times had followed the war. Men who were out of work and pinched for money wished to find new homes beyond the mountains—and the "Proclamation Line" forbade it. Trade was bad and hard cash very scarce; yet the Crown seized this moment to drain gold and silver out of the country by new tariff levies, strictly enforced. Under the Stamp Act it was meanwhile taxing the colonists without their consent. The moneys thus raised were being used to maintain a standing army, for which most colonists saw no real need; and this grim garrison was in turn to help enforce the burdensome customs regulations and the unfair tax laws. To Crown officers it seemed proper to ask the courts for "writs of assistance." But to the colonists these writs, applying to everybody, giving absolute power to officers who held them, and allowing every man's home or shop to be ransacked, were intolerable. The British government had passed certain laws for restricting or forbidding manufactures in the colonies. The Crown thought this fair, for it believed that the empire would prosper best if the colonies concentrated on raw materials and Britain on manufactured goods. But many colonists resented the interference.

And behind these disputes over practical matters lay a theoretical disagreement which gave the whole quarrel depth and created an unbridgeable gulf.

Most British officials held that Parliament was an imperial body which exercised the same authority over the colonies as over the homeland. It could pass laws for Massachusetts as it passed laws for Berkshire. The colonies, to be sure, had governments of their own. But the colonies were nevertheless merely corporations and, as such, subject to all English law; Parliament could limit, extend, or dissolve their governments whenever it pleased. This is not so, said the American leaders, for no "imperial" parliament exists. Their only legal relations, they argued, were with the Crown. It was the Crown which had agreed to establish colonies beyond the sea, and the Crown had provided them with governments. The king was equally a king of England and a king of Massachusetts. But the English Parliament had no more right to pass laws for Massachusetts than the Massachusetts legislature had to pass laws for England. If the king wanted money from a colony, he could get it by asking for a grant; but Parliament had no authority to take it by passing a Stamp Act or other revenue law. In short, a British subject, whether in England or America, was to be taxed only by and through his own representatives.

It must be realized, however, that both in Britain and in America feeling was sharply divided on the main issues; that the developing contest was not so much a struggle between colonies and motherland as a civil conflict within the colonies and also within Great Britain. In Parliament the eminent Whig leaders, Chatham, Burke, Barré, and Fox, leaned strongly toward the side of the American patriots;

in the colonies a stanch body of Tories upheld the British government. It must also be realized that some extreme men on both sides were glad to use the quarrel to further their own views. Lord Bute would have been glad to drive roughly over the colonists in order to diminish the spirit of democracy that was expressed by John Wilkes and others in England. Samuel Adams in Massachusetts and Patrick Henry in Virginia were equally willing to use the conflict to advance their radical ideas in colonial politics and remake society on a basis more friendly to the plain man.

Organizing a Revolt

The revolt against the British government was not a vast, spontaneous movement. Instead, it was carefully planned by shrewd men and laboriously and sagaciously executed by some of the most active spirits on the continent. It could never have succeeded if it had been left unorganized. It was because the patriots were well organized, and because the Tories or loyalists were not, that the former won the day.

The first step in the movement was the appearance of sporadic and unconnected rioting in resistance to the British measures. The Stamp Act of 1765 produced this response in several colonies. Legislatures protested, and Virginia in especial passed influential resolutions. But the most effective action was that taken by mobs which in Massachusetts, New York, Virginia, North Carolina, and other provinces destroyed stamps and other property, compelled the stamp collectors to resign or flee, and even menaced the lives of the royal governors. This rioting had much popular support at first, but the orderly and wealthy citizens soon showed their disapproval of it. Organizations called Sons of Liberty also sprang into existence to maintain a popular opposition to Parliamentary oppression.

The second step was the institution of an economic boy-cott by groups of merchants, sometimes supported by the provincial assemblies. This was called forth by the Towns-hend Act of 1767, imposing duties on tea, paper, glass, and painters' colors. Merchants and substantial citizens in nu-merous communities adopted nonimportation or noncon-sumption agreements, boycotting the articles on which British taxes had been laid. This measure was adopted in Boston in March, 1768, and spread through the colonies till within two years it had affected all of them. In some colonies English imports fell off by nearly one half; in others the agreements were badly enforced. The movement ended in 1770, when Parliament repealed all the Towns-hend duties save that on tea.

The third step was the formation of a system of local and intercolonial committees of correspondence. Sam Adams of Massachusetts, a born propagandist and organizer, was the principal leader in this undertaking. He was the most pow-erful figure in the general assembly of freemen which, meeting in Faneuil Hall, controlled Boston, while he played a leading role in the Massachusetts legislature. In the sum-mer of 1772 citizens learned that the royal government in-tended to give both the governor and the superior judges permanent salaries, thus freeing them from popular control. A town meeting was summoned on November 2 and took the step which "included the whole Revolution." It set up a Committee of Correspondence to communicate with other towns throughout the province. Soon every locality had a similar committee, and the province was humming like an angry beehive. The people from Massachusetts Bay to the Berkshires were brought into a well-marshaled array. A Tory writer later testified, "This was the source of the re-bellion. I saw the small seed when it was implanted. It was as a grain of mustard. I have watched the plant until it has become as a great tree." Other colonies set up similar local committees; and the Virginia Burgesses in 1773 appointed the first of a system of intercolonial committees which rapidly overspread the whole continent.

The fourth step toward revolt was the creation of revolutionary legislatures, or, as they were generally called, provincial congresses. The old regular legislatures would not serve the radicals for two reasons. They were in large part composed of conservative men, property holders attached to the existing order, and slow to act; and they were partly under the control of the royal governors, who could prorogue or adjourn them when he liked. The first provincial congresses appeared in 1774, as a result of news of the passage of the Boston Port Act. The means by which they were created was usually very simple.

In Virginia, for example, news of the Boston Port Act arrived in May, 1774, and electrified the province. The legislature was sitting at the time. Jefferson, Patrick Henry, Richard Henry Lee, and four or five others at once held a meeting in the council chamber. They decided to proclaim a day of fasting and prayer. This was an unusual solemnity, for there had been none since the Seven Years' War. They looked over the precedents of Parliament under Cromwell and induced the Burgesses to appoint June 1, 1774, as the day. Governor Dunmore promptly dissolved the Burgesses as insubordinate. They marched eighty-nine strong down the long street to the Raleigh Tavern, where in the Apollo Room, the scene of many balls and feasts, they came to order with Speaker Peyton Randolph in the chair. The radical members proposed a new nonimportation agreement. Richard Henry Lee wanted additional steps taken, but some held back—for "a distinction was set up between their then state and when they were a House of Burgesses." But they did not hold back long. On May 29, horsemen from Boston rode in, bearing letters from other colonial capitals. They brought the news that a stoppage of all trade with England was now proposed. Peyton Randolph, with twenty-five Burgesses advising him, decided to call the members of the late House together on August 1; and with this call the first Provincial Convention, or revolutionary legislature, in the colonies was born.

Chapter Four

THE REVOLUTION AND CONFEDERATION

The Resort to Arms

LITTLE by little the irritation and turbulence in the colonies' increased. The presence of British troops in various cities gave the radical leaders an opportunity to excite the populace. In New York in 1770 occurred the bloodless "Battle of Golden Hill." As Cadwallader Colden put it, "an ill-humor had been artfully worked up between the townspeople and the soldiers"; at length, "some townspeople began to arm, and the soldiers rushed forth from their barracks to support their fellow-soldiers"; and only the interposition of army officers and magistrates prevented a conflict. In Boston a more serious collision took place. The noise of the fife and drum when the two regiments of the garrison changed guard on Sunday angered some puritanical townspeople, while rougher elements liked to jeer and bait the "lobster-backs." As the troops were ordered to show the greatest restraint, this baiting grew more and more impudent.

Finally, on March 5, two soldiers were attacked and beaten by townsfolk. Bells were rung to call people into the streets. A sentinel posted at the customhouse was reviled and pelted with ice and other missiles. When Captain Preston and a small squad came up to protect him, the jeering and pelting increased. "Fire if you dare—fire and be damned!" cried the mob. The troops behaved well until finally somebody clubbed a soldier to the ground, and ris-

ing, he discharged his musket. A general melee ensued, and
other soldiers, without orders, fired, too. Three men were
killed outright and two mortally wounded. As the drums
beat for a general turnout of troops, the governor appeared
and restored order. One of the mortally wounded men said
on his deathbed "that he had seen mobs in Ireland, but
never knew troops to bear so much without firing as these
had done." But the Boston Massacre seemed to many a
climactic instance of British tyranny. Its anniversary was
solemnly celebrated, and it aroused the populace as nothing
had theretofore done.

The British ministry, headed by Lord North, failed to
draw the proper lesson from this rising suspicion and hostility. In 1772 another significant incident occurred. The
little eight-gun warship *Gaspee,* busy enforcing the laws
against smuggling in Rhode Island waters, ran ashore in
June near Providence. A body of citizens attacked it, over-
mastered the crew, and burned the hated craft. All duties
imposed by the Townshend Acts had been repealed save
that on tea, which was maintained to enforce the principle.
Tea drinking practically ceased in the colonies, and the
East India Company fell into financial difficulties. To help
it, the ministry in 1773 allowed it to send tea to America
under conditions which made the product very cheap; but
Lord North still insisted on maintaining the threepence-a-
pound duty in the colonies, saying that the king regarded
it as a test of authority. That test led directly to American
revolt. Keen indignation was aroused by what seemed to
Americans a subterfuge. The company sent over a number
of ships. At every port the people were determined to resist.
In Charleston the tea was locked up in vaults; from Philadelphia and New York it was sent back in the ships which
had brought it. In Boston excitement ran especially high.
On the night of December 16, 1773, a party of about fifty

men disguised as Indians, led by Sam Adams himself, boarded the ships, burst open 343 chests of tea, and emptied them into the harbor. No town official attempted to prevent the destruction of property. By this act of violence, which was applauded from Maine to Georgia, Boston threw down its gage at the feet of the Crown—and the British government swiftly took it up.

George III and the majority in Parliament were determined to punish rebellious Boston. Burke and Chatham pleaded for a conciliatory course. But the ministry carried through Parliament a series of five drastic acts. One radically changed the much-cherished charter of Massachusetts by destroying some of its most liberal features. One made the British military commander in America, General Gage, the governor of Massachusetts, with four regiments for his support, and authorized the quartering of troops in the homes of the people. One provided that officers charged with capital crimes while executing their duties might be sent to England, with witnesses, for trial. One shut the port of Boston to all commerce until compensation was paid for the tea destroyed and evidence was furnished that the duties would be loyally paid. Finally, the Quebec Act extended the boundaries of Canada over the entire territory north of the Ohio and west of the Alleghenies. This last measure was not punitive in character; it had long been in contemplation, was based on much expert study, and was intended to provide a better regulation of the Northwestern fur trade and to put the French Catholic inhabitants of the Michigan and Illinois country under a congenial authority. But it was ill-timed, and the people of the seaboard colonies naturally thought that it closed the Northwest to them.

These harsh acts of Parliament aroused anger and consternation. The intercolonial Committees of Correspondence were galvanized into action. Meetings were held, newspaper articles written, pamphlets scattered broadcast. When the Virginia legislators, at their Raleigh Tavern meeting, sent out a summons for an annual congress to discuss "the united interest of America," the response was instant and enthusiastic. Virginia's Provincial Convention elected delegates, and other provinces followed. On September 5, 1774, the first Continental Congress assembled in Philadelphia, with every colony except Georgia represented. Its fifty-one delegates included Washington, Benjamin Franklin, John Adams, and other able men. Studiously ignoring Parliament, they adopted addresses to the king and to the people of Britain and America. They drew up a stiff declaration of colonial rights, in which they asserted that the provinces had "exclusive power" to legislate on their own affairs, subject to a royal veto, but promised that they would agree to parliamentary acts upon external commerce made for the bona fide interest of the empire.

But above all, the Continental Congress adopted two measures which pointed straight toward a breach with the British ministry. One was the preparation of an agreement to be scattered broadcast, binding its signers to stop within three months all imports of English goods and within a year all exports to British ports, including the West Indies. This meant grim sacrifice. Virginia planters could no longer ship their tobacco to English consumers; Massachusetts skippers could no longer engage in the profitable West India trade. Eleven of the colonies (New York and Georgia holding aloof) ratified the "association," while in all thirteen energetic local committees undertook to enforce it. They administered oaths, published lists of violators, and sometimes resorted to the whipping post or tar and feathers. The other step was the drafting of a resolution—practically an ultimatum—by which Congress not only approved the opposition of Massachusetts to the recent acts of Parliament, but declared that if force were used against the people of that colony, "all America ought to support them" in resistance.

A collision had now become inescapable. Either the Acts of Parliament would be made nullities or force would have to be used in executing them. Neither side could recede. Parliament declared that Massachusetts was in rebellion and offered the Crown the resources of the empire to suppress the revolt. All over the country arms were being bought and military companies were drilling. Gage in Boston believed that the spring of 1775 would bring an attack on his force. Deciding to seize some illegal military stores at Concord, on the evening of April 18, he set a column of eight hundred men in motion. Patriots were on the watch, and a lantern in the tower of North Church flashed word to Paul Revere beyond the Charles River, who galloped off to arouse the countryside. The embattled farmers gathered at dawn with their muskets and, as Emerson later wrote, fired the shot heard round the world. Sam Adams was not far away, and as he heard the rattle of the guns he exclaimed: "What a glorious morning is this!"

The Revolutionary War

Within a few days an undisciplined and half-armed but formidable mass of patriot troops had besieged Gage and his army in Boston; within a few weeks the last royal governments were being overturned all over the country. The second Continental Congress, meeting in Philadelphia on May 10 as a frankly rebellious body (though it sent a last conciliatory address to the king), organized the troops about Boston into the "American continental army" and appointed George Washington to take command. The fortress of Ticonderoga, commanding the main approach to

Canada, was brilliantly captured by a force under Ethan Allen, leader of the Green Mountain Boys. As the American lines were pushed closer about Boston, Gage realized that his position could be threatened from Dorchester Heights on the south, and from the hills behind Charlestown on the north. When the patriots took steps on June 16–17 to occupy the latter position, they precipitated the first great battle of the war, Bunker Hill.

Like Bull Run eighty years later, Bunker Hill had an importance out of all proportion to its immediate results. The Americans, about thirty-five hundred strong, had planted themselves during the night on both Breed's Hill, where they built a redoubt, and Bunker Hill. At dawn their activities were observed. Gage called a council of war and, though he might have cut off the American works in the rear, decided to attack them in front. This piece of hardihood was probably inspired by the British impatience for a square stand-up fight. Infantry were landed below the American position, formed in line, and at three o'clock in the afternoon of a broiling day sent to the attack. In full-dress uniform, with knapsack, three days' rations, ammunition, and musket, a total load of perhaps 125 pounds each, they advanced slowly in beautiful order. When they were forty yards from the entrenchments the Americans, aiming at the waistline, opened fire with terrible effect; the British recoiled, were re-formed, and came on again to meet another murderous fire at twenty yards; they recoiled once more, were again rallied, and this time swept over the entrenchments as the patriots fired their last two rounds. It was magnificent, but it was criminally unnecessary. An equal force, occupying Charlestown Neck under naval protection, could have starved the Americans into early surrender. Altogether, the British losses were 1054 men, the American losses only 441.

The battle proved to the Americans that even without proper organization or equipment, they could repulse the best regular troops of Europe, and they gained enormously in confidence. Howe, in immediate command on the British side, was so sickened by the carnage that he never forgot it. When he replaced Gage, who was recalled to England in disgrace, he showed a timidity in pressing American troops to battle that helped cost England the war.

American Disadvantages

The conflict dragged over six years, with fighting in every colony, and a dozen pitched battles of importance. Repeatedly the patriot forces came close to total disaster. It was difficult for Washington to form a true army out of the mixed and ill-trained forces at his disposal and still harder to hold it together. Loyalist sentiment was widely diffused, and indifference was even more general. In New England, Virginia, and parts of the Carolinas the people showed a vigorous fighting temper. But New York seemed quite as much Tory as patriot; in Pennsylvania the Quakers would not fight, while most Germans were averse to leaving their farmsteads; in North Carolina many upland settlers, hating the lowland people, rallied to battle for the king; and much of Georgia, threatened by the Creeks and grateful for a special royal subsidy, held back from the struggle. At the lowest computation, twenty-five thousand Americans bore arms for the Crown; and had the loyalists been sedulously cultivated, carefully marshaled, and ably led, the outcome of the war would have been different.

The patriot forces were at first wretchedly organized. When Baron von Steuben, a staff officer of Frederick the Great, arrived in 1778 as a volunteer to improve the situation—soon rising to be inspector general—he found the regiments ranging from three to twenty-three companies in

MOUNT VERNON

GEORGE WASHINGTON

strength. The quality of the commissioned officers was poor, for in some colonies any glib-tongued man with a pleasing personality could induce men to enlist under him as captain, or with the use of rum and money might get himself elected to higher rank. Democracy in New England and elsewhere made for insubordination; the farmer or villager who knew his captain as a neighbor was loath to take orders from him, so that Washington wrote that the Yankees regarded their officers "as no more than broomsticks." Nor were many privates moved by any strong sense of responsibility. They felt that they had enlisted for periods terminable at their convenience. When cold winter weather came on, when they heard that crops were ripening without hands to harvest them, or when they grew homesick and discouraged, they slipped out of camp. Washington besought Congress for long-term enlistments, which were authorized in September, 1776; but this by no means fully met the evil. To stiffen the discipline, Washington finally urged Congress to give courts-martial the power to inflict a maximum of five hundred lashes upon offenders.

Repeatedly the army almost faded away. After the patriots took possession of Boston in March, 1776, and Washington transferred his troops to New York, he found that he had only eight thousand men fit for duty; the total British forces were thirty-five thousand, and Howe landed on Long Island with at least twenty thousand effectives. Naturally he had no difficulty in smashing the little force of patriots which he found at Flatbush. There were left in front of him only some fifty-five hundred troops, and he might have overwhelmed and captured them all if he had moved promptly; but he let the opportunity slip until Washington escaped to Manhattan Island under cover of fog. Then came the patriot defeats on Manhattan and at White Plains; and as Washington retreated across New

Jersey, his army melted away almost to nothing. The New York and New England militia deserted in droves. He lost much of his food, baggage, and cannon. Before he had reached the Delaware River the New Jersey and Maryland militia had also forsaken him. When he took up winter quarters he had about thirty-three hundred men, half of them men whose steadiness he could hardly trust. Only his daring and skill that winter, in his brilliant blows at Trenton and Princeton, saved the country. He was able to begin the campaign of 1777—"the year of the three gallows," said the Tories—with eleven thousand troops. That was the number he had when he marched through Philadelphia on August 24, 1777, with what one writer of the time called "ragged, lousy, naked regiments." Howe moved on Philadelphia with twenty thousand trained troops, and Washington, defeated at Germantown, was driven back to spend a cruel winter at Valley Forge.

The patriots were also fearfully handicapped by their inability to finance the war effectively. They had no way to float bond issues. Taxation was almost out of the question. No continental agency had power to lay taxes; Congress had to request the thirteen states for tax levies; and since the states were jealous, stingy, and badly governed, they gave but grudging and inadequate help. The whole amount raised for national purposes by state taxation, down to 1784, came to less than six million dollars in specie value, or not two dollars per capita! Loans brought in quite inadequate sums—domestic loans nearly twelve million dollars, loans from abroad (chiefly France, with Holland and Spain contributing) not quite eight millions. The principal reliance of the United States in fighting the Revolution had to be placed upon paper money.

First and last, the country was snowed under with paper bills. They depreciated so rapidly that although their face value ran up to about $240,000,000, the actual return to the treasury in specie was less than $38,000,000. By the spring of 1781 continental notes were so near zero that barbershops were papered with them and frolicsome sailors returning from their cruises took the bundles of worthless money in which they were paid, had suits of clothes made from them, and paraded through the streets in this tattered finery. Naturally, the depreciating bills were a source of great injustice, discontent, and disorganization. As a contemporary observer, Pelatiah Webster, wrote: "Paper money polluted the equity of our laws, turned them into engines of oppression, corrupted the justice of our public administration, destroyed the fortunes of thousands who had confidence in it, enervated the trade, husbandry, and manufactures of our country, and went far to destroy the morality of our people."

The patriot cause suffered heavily, again, from the keen distrust of Congress by the separate colonies and from their jealousy of one another. It was quite impossible to set up a strong continental government. The colonies were in revolt against a centralized control and believed in local home rule. Moreover, after the first flush of patriotic ardor had passed away they had little sisterly feeling. Virginians disliked the Yankees as a set of vulgar, grasping, and ultra-democratic schemers, and even the reserved Washington wrote caustically of their bad manners. The Yankees thought the Southerners inclined to be proud and aristocratic. Each colony had lived so much to itself that when John Adams rode to the Continental Congress he hardly knew the names of the principal New York and Pennsylvania leaders. Congress had to beg on bended knee for support of the army and the treasury, and its pleas often went unheeded.

Then, too, the Americans had practically no navy—

though John Paul Jones soon performed some striking exploits at sea, raiding boldly in British waters. Until 1778 the British held general control of the ocean, and partial control thereafter. They could attack almost anywhere they liked along a fifteen-hundred-mile coastline. They had plenty of money and supplies; they brought over nearly thirty thousand German mercenary troops; and their officers possessed a superior training in military affairs. It is not strange that at first they confidently expected victory.

American Advantages

But the Americans had great advantages as well as handicaps, and in the end these turned the scale. One lay in the theater of conflict. They fought in their own sparsely populated land, much of it still wilderness, three thousand miles from Britain. An army might be beaten in one place, and another would spring up hundreds of miles away. The British could no more hold down such a vast territory than they could nail currant jelly to a wall. To transport men and supplies over the wide ocean was costly and difficult, while proper strategic management of the whole British force from London was impossible. Another advantage lay in the superb fighting spirit which American troops at certain critical moments did exhibit. These farmer-soldiers, fresh from the hunting path and plow trail, individualistic and erratic, might be exasperating three fourths of the time, but they sometimes fought like men inspired. The Northern troops who rallied to destroy Burgoyne's invading army in 1777, and the Southern soldiers who took defeat after defeat in 1780–1781, always returning to the attack till final victory came, proved that a patriotic yeomanry could be unbeatable. Still another advantage after 1778 was the alliance with France, burning to revenge herself upon Britain —an alliance that brought men, money, encouragement, and, at the final crucial moment, command of the coast. And by no means least among the patriot blessings was the stupid mismanagement which Burgoyne, Howe, and Clinton gave the British troops. Wolfe was dead, and no Wellington emerged.

The culminating American advantage was that of leadership—for the Americans had George Washington. Chosen by Congress with little knowledge of his capacities, he proved all in all to the patriot cause, its best guide, and support. He can be criticized on narrow military grounds. He never handled an army larger than a modern division, he made many missteps, he was defeated again and again. Yet, taking command at forty-three, he became the soul of the war. This Virginia planter and frontier colonel was its informing spirit because of his unflagging patriotism, his calm wisdom, his serene moral courage; because in the gloomiest hours he never lost his dignity, poise, or decision; because he knew how to combine enterprise and caution; because his integrity, elevation, and magnanimity never failed, his fortitude never faltered. He knew how to bide his hour to strike, so that his patient vigilance gave him the title of "Fabius."

He could lose his temper fiercely when provoked beyond endurance, as the traitorous Charles Lee learned at the battle of Monmouth; but in general he had an iron self-control, so complete that when in later years the news of Wayne's terrible defeat at the hands of the Indians was brought him at a presidential dinner party he betrayed no emotion to his guests. Scrupulous in everything, he drove his troops hard and punished army offenses severely, but his justice and devotion to his men won their utter loyalty. When he began his address to the unpaid and discontented troops at Newburgh with the words, "Gentlemen, you will permit me to put on my spectacles, for I have not only

grown gray, but almost blind in the service of my countrymen," many shed tears. It was characteristic of him that he
accepted nothing but his expenses for his Revolutionary
services and kept account of these expenses with minute
care. When the war was done, like Cincinnatus he thought
only of going back to his beloved farm, which he wished to
make the best in America; "Agriculture has ever been the
most favorite amusement of my life," he wrote. But he remained at the call of duty. Less humanly appealing than
some other heroes of the republic, he has remained pre-
eminent in the massiveness of his character, the fixed elevation of his aims, and the wisdom and breadth of his mind.
Goldwin Smith has justly remarked that the three finest
things in the Revolution "are the character of Washington,
the behavior of his army at Valley Forge, and the devotion
of the better class of loyalists."

Independence

What had begun as a war for the "rights of Englishmen"
and the mere redress of grievances became in little more
than a year a war for independence. This was perfectly natural. At first, Congress warmly protested its loyalty to the
Crown. But the bitterness caused by bloodshed and destruction, the resentment aroused by the implacable attitude
of George III, and a sense of the natural right of Americans
to determine their own destiny soon led to complete separation. Early in 1776 Washington's army raised a distinctive
American flag. At the same time a profound effect was
being produced by the pamphlet *Common Sense,* written
by a brilliant young radical, Thomas Paine, lately come
from England. He argued that independence was the only
remedy, that it would be harder to win the longer it was
delayed, and that it alone would make American union
possible. As June arrived, many members of Congress be-

Charles Edouard Armand Dumaresq

SIGNING THE DECLARATION OF INDEPENDENCE

came impatient. A Virginia delegate, Richard Henry Lee, moved a resolution for independence, which John Adams seconded. A committee of five, for whom Thomas Jefferson held the pen, then drew up a formal declaration of independence, which Congress adopted on July 2 and proclaimed on July 4, 1776.

The men who drew up and adopted this epoch-making document were not content with a mere declaration of independence. They confessed to "a decent respect for the opinions of mankind," and they were at pains to set forth in detail the causes that "impelled them to separation" and the philosophy that justified it. Nor were these causes—some twenty-five or thirty of them are listed—cited as in themselves justifying so drastic a step. They were listed, rather, in order to prove, on the part of George III, "a design to reduce them under absolute despotism." It is significant that at the very beginning of their national history Americans took their stand on principles and proclaimed a philosophy.

And what are these principles of government here given immortal expression? "We hold these truths to be self-evident," wrote Jefferson:

> That all men are created equal, that they are endowed by their Creator with certain unalienable Rights, that among these are Life, Liberty and the pursuit of Happiness.—That to secure these rights, Governments are instituted among Men, deriving their just powers from the consent of the governed,—That whenever any Form of Government becomes destructive of these ends, it is the Right of the People to alter or to abolish it, and to institute new Government, laying its foundation on such principles and organizing its powers in such form, as to them shall seem most likely to effect their Safety and Happiness.

What we have here, of course, is the philosophy of democracy, a philosophy which had never before been given so succinct or so eloquent a statement. There are certain things—so the Americans said—that no reasonable man can doubt—self-evident truths. There is the truth that all men are created equal—that all men are equal in the sight of God and equal before the law. There were, to be sure, even as Jefferson wrote, many inequalities in America: the inequality of rich and poor, of men and women, of black and white. But the failure of a society to live up to an ideal does not invalidate the ideal, and the doctrine of equality, once announced, worked as a leaven in American thought. Soon men everywhere were asking: if all men are created equal, why do we find them unequal? And under the impact of this great ideal they set about the task of realizing it in fact.

Another great truth proclaimed in the Declaration is that men are "endowed" with "unalienable" rights—among them life, liberty, and the pursuit of happiness. These are not rights granted to men by some benevolent government and held at the pleasure of that government. They are rights with which all men are born and which they cannot lose. This principle, too, worked as a ferment in the American mind—and in the minds of men elsewhere in the world, until in time it came to be seen that no government which denied any of these great rights to men had the right to exist.

For, as the Declaration pointed out, it was precisely to secure these rights that governments were organized in the first place. What we have here is the "compact" theory of government—the theory that men once lived in a "state of nature," that in such a state they were continually in danger, and that in order to protect themselves they came together and set up governments, granting to those governments just enough power to protect their lives, their liberty, and their property. In short, men made government to do good, not evil; made it to protect them, not to injure them. And the moment government failed of the purposes for which it was established, it no longer deserved the support or allegiance of men.

If men could make governments, they could unmake them, for it is their right to alter or abolish a bad government and to institute a new one. This, to be sure, had always been considered revolution and had always been carried through with violence and bloodshed. But now Americans were saying that this was neither a revolutionary nor necessarily a violent act, but a proper and lawful one.

And they shortly proved that this was not mere theory. Even as the Revolution was under way, during the stress and turbulence of war, they set about to translate this idea into reality. Meeting together in conventions they did, legally, abolish their old governments and set up new ones; they wrote into their constitutions solid guarantees of life and liberty and happiness. The ideas that had for centuries been the property of philosophers were taken out of the realm of philosophy and made law.

Marches and Battles

The great decisive battle of the war, its turning point in a military sense, was Saratoga. At the beginning of 1777 the British had large forces in Canada, and a strong army in New York under Howe. Had these troops been concentrated at New York, the Crown could have put thirty-five thousand strongly equipped regulars in the field. If an energetic British commander had then used them to strike relentlessly at Washington's little army of eight thousand Continentals in New Jersey, as Grant in 1864 struck relentlessly at Lee in Virginia, the revolt would almost certainly have been crushed. What Washington most dreaded was this concentration of troops to destroy him. But the authorities in London, badly advised by Burgoyne, who had gone home on leave, decided to keep their forces divided. One army, under Burgoyne, was to move from Canada southward upon Albany, at the head of navigation on the Hudson; Howe's army in New York was to move northward up the Hudson to Albany. The king endorsed the plan. Full instructions were then sent from London to the Canadian authorities to launch the northern half of the joint expedition. But no definite instructions were sent to Howe —who moved against Philadelphia instead of Albany!

A radical defect of the Burgoyne scheme was that it prevented an irresistible unification of British forces. Another radical defect was that once the northern army had advanced into American territory, it was much too far from its base. When Burgoyne reached Fort Edward in upper New York, he was 185 miles from Montreal, and every forward step put more difficult terrain between him and his supplies. He had to look about for provisions in the surrounding country. At Bennington, in the southern part of what is now Vermont, were large stores of breadstuffs and cattle, guarded only by a few militia. To seize them, and to strike a blow at a district which, he wrote, "abounds in the most active and most rebellious race of the continent, and hangs like a gathering storm on my left," he sent some thirteen hundred Germans and others against Bennington. They ran into a hornets' nest. The yeomen soldiers of New England, mustering two thousand strong under a veteran of the French war named John Stark, overwhelmed them.

Meanwhile, a fast-increasing American army confronted Burgoyne's main force on the upper Hudson. When the two armies clashed at Freeman's Farm on September 19, 1777, the Americans numbered about nine thousand men, the British about six thousand. Other engagements completed the discomfiture of Burgoyne, who was soon mired down in the wilderness, exhausted, and losing heavily while the American army rose to twenty thousand. On October 17, surrounded on all sides, his troops laid down their arms. He had proved the folly of taking an army nearly two hundred miles from its base into a wild country swarming with hostile recruits.

Burgoyne's defeat had far-reaching consequences. At one stroke nearly one fourth of the king's effective troops in America were lost. The Hudson was placed permanently under American control. The patriots took new heart. In Paris Benjamin Franklin had been laboring manfully to induce Vergennes, the Foreign Secretary, to send aid to the Americans. When news came that Howe was in Philadelphia and that Burgoyne had taken Ticonderoga, French enthusiasm had cooled. But when word arrived of Saratoga, Franklin's friend Beaumarchais is said to have dislocated his arm in hurrying joyously to inform the king. On February 6, 1778, France and the United States signed a treaty of alliance which placed a wholly new aspect upon the war. Already the gallant Lafayette, who came to the United States at his own expense to serve in any capacity, had been made a major general by Congress. Already the kings of France and Spain had made secret loans, with which large quantities of arms and munitions had been purchased. Now the French prepared to send over six thousand excellent troops under Rochambeau to reinforce Washington; they furnished money and supplies in larger quantities; and the operations of the French fleets greatly aggravated the difficulties of the British in supplying their forces.

Having failed to conquer the North, the British turned to the South. Their plan was to seize Georgia, which was notoriously weak, and move irresistibly northward, gaining loyalist aid as they went. In the closing days of 1778 they took Savannah and in 1779 occupied interior areas of Georgia and South Carolina. The Americans sent General Benjamin Lincoln to meet the situation. But he allowed himself to be shut up in Charleston, and in May, 1780, the British captured him, his five thousand men, and the principal Southern seaport together. It was one of the heaviest blows of the Revolution. All South Carolina was soon overrun. A second American commander, the "hero of Saratoga," Horatio Gates, went south to stay the tide. Instead, his little army of three thousand, half of it raw militia, was crushed by Lord Cornwallis at Camden (August 16, 1780). Their total loss in killed, wounded, and captured was two thousand, and Gates did not halt in his flight till he had covered nearly two hundred miles.

But at Kings Mountain a force of a thousand loyalists from western Carolina had meanwhile been defeated by a larger patriot army. A third American commander, Nathanael Greene, far abler than his predecessors, now arrived on the Southern scene. He, too, was defeated—at Guilford Courthouse early in 1781—but he showed astonishing skill in long and rapid marches. Indeed, while in nine months he lost four important battles, he wore the British troops out, and his threats in combination with the hostility of the inhabitants finally forced them back into Charleston and Savannah. Like Washington, Greene lost engagements but won his campaigns.

And while Greene was clearing the lower South, another British army was nearing its doom. Cornwallis left the Cape Fear country in late spring and moved northward to join the force of the traitor Benedict Arnold in Virginia. After an ineffectual pursuit of American forces under Lafayette, he withdrew to Yorktown at the mouth of the York River,

E. A. Abbey

From a Copley print, copyright, Curtis-Cameron Company

GENERAL VON STEUBEN DRILLING TROOPS AT VALLEY FORGE

The
AMERICAN REVOLUTION
▪ ▪ ▪ ▪ ▪   WASHINGTON 1776-77
━━━━━   BURGOYNE - ST. LEGER 1777
—o—o—   HOWE 1776-1777
—x—x—   CORNWALLIS 1778-81
╋╋╋╋╋   WASHINGTON 1781

which he fortified. At this time Washington had some six thousand men near New York and Rochambeau had about five thousand at Newport, Rhode Island. Just as Cornwallis retired to the coast, word came from the French admiral in the West Indies, De Grasse, that he could offer his co-operation. Washington saw his opportunity and brilliantly seized it. By marches of magnificent rapidity, he brought a combined American and French army of sixteen thousand men before Yorktown. Cornwallis' eight thousand troops were cut off from escape by sea by De Grasse's fleet. His outer redoubts were taken; his inner defenses were battered down by American artillery. On October 19 he sent his sword to Washington, who ordered it received by General Lincoln, and the British troops stacked their arms while their band played *The World Turned Upside Down*.

The war was now practically ended. For a time King George stubbornly refused to acknowledge defeat. But during 1782 the Southern ports were all abandoned, and the royal forces soon exercised no authority whatever beyond the sound of the garrison bugles in one city, New York.

The Peace Treaty

In the treaty which in 1783 ended the war, Great Britain made generous terms. Had her government chosen, it might have driven a hard bargain as to boundaries. The British fleet under Rodney had just won a decisive victory over the French in the West Indies, and the British forces in New York could not be dislodged. It is true that American riflemen under George Rogers Clark had penetrated the wild country north of the Ohio River, capturing British posts in what is now Indiana, Illinois, and Michigan. The leading British minister, Shelburne, who dealt with the American plenipotentiaries, Benjamin Franklin, John Adams, and John Jay, might have tried to draw a tight line around these conquests. Instead, he conceded to the new republic all the country between the Alleghenies and the Mississippi, with the northern boundary nearly as it now runs; while he handed Florida over to Spain and gave Americans large fishing rights off the Canadian coast.

This generosity bore valuable fruit. Had the British tried to hold a great part of the Northwest, friction with the United States (by no means lacking anyhow) would have been constant and serious. The natural march of the republic was westward, and its expansive energies were exerted in a direction which finally compelled the French to cede Louisiana and the Mexicans to cede the area north of the Rio Grande—but which, especially after 1815, gave little anxiety to the British Empire. Indeed, Canada and the United States expanded to the Pacific side by side and today hold the best part of the continent as fast friends and allies.

The Growth of Democracy

In external relations, America had accomplished a memorable revolution. But internally an equally important change had taken place. Quite as important as the cutting of the British connection was the profound alteration which these years brought to American society.

Separation from England, of course, meant an immediate gain in political democracy. Governors were now chosen by the people and not by the Crown, the upper chambers of the legislatures were made elective instead of appointive, and laws demanded by the populace were safe from a veto. But equally important were the internal reforms which broadened the suffrage and made representation more equitable. In Pennsylvania a tremendous demand arose in 1775–1776 for two democratic steps: one giving the long-slighted western counties a representation in the Assembly commensurate with their population, the other abolishing the property qualifications and naturalization requirements which had restricted voting to a small favored class. Both reforms were decisively won. In March, 1776, the legislature admitted seventeen additional members, most of them from the western area, while the suffrage was soon broadened to permit any male taxpayer to vote. In some states, like Virginia, the old-settled sections still held an unfair predominance in the legislature, and in others, like Massachusetts, property qualifications were still demanded for the ballot. But in Pennsylvania, Delaware, North Carolina, Georgia, and Vermont the ballot was freed, so that soon any taxpaying "biped of the forest," as one disgusted conservative put it, might vote.

The dispersion of the loyalists made another great contribution to democracy. Many conservative and propertied Tories had shown dislike for those whom Dorothy Hutchinson called "the dirty mob." Devoted to the old order, they exiled themselves in a passionate mixture of scorn and sorrow. When Howe evacuated Boston, almost a thousand loyalists sailed with him, and another thousand soon followed—their motto, "Hell, Hull, or Halifax." Nearly all the important property owners of the province of New York were Tories. When the British evacuated Charleston, a great crescent-shaped fleet of a hundred ships sailed down the bay with departing loyalists—a magnificent and tragic sight. Upper Canada and the Maritime Provinces received more than sixty thousand refugees, the West Indies thousands more, and England a dejected host. "There will scarcely be a village in England without some American dust in it by the time we are all at rest," wrote one. Following their departure the homely, hard-working farmers, shopkeepers, and artisans were free to create a civilization after their own hearts. Dignity, leisure, and culture

ARNOLD'S MARCH TO QUEBEC

From a painting by N. C. Wyeth

thenceforth counted for less, energy and rude self-assertion for more. The pushing trader and speculator were more prominent in American society. Everybody was counted equal, everybody was in a hurry, and nearly everybody thought more of the dollar.

A strong impetus toward democracy was also supplied by the successful attack on three bulwarks of privilege—the destruction of primogeniture and entail, the breakup of great Tory estates, and the overthrow of the Anglican Church establishment wherever it existed. Virginia was the colony in which entail and primogeniture were most firmly rooted. Their effect had been to preserve great family estates intact. As Jefferson said in his *Notes on Virginia,* the province was thus given a set of great aristocratic families, who were "formed into a patrician order, distinguished by the splendor and luxury of their establishments." The holders of Westover, Shirley, Tuckahoe, and other manorial dwellings looked out across princely domains. Thomas Jefferson led the attack on entail in the Virginia legislature and, at almost the first assault in 1776, swept it away. All estates were thereafter subject to unrestricted sale. In 1785 Jefferson also succeeded in abolishing primogeniture. Someone proposed that the eldest son should get at least a double share. "No, unless he eats a double allowance of food and does a double amount of work," Jefferson retorted. When the French traveler, Brissot de Warville, shortly visited Virginia, he was able to record: "The distinction of classes begins to disappear." Great estates were rapidly broken up among the sons or were sold in parcels to newcomers while the children took the money and went west. Other Southern States—Georgia, South Carolina, Maryland—rapidly followed Virginia's example.

Similarly, the confiscation of the huge land tracts of the proprietaries and the rich Tories made for a democratic system of smallholders. The two principal proprietors were the Penn family in Pennsylvania and the Lord Baltimore family in Maryland. In memory of her founder, Pennsylvania granted the Penns £130,000, but Harford received only £10,000 from Maryland. Virginia confiscated a number of estates, notably that of Washington's genial friend, the sixth Lord Fairfax. North Carolina seized the Granville holdings of millions of acres. New York took over all the Crown lands and in addition fifty-nine specified Tory estates, including the Philipse holdings of about three hundred square miles. The De Lancey estate in Westchester and the Roger Morris lands in Putnam County were sold to more than five hundred holders. The confiscated estate of Sir John Johnson in upper New York ultimately gave homes to ten thousand farm people. Massachusetts seized a number of holdings, including that owned in Maine by Sir William Pepperell, a baronet who could ride thirty miles in a straight line on his own land. All the way from New Hampshire, where Sir John Wentworth lost his domain, to Georgia, where Sir James Wright suffered the same fate, small farmers jubilantly moved on to rich lands that would once have taken them only as tenants.

The religious aristocracy connected with the British regime went down along with the landed and official aristocracy. In New England the special privileges of the Congregational Church, which had nothing to do with the Crown, persisted. Massachusetts even strengthened them. But in the South the privileges of the Anglican Church crumbled away.

The Revolution utterly wrecked the establishment in North Carolina, where not one of its pulpits was left occupied. In other states it gave the political radicals, and the dissenting sects like the Baptists and Presbyterians, a golden opportunity. North Carolina adopted a Constitution in 1776 which guaranteed religious freedom and forbade any establishment. South Carolina took the same step in her Constitution of 1778. Georgia did so in her Constitution of 1777. But the fiercest fight was waged in Virginia. Here the establishment was strongly entrenched, for most of the aristocratic families were Anglicans. Even such a political firebrand as Patrick Henry believed that state support of religion was indispensable to piety and good morals. But the dissenting sects found leaders in two great liberals bred within the Church of England, Thomas Jefferson and James Madison.

It was easy for these leaders to carry the first trench by obtaining a guarantee of religious toleration. Madison wrote into the Constitution of 1776 the simple declaration: "All men are equally entitled to the free exercise of religion." But the establishment remained, and a ten years' battle was required to overthrow it. Jefferson called it "the severest contest in which I have ever been engaged." Beginning in 1776, he and his friends succeeded year by year in suspending the ecclesiastical taxes and in 1779 abolished tithes forever. But their antagonists carried resolutions in 1776 declaring that the question of a general tax levy for all churches should be reserved, and behind this demand for a general religious tax rallied a powerful party. In essence the plan would have established all Christian denominations, made them equally state religions, and supported them out of the public purse. Its most redoubtable advocate was the eloquent Patrick Henry.

The crisis came in 1784–1786. Henry, by his irresistible forensic power, carried in the House of Burgesses a resolution declaring: "The people of this commonwealth ought to pay a moderate tax or contribution for the support of the Christian religion, or of some Christian church or denomination, or community of Christians." But when an effort was made to implement this expression by a specific bill, the opposition rallied all its forces. In a tremendous debate between Henry and Madison, the latter carried off all the honors. The bill was postponed, and this allowed the liberal leaders to wage a campaign of education. In 1786 the measure was finally buried out of sight, and at the same time Jefferson's famous bill for religious freedom was passed—a bill declaring that the government must not interfere in Church affairs or matters of conscience or impose any disabilities for religious opinion. This epochal measure became the cornerstone of religious freedom not only in Virginia, but also in many new states of the West.

Much, too, might be said of the measures soon taken in various states to strengthen the foundations of education. The conflict had a distressing effect upon private schools and colleges. Yale College was for a time closed; so was King's College, now Columbia. As late as 1797 the president of William and Mary was teaching a group of barefoot boys, while in 1800 the Harvard faculty consisted of the president, three professors, and four tutors. During the years 1780–1784 not a single bookseller advertised in the principal newspaper of Boston.

But the Revolution had one happy effect in arousing a general demand for popular training—for free public schools. It was at once seen that democratic self-government required an educated electorate. Governor George Clinton of New York remarked in 1782: "It is the peculiar duty of the government of a free state where the highest employments are open to citizens of every rank to endeavor by the establishment of schools and seminaries to diffuse that degree of literature which is necessary to the establishment of public trusts." Jefferson wrote: "Above all things, I hope the education of the common people may be attended to; convinced that on their good sense we may rely with most security for the preservation of a due degree of liberty." Poverty at first hampered the states, but this new demand in time resulted in far better facilities for elementary instruction than before the war. And, of far-reaching importance for education were the provisions of the Land Ordinance of 1785 making available millions of acres of public land as an endowment for public schools.

Lack of a National Government

The outlook of the young republic was thus hopeful and progressive. Yet one dark cloud lay on the horizon. The thirteen states had never succeeded in setting up a really *national* government. They had adopted in March, 1781, certain Articles of Confederation, but this system, which was simply a "league of friendship," was feeble and inadequate. No true national executive existed. No national system of courts had been set up. The Continental Congress, which consisted of one house in which each state had a single vote, was too weak to be effective. It could not levy taxes, enlist troops, punish men who broke the laws it passed, or compel the states to observe the treaties it made with other countries. Worst of all, it could not raise enough money to carry on the functions of government or pay interest on the national debt.

The Revolution, in short, had given the American people an independent place in the family of nations. It had given them a changed social order, in which heredity, wealth, and privilege counted for less, and human equality for more; in which the standards of culture and manners were temporarily lowered, but those of equity were raised. It had given them a thousand memories to deepen their patriotism: Washington unsheathing his sword under a Cambridge elm, the bloody slopes of Bunker Hill, the death of Montgomery under the walls of Quebec, Nathan

Hale saying "I only regret that I have but one life to lose for my country," the prison ships in the Hudson, Benedict Arnold foiled as he tried to betray his country, the piercing cold of Valley Forge, Marion's guerrilla fighters in South Carolina earning him the nickname of "the swamp fox," Benjamin Franklin saying "We must all hang together or we shall all hang separately," Robert Morris, the patriot financier, patiently collecting money for the cause, Alexander Hamilton storming the redoubt at Yorktown, the British fleet sailing out of New York Bay in its grand evacuation.

But the American people still had to show that they possessed a genuine capacity for self-government—for making a success of their republic. They still had to show that they could solve the problem of imperial organization. They had not yet proved it. Their "league of friendship" seemed to be turning into a league of dissension. Their Congress was sinking into utter contempt. The quarrels among the states were growing positively dangerous. No group suffered more from the chaotic state of affairs than the army, which failed to receive the food, clothing, or pay it needed. Its officers had a frequent toast: "Here's to a hoop for the barrel"—and if a hoop were not furnished, the barrel seemed likely to collapse into a pile of staves.

Chapter Five

MAKING THE CONSTITUTION

An Epochal Achievement

By common agreement the United States has one of the most ingenious and effective constitutions ever prepared, a constitution which, unlike Britain's, is written, but which has expanded flexibly with the nation. The story of how it came into existence is of unusual interest. Gladstone said that "As the British Constitution is the most subtle organism which has ever proceeded from progressive history, so the American Constitution is the most wonderful work ever struck off at a given time by the brain and purpose of man." Actually it, too, was largely an evolutionary product. But it took general shape in one of the most remarkable conventions of modern times.

It was probably fortunate that the Articles of Confederation, which the states adopted near the close of the Revolution, were so clearly defective. Had they offered a somewhat better framework of government, efforts might have been made to patch them up, and the country might have labored for many decades under a poor constitution. Because they broke down almost completely, they were thrown aside; because the breakdown sprang from their weakness, the new Constitution was made exceptionally strong. It was fortunate also that American affairs reached so desperate a pitch as they attained by 1786, when a serious commercial depression reigned. Only a manifest crisis could lead many suspicious Americans to accept the powerful new central government.

Weakness of the Confederate Government

For in 1786 the outlook seemed black. Not only was the country without any really vigorous national machinery of government; the thirteen states had become so disorderly that men spoke of possible war between some of them. They were quarreling over boundary lines—in Pennsylvania and Vermont even breaking heads over them. Their courts were handing down decisions which conflicted with one another. The national government, which should have had the power to lay whatever tariffs were necessary and to regulate commerce, did not. This government should have had authority to levy taxes for national purposes: again it did not. It should have had the sole control of foreign relations, but a number of states had begun their own negotiations with foreign countries. The nation should have had exclusive control over Indian relations, but several states managed the savages to suit themselves, and Georgia began and ended an Indian war.

When internal disorders threatened the security of property in great areas, the sober middle classes grew alarmed. When the depression became heaviest in 1785–1786, it produced intense hardship wherever people lived close to the subsistence level. All along the frontiers money was scarce, markets were prostrated, and crops rotted on the ground for want of takers. People resorted to barter. Debtor groups demanded that the state governments manufacture paper money to move their crops and pay their obligations. They asked for a moratorium on debt collection and for statutes making cattle or grain legal tender. The petition of the town of Greenwich, Massachusetts, in January, 1786, recited that foreclosure sales of land took place daily at one third the true value, that cattle sold at half price, and that taxes during the preceding five years had equaled the whole rental of the farms. Political contests assumed the form of struggles between creditor and debtor classes. In many states the antagonism between poor and well-to-do became intense. A typical pronouncement was that of a South Carolina group which denounced Governor Rutledge and other aristocrats: "the nabobs of this state, their servile toadeaters the bobs, and the servilely servile tools and lickspittles of both, the bobbetts."

Seven state legislatures were carried by the paper-money forces in 1786. In Rhode Island they passed measures under which every man could satisfy his obligations by practically worthless currency. As a rhymester wrote:

> *Bankrupts their creditors with rage pursue;*
> *No stop, no mercy from the debtor crew.*

Since the rag money was a full tender for debts owed to people in other states, Connecticut and Massachusetts indignantly passed retaliatory measures. The paper-money forces failed, however, to carry the two legislatures which dominated all northern New England, those of Massachusetts and New Hampshire; and here armed disturbances broke out. The existing Massachusetts Constitution was very conservative. It had erected special defenses for property in suffrage qualifications and officeholding qualifications. The conservative legislature had then levied heavy taxes to pay the Revolutionary debt, which was largely held by speculators. It is not strange that an agrarian revolt occurred. The adjournment of the legislature in July, 1786, gave the signal for the uprising which, led by a veteran of Bunker Hill, has gone down in history as Daniel Shays's Rebellion.

The state acted energetically under Governor Bowdoin,

General Lincoln, and some wealthy men who lent their money in the crisis, and it was easy to stop Shays's march when he tried to plunder the national arsenal at Springfield, and to scatter his forces. But the brief struggle profoundly alarmed conservative circles all over the nation. It seemed to presage a revolutionary movement toward the left. General Knox wrote Washington that New England had twelve or fifteen thousand desperate men who held what would now be called Communist views. "Their creed is, that the property of the United States has been protected from the confiscations of Britain by the joint exertions of all and therefore ought to be the common property of all." They had shocked "every man of principle and property in New England." Washington, who thought that the Massachusetts authorities should have been even more rigorous, wrote in evident consternation: "There are combustibles in every state which a spark might set a fire in." That was the general view. And the logical inference was that a stronger national government was needed to help the states deal with disorder. "It is clear in my mind," wrote Stephen Higginson of Massachusetts to Nathaniel Dane, "that we cannot long exist under our present system; and unless we soon acquire more force to the Union by some means or other, Insurgents will arise and eventually take the reins from us. We shall inevitably be thrown into . . . convulsions which will result in one or more Governments, established with the loss of much blood."

The quarrels of the state governments had already produced severe distress among the groups whose livelihood depended upon some measure of co-ordination. Merchants were in desperation over the lack of a uniform currency. They had to deal with a curious hodgepodge of coins minted by a dozen nations, many clipped and short in weight; with counterfeit pieces, and with a maddening variety of state and national paper bills, fast depreciating in value. It was clear that nothing less than a standard national currency would suffice. All exporters bemoaned the lack of protection for their enterprise in trying to market American goods abroad. The feeble Continental Congress had found it impossible to re-establish the old commercial relations with the British Empire and especially with the West Indies. Spain had defiantly closed the mouth of the Mississippi to American commerce. Even at home no means existed by which traders could be sure of collecting money due them. A New Yorker who sued for payment in Pennsylvania was at the mercy of Pennsylvania courts and juries, which naturally stood by their own fellow citizens. The fast-growing body of American manufacturers were at the mercy of price-slashing competition from Europe.

But the worst evils arose from the deliberate impediments raised against commercial intercourse among the states. A number, anxious to prevent the dumping of European goods and to gain revenues, laid tariffs on all imports. Three main stages appeared in the process. During the war, Virginia alone had levied duties upon a broad range of goods, for she maintained a considerable commerce, exporting tobacco and importing various commodities, and could afford to do this. Then in the first three years after the peace all the states, except New Jersey, placed duties on imports, but for revenue only, not protection. Finally, by 1785 New England and most of the Middle States had developed promising home industries and suffered from European competition. They therefore set up protective tariffs.

An element of interstate retaliation quickly crept in. The Southern States and some small Northern States had few manufactures and needed imported goods. Delaware and New Jersey created free ports for European wares, while

Connecticut also passed laws to encourage the direct shipment of European goods. Restrictions were also laid on the movement of vessels, so that New Jersey men, for example, could not cross the Hudson to sell vegetables in New York without paying heavy fees. Naturally, feeling among the states grew savage. North Carolinians, denouncing Virginia and South Carolina, compared their state to a cask broached at both ends. Oliver Ellsworth said that his little Connecticut was like "Issachar of old, a strong ass crouching down between two burdens."

A wide variety of creditor groups besides the merchants and manufacturers deplored the want of any national authority which could place effective restraints upon the "leveling" tendencies of radical legislatures. They included moneylenders and mortgage holders who were distressed by state "stay" laws and by the wholesale issues of rag money. They included American holders of British claims, for the radical groups in control of some legislatures and courts had made debts owed to Britons uncollectible. They included many officers and soldiers who had received land warrants in part payment for their Revolutionary services. They included the land speculators who had bought up great areas, either in soldiers' lands or in confiscated lands, at cheap rates, and were anxious to resell them. These landholders wanted a national government strong enough to protect the frontier against Indians, to ensure order in newly settled areas, and to protect titles.

Finally, an important body of holders of Federal and state securities viewed with anguish the chaotic financial conditions of the time and the popular aversion to taxes. In the last fourteen months under the Articles of Confederation, interest on the internal and external debt of the nation was approximately $14,000,000, while the national revenues were only $400,000! Washington summed up the situation when he wrote James Warren in 1785: "The wheels of government are clogged."

The Northwest Ordinance

One great success was scored by the government of the Confederation. Faced with the question of what to do with the unsettled lands west of the Alleghenies (for the states one by one ceded their claims here to the general government), it devised a wise plan which did much to make the United States the country it is. It decided to open them to orderly and progressive settlement; to encourage the inhabitants to develop self-government by regular stages; and, finally, to erect new states, similar in powers to the original thirteen. This scheme was embodied in the Northwest Ordinance (1787), which covered the region north of the Ohio and provided for the ultimate creation of from three to five states. Slavery was never to enter. Three regular stages of government were arranged. Congress was first to create a "territory," appointing a governor and judges who were to make laws subject to a Congressional veto. Later, when the population reached five thousand, the people were to have a legislature of two chambers, electing the lower house themselves. Finally, when the territory attained sixty thousand people, it was to be made into a full-fledged state. Thus the United States solved its "colonial problem." A pattern was established which the nation followed as it expanded to the Pacific and which finally gave it forty-eight states.

But in most other ways the Confederation was a disappointment. Washington wrote that the states were united only by a rope of sand, and another observer declared that "our discontents were fermenting into civil war." Congress now had too few members of ability, and its prestige was too low, to enable it to devise a better form of government. Thomas Paine had long before suggested that "a continental conference be held, to frame a continental charter." A few farsighted leaders who gathered to discuss commercial questions brought this about.

Calling the Convention

The preliminaries of the Constitutional Convention are a familiar story. While thoughtful men were growing sick of national weakness and the bickerings of the states, a special commercial problem was demanding attention. Maryland held sovereignty over the entire Potomac River, where it divides her from Virginia, to the southern bank. Virginians feared that Maryland would interfere with their free navigation of that noble stream; and in 1785 representatives of Virginia and Maryland met at Mount Vernon with George Washington to discuss the navigation of the Potomac and Chesapeake Bay. Madison, who was there, had been greatly depressed by the general disorder of commerce and believed that a larger conference should be held with the object of getting the states to vest its regulation in Congress. This body met at Annapolis in 1786; when delegates from only five states appeared, it seemed an utter failure.

Fortunately, one of the delegates was the audacious Alexander Hamilton, who snatched victory out of defeat. He induced the gathering to call upon the states to appoint commissioners who should meet in Philadelphia the following May to consider the situation of the United States and to "devise such further provisions as shall seem to them necessary to render the Constitution of the Federal government adequate to the exigencies of the Union." The Continental Congress was at first indignant over this bold step, but its fatuous protests were cut short by the news that Virginia had elected Washington a delegate. Congress then fell into line, fixing the second Monday in May, 1787, as the date of meeting. During the fall and winter all the states but contumacious little Rhode Island elected delegates.

The delegates were chosen by the state legislatures. Some legislatures were controlled by radical agrarian groups, and in all of them the defenders of state sovereignty were strong. Yet most of them instructed their delegates to create a strong national government, and sent to Philadelphia a body of men who were overwhelmingly conservative in their general philosophy of politics and overwhelmingly nationalist in their views. This was partly because men as yet hardly comprehended the idea of parties in the modern sense, partly because the emphasis on new commercial regulations suggested that men expert on commercial matters should be chosen, and partly because the early announcement that Virginia had selected George Washington put other states on their mettle to choose strong and sober men.

Early May found the delegates straggling into Philadelphia by ones and twos. Washington was characteristically punctual, arriving on the thirteenth; and clad in black velvet, wearing a ceremonial sword, he was immediately a cynosure of attention. Benjamin Franklin on the sixteenth gave a long-remembered dinner for the delegates then in town, broaching a cask of porter that a friend had sent him and doubtless opening plenty of old Madeira. His guests included James Madison of Virginia, diminutive in stature but a giant in his powers of political analysis. A graduate of Princeton, and a lawyer-planter who spent much time in his fine library, he was next to Franklin the most learned member of the Convention. He was to prove the most industrious and constructive-minded of the delegates. Another guest was the sixty-five-year-old George Wythe, who had taught Jefferson, Madison, John Marshall, and other luminaries of the Virginia bar much of their law. Still another was the governor of Virginia, Edmund Randolph, the owner of some seven thousand acres with two hundred slaves.

Among the Pennsylvanians were Robert Morris, the portly banker who had raised the money which kept Washington's armies in the field during the gloomiest days of the Revolution. It was at Morris' handsome house that Washington stayed during the sessions. Gouverneur Morris was there, son of a wealthy New York family, and now a leading lawyer and speculator of Philadelphia. Jared Ingersoll, who had studied in the Middle Temple and risen to be one of the best lawyers in Pennsylvania, was present, and so was James Wilson, a brusque, hardheaded man of Scottish birth and education, the best-read jurist in America. It would have been difficult to assemble at a dinner table anywhere in the world in 1787 more talent and character; certainly no Old World group could have boasted more impressive figures than the grave, dignified Washington and the delightfully wise and benevolent Franklin, who, as a contemporary wrote, seemed "to diffuse an unrestrained freedom and happiness."

It is worth noting that some of those who had been most active in bringing on and fighting the Revolution were not delegates to the Convention. Jefferson was in France; Patrick Henry had refused election; those three firebrands, Tom Paine, Sam Adams, and Christopher Gadsden, had not been chosen. The radicals, in short, were not adequately represented.

The Convention at Work

The Convention was that rare creation, a truly deliberative body. In view of the fact that each state had been allowed to send as many delegates as it liked—for every state voted as a unit—this was remarkable. But for reasons of economy, most states sent small delegations. Only fifty-five men in all attended; some came but for a short time, so that at the close only thirty-nine were present; and a few, including Washington, were habitually silent in debate. About half were college graduates, and a heavy majority were lawyers, so that they expressed themselves concisely and well. No verbatim report of debates was kept, and the versions given in the journals of Madison and others doubtless eliminate much verbosity; but no one can read these summaries without being impressed by the logical cogency of most of the utterances. They were aided in their discussions by the rule of secrecy which the Convention strictly kept. Publicity would have magnified the dissensions; it would have tempted members to make speeches for the galleries or press; and it would have laid them open to pressure from their constituents. The sober citizens of Philadelphia deserved praise for their refusal to pry into the Convention's work. Once at his dinner table Franklin mentioned to friends the old fable of the two-headed snake which starved to death because the heads could not agree on which side of a tree to pass; he said he could give an illustration from a recent occurrence in the Convention; but his friends reminded him of the rule of secrecy and stopped him.

At the outset the delegates tacitly agreed that they would not revise the Articles of Confederation, but write a wholly new Constitution. In this decision they exceeded their powers. The Continental Congress had called the Convention "for the sole and express purpose of revising the Articles of Confederation." But, as Madison later wrote, the delegates, "with a manly confidence in their country," simply threw aside the Articles and went ahead with a new form of government. It was, as Hamilton remarked, a revolutionary step, and an eminent authority, John W. Burgess, later declared that if Napoleon had done such a thing, it would have been pronounced a *coup d'état,* yet we must remember that many of the states had specifically instructed their delegates to create a union adequate to all the exigencies of the crisis.

In describing the work of the Convention, it is important to lay emphasis upon a few great general considerations. The delegates knew that a complex mechanism had to be set up, that no simple government would suffice. To begin with, they had to reconcile, with scrupulous nicety, two different powers: the power of local control which was already being exercised by the thirteen semi-independent states and the power of the newly created central government. It was a task for which only the history of the British Empire afforded precedent. In the empire as it existed prior to 1763 there was, to all intents and purposes, a federal system—a division of governing powers between central and local authorities. But the other federations created up to that time had without exception been small in area; they had almost without exception been exceedingly loose; and they had seldom been successful for any long period. James Madison and a few others had made an intensive study of government in general, and of the Greek, Helvetic, and Dutch Confederations in particular, while most of the delegates were well read in political thought. The principle adopted was that the functions and powers of the national government should be carefully defined, while all other functions and powers should be understood as belonging to the states. The powers of the national sovereignty, being new, general, and inclusive powers, simply *had* to be stated.

The Final Handiwork

Hand in hand with this process of statement went the construction of the national machinery. Here also a general principle underlay the work. It was understood that three distinct branches of government should be set up, each equal and co-ordinate with the others: the legislative, executive, and judicial powers, so adjusted and interlocked as to permit of their harmonious operation, but at the same time so well balanced that no one interest could ever gain control. This eighteenth-century idea of the balancing of powers was a Newtonian conception of politics. The principle was naturally derived from colonial experience and strengthened by the writings of Locke and Montesquieu, with which most of the delegates were familiar. The American definition of a tyrannical government was one in which a single element assumed a dominant role. It was natural also to assume that the legislative branch, like the colonial legislatures and British Parliament, should consist of two houses. Not everyone believed in a single executive; but the advocates of a plural executive were silenced by an appeal to the general example of the colonies and states.

The decision to set up a legislature of two branches made it much easier to adjust the fundamental quarrel in the Convention over the powers of the small states and the large states. The small states asserted that, as under the Confederation, they were entitled to precise equality with their greater sisters; that little Connecticut should never be trampled over by great New York, or little Maryland by great Virginia. The large states asserted that power should be proportioned to size, population, and wealth.

By the compromise finally adopted, the small states were given equal representation with the large in the Senate, but in the House of Representatives the seats were to be based upon population. When it came to the executive, the greatest difficulty lay in fixing upon a mode of election. Should the President be chosen by Congress? That would go far toward making him dependent on the legislative branch, and so upsetting the balance of power. Should he be chosen by popular vote? The people of the United States were scattered over an immense and expanding area, and communications were poor. It would, therefore, be difficult for them to concentrate upon one or a few candidates; a great number of choices would be made, and no one man would have any approach to a majority of votes. It was finally decided, therefore, to set up an electoral college, each state having as many electors as it had Senators and Representatives. This system by no means operated as its authors had intended, for they failed to foresee the party development which immediately took place. As for the third branch, the Federal judiciary, the judges were to be appointed by the President, by and with the advice and consent of the Senate, for life terms during good behavior.

The ingenuity as well as the wisdom of the authors of the Constitution challenges our admiration. They set up the most complex government yet devised by man, and also the most nicely poised and guarded. Each of the three branches was independent and co-ordinate, and yet each was checked by the others. Congressional enactments did not become law until approved by the President; the President in turn had to submit many of his appointments and all of his treaties to the Senate and might be impeached and removed by Congress. The judiciary was to hear all cases arising under the laws and the Constitution and, therefore, had a right to interpret both the fundamental law and the statute law. But the judiciary were appointed by the President and confirmed by the Senate, while they, too, might be impeached by Congress. Since the Senators were elected by the state legislatures for six-year terms, since the President was chosen by an electoral college, and since the judges were appointed, no part of the government was exposed to direct public pressure except the lower house of Congress. Moreover, officers of government were chosen for such a wide variety of terms, ranging from life to two years, that a complete change in personnel could not be effected except by a revolution.

The decisions by which the Convention made certain that the Federal government would be strong enough to maintain order and protect property might, under other circumstances, have been dangerously explosive. But most of them were taken after brief and calm debate. The Federal government was freely and fully given the power to lay taxes, thus ensuring it the means to pay the debt so long overdue, to restore its credit, and to raise money for the general welfare. It could borrow money, and lay uniform duties, imposts, and excises, and pass uniform bankruptcy laws. It was given authority to coin money, fix weights and measures, grant patents and copyrights, and establish post offices and post roads. It was empowered to raise and maintain an army and navy. It could regulate interstate commerce. It was given the whole management of Indian relations, of international relations, and of war. If "domestic violence" broke out in any state, and the legislature or governor asked for help, it might intervene to restore order. It could pass laws for naturalizing foreigners. Controlling the public lands, it could admit new states on a basis of absolute equality with the old. It was to have its own capital in a district not more than ten miles square. In short, the national government was strong from the beginning—and was soon to be made still stronger by the interpretations which the Supreme Court gave the Constitution. This strength was a natural reaction from the weakness of the Confederation.

Yet the states also remained strong. All the powers of local government were kept in their hands, and they regulated most of the daily concerns of the people. Schools, local courts, policing, the chartering of towns and cities, the incorporation of banks and stock companies, the care of bridges, roads, and canals—these and many other matters were in state hands. The states were to decide who should vote, and how. They were mainly responsible for the protection of civil liberties. For a long time many people felt themselves Georgians, or Pennsylvanians, or Virginians before they felt themselves Americans.

Finally, the Convention faced the most important problem of all: how should the powers given to the new national government be enforced? The old Confederation had possessed large, though by no means adequate, powers, on paper. But in practice its powers had come close to zero, for the states paid no attention to them. What was to save the new government from meeting precisely the same obstacles and refusals? At the outset most delegates furnished but one answer—the use of force. Virginia proposed that Congress should be given power to "call forth the force of the Union against any member . . . failing to fulfill its duty under the articles thereof." This was wrong in theory, for force is an instrument of international law. It would have been fatal in practice, for it would have meant civil war. Application of force would quickly have broken up the Union amid bloodshed and destruction.

What, then, was to be done? As the discussion went on, a new and perfect expedient was evolved. The government, it was decided, should not act upon the states at all. Instead, it should act directly upon the people within the states. It was to legislate for and upon all the residents of the country, ignoring the state governments. As Madison wrote Jefferson: "A voluntary observance of the Federal law by all the members could never be hoped for. A compulsive one could evidently never be reduced to practice, and if it could, involved equal calamities to the innocent and the guilty, and in general, a scene resembling much more a civil war than the administration of a regular government. Hence was embraced the alternative of a government which, instead of operating on the States, should operate without their intervention on the individuals composing them. . . ." The Convention adopted as the kingpin of the Constitution the following brief article:

> This Constitution, and the Laws of the United States which shall be made in Pursuance thereof; and all Treaties made, or which shall be made, under the Authority of the United States, shall be the supreme Law of the Land; and the Judges in every State shall be bound thereby, any Thing in the Constitution or Laws of any State to the Contrary notwithstanding.

Under this provision, the laws of the United States became enforceable in its own national courts, through its own judges and marshals. They were also enforceable in the state courts, through the state judges and state law officers. This provision breathed a vitality into the Constitution which it might never otherwise have gained, and offers perhaps the best single illustration of that combination of common sense and inspiration, of practical ingenuity and farsighted vision, which marked the instrument as a whole.

On Monday, September 17, after one of the best summer's work yet done by any deliberative assemblage in the world, the Convention held its last meeting.

Only three of the delegates present refused to sign, and most of the members were delighted. The aged Franklin declared that while he did not approve all parts of the Constitution, he was astonished to find it so nearly perfect. He begged any men who did not like some of its features to doubt their own infallibility a little and accept the document. Dashing young Alexander Hamilton made a somewhat similar plea. He had wished a far more centralized and more aristocratic form of government, but, he asked, how could a true patriot hesitate between anarchy and convulsion on one side, order and progress on the other? Delegates representing twelve states came forward to sign. Many seemed oppressed by the solemnity of the moment, and Washington sat in grave meditation. But Franklin relieved the tension by a characteristic sally. Pointing to the half sun painted in brilliant gold on the back of Washington's chair, he remarked that artists had always found it difficult to distinguish between a rising and a setting sun. "I have often and often, in the course of the session, and the vicissitudes of my hopes and fears as to its issue, looked at that behind the President, without being able to tell whether it was rising or setting; but now, at length, I have the happiness to know that it is a rising, and not a setting, sun."

Ratification

But would the states ratify the new Constitution? To many plain folk it seemed full of dangers, for would not the strong central government that it set up tyrannize over them, oppress them with heavy taxes, and drag them into foreign wars? The Convention had decided that it should go into effect as soon as approved by nine of the thirteen states. Before 1787 ended, Delaware, Pennsylvania, and

FRANKLIN AS A MIDDLE-AGED MAN

From a painting by Mason Chamberlin

New Jersey had ratified, but would six others follow? Great anxiety was felt by the authors of the new system.

The struggle over ratification brought into existence two parties, the Federalists and Antifederalists; those who favored a strong government and those who wanted a mere league of states. The contest raged in the press, the legislatures, and the state conventions. Impassioned arguments were poured forth on both sides. The ablest were the *Federalist Papers,* written in behalf of the new Constitution by Alexander Hamilton, James Madison, and John Jay, a series that has become a classic work on politics. The three states in which the battle proved sternest were Massachusetts, New York, and Virginia. In Massachusetts the strong support of the Boston shipwrights, metalworkers, and other mechanics, reinforcing the lawyers, merchants, and a good part of the farmers, carried the Constitution to victory. In New York the eloquence of Alexander Hamilton finally converted the principal opposing debater, broke down the enemy forces, and obtained ratification by a handsome majority. In Virginia the influence of George Washington (which was powerful everywhere), and the strong arguments of Madison, won the day. By the time that Virginia finally acted, nine other states had given their approval, so that the government was certain to go into effect; but the full support of Washington's state was felt indispensable and was received with tumultuous rejoicings.

Philadelphia mustered a great procession on July 4, 1788, to celebrate the acceptance of the new form of government. One symbolic float showed how the battered scow *Confederacy* (representing the weak government under the Articles of Confederation), with Imbecility for captain, had foundered; another showed the stanch ship *Constitution* ready to take the high seas. And ready she was. Arrangements were made for the choice of President and Congress and for putting the new government into force in the spring of 1789. One name was on every man's lips for the new chief of state, and Washington was unanimously chosen President.

Thus it was that after the gloom of recent years the country witnessed the bright sunrise which Franklin had hailed in Independence Hall. One of the delightful episodes of early American history, at once idyllic and moving, was the journey which Washington made from his beautiful estate on the Potomac to take up the reins of government in New York. He set out in mid-April, as full spring was breaking over the Virginia hills. He moved northward over roads that at some points closely paralleled the route he had taken in 1781 to capture Cornwallis. In every hamlet, town, and city the people poured forth to give him lusty cheers. At Philadelphia cavalry paraded, and he rode under triumphal arches of evergreen and laurel. He reached Trenton on a sunny afternoon, where twelve years earlier he had crossed the ice-filled Delaware in darkness and storm to strike one of his most famous military blows. Here a party of white-clad maidens strewed flowers before him and sang an ode. On the shores of New York Bay he was escorted aboard a handsome barge manned by thirteen men in white uniforms, and as he approached the city thirteen guns boomed; while he landed to find the city filled with joyful crowds, which included many Revolutionary veterans. On April 30, in the presence of an immense multitude, he stood on the balcony of Federal Hall in Wall Street to take the oath of office. The chancellor of New York administered it and then, turning to the crowd, exclaimed: "Long live George Washington, President of the United States!" From the host below rose a thunderous shout.

America in 1789

It was a lusty republic that was now ready to begin its career. A census taken the year after Washington's inauguration showed that it had nearly four million people, of whom about three and a half million were whites. This population was almost wholly rural. Only five cities worthy of the name existed: Philadelphia with 42,000 people, New York with 33,000, Boston with 18,000, Charleston with 16,000, and Baltimore with 13,000. The great mass of the population lived on farms and plantations or in small villages. Communications were poor and slow, for the roads were wretched, the stagecoaches uncomfortable, the sailing vessels uncertain. But turnpike companies were beginning to be formed (a model road was soon made from Philadelphia to Lancaster), and canals were soon dug. Most people lived comparatively isolated lives, with poor schools, few books, and rare newspapers. The impression which America made upon European travelers was one of rudeness, discomfort, rough manners, and thin culture, along with independence, material well-being, and boundless self-confidence. Yet culturally as well as materially its condition was improving.

For the country was growing sturdily. Immigration from the Old World came in such volume that Americans sometimes thought that half of western Europe was flowing into the land. Good farms were to be had for small sums; labor was in strong demand and well paid. The government looked with favor on this immigration, and Washington particularly liked the idea of bringing expert farmers over from Britain to teach Americans better agricultural methods. The rich stretches of the Mohawk and Genesee valleys in upper New York, of the Susquehanna in upper Pennsylvania, and of the Shenandoah in Virginia soon became great wheat-growing areas. New Englanders and Pennsylvanians were moving into Ohio, Virginians and Carolinians into Kentucky and Tennessee.

Manufactures, too, were growing and were encouraged by state bounties. Massachusetts and Rhode Island were laying the foundation of important textile industries, surreptitiously obtaining their models of jennies and Arkwright machinery from England. Connecticut was beginning to turn out tinware and clocks; the Middle States paper, glass, and iron. But America as yet had no mill towns with a population exclusively devoted to factory work. Indeed, much of the manufacturing was still done in households. Farmers in the long winter evenings could make coarse cloth, leather goods, pottery, simple iron implements, maple sugar, and wooden contrivances. When mills and factories did spring up, the owner usually labored alongside his hands.

Shipping was beginning to flourish, and the United States was taking second place on the ocean only to England. Vessels were built in great numbers for the coastal trade, for the codfisheries, for whaling, and for carrying breadstuffs, tobacco, lumber, and other goods to Europe. The Revolution had scarcely ended when the ship *Empress* made a voyage to Canton and brought back news of the possibilities of the Oriental trade, which stirred New Englanders. A new commerce sprang up. It became so brisk that in 1787 five ships carried the Stars and Stripes to China. The Orientals were eager to obtain furs; and some Boston merchants determined to send ships to the Northwest coast, buy pelts from the Indians, carry them to China, and bring home teas and silks. The new scheme proved successful. What was more, it led the Yankee captain Robert Gray, master of the ship *Columbia,* to enter the great river on the upper Pacific Coast which he named after his vessel, and so lay a basis for the United States claim to Oregon.

The main impulse of American energy was westward —ever westward. From the oak clearings of Ohio to the pine glades of Georgia the backwoodsman's ax rang out as the drumbeat of advancing hosts. Up the long slopes of the Alleghenies climbed the white-topped Conestoga wagons of the emigrant trains; through the Cumberland Gap into Kentucky wound the buckskin-clad hunters and the pioneers with carts of furniture, seeds, simple farm implements, and domestic animals. In many a rough clearing, where the hickory and walnut trees, tokens of a rich soil, had been killed by girdling, the frontier farmer and his neighbors lifted a log cabin, its timbers chinked with clay, its roof covered with thin oak staves. Year by year the Ohio and Mississippi saw more American rafts and flatboats floating downward to New Orleans with grain, salt meat, and potash. Year by year the western towns, such as Cincinnati on the Ohio, Knoxville in the heart of Tennessee, and Lexington in Kentucky, grew more important. Indian warfare, malaria, wild beasts, the roving highwaymen of the remote borders, and other perils had to be faced; hardship, poverty, and disease took a heavy toll. But still ten thousand rivulets of settlement spilled into the wilderness, still the frontier line advanced, still Bishop Berkeley's statement of colonial days held good: "Westward the course of empire takes its way."

Chapter Six

THE REPUBLIC FINDS ITSELF

Organizing the Government Under Washington

THE year 1789 found New York blossoming temporarily into a national capital. Its best houses were renovated with all possible elegance; its streets that summer were crowded with Congressman, expectant officeholders, lobbyists, and spectators. President Washington at first occupied a residence just out of town on Franklin Square and then took the imposing McComb mansion in lower Broadway, with a beautiful reception room. Vice-President John Adams occupied a large house on Richmond Hill. Congress sat in Federal Hall at Wall and Broad Streets—for the nation's first political capital was on the site of its subsequent financial capital. Levees were held and balls arranged. The President gave dinner parties of chilly dignity and went frequently with friends to the theater in John Street. When he visited Congress it was in state, riding in a heavy cream-colored coach, drawn by six spirited white horses of Virginia breed, with postilions and outriders. Citizens were not admitted to the Congressional debates, but knots gathered in the streets outside to discuss the grave issues of the day.

The wise leadership of Washington was indispensable to the new government. Politically, he was not a man of imagination or brilliant initiative; he was a stiff writer and a poor public speaker; he knew little about principles of administration. But he commanded not merely obedience but a sort of awe, and he typified the idea of union as nobody else could. Responsible men of every party and section trusted his fairness, breadth of view, and sagacity. Always dignified, his "republican court" was marked by a grave formality. At receptions he would enter dressed in black velvet and satin, with diamond knee buckles, his powdered hair tied in a bag, his military hat under his arm, and a dress sword in a green scabbard at his side. In his relations with Congress and administrative officers he held aloof from party or faction, essaying to represent the national idea alone—though his sympathies were with the Federalists. Vigilant and laborious as ever, he worked by fixed schedules for long hours. He toiled successfully to give the government elevation and principle and to impress upon the country the admonition which he put into his "Farewell Address" in 1796: "Be united—be Americans."

In August Congress adjourned to meet again in Philadelphia that December—for Philadelphia, clean, quiet, and sociable as ever, was to be capital for ten years. Meanwhile, much was done to set national affairs in order.

The organization of the government was no small task. Congress in rapid succession created a Department of State, a Department of War, and a Department of the Treasury. Washington appointed to the first post Thomas Jefferson, just returned from his service as minister to France; to the second post Henry Knox of Massachusetts, a mediocre but popular general; to the third Alexander Hamilton, known for his special knowledge of finance. Congress also established the office of Attorney General, who was at first not a departmental head but merely legal adviser to the government; and Washington filled it with Edmund Randolph, a Virginian. Hamilton and Knox were understood to be of Federalist leanings, Jefferson and Randolph of Antifederalist views. Congress simultaneously

moved to create a Federal judiciary. It set up not only a
Supreme Court, with one Chief Justice and five Associate
Justices (a number later enlarged), but three circuit courts
and thirteen district courts. All the judges, like the heads
of the Federal departments, were to be appointed by the
President and confirmed by the Senate. By the end of 1790
the three first national departments and the national courts,
with a considerable number of subordinate employees, were
hard at work.

Already party politics had appeared—though many
Americans had dreamed of a republic unstained by politics! One of its early manifestations came in the struggle
over amending the Constitution. A number of states had
accepted the instrument with urgent recommendations for
changes. At first it seemed that Congress would pay no
attention to these suggestions. Patrick Henry and others
then set up a clamor which had to be heeded, and Congress referred the proposals to a committee. The upshot
was that the Congressional majority threw out all suggestions for altering the scheme of government, but sent the
states twelve amendments in the nature of a bill of rights.
Ten of these safeguards of civil liberty were ratified. The
Antifederalists were indignant that more was not done,
and made the welkin ring with their protests. But by this
time the original Federalist-Antifederalist alignment was
disappearing, for the country took the Constitution as a
permanent fixture. New issues were emerging, the Federalist party of a strong central government and rising
business and commercial interests and the Antifederalist
party of state rights and agrarianism were assuming a new
character, and new leaders were stepping into view.

As revolutionary America had produced two commanding figures who gained world-wide renown, Washington
and Franklin, so the youthful republic raised into fame two

brilliantly able men whose reputation spread beyond the seas—Alexander Hamilton and Thomas Jefferson. But it was not the striking personal gifts of these two men, great though their talents were, which best entitle them to remembrance. It was the fact that they represented two powerful and indispensable, though to some extent hostile, tendencies in American life: Hamilton the tendency toward closer union and a stronger national government, Jefferson the tendency toward a broader, freer democracy. The most significant facts in American history between 1790 and 1830, next to the irresistible westward march, are the triumphs scored by nationalism and democracy.

Alexander Hamilton

Hamilton had been born in Nevis, a little sugar-growing island of the Lesser Antilles, to a Scottish father and a Huguenot mother. He grew up a man of the Scottish type portrayed by Stevenson in Alan Breck of *Kidnapped*— ambitious, generous, devoted, proud, quick to take offense and to forgive, of flashing mind and inexhaustible energy. His achievements all arose from his combination of brilliancy, self-confident ambition, and industry. It is noteworthy how precociously he displayed these traits. A poor boy, he had no money to go to college. But a terrible hurricane swept the Antilles, and he wrote a description of it which attracted so much attention that his aunts sent him to the American mainland. He entered King's College in New York, a happy choice, for it threw him into easy contact with the radicals of the town who were leading the revolt against royal authority. By publishing two long pamphlets, one just before he was eighteen, the other just afterward, he measured himself effectively against the leading Tory divine of the province. When at twenty he became captain of an artillery company, he showed his

omnivorous mind by taking his books to camp and studying far into the night.

Besides brilliancy and ambition, Hamilton had other
qualities which served him well. He possessed great personal attractiveness. With reddish-brown hair, bright brown
eyes, fine forehead, and firm mouth and chin, he was exceptionally handsome, his face animated and pleasant when
he talked, severe and thoughtful when he was at work.
He liked a lively dinner party and shone in any circle
which offered good wine, intellectual companions, and
lively talk. As shrewd as he was quick, he had the great
quality of *address*—of doing the right thing at the right
time. His address made him leader of the New York patriots, it brought him to Washington's notice and made
him the general's principal aide, it enabled him to lead a
dramatic assault at the siege of Yorktown, it lifted him to
the leadership of the New York bar, it rendered him the
principal figure in Washington's administration, and it
gave him command of a great party. He had remarkable
talents as an executive and organizer. He wrote and spoke
with admirable dash and vigor. Yet he also showed striking
defects. He was excitable, quick-tempered, and when
thwarted decidedly petulant. At the battle of Monmouth,
when Washington rebuked General Charles Lee for re-
treating, he leaped from his horse, drew his sword, and
shouted, "We are betrayed!" Washington silenced him by
the quiet command: "Mr. Hamilton, mount your horse."
He quarreled with Washington near the end of the war,
wrote his father-in-law a pompous, conceited letter about
the incident, and rejected the advances that Washington
made to heal the breach. His hot impetuosity, his readiness
to embark hastily upon a quarrel, and his petulant arrogance of spirit brought him into unnecessarily harsh
conflicts—with Jefferson, disrupting the Washington ad-

ALEXANDER HAMILTON

From a painting by John Trumbull

ministration, with John Adams, disrupting the Federalist party, and with Aaron Burr, ending in his own death in a duel.

The keynote of Hamilton's public career was his love of efficiency, order, and organization, a dominant impulse which explains his unforgettable service to the young nation. From 1775 to 1789 he saw spread all about him the evidence of inefficiency and weakness. He thoroughly detested the resulting disorder. As Washington's secretary he was the agent through whom the commander conducted much of his business. We need only glance at Washington's letters for the Revolutionary period to see in what a continual fret the general was kept by the feebleness of the government. He fretted because the states would not supply him with enough troops, because they sent insufficient munitions, clothing, and money, because while one part of the country acted energetically, others hung back. He fretted over the lack of discipline in the army, for the troops straggled, looted, and on the slightest excuse often packed up and went home. All this anxiety Hamilton shared. And later, in the dark Confederation years, Hamilton was an active attorney close to the mercantile groups in New York and intimately acquainted with their worries over the obstacles to trade and the insecurity of property. His reading gave him a European rather than an American conception of the proper character of the state, and throughout his life he thought the English the most admirable form of government. It is easy to see why he desired efficiency and vigor in the government—a strong Federal authority.

Thomas Jefferson

When we turn to Jefferson, we turn from a man of action to a man of thought. As Hamilton's talents were executive, Jefferson's were meditative and philosophical.

Hamilton delighted in setting up strong machinery and watching its efficient operation; Jefferson delighted in people and in seeing them contented whether efficient or not. His inefficiency as governor of Virginia has been exaggerated, but he nevertheless left the office in discredit, and he was not a particularly efficient Secretary of State. But as a political thinker and writer, in his own generation he was without a peer, after the death of Burke, anywhere in the world. When he suggested the inscription on his gravestone, he proposed not a record of his offices and acts but of his three major contributions to thought. The stone reads:

HERE WAS BURIED THOMAS JEFFERSON
AUTHOR OF THE DECLARATION OF AMERICAN INDEPENDENCE
OF THE STATUTE OF VIRGINIA FOR RELIGIOUS FREEDOM
AND FATHER OF THE UNIVERSITY OF VIRGINIA

Jefferson had been reared in the loose, genial, and carelessly intellectual atmosphere of Virginia. As a youth he engaged in "dancing, junketing, and high jinks"; he was fond of riding, observing wild life, and playing the violin; he read novels—Fielding, Smollett, and Sterne—and was enthusiastic over Ossian. His later life, full of wide contacts with nature, books, and men, merely stimulated his intellectual versatility. He acquired a knowledge of half a dozen languages, of mathematics, surveying, and mechanics, of music and architecture, and of law and government. He eagerly gathered a large library and a remarkable collection of prints. He wrote about plants and animals, about history, politics, and education—and always with originality and insight. He designed his famous house at Monticello and the beautiful halls of the University of Virginia. A lover of talk, deep, discursive, and many-sided, he was one of the best conversationalists of his time. The sage of Monticello, often putting fifty people up over night, showed as much courtesy and warmth to a learned Negro as to a European nobleman. Throughout his life he liked freedom, leisure, and breadth of contacts.

Politically all Jefferson's instincts were opposed to Hamilton's, and his training confirmed them. He was identified for many years with Virginia, first as legislative leader and then governor. In this early period he was never in a position to understand clearly the anxieties which troubled Washington and other continental leaders. On the contrary, he saw plainly how difficult it was for the states to meet all the demands upon them. When he went abroad as minister to France, where he was pressed for repayment of the loans to America, he did realize that a strong national government could be of value in foreign relations, but he did not want it strong in many other respects, frankly declaring: "I am not a friend to a very energetic government." He even said that the weak Articles of Confederation were "a wonderfully perfect instrument." He feared that a strong government would fetter men. He fought for freedom from the British Crown, freedom from Church control, freedom from a landed aristocracy, freedom from great inequalities of wealth. He was an egalitarian democrat. He disliked cities, great manufacturing interests, and large banking and trading organizations—they promoted inequality; and though in his later years he admitted that industrialism was necessary to give the country an independent economy, he believed that America would be happiest if it remained chiefly a rural nation.

Hamilton's great aim was to give the country a more efficient organization; Jefferson's great aim was to give individual men a wider liberty. The United States needed both influences. It required a stronger national government and it required also the unfettering of the common man. The nation would have suffered had it possessed Hamilton alone, or Jefferson alone. It was a piece of great good fortune that it had both men and could in time fuse and to a great extent reconcile their special creeds.

Hamilton's Financial Measures

Becoming Washington's Secretary of the Treasury, Hamilton carried through a set of measures that made him the greatest finance minister in American history. His program was not only impressive in extent but creative in character. Many men wished to repudiate the national debt of about $56,000,000, or to pay only part of it; against their opposition Hamilton put into effect a plan for reorganizing and paying off all of it. He carried out a plan by which the Federal government took over the unpaid debts of the states, incurred in aid of the Revolution, some $18,000,000 more. He set up a Bank of the United States modeled largely on the Bank of England. He established a national mint. Writing a famous *Report on Manufactures,* he argued in favor of laying moderate tariff duties in order to develop national industries; and Congress did pass a tariff law which, though it imposed only low duties, gave definite aid to American manufacturers. Finally, Hamilton had a law enacted levying an excise tax to be collected upon all distilled liquors.

These measures had an instant effect, which reached in three directions. They placed the credit of the national government on a foundation strong as bedrock and gave it all the revenues it needed. They encouraged industry and commerce. And most important of all, they attached powerful groups of men in every state to the national government. The refunding of the national debt, and the assumption of the state debts, made a host of men who held continental and state paper look to the new government for their money. Manufacturers who depended on the new tariff law for their prosperity looked in the same direction. The national bank secured the support of influential groups of moneyed men, for it made all financial transactions easier and safer. The excise tax not only furnished revenue, but, being collected at every local still, brought home to plain citizens the authority of the Federal government. Altogether Hamilton's policies created a solid phalanx of propertied men who stood fast behind the national government, ready to resist any attempt to weaken it; and it made that government much more impressive than before.

Interpretation of the Constitution: "Implied Powers"

Nor was this all, for Hamilton's measures required a new and profoundly important interpretation of the Constitution. When he brought forward his scheme for a national bank, Jefferson—speaking for all believers in state rights as against national rights, and for those who feared great corporations and a money power—objected. He sent Washington a strong argument. The Constitution, he declared, expressly enumerates all the powers belonging to the Federal government and reserves all other powers to the states; and it nowhere says that the Federal government may set up a bank. This seemed good logic. Washington was on the point of vetoing the bill. But Hamilton submitted a more convincing argument. He pointed out that all the powers of the national government could not be set down in explicit words, for that would mean intolerable detail. A vast body of powers had to be implied by general clauses, and one of these authorized Congress to "make all laws which shall be necessary and proper" for carrying out other powers granted. In reading this clause Hamilton emphasized the word "proper." For example, under the war powers of the Constitution the government clearly had a right to conquer territory. It followed that it properly had a "resulting power" to administer this territory, even though the Constitution said nothing about it. The Constitution said that the government should regulate commerce and navigation; and it followed that it had a "resulting power" to build lighthouses. Now the Constitution declared that the national government should have power to lay and collect taxes, to pay debts, and to borrow money. A national bank would materially assist it in gathering taxes, in sending money to distant points to pay bills, and in borrowing. It was therefore entitled to set up the national bank under its "implied powers." Washington accepted this argument and signed Hamilton's measure.

The Whisky Rebellion; Jay's Treaty

Jefferson thought that Hamilton's excise law of 1791 was "odious" and wrote Washington that it was also unwise, for it committed "the authority of the government in parts where resistance is most probable and coercion least practicable." By this he primarily meant western Pennsylvania. This country was filled with hardy Scotch-Irish. They had no means of getting their grain eastward across the mountains to market; they needed money; and knowing the Scottish art of whisky-making, they set up stills on nearly every farm to produce an easily transported commodity. The excise tax seemed to fall unfairly on this money crop. Moreover, it was inquisitorial. Four counties in the area just south of Pittsburgh were soon being lashed to open resistance by angry leaders. Washington issued a proclamation of warning, but it was disregarded; and in 1794, when the government tried to arrest men who had defied the revenue officers, violence broke out. Mobs forced a Federal inspector to flee for his life and threatened the little garrison in Pittsburgh. The governor should have used the militia, but, fearing to make himself unpopular with the western voters, he failed to do so.

Thereupon Washington, closely advised by Hamilton, decided to take stern action. A force of a thousand soldiers could easily have suppressed the "insurrection," which was really nothing more than a disorderly demonstration. But Hamilton was anxious to furnish an illustration of the overwhelming strength of the government. Fifteen thousand troops were therefore called out from Virginia, Maryland, and Pennsylvania—an army almost as large as that which had captured Cornwallis. Marching upon the disaffected area, the soldiery quickly overawed the malcontents. Hamilton went with them and saw that eighteen men were carried to Philadelphia for trial. But only two were convicted, and Washington pardoned them.

This Whisky Rebellion created great excitement, the Federalists extolling the government's stern measures and the Antifederalists denouncing them as arbitrary and militaristic. Unquestionably Hamilton's policy enhanced the prestige of the national authorities. But it is also unquestionable that it aroused much popular antagonism and distrust and was a mistake. As soon as the Jeffersonians came into power the excise was repealed.

Equally unpopular with many was the course of the Washington administration with respect to foreign affairs. In 1793 war began in Europe between France and Britain. Strong feeling was aroused in the United States. The trading classes and many religious people, especially in New England, feared and hated the Republic which had overturned property interests and set up a goddess of reason; the Southern farmers and urban mechanics sympathized with the French. Washington wisely issued a proclamation of neutrality. This was so fiercely denounced that the hotheaded French minister to the United States, Genêt, thought that he could disregard it. He wrote his government that Washington was a weak old man under British influence; he talked of appealing to the populace; and when the government forbade him to use American ports as a base of operations for French privateers, he disobeyed the order. Is he, Washington angrily demanded, "to set the acts of this government at defiance with impunity"? Genêt was ordered to return home. But knowing that the guillotine waited him, he did better—he stayed in the United States, married the daughter of the governor of New York, and lived prosperously to old age. His indiscretions had embarrassed the pro-French party in America. Nevertheless, this party in 1794 began to demand war with England, chiefly on the ground that the British were illegally seizing American ships bound for the French West Indies, and that they were holding trading posts in the Northwest Territory in flagrant violation of the Treaty of 1783.

Nothing could have then been more disastrous to America at this time than such a war; and to settle a variety of disputes with Great Britain, Washington sent John Jay, an experienced diplomatist who was now Chief Justice, to London as envoy extraordinary. He could have made no better choice. Jay believed that "a little good-natured wisdom often does much more in politics than much slippery craft." Acting with moderation and enlightenment, he made a treaty which gained as much as the United States could rightfully expect. That is, he obtained a promise that the Western posts which the British still held should be given up within two years. He got the American claim for damages arising from British ship seizures referred to a commission. Finally, he obtained important commercial privileges in both the British East Indies and West Indies. The treaty was received with a fierce outburst of indignation. Jay was burned in effigy by wild mobs; angry orators and editors heaped execration upon Washington. But Washington and Jay were too wise and too philosophic to be moved by a temporary public clamor. With certain amendments, the Senate accepted the treaty. Merchants and shipowners again had reason to look gratefully to the national government.

John Adams

As Washington retired, John Adams, able and high-minded, but stern, obstinate, and full of idiosyncrasies, took the helm. His headstrong, tactless traits made it certain that his presidency would be troubled. Too independent to accept Hamilton's guidance, he had quarreled with that leader even before he entered the presidency. Thus he was handicapped by having a divided party behind him and a divided Cabinet at his side—for the heads of departments took Hamilton's views in party matters. Many Southerners disliked Adams as a New Englander, and party feeling grew intensely bitter. To make matters worse, the international skies became more heavily clouded than ever.

This time it was with France that war threatened. The Directory which governed the French Republic, angered by Jay's treaty, refused to accept the minister whom Adams sent over and actually threatened him with arrest. This humiliating episode aroused strong American feeling. When Adams sent three commissioners to Paris to try to adjust the difficulties, they were met with fresh contumely. Talleyrand, in charge of foreign affairs, curtly declined to deal with them. Confidential agents, later described by the American envoys as X, Y, and Z, suggested that something might be done if they were paid a bribe of $250,000. Finally Talleyrand practically broke off negotiations by a coarsely insulting message in which he accused the United States of double-dealing. The publication of the X Y Z papers, as the correspondence was called, raised indignation in America to an excited pitch. Troops were enlisted, the navy was strengthened, and in 1798 a series of sea battles took place in which American ships uniformly defeated the French. For a time open war seemed unescapable.

In this crisis Adams' stern individualism served the nation well. Thrusting aside Hamilton, who wanted war, he suddenly sent a new minister to France—and Napoleon, who had come to power, received him cordially. The danger of conflict swiftly disappeared. Unfortunately, in home affairs, Adams meanwhile, behaved with a narrowness and tactlessness that the American people found unforgivable. He and the Federalist Congress made themselves responsible for four unhappy laws which did much to ruin the administration. The first extended from five years to fourteen the period for which an alien must reside in the United States before becoming a citizen. The second gave the President power for two years to order any dangerous alien out of the country. The third provided that in time of war aliens might be deported, or imprisoned as long as the President decreed. The fourth made it a high misdemeanor to conspire against any legal measure of the government, or to obstruct or even to criticize a public officer.

These Alien and Sedition Laws seemed outrageously severe, a gross infringement of personal and civil liberties. Jefferson and Madison, who believed that the Federalists were concentrating a dangerous power in the national government, determined to take a stand against them. They wrote two sets of resolutions, of which Jefferson's were adopted by the Kentucky legislature and Madison's by the Virginia assembly. Setting forth the theory that the national government had been founded by a compact among the states, these Kentucky and Virginia Resolutions declared that a state might take step. to veto an unconstitutional act.

The year 1800 found the country ripe for a change. Indeed, it proved the year of a great political upheaval. Under Washington and Adams, the Federalists had done a great work in establishing the government and making it strong. Nobody now doubted, as many had in 1789, that the nation and the Constitution would endure. But the Federalists had failed to recognize that the American government was meant to be essentially popular in character. They had followed policies w   did much to give its control and benefits to special cla   Jefferson, a born popular leader, had steadily gathered   ind him the great mass of small farmers, mechanics, sh   keepers, and other workers. They meant to see that the nation had a people's government, not a government of special interests, and they asserted themselves with tremendous power. In the election of 1800 Adams carried New England. But the opposition swept the Southern States and gained a heavy majority in the Middle States. The clumsy electoral system resulted in a tie between Jefferson and Aaron Burr, a plausible but unprincipled New Yorker of the same party. But the people had manifestly intended that Jefferson should be President, and Hamilton, in one of those fine acts which so frequently marked his career, saw to it that the House of Representatives decided in his favor.

"The tough sides of our Argosie have been thoroughly tried," wrote Jefferson to a friend. "We shall put her on her republican tack, and she will now show by the beauty of her motion the skill of her builders."

Chapter Seven

THE RISE OF NATIONAL UNITY

Jefferson's Administration

THE manner in which Jefferson assumed the presidency in 1801 emphasized the fact that democracy had come into power. The ceremonies were the first to be held in Washington, which had just been made the capital. It was then a mere forest village on the north bank of the Potomac, its muddy roadways built through bushes and across sloughs, with only a few shabby houses—"most of them small, miserable huts," according to one of the outgoing Cabinet. Gouverneur Morris sarcastically remarked that the capital had a great *future*. "We want nothing here but houses, cellars, kitchens, well-informed men, amiable women, and other trifles of this kind, to make our city perfect." Jefferson, carelessly garbed as usual, walked from his simple boardinghouse up the hill to the new Capitol, with a number of friends at his heels. Entering the Senate chamber, he shook hands with Vice-President Burr, his recent unscrupulous rival. Another man whom he distrusted stood at hand, John Marshall of Virginia, a distant kinsman whom Adams had recently appointed Chief Justice. Jefferson took the oath of office and quietly delivered one of the best addresses ever made by an incoming President.

Part of Jefferson's address was a much-needed plea for conciliation. The political canvass just ended had been so bitterly vituperative that many people, especially in New

PRINCIPAL HIGHWAYS AND CANALS USED
IN WESTWARD EXPANSION 1825-1850

England, believed that Jefferson was an atheist, a leveler, and even an anarchist. He begged the citizens to remember that political intolerance is as bad as religious intolerance and to unite as Americans in preserving the Union, making representative government effective, and developing the national resources. The remainder of the address laid down the political principles of the new administration. The country, he said, should have "a wise and frugal government," which should preserve order among the inhabitants, but "shall leave them otherwise free to regulate their own pursuits of industry and improvement, and shall not take from the mouth of labor the bread it has earned." It should preserve the rights of the states. It should seek honest friendship with all nations, but "entangling alliances with none"—a long-remembered phrase. Jefferson promised to sustain the Union "in its whole constitutional vigor," to preserve "the supremacy of the civil over the military authorities," and to support popular elections as the only arbiter short of revolution.

The very fact that Jefferson was in the White House for two terms greatly encouraged democratic procedures throughout the country. He abolished all the aristocratic trappings with which Washington had surrounded the presidency. The weekly levees were given up, court etiquette was rigidly pruned, and titles of honor like "Excellency" were abandoned. To Jefferson the plainest citizen was as worthy of respect as the highest officer. He taught his subordinates to regard themselves simply as trustees for the people. He encouraged agriculture and promoted land settlement by purchasing the Indians' titles and helping them migrate westward. Believing that America should be a haven for the oppressed, he encouraged immigration by a liberal naturalization law. He tried hard to keep peace with other nations, for war would mean more government activity, more taxes, and less freedom. Appointing Albert Gallatin, a farsighted financier of Swiss birth, his Secretary of the Treasury, Jefferson encouraged him to reduce expenses and pay off the national debt; with the result that by 1806 the national revenues were $14,500,000, the expenses $8,500,000, and the surplus $6,000,000. By the end of 1807 the thrifty Gallatin had reduced the national debt to less than seventy millions. As a wave of Jeffersonian feeling swept over the nation, all commoners rejoiced. State after state was abolishing property qualifications for the ballot and for office and passing more humane laws as for debtors and criminals.

Yet fate turned Jefferson and the country in a direction that he had not intended. By two steps he, the apostle of a "strict construction" of the Constitution, stretched the powers of the Federal government to the utmost; and, when he left office, the war that he hated lay just ahead.

The Louisiana Purchase; The Burr Conspiracy

One of his steps doubled the area of the nation. Spain had long held the country west of the Mississippi, with the port of New Orleans near its mouth. But soon after Jefferson came into office Napoleon forced the weak Spanish government to cede the great tract called Louisiana back to France. The moment he did so intelligent Americans trembled with apprehension and indignation. New Orleans was an indispensable port for the shipment of American products grown in the Ohio and Mississippi valleys. Napoleon's plans for a huge colonial empire just west of the United States, balancing the Anglo-Saxon dominion in North America, menaced the trading rights and the safety of all the interior settlements. Even feeble Spain had made a great deal of trouble for the Southwestern country. What might not France, the most powerful nation in the world, do?

· Jefferson asserted that if France took possession of Louisiana, "from that moment we must marry ourselves to the British fleet and nation"; and that the first cannon shot fired in a European war would be the signal for the march of an Anglo-American army against New Orleans. Napoleon was impressed by the certainty that the United States and England would strike. He knew that another war with Great Britain was impending after the brief Peace of Amiens and that when it began he would surely lose Louisiana. He was discouraged, too, by his inability to crush the great revolt of the Negro leader Toussaint l'Ouverture in French-ruled Haiti, where in 1802 the insurgents and yellow fever together destroyed a force of twenty-four thousand men. He therefore resolved to fill his treasury, to put Louisiana beyond the reach of the British, and to bid for American friendship by selling the region to the United States. For $15,000,000 this vast area passed into the possession of the republic. Jefferson "stretched the Constitution till it cracked" in buying it, for no clause authorized the purchase of foreign territory, and he acted without Congressional consent.

By this happy stroke the United States obtained more than a million square miles and with it the valuable port of New Orleans, picturesque brick and stucco city built on a crescent sweep of the Mississippi, with the dark cypress forest as background. On an autumn day in 1803 a motley gathering on the Place d'Armes—French soldiers in gay uniforms, Spaniards and French Creoles in fashionable dress, pioneers in hunting shirts, tawny Indians, ebony slaves—saw the ensign of France fall and the Stars and

Stripes rise. The United States gained a sweep of rich plains that within eighty years was one of the world's granaries. It gained control of the whole central river system of the continent. For the first time Americans could say, as Lincoln said later in Civil War days, that the Father of Waters went unvexed to the sea. Within four years Robert Fulton's introduction of a successful steamboat on the Hudson solved the problem of using these inland waters easily and cheaply. Puffing vessels soon filled all the Western streams, taking emigrants to settle on the land and bringing furs, grain, cured meats, and a hundred other products back to market.

As the end of his first term approached, Jefferson had gained widespread popularity, for Louisiana was manifestly a great prize, business was prosperous, and the President had tried hard to please all sections. His re-election was certain, and in 1804 he actually received all but fourteen of the 176 electoral votes, carrying every state even in New England, except Connecticut. Able to rule his party with a strong hand, he had taken steps to crush the ambitious and constantly intriguing Aaron Burr. The crafty New Yorker, deprived of all share in the distribution of Federal offices and practically read out of the party, turned to a flirtation with the bitterest Federalists of New England. He ran for governor of New York on the Federalist ticket in the spring of 1804, but largely through the opposition of Hamilton—who correctly suspected that Burr and such Yankee schemers as Timothy Pickering were plotting disunion—suffered a humiliating defeat. To obtain revenge, the unprincipled Burr then provoked Hamilton to a duel which, fought at dawn of a July morning on the Jersey shore of the Hudson, ended in Hamilton's death. The loss of so brilliant and beloved a leader threw the community into a paroxysm of angry grief, and Burr had to go into hiding for safety. His career in the East was blasted, but with unchastened insolence he turned to the West for new adventures.

Ordinary prizes and distinctions did not suffice for so overmastering an ambition as Burr's. Rule or ruin was his motto, and he laid plans to found a state of his own. Just where it was to be, and just how he was to create it, are still disputed questions. Many students believe that he intended to collect a little army in the West, descend the Mississippi, seize control of New Orleans, and wrench Louisiana away from the United States. Describing some such intention to British and Spanish officers, he tried to get money from London and Madrid. He told the British that he would place his state under their protection, while he informed the Spaniards that he would make it a buffer state between Mexico and the United States. Neither supported him. But other students believe that Burr's real object was to recruit his army and lead it against the Spanish authorities in Vera Cruz and Mexico City, gaining control of Mexico. Indeed, he told such leaders as Andrew Jackson of Tennessee, who hated Spain, that this was his intention. Possibly he did not know himself whether he was aiming at Louisiana or Mexico; possibly he even aimed at both!

At any rate, Burr came to a fall as complete as Lucifer's. Loyal men in the Southwest got wind of his conspiracy and late in 1806 brought charges against him. He was arrested and sent to Richmond, Virginia, for trial on an indictment for treason. John Marshall presided over the case, and his principal rulings were favorable to Burr, while the evidence was necessarily vague. Burr was therefore acquitted—but he was now ruined beyond all redemption.

American Neutrality: The Embargo Act

Jefferson made his second extraordinary use of Federal authority in attempting to maintain American neutrality during the colossal struggle between Great Britain and Napoleon. He knew that the young and immature republic needed peace; and as war raged on land and sea, he hoped to keep the United States outside the circle of flames. Great Britain was fighting to prevent the conquest of all continental Europe by a single power. Naturally, commercial warfare was one of her best weapons. Realizing its value, the British hastened to blockade Napoleon's empire, and Napoleon retaliated by the Berlin and Milan decrees for blockading Great Britain. In their combat both powers struck heavy blows at American commerce. The British acted to cut off the rich carrying trade of American vessels with products of the French West Indies and to shut them out of practically the whole European coast from Spain to the Elbe. The French ordered the seizure of any American ship which submitted to British search or touched at a British port. That is, the war soon reached a point where no American craft could trade with the broad region controlled by France without being seized by the British, and none could trade with Britain without being seized (if it ever got within reach) by France! Under these conditions commerce was almost impossible. The British government was fairly rigorous, while the French confiscated American vessels on the slightest excuse.

What especially aroused American feeling against Great Britain was the impressment question. To win the war the British were compelled to build up their navy to a point where it had more than seven hundred warships in commission, with nearly 150,000 sailors and marines. This oaken wall kept Britain safe, protected her commerce, and preserved her communications with her colonies. It was vital to Britain's existence. Yet the men of the fleet were so ill-paid, ill-fed, and ill-handled that it was impossible to obtain crews by free enlistment. Many sailors deserted and they were particularly glad to find refuge on the pleasanter and safer Yankee vessels. In these circumstances British officers regarded the right of searching American ships and taking off British subjects as essential. They did not claim the right to impress American seamen, but they refused to admit that a Briton could be naturalized into an American citizen. The American view, however, was thoroughly hostile to this claim. It was humiliating for American vessels to lay to under the guns of a British cruiser while a lieutenant and a party of marines lined up the crew and examined them. Moreover, many British officers were arrogant and unfair. They impressed true American seamen by scores and hundreds—ultimately, it was alleged, by thousands.

To bring Great Britain and France to a fairer attitude without war, Jefferson finally had Congress pass the Embargo Act, a law forbidding foreign commerce altogether. It was a grim experiment. First the shipping interests were almost ruined by the measure, and discontent rose high in New England and New York. Then the agricultural interests found that they were suffering heavily, for prices tumbled when the Southern and Western farmers could not ship their surplus grain, meat, and tobacco overseas. Observers compared the measure to a surgeon's amputation of a leg in an effort to save a life. In a single year American exports fell to one fifth their former volume. But the hope that the embargo would starve Great Britain into a change of policy failed—the British government would not budge. As the grumbling at home increased, Jefferson turned to a milder measure.

A Nonintercourse Law was substituted for the embargo. This forbade commerce with either Britain or France, including their dependencies, but promised that it would be suspended with reference to either country as soon as that country ceased its attacks upon neutral commerce. Napoleon in 1810 officially announced that he had abandoned his measures. This was a lie—he was maintaining them. But the United States believed him and limited its nonintercourse to Great Britain.

The War of 1812

This made relations with Great Britain worse, and the two countries drifted rapidly toward war. Ill-feeling had been aroused by various incidents. For example, the British warship *Leopard* had ordered the American warship *Chesapeake* to give up certain British deserters—though actually only one was aboard; meeting some hesitation, it fired into the *Chesapeake* for fifteen minutes and then boarded her, the decks wet with blood, and took off four men. A little later the President laid before Congress a detailed report, showing 6057 instances in which the British had impressed American citizens within three years. Other factors entered into the situation. Northwestern settlers had suffered from the attacks of a league of Indian tribes formed by the able chief Tecumseh, and they believed that British agents in Canada had encouraged the savages. Many land-hungry men in the West, ably represented in Congress by the eloquent Henry Clay of Kentucky, wished to annex Canadian territory, while some Southerners hoped to conquer Florida from Spain, now Britain's ally. The result was that, with Madison in the White House, war was declared on Britain in 1812.

This War of 1812 was in many ways one of the most unfortunate events in American history. For one reason, it was needless; the British Orders in Council that had caused the worst irritation were being unconditionally repealed just as Congress declared war. For another, the United States suffered from internal divisions of the gravest kind. While the South and West favored war, New York and New England in general opposed it, and toward its end important New England groups went to the very edge of disloyalty. For a third reason, the war was far from glorious in a military sense.

The American army, which Jeffersonian economy had reduced by 1809 to fewer than three thousand troops, supported by a rabble of undrilled, undisciplined militia, was in wretched shape to fight. Many regular soldiers were the offscourings of jails and pothouses. Winfield Scott, a young Virginian who had begun his brilliant military career a few years earlier, tells us that the commanders fell into two main groups. "The old officers had very generally slunk into either sloth, ignorance, or habits of intemperate drinking." The newer officers had for the most part been appointed for political reasons; a few were good, but the majority were either "coarse and ignorant men," or if educated were "swaggerers, dependents, decayed gentlemen, and others unfit for anything else." The senior major general when the war began was the incompetent Henry Dearborn, well past sixty, who had never commanded a larger unit in the field than a regiment. The senior brigadier general was James Wilkinson, now known to have been a traitor to the United States, a pensioner of Spain, and an accomplice of Aaron Burr: corrupt, profligate, and insubordinate, he was despised by all who knew him. The only brigadier general who possessed valuable experience was William Hull, who had attained the rank of colonel in the Revolution, but was now infirm and senile. He began the war by surrendering Detroit without firing a shot.

Disaster then followed disaster. The American efforts to invade Canada ended in general failure. During the first year, as a British historian puts it, "the militia and volunteers do not seem to have made up their minds whether they wanted to fight or did not." The hardest fought contest on the northern frontier, that of Lundy's Lane near Niagara, was a drawn battle which both sides later claimed as a victory (July, 1814). But as it temporarily shattered American plans for pushing forward into Canada, the British had the better title to exultation.

When Napoleon's forces were defeated in Spain, the British were able to reinforce their armies heavily with Wellington's veterans. A seasoned force drove into New York at Plattsburg on Lake Champlain, but the British fleet on those waters was decisively defeated by a youngster of twenty-eight, Commodore Thomas MacDonough, and the British army, its communications thus rendered precarious, was forced to retreat. Another British army of less than five thousand men landed near Washington and met a slightly larger force, chiefly militia, at Bladensburg. The unheroic defenders gave way after losing ten killed and forty wounded and ran for Washington so rapidly that many Britons suffered sunstroke in trying to keep up. In retaliation for the American destruction of public buildings at York (now Toronto), British troops fired the Capitol and White House. However, when the British fleet subjected Fort McHenry near Baltimore to a long-range night bombardment—shoals making closer fire impossible—it accomplished nothing; and a young Washington attorney, Francis Scott Key, who had been on a British warship trying to arrange an exchange of prisoners, was inspired by the sight of the national flag waving in the morning breeze to write *The Star-Spangled Banner*.

Only at sea did the Americans win any laurels. The navy, systematically built up under Washington and Adams, had acquitted itself magnificently in the short war with France and the operations of 1803–1804 against the Tripolitan corsairs, whose depredations upon American shipping had become intolerable. Unlike the army, it had been blessed with one great early organizer. This was Edward Preble, who gave the Mediterranean squadron a harsh but efficient administration, instilled into his men a spirit of pluck, gallantry, and obedience which became a tradition, and trained young officers like Stephen Decatur to high capacity. Numerically the navy was small, for Jefferson had followed a fatuous policy of building shore-defense gunboats. In 1810 it numbered only a dozen vessels of any power. But in a series of single-ship actions, like that of the *Constitution* ("Old Ironsides") and the *Guerrière,* the *United States* and the *Macedonian,* the Yankee captains consistently defeated equal or heavier British vessels. On the Great Lakes, too, the Americans proved their mettle. Captain Oliver Hazard Perry, another officer well under thirty, built a fleet on Lake Erie, searched out a smaller British force, and after a dogged action thrilled the country with his laconic dispatch: "We have met the enemy and they are ours." Yet in the end the stronger British navy established full command of the seas, drove American commerce into shelter, and kept a close blockade of the American coast.

When the war closed, the Treaty of Ghent (1815), negotiated by John Quincy Adams, Henry Clay, and others, said not a word about impressment and neutral rights, ostensibly its chief causes. Only the dramatic victory which a bizarre but formidable army of frontiersmen under the veteran Indian fighter, Andrew Jackson, won at New Orleans over a strong British force commanded by Wellington's courageous lieutenant, Edward Pakenham, gave the country any real exultation. This was January 8, 1815, after the peace treaty was signed, but before it was known in America. It made the fiery, imperious Jackson a tremendous national hero.

National Unity

Yet in one respect the war did contribute signally to the development of the republic. Begun and continued amid discontent and bickering, it nevertheless strengthened the sentiment of national unity and patriotism. For this several reasons can be assigned. The scattered successes, and especially the naval victories and the defeat of Pakenham's veterans at New Orleans, gave Americans a new basis for pride and self-confidence. They dispelled the feeling of inferiority that Jefferson's "submission policy" had fostered. In the second place, the fact that men of different states again fought side by side, and that a Virginian, Winfield Scott, was the ablest commander the Northern troops found, added to the sense of national unity. The Western troops won some battles that they did not forget, and they had less attachment to their state and more loyalty to the nation than many people of the original thirteen. From this time onward the West counted for much more in American life, and the West was always national in sentiment.

Finally, the people came out of the war disgusted with the unpatriotic temper that some selfish and narrow groups had shown. The malcontents of New England late in the war had sent delegates to a convention in Hartford to consider their grievances, and this "Hartford Convention" became a byword of contempt and reproach.

Altogether, this ill-starred war did a great deal to make the republic more mature and more independent; to knit it together and strengthen its character. Albert Gallatin asserted that before the conflict, Americans were becoming too selfish, too materialistic, and too prone to think in local terms. "The war," he said, "has renewed and reinstated the national feeling and character which the Revolution had given, and which were daily lessening. The people have now more general objects of attachment, with which their pride and political opinions are connected. They are more Americans; they feel and act more as a nation; and I hope that the permanency of the Union is thereby better secured." Because the war had been so closely fought, it left little ill-feeling. When next Britons and Americans met on a battlefield, more than a hundred years later, it was as comrades in arms and in sentiment.

Events had proved that no matter which party was in control, whether Hamilton's Federalists or Jefferson's Democrats, the national unity grew and the power of the central government increased. This was because the conditions of national growth demanded it. To acquire Louisiana, to wage a commercial contest with France and Great Britain, to attack the Barbary pirates, to carry on war with the British—all this required a vigorous central authority.

And we should add that the government was being greatly strengthened at the same time by the decisions of the Supreme Court. The convinced Federalist, John Marshall of Virginia, who was made Chief Justice just before Jefferson entered the presidency, held that office until his death in 1835. The court had been weak and little regarded; he transformed it into a powerful and majestic tribunal, occupying a position as important as that of Congress or President. In his tastes and manners Marshall

JOHN MARSHALL

From the portrait by Robert M. Sully

belonged to the easygoing planter society of his native state. He dressed plainly, he carried his own dinner home from market, he loved cards, punch, and a rollicking game of horseshoes or quoits. But in ideas he represented rather the business and professional circles of cities like Boston and New York. His memorable decisions, the work of a penetrating mind, showed that he was dominated by two cardinal principles—one, the sovereignty of the Federal government; the other, the sanctity of private property.

Marshall was a great judge. His decisions were written with a masterly logic which in nearly every instance carried conviction to the reader. Simple in style, they rested upon an impressive learning and an exhaustive analysis. His habit was first to establish his major premise fully; then to go on to the deductions, demolishing every objection to them; and finally state his conclusion, amply supported by citations and illustrations. Master of the Supreme Court, he gave it harmony, so that discordant views and dissenting opinions were rare. But Marshall was more than a great judge—he was a great constitutional statesman. Deciding nearly half a hundred cases which involved clear constitutional issues, he dealt with them on the basis of a well-matured political philosophy. They concerned nearly all the important parts of the Constitution. In consequence, when he finished his long service, the Constitution as the courts applied it throughout the country was in great degree the Constitution as Marshall interpreted it. He may be said to have remolded the instrument according to his own clear vision.

It is impossible to do much more than enumerate his principal decisions. In Marbury vs. Madison (1803), he decisively established the right of the Supreme Court to review any law of Congress or of a state legislature. "It is emphatically the province and duty of the judicial department to say what the law is," he wrote. In Cohens vs. Virginia (1821), he swept aside the arguments of those who declared that the decision of a state court in cases arising under state laws should be final. Pointing out the confusion into which this would lead the country—for the states would take numerous different views as to the validity of laws under the Federal Constitution or Federal treaties—he insisted that the final judgment must be that of the national courts. In McCulloch vs. Maryland (1819), he dealt with the old question of the implied powers of the government under the Constitution. Here he stood boldly forth in defense of the Hamiltonian theory that the Constitution by implication gives to the government powers which it does not expressly state. In Gibbons vs. Ogden (1824), Marshall amplified this doctrine. The Constitution gave to Congress the right to regulate interstate commerce; and in a case arising out of a dispute over steamboat rights on the Hudson, Marshall held that this right of national regulation was to be interpreted broadly, not narrowly. In the Dartmouth College case, Marshall applied the contract clause of the Constitution to sustain the validity of a corporate charter, denying the state subsequent power to amend it. Altogether, Marshall did as much as any leader to make the central government of the American people a living, growing force.

Nationalism was irresistibly advancing. A national literature was being born—William Cullen Bryant's *Thanatopsis* appeared in 1817, Irving's *Sketch Book* in 1819, and the first of Fenimore Cooper's many novels in 1820, while 1815 saw the beginning of the great *North American Review*, modeled on the British quarterlies but devoted largely to American interests. The Hudson River school of painters, though still strongly under European influences, concerned themselves with a celebration of the American scene. Jefferson skillfully adapted Italian and classical architecture to American needs, and in the buildings of the University of Virginia presented a harmonious architectural group that compared favorably with anything then being done abroad. A better national land system was being established, the law of 1820 reducing the price of government holdings from $2 to $1.25 an acre. Commerce was cementing the American people into a national unit. The tariff of 1816 continued the fairly high wartime rates and gave manufacturers a taste of real protection. In that same year the second Bank of the United States (for the first had been allowed to die) was incorporated to assist the financial operations of the government and to furnish a sound paper currency. A national system of internal improvements was being warmly advocated by Henry Clay, the South Carolina leader John C. Calhoun, and others who pointed out that better roads and canals would bind the East and West together. And as national unity advanced, so also did democracy.

Chapter Eight

JACKSONIAN DEMOCRACY SWEEPS IN

The Monroe Doctrine

The "little withered applejohn" James Madison gave way in 1817 to tall, rawboned, awkward James Monroe, who presented that not unusual combination, a commonplace man with a highly distinguished public career. He had held one position after another—Senator, governor, minister to France and England, Secretary of State—until he became President. Though the era was rather one of bad feeling than good, political parties were temporarily in abeyance. Monroe therefore had the distinction in 1821 of being reseated by all the electoral votes except one, cast by a New Hampshire elector who wished Washington alone to have the honor of unanimity. Yet Monroe, who lacked magnetism, was never very popular, and his wife, a stiff, reserved, handsome woman, was liked far less than the vivacious Dolly Madison. Monroe's two exceptional qualities were his shrewd common sense and strong will. As John Quincy Adams put it, he had "a mind sound in its ultimate judgments, and firm in its final conclusions."

The event of his administration which has given his name immortality was his enunciation of the so-called Monroe Doctrine. Two main ideas were bound up in this doctrine which was actually but part of Monroe's annual message to Congress for 1823. One was the idea of noncolonization, an assertion that Europe should be for-

174

bidden to establish any new dependencies in the Western Hemisphere. The other was the idea of nonintervention, a declaration that Europe must no longer interfere in the affairs of New World nations in such a way as to threaten their independence. These ideas arose from two distinct situations.

The first was called forth primarily by the claim of Russia to the territory south of Alaska, reaching down as far as the fifty-first parallel, a pretension which conflicted with American and British claims in the Pacific Northwest. The second was evoked by the threat which the reactionary Holy Alliance in Europe offered to the newly liberated nations of Latin America. The allied powers had taken steps to crush democratic movements in Spain and Italy. Holding a congress at Verona in 1822, they discussed sending forces across the ocean to South America in order to compel at least some of the weak new republics to return to Spanish allegiance. France would take the leading part in such an expedition and might obtain lands of her own.

On hearing the news the brilliant British Foreign Secretary, George Canning, was deeply alarmed. He suggested that the United States and Great Britain take concerted steps to block such intervention; and for a time the American government seemed likely to assent. Jefferson and Madison counseled Monroe in favor of joint action. But John Quincy Adams, as Secretary of State, rightly insisted that the United States ought to move alone, and Monroe finally swung to this view. In his message to Congress he declared, first, that the American continents "are henceforth not to be considered as subjects for future colonization by any European powers"; and, second, that any European interposition "for the purpose of oppressing" the Latin American states, "or controlling in any other manner their destiny," would be treated as evidence of unfriendliness toward the United States.

The Missouri Compromise

Although it had thus far received little public attention, slavery had rapidly been growing into a great power, and in 1819, with startling suddenness—"like a fire bell in the night," wrote Jefferson—the terrible problem it offered was called to public attention. In the early years of the republic, when the Northern States were providing for immediate or gradual emancipation, many leaders had supposed that slavery would presently die out everywhere. Washington wrote Lafayette in 1786 that he devoutly wished that some plan might be adopted "by which slavery may be abolished by slow, sure, and imperceptible degrees." In his will he emancipated his slaves. Jefferson held that slavery ought to be wiped out by a combination of emancipation and deportation. "I tremble for my country," he declared, "when I reflect that God is just." Patrick Henry, Madison, Monroe, and many others made similar utterances. As late as 1808, when the slave trade was abolished, numerous Southerners thought that slavery would prove but a temporary evil.

But during the next generation the South was converted into a section which for the most part was grimly united behind slavery. How did this come about? Why did the abolitionist spirit in the South almost disappear? For one reason, the spirit of philosophical liberalism which flamed high in Revolutionary days gradually became weaker. For another reason, a general antagonism between puritanical New England and the slaveholding South became evident; they differed on the War of 1812, the tariff, and other great issues; and the South felt less and less liking for the so-called Northern idea of emancipation. But above all, certain new economic factors made slavery far more profitable than it had been before 1790.

One element in the economic change is familiar—the rise of a great cotton-growing industry in the South. This was based in part on the introduction of improved types of cotton, with better fibers, but in much larger part on Eli Whitney's epochal invention in 1793 of the "gin" for cleaning cotton. Cotton culture rapidly moved westward from the Carolinas and Georgia, spreading over much of the lower South to the Mississippi River and, eventually, on into Texas. Another factor which placed slavery upon a new basis was sugar growing. The rich, hot delta lands of southeastern Louisiana are ideal for sugar cane; and in 1794–1795 an enterprising New Orleans Creole, Étienne Boré, proved that the crop could be highly profitable. He set up machinery and vats, and the crowds which had come from New Orleans to watch the boiling-off broke into cheers when the first sugar crystals showed in the cooling liquid. The cry, "It granulates!" opened a new era in Louisiana. A great boom resulted, so that by 1830 the state was supplying the nation with about half its whole sugar supply. This required slaves, who were brought, in thousands, from the Eastern seaboard.

Finally, tobacco culture also spread westward and took slavery with it. Constant cropping had worn out the soil of lowland Virginia, once the greatest tobacco region in the world, and the growers were glad to move into Kentucky and Tennessee, taking their Negroes with them. Thereafter the fast-multiplying slaves of the upper South were largely drained off to the lower South and West. This diffusion of slavery relieved many observers, because it lessened the risk of such a slave insurrection as Nat Turner's Rebellion, a revolt of sixty or seventy Virginia slaves in 1831—which, incidentally, did much to increase Southern fear of emancipationist doctrines.

As the free society of the North and the slave society of the South spread westward, it seemed desirable to maintain a rough equality between them. In 1818, when Illinois was admitted to the Union, there were ten slave and eleven free states. In 1819 both Alabama and Missouri applied for admission. Now Alabama by the terms of Georgia's original land cession had to be a slave state, and its admission would restore the balance between slave and free. But many Northerners at once rallied to oppose the entry of Missouri except as a free state. Representative Tallmadge of New York introduced an amendment to the admission bill requiring Missouri to adopt gradual emancipation. A terrific storm swept over the country. For a time Congress, with the free-soil men controlling the House, the slavery men controlling the Senate, was at a complete deadlock. Men even feared bloodshed.

Then, under the pacific leadership of Henry Clay, a compromise was arranged. Missouri was admitted as a slave state, but at the same time Maine came in as a free state; and Congress decreed that slavery should be forever excluded from the territory acquired by the Louisiana Purchase north of the parallel 36° 30', the southern boundary of Missouri. The skies became sunny again. But every farsighted observer knew that the storm would recur. Jefferson wrote that this fire bell in the night had seemed to him the knell of the Union. "It is hushed, indeed, for the moment. But this is a reprieve only, not a final sentence. A geographical line, coinciding with a marked principle, moral and political, once conceived and held up to the angry passions of men, will never be obliterated; and every new irritation will mark it deeper and deeper."

Two clouds no bigger than a man's hand might have announced to the South the impending tempest. In 1821 a young Quaker named Benjamin Lundy founded in Ohio an antislavery journal called *The Genius of Universal Emancipation*. In 1823 the English reformer, Wilberforce, established an antislavery society which was joined by Zachary Macaulay and other men of note.

The Emergence of Jackson

The year 1824 found five important candidates for the presidency before the country. Of these five, John Quincy Adams, Clay, and Calhoun were all men of consummate ability, and W. H. Crawford of Georgia was a most astute politician. But beyond question the most popular aspirant was the fifth, Andrew Jackson. Western admirers of the hero of New Orleans regarded him as the greatest living soldier. Some thought that Caesar, Napoleon, and Marlborough were nobodies compared with him. In the East many conservative men distrusted him. They recalled with Jefferson that in the Senate debates he used to choke with rage until he could not speak; they remembered how impetuously as a military commander he had invaded Spanish Florida and how highhandedly he had hanged two Englishmen there. Adams thought he would make an ideal Vice-President. It would be a dignified office for him; his fame would restore its luster; and there would be no danger that he would hang anybody!

But the election showed Jackson far ahead in the popular vote. No man had a majority of the electoral college, however, and the choice went to the House, which finally selected the learned, experienced, and statesmanlike, but stubbornly untractable Adams.

Adams entered office with two great national achievements to his credit: for the Monroe Doctrine was primarily his work, while it was he who in 1819 had pushed the Spanish government into a treaty which ceded Florida to the United States. He was a man of extraordinary talents, fine character, and great public spirit, but handicapped by his icy austerity, brusque manners, and violent prejudices. As President he was able to accomplish little, for 'the virulent hostility of the Jacksonians—who charged that he had reached the White House by a corrupt bargain with Clay—thwarted him at every turn. Party antagonism has seldom risen higher than in these years. The caustic John Randolph of Roanoke, with a reference to Fielding's *Tom Jones,* spoke of Adams and Clay as "the coalition of Blifil and Black George—the combination, unheard of till then, of the Puritan with the Blackleg." Adams was provoked by such assaults to write in his diary: "The skunks of party slander have been squirting around the House of Representatives, thence to issue and perfume the atmosphere of the Union." He called Randolph "a frequenter of gin lane and beer alley."

During the administration new alignments took shape, the followers of Adams and Clay assuming the name of National Republicans, later to be replaced by that of Whigs, and the Jacksonians giving a new character to the Democratic party. Adams governed honestly and efficiently and strove in vain to institute a national system of internal improvements. His untiring industry is well described in a paragraph of his diary:

> The life that I lead is more regular than it has perhaps been at any other period. It is established by custom that the President of the United States goes not abroad into any private companies; and to this usage I conform. I am, therefore, compelled to take my exercise, if at all, in the morning before breakfast. I rise usually between five and six; that is, at this time

of year, from an hour and a half to two hours before the sun. I walk by the light of moon or stars, or none, about four miles, usually returning here in time to see the sun rise from the eastern chamber of the [White] House. I then make my fire, and read three chapters of the Bible, with Scott's and Hewlett's Commentaries. Read papers till nine. Breakfast, and from nine till five P.M. receive a succession of visitors, sometimes without intermission—very seldom with an interval of half an hour—never such as to enable me to undertake any business requiring attention. From five to half-past six we dine; after which I pass about four hours in my chamber alone, writing in this diary, or reading papers upon some public business, excepting when occasionally interrupted by a visitor. Between eleven and twelve I retire to bed, to rise again at five or six the next morning.

The election of 1828 was like an earthquake, the Jacksonians overwhelming Adams and his supporters. So bitter had feeling become that on arriving in Washington, President-elect Jackson refused to pay the usual visit of respect to the President, while Adams declined to ride to the Capitol with his successor.

Jackson's inauguration has long been regarded as opening a new era in American life. It was such an inauguration as the country had never before witnessed. Washington observers compared it with the invasion of Rome by the barbarians. Daniel Webster wrote several days before that the city was full of speculators, office hunters, triumphant politicians, and plain Westerners and Southerners. People had come five hundred miles to see their hero made President and they talked as if the country had been rescued from some awful danger. As they surged through the streets shouting "Hurrah for Jackson!" many were so boisterous that gentlemen shrank from them. One observer has left a graphic record:

On the morning of the inauguration, the vicinity of the Capitol was like a great, agitated sea; every avenue to the fateful spot was blocked up with people, insomuch that the legitimate procession which accompanied the President-elect could scarce make its way to the eastern portico, where the ceremony was to be performed. To repress the crowd in front, a ship's cable was stretched across about two-thirds of the way up the long flight of steps by which the Capitol is approached on that side, but it seemed at times as if even this would scarce prove sufficient to restrain the eagerness of the multitude, every man of whom seemed bent on the glory of shaking the President's hand. Never can I forget the spectacle which presented itself on every side, nor the electrifying moment when the eager, expectant eyes of that vast and motley multitude caught sight of the tall and imposing form of their adored leader, as he came forth between the columns of the portico; the color of the whole mass changed as if by a miracle; all hats were off at once, and the dark tint which usually pervades a mixed map of men was turned, as by a magic wand, into the bright hue of ten thousand upturned and exultant faces, radiant with sudden joy. The peal of shouting that arose rent the air and seemed to shake the very ground.

But the most characteristic scene of the day was that which followed the ceremony. The motley concourse of enthusiastic Democrats made a rush for the White House. Everyone knew that refreshments were to be distributed there; everybody wanted to see the new President at home. Barrels of orange punch stood ready, but the crowd upset the waiters with pails and glasses. They forced Jackson against the wall, so that his friends had to link arms to protect him. They stood in muddy boots on the satin-covered furniture. "I never saw such a mixture," wrote Justice Story. "The reign of King Mob seemed triumphant."

Jackson's Ideas

Jackson was one of the few Presidents whose heart and soul were completely with the plain people. He sympathized with and believed in them partly because he had always been one of them. He had been born in utter poverty. His father, a poor Ulster Scottish linen draper, who had come to the woods of North Carolina and cleared a farm, died while Andrew was still unborn; the family was unable to buy him even a headstone. His mother became a poor-relation housekeeper to a brother-in-law. The boy, reared in hardship and insecurity, dressed in the cheapest linsey-woolsey, and subject to a nervous disease, was probably humiliated again and again. A childhood sense of inferiority may help to explain his explosive temper, his keen sensitiveness, and his lifelong sympathy with the oppressed. As a mere lad, he fought in the Revolution, which cost the lives of two brothers.

Jackson also imbibed, partly from his Western frontier environment and partly from unfortunate personal experiences, an intense distrust of Eastern capitalistic organizations. After studying law, he went to Tennessee, where he tried to push forward in the world. He bought and sold land, traded in horses and slaves, and for a time owned a general store. A lawyer almost had to be a trader in that area, for he received many fees in bearskins, beeswax, leather, cotton, and land. In 1798 Jackson bought nearly $7000 worth of goods in Philadelphia, selling land to pay for them to a merchant whose notes (endorsed by Jackson) presently went to protest. This saddled him with a heavy debt, and he paid it with a feeling that somehow the financial system of the East had victimized him. He had not gambled; he had simply taken some of the paper circulating among Philadelphia merchants, and when the fog blew away the merchants had his land and his cash.

Moreover, as a frontier lawyer, planter, and merchant Jackson learned that the East exercised absolute sway over much Western commerce. He had to sell his cotton, corn, and hogs down the river in New Orleans; he had to buy general merchandise for his Nashville store in Philadelphia. In both cities the markets kept fluctuating. He might send his orders to Philadelphia and find that prices of goods there had risen to a ruinous level. He might send his produce down the Mississippi and find the bottom had fallen out of the market. At both ends of the line the men who controlled credit grew fat, while Jackson and his neighbors had difficulty in making both ends meet. From this fact grew a distrust and hatred of banks—the same distrust that has always marked the West. The money power, Jackson believed, was paid too much for its services. It was monstrous that easy-living bankers in Philadelphia and New York should have power to ruin the hard-working people of Tennessee.

In the third place, Jackson had the Western faith that the common man is capable of uncommon achievement. Westerners believed that an upstanding man who could command a militia company, run a plantation, and make a good stump speech was fitted for almost any office. They did not believe for a minute that the great prizes of public life were reserved for the rich, the well born, and the educated. The coon hunter had as good a right to them as the Harvard graduate. They had some reason for this view. In Tennessee the Indian fighter Jackson, whose wife smoked a corncob pipe and who spelled Europe "Urope,"

ANDREW JACKSON IN 1819

From a painting by C. W. Peale

got a training that made him a great national leader. In Illinois was growing up a lanky rail splitter who was totally ignorant of drawing-room manners and Latin conjugations, but who was destined to save the Union. Jackson had seen the backwoodsmen whip Wellington's veterans. He had seen self-made men like Benton and Clay dominate the national Congress. He knew the tremendous energy of the West and its strength of character.

Altogether, Jackson's main creed can be summed up in a few phrases: faith in the common man; belief in political equality; belief in equal economic opportunity; hatred of monopoly, special privilege, and the intricacies of capitalistic finance.

Two principal elements could be distinguished in the heterogeneous Democratic party supporting Jackson. Much the largest was composed of the agrarian voters of the nation, the pioneers, farmers, small planters, and country shopkeepers. The trans-Allegheny West, which by 1830 had roughly one third of the population, was marked by special characteristics. It was highly nationalistic in feeling; the new areas had far less state feeling, far more attachment to the Union, than the thirteen original states. In the West, moreover, political equality was taken for granted. Every adult white male there was eligible to vote and to hold office. Restrictions on suffrage long survived in the East, and the movement to abolish them was denounced with horror by such conservatives as Webster in Massachusetts, Chancellor James Kent in New York, and John Marshall in Virginia. But Alabama and Missouri, Indiana and Illinois, gave every white man the vote.

The West, again, liked a direct form of democracy. Jackson's followers attacked the old method of nominating presidential candidates by Congressional caucus and supported the new method of direct nominating conventions, which became firmly established by 1836. They preferred elected judges to appointed judges. Finally, the agrarian voters of the West were interested in a new set of political demands. They disliked banking institutions under Eastern control; they favored the debtor as against the creditor; and they hated anything like monopoly, from steamboat and bank charters to patent rights. They wanted the right to buy public lands cheap and on easy terms.

The other prominent element in the Jacksonian democracy was the mass of toilers in Eastern towns and cities. Stimulated by the Embargo, the War of 1812, and the protective tariff, factories were beginning to grow important in New England and the Middle States. The Merrimack Valley and the region around Providence became thriving textile centers. Lowell in Massachusetts had about five thousand factory hands in 1830. By that year a great part of New York's two hundred thousand people were workers in the factories and shipyards. Most immigrants—English, Irish, German—found the Democratic party more congenial than the Whig. The new working classes converted New York from a Federalist to a Democratic city with a rush and made Philadelphia and Pittsburgh centers of Jacksonian sentiment. They formed many unions (at first usually called trade associations) in this Jacksonian period, and under such leaders as the fiery William Leggett fiercely assailed the reactionary courts which punished strikes under the old conspiracy laws. They warmly applauded Jackson when in 1836 he established the ten-hour day (for the Massachusetts factories then worked men twelve or fourteen hours daily for five dollars a week) in the national shipyards.

Jackson's Measures

Once in power, Jackson vigorously carried his main ideas

into practice. Objecting to the way in which Congress was voting money for local roads and canals, he sharply checked these raids on the treasury by his "Maysville veto"—disapproving a road from Maysville to Lexington in Kentucky. He dealt sternly with South Carolina when it attempted to nullify the protective tariff of 1828. At a Jefferson Day banquet in 1830 he looked the South Carolina leader, Calhoun, squarely in the eye as he gave an immortal toast: "Our Union—it must be preserved." When South Carolina continued on her willful course, he showed that he meant business by sending General Scott and a naval force to Charleston and by issuing a proclamation in which he declared that "disunion by armed force is treason." He was ready to hang Calhoun if necessary, and in later years regretted that he had not. Daniel Webster, in a masterly speech, overwhelmed South Carolina's principal champion in the Senate, Robert Y. Hayne; and his peroration, "Liberty and Union, now and forever, one and inseparable!" became a national rallying cry. Fortunately, South Carolina, unable to unite the South, gave up nullification as Clay, always a friend of peace, arranged a compromise in the reduction in the tariff.

Jackson fought a desperate and successful battle with the second Bank of the United States, overthrowing that citadel of Eastern finance and monopolistic power. Its head, the dexterous Nicholas Biddle, was supported by Henry Clay and the Whigs. On the whole, the bank had been well conducted and had rendered valuable services to the nation. But Jackson sternly vetoed a bill for its recharter. Then, removing the government deposits from the bank, he placed them with leading state banks, so that these would be able to take over the functions of the central institution. Beyond question the bank had meddled with politics; beyond question it was also a private monopoly which had unduly enriched a small group of insiders. Public sentiment was behind Jackson, and though he had to fight hard to bring his whole party behind him, he made his will effective.

In foreign affairs also the President acted with stern decision. When France suspended payment on certain obligations to the United States, he recommended the seizure of French property and brought her to terms. When Texas revolted against Mexico and appealed to the United States for annexation, he wisely took a waiting attitude. To the end of his second term he retained his vast popularity.

Other Democratic Tendencies

The great new democratic wave which rose to flood tide in Jackson's day reached much higher levels than Jeffersonian democracy had touched. Manhood suffrage meant an increased interest in national affairs. In 1824 the aggregate vote cast in the presidential election was only 356,000; in 1836 it rose to 1,500,000; and in 1840 the vote was 2,400,000—seven times as much as only sixteen years earlier. While part of this increase resulted from the growth of population, most of it could be traced to the unshackling of the ballot and the mounting interest in politics. Presidential electors ceased (except in South Carolina) to be chosen by the legislatures, and were elected by popular vote. In national affairs a more rapid rotation in office became the rule. Jackson, frankly announcing his belief in this, displaced many political opponents. Though he made fewer removals than later Presidents, he accepted the rule defined by William L. Marcy of New York: "to the victors belong the spoils."

Manners were becoming more democratic, less formal and punctilious. Foreign observers were shocked by the general tobacco spitting, the rapid feeding at table, the impertinent curiosity, the widespread bumptiousness and bragging, and the nervous hurry of the Northern cities. American culture was stamped also by recklessness and violence. As was natural in a fast-developing country, the job in hand seemed more important than human life. Steamboats and railroads paid little attention to safety. Dueling had become common, and in the South and West, family feuds, marked by free use of the bowie knife and pistol, were frequent. In areas where courts and law officers were undependable, lynching naturally took root. When William Henry Harrison was elected President by the Whigs in 1840, the party had to pretend that this educated and moderately wealthy man, living as a country gentleman on his two thousand acres near Cincinnati, was really a rough pioneer who had dwelt in a log cabin, drinking hard cider. Yet actually the average level of manners was not lower than in the early days of the republic. They were worse than the manners of the aristocracy had then been; but they were better than the manners of the ignorant and brutish workingmen. The old cleavage so sharply visible between good deportment of the gentry and the wretched deportment of the "mob" had been largely obliterated.

Life was growing more democratic in many ways. A cheap press was arising. Imitating the penny papers of London, Benjamin Day in 1833 launched the New York *Sun* at popular prices, while two years later James Gordon Bennett achieved a more spectacular success by founding the sensational New York *Herald*. The first popular magazine also appeared in the Jacksonian era, for *Godey's Lady's Book* was established in Philadelphia in 1830; while the first widely read literary monthly, the *Knickerbocker,* emerged three years later. In education a tremendous battle was being fought for free public schools, nonsectarian, publicly controlled, and tax supported. In this struggle Horace Mann of Massachusetts took the lead. It was a much fiercer battle, in fact, than later generations would suppose. On the one side were ranged democratic and humanitarian men, intelligent workers, Calvinists, and Unitarians; on the other side stood men of aristocratic views, penurious conservatives, the Lutheran, Catholic, and Quaker supporters of parochial schools, many planters and farmers, and teachers in private schools. After bitter fighting, one by one the states were forced into line. A New Englander declaimed, "Reading rots the mind"; an Indianian asked to have inscribed on his tombstone, "Here lies an enemy to free schools." But laws permitting any county or town to levy a tax for free public schools were followed in the Middle States and the West by laws compelling local units to do so.

Even religion, as it followed the frontier westward, became democratized. The sects which flourished most in the West were the Baptists, the Methodists, the Campbellites, and the Presbyterians, all of which were democratic in their form of government and grew more so. The first three sects in particular emphasized two religious elements which the frontier liked: an appeal to the emotions, with much shouting, singing, and fervent prayer; and the idea of personal conversion, which led to enthusiastic revivals and uproarious camp meetings of the kind described in Mark Twain's *Huckleberry Finn*. Literature, too, revealed democratic tendencies. Bryant, Fenimore Cooper, and Washington Irving were all ardent supporters of Jackson. Cooper's books on Eastern society, and Irving's volumes on the wild West, alike stressed democratic ideas. Popular works like David Crockett's *Autobiography* (1834) and Augustus B. Longstreet's *Georgia Scenes* (1835) revealed the influence of the frontier. The first volume of George Bancroft's *History of the United States* unmistakably "voted for Jackson."

Chapter Nine

THE WEST AND DEMOCRACY

The Moving Frontier

ONE of the forces which did most to shape American life from the beginning was the frontier, which may be defined as the border area whose sparse population (not more than six to the square mile) was engaged chiefly in clearing and breaking land and building homes. Moving across the continent as population advanced from the Atlantic to the Rockies, it profoundly affected the American character. It was more than a line—it was a social process. It encouraged individual initiative; it made for political and economic democracy; it roughened manners; it broke down conservatism; it bred a spirit of local self-determination coupled with respect for national authority.

When we think of the frontier we think of the West. But the Atlantic coastal strip was the first frontier and long contained frontier areas; Maine, which drew forty thousand settlers from older New England in 1790–1800, was frontier country for a generation after the Revolution. The second frontier was the region about the headwaters of the coastal rivers and just over the Appalachians. The close of the Revolution found the border in western New York, where two capitalists in 1787 obtained title to six million acres of wild lands; in the Wyoming Valley of Pennsylvania, where Connecticut settlers established homes; about Pittsburgh, which in 1792 had 130 families and "36 Mechanics"; in the eastern

Tennessee area, where in 1784 independent-minded pioneers organized the short-lived "State of Franklin"; and in upland Georgia. Then by 1800 the Mississippi and Ohio valleys were becoming a third great frontier region. "Hi-o, away we go, Floating down the river on the O-hi-o," became the song of thousands of emigrants. In the spring after the writing of the Constitution, Rufus Putnam had taken the first emigrants westward to found Marietta, thus opening an area of about two million acres transferred by Congress to the Ohio Company. That same year another group of land speculators founded Cincinnati. Population was meanwhile pouring into Kentucky and Tennessee with startling rapidity. The first year after peace, ten thousand settlers entered Kentucky; and first national census in 1790 gave it and Tennessee together a population of over a hundred thousand.

Without pause the westward stream flowed over the whole Northwest and Southwest. By 1796 Kentucky and Tennessee were full-fledged states, and Ohio, with a belt of settled lands along the Pennsylvania border and Ohio River, was about to become one; by 1820 Indiana and Illinois, in the Northwest, Alabama and Mississippi in the Southwest, were all states. The first frontier had been tied closely to Europe; the second was tied to the coast settlements; but the Mississippi Valley was independent, and its people looked West rather than East.

The Frontier Settlers

Naturally the frontier settlers were a varied body of men, but most early observers distinguish three main groups. In the van of emigration marched the hunter or trapper. An English traveler named Fordham pithily described the wilder sort of pioneer, usually unmarried:

A daring, hardy race of men, who live in miserable cabins, which they fortify in time of war with the Indians, whom they hate but much resemble in dress and manners. They are unpolished but hospitable, kind to strangers, honest and trustworthy. They raise a little Indian corn, pumpkins, hogs, and sometimes have a cow or two, and two or three horses belonging to each family. But the rifle is their principal means of support.

When they heard the sound of a neighbor's gun, it was time to move on. Fenimore Cooper has given a good picture of the pioneer hunter in Natty Bumppo, and of backwoods life in *The Prairie*. These men were dexterous with the ax, rifle, snare, and fishing line; they blazed the trails, built the first log cabins, held back the Indians, and so made way for a second group.

This second body Fordham describes as the first true settlers, "a mixed set of hunters and farmers." Instead of a cabin, they built a "log house," which had glass windows, a good chimney, and partitioned rooms, and was as comfortable as an English farm cottage; instead of using a spring they sank a well. An industrious man would rapidly clear land of timber, burning the wood for potash and letting the stumps decay. Growing his own grain, vegetables, and fruit, ranging the woods for venison, wild turkeys, and honey, fishing the nearest streams, looking after some cattle and hogs, he would worry little over the loneliness and roughness of his life. The more enterprising bought large tracts of the cheap land on the theory that it was wise, as a character in Edward Eggleston's *Hoosier Schoolmaster* put it, to "git a plenty while you're agittin' "; then, as land values rose, they sold their acres and moved westward. Thus they gave way to the third group, the most important of all.

The third body included not only farmers, but also doctors, lawyers, storekeepers, editors, preachers, mechanics, politicians, and land speculators—all the materials to furnish the fabric of a vigorous society. But the farmers were the most important. They intended to stay all their lives where they settled and hoped their children would stay after them. They built larger barns than their predecessors and then sounder brick or frame houses. They constructed better fences, brought in improved livestock, plowed the land more skillfully, and sowed more productive seed. Some of them erected flour mills, sawmills, or distilleries. They laid out good highways, built churches and schools. As towns grew up, many of this third group, as bankers, merchants, or land dealers, became men of wealth. In short, they represented American civilization. So rapidly did the West grow that almost incredible transformations were accomplished within a few years by this third wave. Chicago in 1830 was merely an unpromising trading village with a fort; before some of its first settlers died it was one of the largest and richest cities in the world.

Many different peoples mingled their blood in the new West. Farmers of the upland South were prominent, and from this stock sprang Abraham Lincoln and Jefferson Davis, born in Kentucky log cabins in the same year. Hard-headed Scotch-Irish, thrifty Pennsylvania Germans, enterprising Yankees, and men of other origins played their part. All these people had two traits in common—individualism and democracy. By 1830 more than half the Americans had been brought up in an environment in which Old World traditions and conventions were absent or very weak. Men in the West had to stand on their own feet. They were valued not for family, inherited money, or years of schooling, but, like the castaways in Barrie's *The Admirable Crichton,* for what they could do. People could get farms for a price not beyond reach of any thrifty person; government land after 1820, as we have seen, could be obtained for $1.25 an acre, and after 1862 for merely settling on it. They could easily get the tools to work it. Then, as Horace Greeley said, they could "grow up with the country." This equality of economic opportunity bred a sense of social and political equality and gave natural leaders a chance to come quickly to the front. It should be added that the sea was practically another frontier in its effect upon American character. Vessels were small and had small crews, while many fishing ships and whalers were worked on a partnership basis. Initiative, courage, individual vigor, and hard sense were the requirements of a good pioneer hunter, frontier farmer, or Eastern sailor alike.

Frontier Virtues and Vices

By contagion and example this democracy and individualism became marked traits in the cities of the young republic. The upright independence that William Cobbett lauded immediately struck European visitors to New York and Philadelphia. These observers noted that workmen did not tip their hats and say "sir" to earn a shilling. The very porters accepted a job with the attitude of men conferring a favor. Cobbett mentioned approvingly that American servants wore no livery and usually ate with the family and were called "help." He saw only two beggars in America, and both were foreigners. One of Ralph Waldo Emerson's most truly American essays is that on "Self-Reliance." He speaks of the typical Yankee of the day who, going West, was by turns farmer, storekeeper, land dealer, lawyer, Congressman, and judge, a jack-of-all-trades, always landing on his feet. It was not an overdrawn portrait. One of the ablest Civil War generals, W. T. Sherman, was in turn cadet, soldier in the Mexican War, banker in San Francisco, lawyer in Leavenworth, farm manager on the Kansas frontier, head of a military college in Louisiana, and then soldier again.

But if the frontier fostered virtues, it also bred vices. The frontier folk were in general unruly, impatient of discipline, and too aggressively self-confident—too "brash." Many of the military defeats of the War of 1812 were attributable to a frontier dislike of training and subordination. Frontier-trained Americans were inclined to do everything with hurried crudity. So many tasks needed performing that careful finish seemed a waste of time. Americans hurried up rough frame houses instead of durable stone and brick structures, they built rough roads, they made makeshift bridges, they gutted rather than cultivated the soil. New York had fire bells clanging all night because its houses burned like tinder, while in 1836 two of the city's largest business buildings actually collapsed. Railroad collisions and steamboat explosions were frequent. Naturally, little attention was paid to manners or culture; the frontier had no leisure for them. And worst of all, frontier life was marked by a deplorable amount of outright criminality. Some of the scum of society swirled out to the border. Men developed ungovernable tempers and had a taste for settling their quarrels with fists or pistols. Officers of justice had to possess iron nerve and a quick trigger finger.

The Indian Wars

The undisciplined character of the frontiersmen had especially tragic consequences in their dealings with the Indians. They constantly encroached on Indian lands in defiance of treaty; they destroyed the game on which the Indians depended for food and clothing; and many were ready to slay any redskin on sight. When the Indians tried to defend themselves, war ensued. Of course, the savages were often aggressors, but the inexorable westward thrust of the whites was the principal cause of the many conflicts. The most bloodcurdling wars were with the Creeks in the South, where Andrew Jackson won a bloody victory; with the Seminoles in the Florida swamps and thickets; and with Tecumseh's followers in Indiana.

Young Abraham Lincoln was a captain in the Black Hawk War, an especially brutal affair. Some spokesmen for Black Hawk's tribe, the Sauk and Fox Indians, had ceded to the government their title to about fifty million acres. The chief and a great part of the tribe denied the validity of this cession. Before a threat of force Black Hawk withdrew from his corn lands in Illinois to the west bank of the Mississippi. But his tribe suffered from hunger, and next spring they recrossed the river in order to join the friendly Winnebagos in Wisconsin and raise corn there. They had a childlike faith that their amicable intentions would be understood. But the whites immediately attacked them; Black Hawk retreated, making offers of peace, which the two thousand militia ignored. His despairing followers were driven through southern Wisconsin to the Mississippi again, where men, women, and children were mercilessly cut to pieces as they tried to cross. "It was a horrid sight," wrote one rifleman, "to witness little children, wounded and suffering the most excruciating pain, although they were of the savage enemy." This was the frontiersman at his worst.

The idea of a general removal of the Eastern Indians to the Great Plains beyond the Mississippi, long thought to be uninhabitable by white men, was officially adopted under Monroe and energetically pursued under Jackson. Congress authorized the President to exchange lands in the West for the older Indian holdings. An "Indian Country" was created, running at first from Canada to Texas. To this area the Northern Indians were removed without much difficulty. But in the South, where the tribes were larger and stronger, the Indians offered a stubborn resistance, and the result was tragic. The so-called Five Civilized Tribes— Creeks, Choctaws, Chickasaws, Cherokees, and Seminoles —loved their homes. Many of them, especially the Creeks and Cherokees, had learned to be thrifty farmers, had built good houses, acquired herds of cattle, erected gristmills, and educated their children in missionary schools. They clung to their lands to the last, some being driven away only by force. Traveling in great part by wagon and on foot, they suffered from hunger, disease, and exposure, and many died. By 1840, however, nearly all the Indians east of the Mississippi had been taken to their new homes.

This removal facilitated the complete peopling of the Mississippi Valley, the richest and most distinctive part of the country. Wisconsin, the last state east of the Mississippi, was admitted in 1848. Already a tier of states had been erected west of the river, for after Missouri's entry in 1821, Arkansas became a state in 1836 and Iowa ten years later, while Minnesota Territory was organized in 1849. The panic of 1837, in large part a product of overdevelopment in the West, checked the onward movement but briefly. Cyrus H. McCormick, inventor of the reaper, set up a factory in Chicago in 1847 and began turning out machines that made it easy to cover the Western prairies with grain. Railroad building began and soon threw a mesh of tracks over the level region. In 1854 seventy-four trains a day ran into Chicago, which already boasted itself the largest primary grain market in the world. That year saw the Galena and Chicago Railroad carrying three thousand emigrants a month to Iowa, while other thousands traveled by road. Germans, Scandinavians, and Britons helped fill the upper valley and took homes in Texas or Arkansas as well. An English observer was startled in 1854 to find St. Paul in far-

STEAMBOAT RACE ON THE MISSISSIPPI

off Minnesota a city of seven or eight thousand, with four or five hotels, half a dozen good churches, wharves at which three hundred steamers arrived annually, and "good streets with sidewalks, and lofty brick warehouses, and stores, and shops, as well supplied as any in the Union." New Western leaders came into prominence before 1850; such men as Stephen A. Douglas and Abraham Lincoln in Illinois, David R. Atchison in Missouri, Jefferson Davis in Mississippi, and Sam Houston, the hero of the Texan War for Independence, in the Lone-Star State.

The Settlement of the Nearer West

A major part was played in the development of the Mississippi Valley by several great avenues of transportation. The first main artery to the West was the Cumberland Road, begun in 1811 and built for the most part with Federal money. Running from Cumberland, Maryland, over the mountains to Wheeling and Zanesville on the Ohio, it was finally pushed on to Vandalia in Illinois. When completed it was about six hundred miles; sixty feet wide, it had in the center a paved strip of twenty feet constructed on McAdam's principles.

Over this "National Pike" ran the Western mails, with special postage. Inns sprang up at convenient distances. The stream of colonists swelled until in summer passengers were never out of sight. "Hundreds of families are seen migrating to the West with ease and comfort," wrote one observer in 1824. "Drovers from the West with their cattle of almost every description are seen passing eastward seeking a market. Indeed, this great thoroughfare may be compared to a street through some populous city—travelers on foot, on horseback, and in carriages are seen mingling on its paved surface." The road connected at Wheeling with the Ohio River, and this also became a crowded artery of travel. At first it was navigated by flatboats, barges, and arks, which "managed to keep up with the current," and took grain, venison, peltry, pork, and flour down to New Orleans. Then Nicholas Roosevelt, of a family later famous, built a steamboat which in 1811 ran from Pittsburgh clear through to New Orleans and back, and he soon had many imitators.

But the most famous highway to the West was the Erie Canal, which linked the Hudson River and Atlantic Ocean with the Great Lakes, thus providing a water road into the very heart of the continent. Men had dreamed of it even in the eighteenth century. It would enable emigrants and trade to flank the wild Appalachian chain. But the task of digging nearly four hundred miles of canal was so formidable that leaders shied away from it. Finally, an indomitable New Yorker, De Witt Clinton, carried on a campaign to convert the vision into reality. He gained the governorship, began the work in 1817, and after arduous years saw "Clinton's Ditch" completed. A joyous celebration in 1825 welcomed the first procession of boats, and before an acclaiming multitude Clinton poured a kegful of Lake Erie water into the Atlantic. The canal, which made Buffalo a thriving port, and along which new towns and cities sprang up, confirmed New York in her position as leader of American trade and finance.

More important than that, however, was its contribution to Western growth. New Englanders and New Yorkers traveled westward on it in a steady stream. This flood of migrants built up Cleveland, Detroit, and Chicago into bustling cities, and gave great parts of the Northwest a decidedly Yankee flavor. It was responsible in itself for a striking shift in the American population, and it did much to help save the Union, for before the Civil War broke out it had tied the upper Mississippi Valley securely to the

North Atlantic states. In this it was aided by Pennsylvania's system of canals. Stung to emulation by the success of Clinton's ditch, the Pennsylvanians spent about forty million dollars upon a transportation system which linked Philadelphia with Pittsburgh, four hundred miles away. In part they used rivers and canals, while they surmounted the high Allegheny ridges by a series of inclined planes, up which boats, cargo, and passengers were hauled by steam. It was a heroic enterprise, and though it almost bankrupted the state, it did a useful work and helped make Pennsylvania one of the leading industrial states.

Population movements tended roughly to follow the parallels of latitude. Alabama and Mississippi were settled mainly by Southerners; Michigan and Wisconsin mainly by Northerners. In such commonwealths as Ohio, Indiana, and Illinois, the two currents met. The Southern stream, pouring along the Ohio, and the Northern stream, pouring along the Erie Canal and Great Lakes, peaceably mingled. Cities like Columbus, Indianapolis, and Springfield were built up by the two stocks, who intermarried with each other and with European immigrants. Here came into being "the valley of democracy."

The Trans-Mississippi West

When we turn to the vast country west of the Mississippi, we find that its settlement offers an even more colorful story. It was first made known to the nation by the exploring expedition which Jefferson sent clear to the Pacific under Meriwether Lewis and William Clark, two young Virginians with a great deal of frontier experience. This famous undertaking, which wrote an immortal chapter in geographical discovery, was financed by a Federal appropriation of only $2500! Jefferson had always been keenly interested in the wonders of the West. He had written at length about the Indians, whom he admired, and of the discovery of remains of the mammoth in the Ohio Valley. But when he sent Lewis and Clark into the wilderness his object was twofold. In addition to scientific inquiry he expected these men to open up the Missouri River country to American fur traders. At that time the Indians of the area carried their furs into Canada to sell to British dealers. They would find it far easier, Jefferson thought, to send the pelts down the river to American buyers.

Both objects were accomplished. Lewis and Clark, ascending the Missouri, crossing the Rockies, and descending the Columbia to the Pacific, accomplished an epic bit of exploration, which has been called "incomparably the most perfect achievement of its kind in the history of the world." They encountered little real danger, for they evaded the warlike Sioux. Covering about four thousand miles on the outward trip in eighteen months, they carefully mapped and described the country. They also laid a basis for American competition with the rich British fur-trading companies. Immediately after their return Clark helped found the Missouri Fur Company, with a chain of forts on the river. It prospered and grew. And soon afterward John Jacob Astor's energetic American Fur Company entered the Northwestern field. It had hitherto traded chiefly about the Great Lakes, but Astor now resolved to plant a trading post at the mouth of the Columbia. In 1811 a ship of his, called the *Tonquin,* rounded Cape Horn, sailed north, and founded Astoria (about which Washington Irving later wrote a delightful book), while an expedition across the continent by land reached the same point the next year.

This was a good beginning. And the development of the West and its trade was hastened by three picturesque occurrences early in the 1820's. One was the opening of a brisk trade along the Santa Fé Trail to the far Southwest, then

WAGON TRAIL ACROSS THE ROCKIES

in Mexican hands. An enterprising Missourian, William Becknell, got together a trading party of about seventy men, placed goods on horses and mules, and, traveling eight hundred miles over a rough, dangerous country, sold his wares in the Mexican outpost of Santa Fé at a handsome profit. The next year he took wagons on the long journey. Other traders imitated him, and the celebrated Santa Fé Trail was fairly open. The traders who used it encountered many perils, for much of the country was semi-desert, parched by heat and drought; they had to ford difficult rivers; and they were likely to be attacked by hostile Comanche, Arapaho, and Cheyenne Indians. While large groups of eighty or a hundred men were fairly safe, small groups of ten or twenty were likely to be overwhelmed. In time the pioneers beat out an American road which did much to win the Southwest for the republic.

The second remarkable occurrence was the founding of the Rocky Mountain Fur Company in 1822 by William Ashley, a St. Louis general of militia, who advertised for a hundred young men to ascend the Missouri and remain about its headwaters for one to three years. This was the first company which depended primarily upon trapping by its employees rather than upon trading with the Indians. Among its men were some of the greatest figures in Western exploration, including Kit Carson, who as trapper, hunter, Indian fighter, scout, and guide was to meet a series of adventures which make his life read like a romance, and Jedediah Smith, who was unsurpassed as an explorer. The third occurrence was a military expedition up the Missouri in 1823 to frighten the Arikaras and other fierce Indians into submission. This "Missouri Legion," fitted out by the national government and the St. Louis fur traders combined, made it clear that the United States would protect the fur seekers.

Missionary activity also helped greatly in the penetration of the Far West. The churches had long been active in frontier work, but a curious incident in 1831 gave new stimulus to their zeal. The Indian tribes on the upper Columbia had learned from British traders some rudiments of religion and wished to obtain further information. The Nez Percé sent four leading men to William Clark in St. Louis to ask for the Book of Heaven. When church journals published the story, keen interest was aroused. The Protestants sent several clergymen, with supporting parties, into the far Northwest, and they established a mission in the Willamette Valley and another near the junction of the Snake and Columbia. The leading figure in this effort was the devoted Dr. Marcus Whitman. These missions did a good deal to Christianize the Indians. They set up model farms, showing the savage converts how to build houses, clear the fields, and grow crops. The enthusiastic letters they wrote about the scenery and climate, meanwhile, fired the interest of relatives and friends; and soon annual caravans of settlers were crossing the plains and mountains to the Oregon country.

The Oregon Trail

The first explorers and fur traders who journeyed from the Missouri River to the Columbia vaguely traced a route which in time became definite as the Oregon Trail and which by the middle forties was a great highway. Some two thousand miles in length, it abounded in dangers and difficulties. Starting at Independence on the Missouri, it traversed the rolling plains to the Rockies, crossed them by the relatively low South Pass, and went on through barren and mountainous stretches to Fort Hall on the Snake River, whence the trail ran through the almost impassable Blue Mountains to the Umatilla River and down to the Colum-

WESTERN U.S. SHOWING THE
OVERLAND TRAILS & ROUTES
OF AMERICAN EXPLORATION

PACIFIC OCEAN

bia. An alternative route beyond Great Salt Lake led to California. The first emigrant train to set out for the Pacific was promoted by John Bidwell and, numbering about eighty men, women, and children, successfully wound its way through the wild country to Oregon in 1841. This was the advance guard of an astonishing movement. In 1843 occurred the "Great Emigration," when not fewer than two hundred families, comprising a thousand people, crossed the plains and mountains, driving hundreds of cattle with them, and reached their goal. At two miles an hour the ox-team caravans could make twenty-five miles on good days; on bad days but five or ten. In 1845 the human rivulet following the Oregon Trail rose to a broad stream. More than three thousand people came into the Willamette Valley that year.

It was an epic migration, this Oregon movement. "Catch up, catch up!" would ring out the cry at dawn; and the long lines of covered wagons, marshaled by chosen leaders, would be got into motion. At nightfall they camped in a circle, the wagons, baggage, and men on the outside, the women, children, and animals within. Sentries were carefully posted. Food was cooked, clothes were washed, on the way. Courtships were carried on, children were born, the feeble died and were buried in unmarked graves. When worn oxen and mules could no longer drag the heavy wagons, dearly prized possessions had to be left by the trail. To some who met Indians, grizzlies, the dreaded cholera, or bitter weather, the trip might be a prolonged agony. Others found it exhilarating. "It was a long picnic, the changing scenes of the journey, the animals of the prairie, the Indians, the traders and trappers of the mountain country," wrote one. This mass movement made Oregon an American community, doing as much as diplomacy to secure it to the United States. It peopled that far-off country

POLITICAL EXPANSION OF THE UNITED STATES

so effectively that it was organized as a territory in 1849 and became a full-fledged state only ten years later.

The Mormons

By far the most striking and important of the religious settlements in the West was that of the Mormons in Utah. The traditions of individualism, dissent, and evangelism in America had led to the formation of numerous curious sects. Most of them were offshoots of existing bodies. But the Mormons were a wholly new organization. The creator of this Church of Latter-Day Saints was Joseph Smith, a youth of upper New York, who asserted that one day in 1820 he retired to the woods to pray for salvation; that two glorious personages appeared to him and asked him to wait for a full restoration of the Gospel; that in time an angel named Moroni came and told him of a record, engraved on buried plates of gold, containing the sacred history of the ancient inhabitants of North America; and that with the aid of instruments presented by this angel, he translated the history. It was published in 1830 as the *Book of Mormon*. A church was organized in that year and grew rapidly. Its headquarters, after various vicissitudes, were transferred to Illinois. Here the Mormons built on the banks of the Mississippi the prosperous city of Nauvoo, founded a university, and commenced erecting a great temple. They also adopted polygamy. Antipathy to this practice and to their religion, together with economic and political jealousies, caused an outbreak of rioting. A mob took Smith and his brother from the county jail and hanged them; and soon afterward the Mormons, now led by the able Brigham Young, were expelled from the state. They crossed the Mississippi, resolved to find peace and safety in the Far West.

The upshot was a remarkable exploit in the settlement

of what many thought a desert region. Brigham Young led his people across the plains and into the valley of the Great Salt Lake, where, surrounded by high mountain ranges, he found fertile land, a healthful climate, and enough water for irrigation. He directed the laying out of fields, selected the site for a city, and saw to communications with the East. The first year witnessed some scarcity, but after that Utah offered a rude plenty for everyone. Farms and irrigation ditches soon extended up and down the whole valley. Brigham Young exercised a despotic power, but his wisdom and benevolence made it endurable. He and his church officers organized the marketing of Utah products; they controlled settlement, choosing sites for new towns and sending each just the craftsmen it needed; and they made Salt Lake City, with its fine broad streets, its rills of sparkling water, and its temple and tabernacle, one of the most interesting places in America. It was the first American experiment with a planned economy, and it was successful. Polygamy for a time continued, serving a sound colonizing purpose —for women were in the majority among the converts, and the frontier had little place for unmarried and childless women. By 1850 Utah was organized as a territory.

The Annexation of Texas

The annexation of Texas, and the conquest of California and the Southwest from feeble Mexico, finally rounded out the American domain in the West. Within a few years in the 1840's the United States extended its boundaries over some of the richest and most scenic regions of the continent. Various writers have treated this wresting of territory from Mexico as immoral aggression. James Russell Lowell said that the South wanted Texas just to have "bigger pens to cram slaves in." This is unjust. A natural and inevitable process brought about the addition of this territory to the United States—a process well hit off by the phrase "manifest destiny."

Texas was at first a part of the Mexican Republic, a land as large as Germany with but a few ranchers and hunters. It early attracted many Americans and some Britons, Stephen F. Austin planting the first Anglo-American settlement in 1821. Free lands, easily accessible to the Southern States, were the principal bait. The Mexican government was inefficient, corrupt, and tyrannical. In 1835 the settlers rose in revolt and after a number of battles won their independence. One episode was the capture by the Mexicans of the Alamo, a fort in San Antonio, where every American defender was killed: "Thermopylae had its messenger of defeat; the Alamo had none." Once established, the Texan Republic flourished and attracted many fresh American settlers. For a time the United States refused to consider any proposal for annexing the country. But for a number of reasons many Americans gradually changed their minds. For one, they thought it a duty to expand over the unpeopled and undeveloped West. For another, they felt that the Texans were a kindred people whose natural place was under the American flag. For a third reason, they feared that Great Britain might intervene in Texas and try to establish a protectorate. And finally, pocket motives were at work. Northerners wished to sell farm products and manufactured goods in Texas; shipowners saw that their vessels could make profitable voyages to Galveston; Yankee mill owners wished to have cheap Texas cotton to spin. Many Southerners wanted to migrate and yet were unwilling to leave the American flag.

In the national election of 1844 a majority of the voters showed that they were ready to take the little republic into the Union, and early the next year it was annexed.

Charles Nahl   *Courtesy of E. B. Crocker Art Gallery*

SUNDAY MORNING IN THE MINES

The Mexican War and the Acquisition of California and New Mexico

Meanwhile many Americans were equally intent upon gaining control of California by the same peaceful means. They thought this possible because of its peculiar position. California had a meager population of but eleven or twelve thousand people, clinging tightly to the coast. They had no money, no army, no political experience. They had more Spanish blood than the Mexican masses and regarded themselves as physically and intellectually superior and they were only nominally dependent upon Mexico. Indeed, they would have thrown off the Mexican authority altogether had it not been for their family jealousies and an old feud between northern and southern California. As it was, Mexico provided no courts, no police, no regular postal facilities, and no schools. Communication between California and Mexico City was rare and uncertain. So frankly did Mexico recognize that its sovereignty was a mere shadow that by the middle forties it showed a disposition to sell the region to Great Britain. Year by year the American element in California was growing in numbers and aggressiveness. American ships had long traded on the coast, while emigrants who wished to settle in the golden climate and make money from cattle and wheat had begun crossing the mountains in the 1830's. By 1846 California had twelve hundred foreign residents, most of them Americans. No wonder that some men believed California would drop like a ripe pear into the outstretched hand of the United States —that no force would be needed.

Perhaps it would have done so had not the Mexican War broken out. The remote cause of this conflict was the increasing distrust between the two nations, while its immediate cause was a dispute over the boundary of Texas. The

United States found it a short and brilliant conflict. One American army under Zachary Taylor was sent into northern Mexico, captured the fortified city of Monterey, and defeated a large Mexican force in the stubborn battle of Buena Vista. Another army under Winfield Scott, hero of the War of 1812, landed at Vera Cruz, pushed westward over the mountains, and after hard fighting took Mexico City. Here Scott hoisted the American flag over "the halls of the Montezumas." When peace was made, the United States was given not only California but the huge area between it and Texas called New Mexico, which included the present Nevada and Utah. Altogether, in this country and in Texas the United States gained about 918,000 square miles.

It also gained a treasure house, for even as the treaty of peace was ratified gold was discovered in the California hills. At once a host of fortune hunters poured forth, some by sea and some by overland trail, to the canyons and gulches where nuggets could be washed out in troughs and pans. The mountains filled with roaring camps; San Francisco sprang overnight into a lusty little metropolis, full of vice, luxury, and energy; and California was converted in a twinkling from a sleepy, romantic community of Spanish-American ranchers into a hustling and populous commonwealth of Anglo-Saxons. These "days of old, and the days of gold, and the days of '49" were among the most colorful in all American history. So fast did California grow that in 1850 it was added to the Union as a state.

The acquisition of these broad new stretches in the West compelled Americans to take an interest in various neglected problems—the problem of the Caribbean; the problem of the Pacific; the problem of an isthmian canal; and above all the problem of slavery, which threatened to expand into the whole area.

Chapter Ten

THE SECTIONAL STRUGGLE

Slavery: The "Peculiar Institution"

HALF a dozen years before the Civil War the shrewd New York observer, Frederick Law Olmsted, visited one of the first-rate cotton plantations in Mississippi. He found a large and handsome mansion; nearly fourteen hundred acres planted to cotton, corn, and other crops; and two hundred hogs. Of the one hundred thirty-five slaves, nearly seventy worked in the fields, three were mechanics, and nine were house or stable servants. They labored from dawn to dark, with Sundays and sometimes Saturdays free. In summer the hoe gang thus spent sixteen hours in plodding labor, with one short interval at noon for rest. The food allowance was a peck of corn and four pounds of pork apiece each week, supplemented by vegetables, eggs, and poultry grown by the slaves themselves. Every Christmas molasses, coffee, tobacco, and calico were generously distributed. The Negroes got their own fuel for their little cabins from a wooded swamp, where on Sundays they could also cut puncheons for sale, using the money to buy small comforts. A black driver walked about among the field hands, urging them on, cracking his whip, and sometimes letting the lash fall lightly on their shoulders. The white overseer told Olmsted that discipline was good, though he had just sold a slave who tried to stab him. "His niggers did not very often run away, he said, because they

213

were almost sure to be caught. As soon as he saw that one was gone he put the dogs on."

This was a typical plantation of the better sort. Olmsted, like other observers, found plantations where slavery was harsher and more brutish; he could have found some where it was kindlier. Critics indicted slavery because of the overwork, the occasional floggings, the cruel disruption of families by sales, the denial of education and advancement to the blacks. Defenders extolled it because it protected the worker in unemployment, sickness, and old age, because it freed the South from strikes and labor clashes, because it Christianized a heathen people and gradually elevated them, because (they said) it made masters chivalrous and servants loyal. As an economic institution, slavery had both attackers and supporters. Olmsted, like the North Carolina writer, Hinton Rowan Helper, author of *The Impending Crisis,* thought that it impoverished the South, but many Southern leaders explained the backwardness of their section in terms of Northern aggrandizement. Socially, Northerners declared that slavery injured blacks and whites alike, but most Southerners deemed it the only feasible method of controlling the great mass of Negroes and maintaining white supremacy.

Actually few Americans, North or South, really understood the nature of the peculiar institution which one side was so bitterly attacking, the other so passionately defending. For the most important fact about American slavery was that it was Negro slavery: most of the features that characterized it were connected with race rather than with status. The whole institution was designed largely to regulate the relationships of black and white rather than of master and slave, and though the status of the Negro was completely changed by the Civil War and the Thirteenth Amendment, the economic and social relationships of Negroes and whites were not greatly changed. Most of the arguments advanced to justify slavery would have applied with equal force and relevance to the doctrine of white supremacy formulated after the Civil War; most of the abolitionist criticism of the peculiar institution could have been polished up for postwar use. When the Yankees argued that slavery retarded Southern progress, when they placed upon it responsibility for the backwardness of agriculture, of industry, of education, in the South, they were really talking about the presence of cheap and ignorant black labor—a situation that persisted long after emancipation. Some Southerners understood this, but instinctively rather than intellectually, and they were unable to explain that slavery was a transitional stage in the evolution of race relationships. And because Northerners did not appreciate this they too did not understand what was involved in emancipation and doomed themselves to grave disappointment in its results.

By 1850, when the total population of the country exceeded twenty-three millions (it passed that of Great Britain during the next decade), the total number of slaves was 3,200,000. In South Carolina and Mississippi they exceeded the whites in number; in Louisiana they nearly equaled the whites, and in Alabama were roughly three sevenths of the population. The South had large areas where slaves were not one tenth of the people, the Appalachian Mountains all the way from Maryland to Alabama being largely free from them. It had other areas where they were heavily predominant. Just north of Charleston they constituted eighty-eight per cent of the population, on the Georgia seacoast eighty per cent, in central Alabama nearly seventy, and in one belt along the lower Mississippi River more than ninety. The slave population was greatest where the climate was hot, the soil flat and rich; it was least where the land was mountainous or barren. Only a minority of Southerners held slaves. Out of a total white population of about six millions in 1850, the census revealed but 347,725 owners. Although most of the blacks were held in small groups, in the cotton, sugar, and rice country of the lower South three or four thousand families owned a majority of the slaves, lived on the best lands, and enjoyed three fourths of the income. Howell Cobb of Georgia, for example, with a thousand Negroes, raised cotton on ten thousand acres. Political power and intellectual leadership were similarly concentrated in a small and generally aristocratic group.

Beginning about 1830, sectional lines had steadily hardened on the slavery question. Abolitionist and above all free-soil feeling grew more powerful in the Northern States. The fiery William Lloyd Garrison founded his *Liberator* in Boston in 1831. But Garrison's importance has been much exaggerated; an equally effective part was played in the movement by a stalwart Ohio group led by the evangelist C. G. Finney and the agitator Theodore D. Weld, and a New York group led by Arthur Tappan. They were able organizers of the demand for "root-and-branch" emancipation. Persecution simply threw oil on the flames. When Elijah P. Lovejoy, trying in 1837 to defend his abolitionist press against a mob in Alton, Illinois, was murdered, the crusade gained intensity. Interferences with civil rights convinced many able men that the cause of human freedom was broadly involved. The eloquent Wendell Phillips of Boston was inspired to join the movement by a mob attack on Garrison; the wealthy Gerrit Smith of upper New York by an assault on an antislavery meeting in Utica; the able Salmon P. Chase of Ohio by attacks on the press in his own state. At no time did the root-and-branch abolitionists command much popular strength. But the free-soil men, who insisted that slavery must not expand one inch farther, grew into a host. Meanwhile, in the South various leaders declared slavery a positive good. Thomas Dew, of William and Mary, published a book defending it; Governor Hammond of South Carolina in 1835 pronounced it "the cornerstone of our republican edifice"; Calhoun, pointing to ancient Athens, asserted that slavery offered the firmest basis for a splendid culture.

From an early date keen-sighted men saw that this sectional dispute endangered the Union. John Quincy Adams in the House repeatedly warned the South that secession would mean war and that "from the instant your slaveholding states become the theater of war, civil, servile, or foreign, from that moment the war powers of the Constitution extend to interference with the institution of slavery." Lincoln was to verify that prophecy.

The Rising Storm

The moment the Texan question and Mexican War made huge annexations of Southwestern territory certain, the slavery quarrel entered upon an acute phase. The fire bell in the night, to use Jefferson's phrase, again clanged ominously. Up to 1844 slavery had merely asserted its right to continue unmolested where it existed. It had been given limits by the Missouri Compromise and had not overstepped them. Now when it declared its right to expand, a host of Northerners rose in opposition. They believed that if kept within close bounds it would ultimately decay; they asserted that Washington, Jefferson, and other founders of the republic had held this view; and they pointed to the Ordinance of 1787, forbidding its expansion into the Northwest, as a binding precedent. As Texas already had slavery, she naturally entered the Union as a slave state. But California, New Mexico, and Utah did not have it. When the United States prepared to take over these areas, a Pennsylvania Democrat named David Wilmot attached to an appropriation bill a proviso declaring that slavery should forever be prohibited in any territory which might be acquired from Mexico. The House passed the Wilmot Proviso; the Senate defeated it.

To Southerners it seemed bitterly unfair that an area which they had helped gain by their blood should not be open to them and Northerners alike, one group free to take in slave property as the other was to take in machine property. To free-soilers it seemed outrageous that virgin territories should be opened to an institution that blighted free enterprise and offended their moral sense. A constitutional question was bound up with this political issue. Did or did not the Constitution permit Congress to exclude or regulate slavery in the national territories? Congress had repeatedly done so; but the instrument was vague, and Calhoun and other Southern radicals asserted that slavery followed the flag into the common domain and could not be shut out. For the first time, in the campaign of 1848 a powerful Free-Soil party appeared. It nominated Martin Van Buren for President and closed its platform with the ringing words: "We inscribe on our banner 'Free Soil, Free Speech, Free Labor, and Free Men,' and under it will fight on, and fight ever, until a triumphant victory shall reward our exertions." The party polled an impressive vote. Largely because of its activities, the Democrats were defeated, and the Whig party elected its last President, the war hero Zachary Taylor.

During and after the campaign it became clear that the lower South would secede before it submitted to the Wilmot Proviso. It was equally clear that Northern antislavery men would never yield to Calhoun's demand that slavery enter all parts of the new acquisitions. Some compromise was imperatively required. One group of moderates suggested that the Missouri Compromise line of 36° 30' be extended to the Pacific, with free states north of it and slave states to the south. Another moderate group, led by Lewis Cass of Michigan and Stephen A. Douglas of Illinois, proposed to refer the question to "popular sovereignty." That is, the national government should take its hands off; it should allow settlers to flock into the new country with or without slaves; and when the time came to organize the region into states, the people should determine the question for themselves. When Congress met at the end of 1849, Southern men openly threatened withdrawal. Robert Toombs of Georgia shouted, apropos of one Northern bill: "If it should pass, I am for disunion!"

Compromise of 1850

In this crisis Henry Clay, for the third time, halted a dangerous sectional quarrel with a well-wrought compromise. His plan proposed that California be admitted as a free state, that New Mexico and Utah be organized as territories without legislation either for or against slavery, that a more efficient machinery be set up for returning fugitive slaves to their masters, that the slave trade be abolished in the District of Columbia, and that Texas be compensated for some territory ceded to New Mexico. Both sides would have to give up something. Most of these proposals came originally from Douglas, but Clay welded them together, and his backing was indispensable. His prestige in all sections, his eloquence, his deep earnestness, and the influence of his courtly, charming personality were needed to carry them to victory.

The debates by which the Compromise of 1850 was hammered into final shape were among the most impressive in American history. The Senate then possessed three parliamentary giants, all approaching the grave—Clay, Webster, and Calhoun. It possessed a galaxy of younger men of high talent—Stephen A. Douglas, Jefferson Davis, William H. Seward, and Salmon P. Chase. Of these men Calhoun and Davis opposed the compromise as unfair to the South. The former wrote an impressive argument, declaring that to prevent a tragic conflict the grievances of the South must be remedied. One by one, he said, the cords which bound the North and South together were breaking. Already the Methodist and Baptist churches had broken into two parts. "If the agitation goes on, the same force, acting with increased intensity, will finally snap every cord, when nothing will be left to hold the states together except force." Too weak to read his speech, he tottered into the Senate to hear it delivered by a Virginia colleague. Seward and Chase opposed the compromise as unfair to the North. But Clay was magnificently supported by Daniel Webster. In a powerful speech on March 7, the last great oration of his life, Webster pleaded "not as a Massachusetts man, nor as a Northern man, but as an American," for unity. Peaceable secession he declared impossible. His support of the compromise outraged radical antislavery men in New England and required high courage; but it was a statesmanlike act—his last great service to the nation. In the end the moderate spirit of Clay, Douglas, and Webster triumphed. The compromise measures were passed, and the country breathed a sigh of heartfelt relief. Zachary Taylor would probably have vetoed the bills, but he had died in early summer, and his successor, Millard Fillmore, gladly signed them.

For three short years the compromise seemed to settle nearly all differences. A majority in both Whig and Democratic parties cordially supported it. Yet under the surface the tension remained and grew. The new Fugitive Slave Law deeply offended many Northerners. They refused to take any part in catching slaves; instead, they helped fugitives to escape. The "underground railroad" became more efficient and unabashed. Some slaves escaped from coastal areas by ship. Some, traveling by night and guided by the North Star, walked from their plantations to the Ohio River and were thence helped into Canada. Some followed the Appalachian chain into Pennsylvania. The Northern States became honeycombed with shelters for runaways, and men like Levi Coffin, the so-called president of the "underground railroad," helped scores to reach safety. In 1850 about twenty thousand escaped slaves who had settled in Northern communities were subject to recapture, but efforts to seize men often provoked riots.

Harriet Beecher Stowe was inspired by the Fugitive Slave Law to write *Uncle Tom's Cabin,* which, appearing in book form in 1852, painted a dark picture of slavery so vividly that it aroused deep feeling in both North and South. Mrs. Stowe had lived in the border city of Cincinnati and visited in the homes of Kentucky planters. She did full justice to the many humane and generous slaveholders; her one brutal slave driver, Simon Legree, was of Yankee origin. But she showed how inseparable cruelty was from slavery and how fundamentally irreconcilable were free and slave societies. Her book was translated into more than a score of languages, sold more than a million copies in the British Empire, and when converted into a play thrilled huge audiences. The rising generation of voters in the North was deeply stirred by it.

Then in 1854 the old issue of slavery in the territories was torn open again, and as the quarrel became more bitter, new leaders stepped forward to take command of both sections. The radical Southerners were determined to get rid of the Missouri Compromise, closing the whole upper Missouri Valley to slavery. When steps were taken to achieve this, the North roused itself like an angry giant.

The country beyond the Missouri River which now comprises the fertile states of Kansas and Nebraska was already attracting settlers. If the Indians were removed and a stable government instituted, it promised a rapid development. The old idea of a "great American desert" in this area had been exploded by the explorer John C. Frémont and others; and many Northerners believed that if the region were organized as a territory, settlers would flock in and a railroad could be built through it from Chicago to the Pacific. This would forestall a Southern project for a railway striking westward from New Orleans. Early action was required, for the Southern route ran through well-settled Texas and New Mexico Territory, it was little exposed to Indian attack, and public lands were available for grants to railroad builders. Nobody was more eager to clear the Northern line than Stephen A. Douglas, who lived in Chicago, was an active real-estate speculator, and had become chairman of the Senate Committee on Territories. But he met stern opposition. Under the Missouri Compromise all this country was closed to slavery, and Missouri objected to letting Kansas, which adjoined her on the west, become a free territory. It would be all too easy for Missouri slaves to run away to this free area. Moreover, Missouri would then have three free neighbors and, yielding to an already strong movement, would probably soon become a free state herself. For a time Missourians in Washington, backed by Southerners, blocked all efforts to organize the region.

Then Senator Douglas in 1854 cut through the opposition with a bill that enraged all free-soil men. It was an application of his favorite doctrine of popular sovereignty. In its final form it declared that the Missouri Compromise had been superseded by the compromise provisions in 1850, leaving Utah and New Mexico free to decide on slavery for themselves; it organized two territories, Kansas and Nebraska, permitting settlers to carry slaves into them; and it authorized the inhabitants to determine whether they should enter the Union free or slave. Douglas' motives were doubtless mixed. He was accused of currying favor with the South in order to gain the presidency in 1856, and his political ambitions were unquestionably strong. His Democratic associates were chiefly Southerners; he had married a Southern woman; he did not dislike slavery or object to its extension. His chief object, however, was to hurry on the development of the region, whose climate he thought unsuitable to slavery anyway.

But if he believed that Northern sentiment would tamely accept his plan, he was quickly undeceived. To open these rich Western prairies to slavery struck millions of men as unforgivable. Angry debates marked the progress of the Kansas-Nebraska Bill. The free-soil press violently denounced it. Northern clergymen assailed it from literally thousands of pulpits. Businessmen who had hitherto befriended the South turned suddenly about-face. Mass meetings were held in all the chief Northern cities to attack Douglas and his measure. He confessed that he could travel from Washington to Chicago by the light of fires built to burn him in effigy. On a March morning the bill passed the Senate amid the boom of cannon fired by Southern enthusiasts. As Chase walked down the Capitol steps he remarked to Charles Sumner of Massachusetts: "They celebrate a present victory, but the echoes they awaken shall never rest until slavery itself shall die." When Douglas did visit Chicago to speak in his own defense, the shipping in the harbor lowered its flags to half mast, the church bells tolled for an hour, and a crowd of ten thousand hooted and groaned until, exhausted in the effort to make himself heard, he finally drew out his watch and according to some auditors exclaimed: "It is now Sunday morning; I am going to church and you can go to hell!"

The immediate results of Douglas' ill-starred measure were momentous. The Whig party, which had straddled the question of slavery expansion into the territories, sank to its death, and a powerful new organization, the Republican party, rose instead. Idealistic, full of enthusiasm, attracting young men of brains and vigor, appealing alike to Eastern business and Western farmers, it was formidable from the beginning. Its primary demand was that slavery be excluded from all the territories. In 1856 it nominated the dashing John C. Frémont, whose five exploring expeditions into the Far West had won him deserved renown, and swept a great part of the North; had it carried Pennsylvania in the October elections, it might even have won over the Democratic nominee, James Buchanan. Such free-soil leaders as Seward and Chase rose to greater influence than ever, and along with them appeared a tall, gaunt attorney of Illinois who showed a marvelous power of logic in discussing the new issues—Abraham Lincoln.

A speech which Lincoln made in Peoria on October 16, 1854, was the best statement of free-soil principles thus far presented. He said that he had no desire to interfere with slavery where it stood. "If all earthly power were given me, I should not know what to do as to the existing institution." He declared that Congress had no more moral right to repeal the Missouri Compromise, a great sectional compact, than to repeal the law against importing slaves from Africa. He asserted that all national legislation should be framed on the principle adopted by the fathers of the republic, that slavery was an institution to be restricted and ultimately abolished. And he contended that the popular-sovereignty principle was false, for slavery in the West was the concern not merely of the inhabitants there, but of the whole United States. "What better moral right have thirty-one citizens of Nebraska to say that the thirty-second shall not hold slaves than the people of thirty-one states have to say that slavery shall not go into the thirty-second state at all?"

The flow of Southern slaveholders and Northern anti-slavery men into Kansas produced a sharp conflict, with savage episodes of guerrilla warfare. Steps were taken in both sections to send forward settlers to hold the country, the Emigrant Aid Society in the North being especially diligent. They went well armed. The popular Brooklyn clergyman, Henry Ward Beecher, attending a meeting at which a deacon called for weapons for one company, declared that a Sharpe's rifle was a greater moral agency than the Bible; and from this remark sprang the familiar phrase, "Beecher's Bibles." It was soon clear that the North held the advantage. The proximity of the large free-soil population of the upper Mississippi Valley, and the risks of taking slaves into a region that might soon be free, assisted it. However, many "border ruffians" crossed the river from Missouri to cast illegal votes or to intimidate Northern settlers, while the slaveholding forces had the support of the Buchanan administration in Washington. The conflict, therefore, dragged on, arousing ever-keener feeling throughout the country. When the blundering Buchanan tried to induce Congress, Democratic in both branches, to admit Kansas under the Lecompton Constitution authorizing slavery, a new storm swept the North, and Douglas himself indignantly broke with the President.

Meanwhile, many Northerners who felt that the bargain made in the Compromise of 1850 had been broken by the South refused to carry out the Fugitive Slave Act, which was part of that bargain. Mob interference in behalf of fleeing Negroes became more common. Many Northern

States passed "personal liberty laws" which openly nullified the Federal statute. When the slave Anthony Burns was caught in Boston, some of the city's most distinguished leaders hastened to his defense. Angry men poured in from all eastern Massachusetts, threatening crowds filled the streets, and it required the united force of the city police, the state militia, and the national army and navy to drag one poor black man back into slavery.

Drifting Into War

Year by year the nation moved closer to war. A great drum seemed to beat out the march to conflict, stroke after stroke. In 1856 a hot-headed South Carolina member of Congress, Preston Brooks, attacked Sumner of Massachusetts at his Senate desk and hammered him so heavily with his cane that Sumner was an invalid for several years. The provocation, a grossly abusive speech by Sumner, had been great, but the act was indefensible. Early in 1857 Chief Justice Taney and a majority of the Supreme Court declared in the Dred Scott case that Congress had no power to exclude slavery from the territories. It was a bad interpretation, badly argued. At once the free-soil press and politicians attacked the court with unprecedented bitterness, declaring they would see to it that in good time it changed this mistaken construction. "Hearafter," wrote the poet-editor William Cullen Bryant, "if this decision shall stand for law, slavery, instead of being what the people of the slave states have hitherto called it, their peculiar institution, is a Federal institution, the common patrimony and shame of all the states, those which flaunt the title of free, as well as those which accept the stigma of being the Land of Bondage; hereafter, wherever our jurisdiction extends, it carries with it the chain and the scourge—wherever our flag floats, it is the flag of slavery. If so, that flag should have the light of the stars and the streaks of running red erased from it; it should be dyed black, and its device should be the whip and the fetter. Are we to accept, without question, these new readings of the Constitution . . . ? Never! Never!"

In 1858 occurred the memorable series of debates in Illinois between Lincoln and Douglas, both seeking a seat in the Senate. Outwardly, these debates had little dignity. Douglas, a squat, dwarfish man with a huge head, and Lincoln, an awkward, lanky giant whose homely countenance was surmounted by a shock of rough black hair, presented an extraordinary contrast. But no arguments in the English language have more shrewdness, luminosity, or Saxon force than those which they presented. They did much to awaken the country to the significance of the issues. Moreover, Lincoln succeeded in forcing Douglas to reiterate, with emphasis, his belief that the Dred Scott decision did not necessarily overthrow the principle of popular sovereignty in the territories. True, the Supreme Court had held that neither Congress nor territorial legislature could interfere there with slavery. But Douglas explained that in hostile communities slavery could not survive unless protected by positive police regulations, and that by simply refusing to pass such laws, a community could blight and destroy it. When Southerners heard this bold avowal, many took sides with Buchanan in reading Douglas out of the Democratic party. He won the senatorship, but after this year Lincoln was a national figure.

Then in 1859 came the raid of John Brown at Harpers Ferry, a fanatical invasion of Virginia by a little group who hoped to liberate and arm the slaves. This quixotic and criminal enterprise completely failed. The South was justly outraged by the attack. But when Brown and six followers were hanged, many Northerners exalted the old abolitionist into the seat of a martyr to liberty. And within two years soldiers were to march to battle to the tune of *John Brown's Body*.

One underlying fact which made these events desperately serious was that North and South had now grown into sections that were widely unlike, economically, socially, and politically. The South was almost wholly rural, with but one considerable city, New Orleans. Great parts of the North had become urbanized, and New York was fast approaching a population of a million. The South had very little manufacturing, though a few such enterprises as the Tredegar Iron Works in Richmond flourished; its textile mills actually handled less cotton than the single town of Lowell in Massachusetts. The North, on the other hand, was now full of thriving industrial establishments, turning out iron, textiles, shoes, watches, farm implements, and a thousand other products on a large scale, building ships, packing meats, and milling flour, and growing steadily in technical skill. Nearly all the heavy stream of European immigration (2,452,000 in the decade 1850–1860) stayed in the North and West, the Irish settling in the cities, many Germans and Scandinavians going to the farms, the British scattering everywhere. Already this section had a painful problem of labor management and another of slums. The South would have welcomed immigration, but got little, for immigrants did not care to compete with Negro slaves. Railroad construction was far more advanced in the North than the South. Three trunk lines from the East were built over or around the Appalachians— the Erie, completed from New York to the Buffalo area in 1851; the Pennsylvania, completed from Philadelphia to Pittsburgh in 1852; and the Baltimore and Ohio, completed from Baltimore to Wheeling in 1853. The greatest of the Western lines was the Illinois Central, endowed by a

SLAVERY & SECTIONALISM

━━━ BOUNDARY OF SLAVE STATES

••••••• BOUNDARY OF 11 CONFED. STATES

▨▨▨ AREA OF THE COTTON STATES

rich land grant of 2,600,000 acres and linking Chicago with the Gulf. Of the twenty thousand miles of railroad built in 1850–1860, most was in the North.

An increasing body of Northerners believed in protective tariffs, while the rural South, wanting its manufactured goods cheaply, detested them. The North was interested in a quicker distribution of the public lands to small holders. A mighty demand for free homesteads to all settlers was arising: "Vote yourself a farm!" became a popular cry. The South wished to see the national domain held and sold only for good prices. The Northwest wanted internal improvements—to which the South was indifferent. The North wanted an efficient national banking system; the South, which accumulated little capital, was hostile to centralized banking. Socially the North, despite growing extremes of wealth and poverty in the large cities, was more democratic than the South, where the slaveholding oligarchy held most of the wealth and power.

Yet these differences, important as they were, would not have divided the sections had not fear and prejudice exaggerated them and demagogy exploited them. The South was keenly aware of the fact that an almost insoluble race problem underlay the slavery problem. It "had the wolf by the ears," as Jefferson said, and could neither hold him nor let him go. The abolitionist agitation engendered a fear that the North would attack slavery where it already existed, disrupt the historic labor system of the South, and array race against race to the destruction of both. Much Northern criticism was indeed of a selfish, canting type, unconstructive and incendiary. On the other hand, even reasonable Northerners like Lincoln feared that radical Southerners would try to spread slavery over the whole nation. They feared, too, that the lower South would attempt to reopen the slave trade, as some of its leaders advocated; and that in an effort to expand its system, it would lead the nation into wars to conquer Cuba, or Mexico, or Central America. The Ostend Manifesto of 1854, an irresponsible statement in favor of Cuban annexation signed by the three Democratic ministers whom President Franklin Pierce had sent to Great Britain, France, and Spain, had aroused a distrust of Southern imperialism. So had the filibustering expeditions of the reckless William Walker in Central America.

Many Northern editors, clergymen, and politicians grossly exaggerated the evils of slavery and the intentions of slaveowners. Many Southern fire-eaters grossly exaggerated the evils of industrial society and the aims of the free-soilers. A wise New York leader said that if the worst agitators on both sides could be packed into a stagecoach and plunged beneath the Potomac for fifteen minutes, sectional peace might be secure; but that was too optimistic a view. Others would quickly have taken their places.

Lincoln's Election: Secession

Republican victory in 1860, which precipitated Southern secession, was made possible by a schism in the Democratic party. Behind this schism lies one of the most dramatic stories of American political history.

For years a growing body of Southern extremists had been demanding that Congress pass laws protecting slavery in the territories. When Douglas declared that the Dred Scott decision giving slavery free entry into all territories could be rendered meaningless by hostile local laws, the demand for this protection was redoubled. It was voiced by Jefferson Davis of Mississippi, William L. Yancey of Alabama, and Robert Toombs of Georgia, three spokesmen of the cotton kingdom. In the Senate early in 1859 Albert G. Brown of Mississippi reiterated the demand

and, turning to Douglas, asked where he stood. "If the territorial legislature refuses to act," he asked, "will you act? If it passes laws hostile to slavery, will you annul them, and substitute laws favoring slavery in their stead?" The South, he said, called for action—"positive, unqualified action." Other Southerners rose to support him.

But Douglas was not to be intimidated. Brown's demand, he declared, was an infringement upon popular rights in the territories. Never in American history had Congress passed either a criminal code for any territory or a law protecting property in a territory. From 1789 onward Congress had left these matters to the territorial legislature. Why should it break its sound rule now? The Democratic party had for years declared that it stood for Congressional nonintervention in the territories. Why should it forsake that sound doctrine now? "If," asserted Douglas, "you repudiate the doctrine of nonintervention and form a slave code by act of Congress when the people of a territory refuse it, you must step off the Democratic platform. . . . I tell you, gentlemen of the South, in all candor, I do not believe a Democratic candidate can ever carry any one Democratic state of the North on the platform that it is the duty of the Federal government to force the people of a territory to have slavery when they do not want it." Jefferson Davis rejoined that Congress must assert the rights of American citizens and that when a territorial legislature did not perform its proper functions in protecting property, Congress must do it. Not at all, exclaimed Douglas. If Oregon will not enact statutes to encourage mules, I won't pass a law in Washington to force mules on them; if Oregon will not encourage longhorn cattle, I will not force cattle on them; and if Oregon will not accept slaves, I will not force slaves on her people.

This was the rock on which the Democratic Convention

in 1860 split, this and the feud between Douglas and supporters of the Buchanan administration. The delegates met in Charleston, the very center of aggressive slavery sentiment—the city of Calhoun, of Hayne, of R. B. Rhett and his radical *Mercury*. They met to continue the battle between Douglas and Davis which had now raged in the Senate for two years. If Douglas won, the Democratic party could continue as a truly national organization, strong in the North and West as well as South. If Davis won on his platform of forcing unwilling communities to foster slavery, the Democracy would become a sectional party, strong only in the south. For a time it seemed that a compromise candidate might be placed on a noncommittal platform. But such Southern extremists as Davis, Yancey, Rhett, Toombs, and Judah P. Benjamin of Louisiana were following a policy of party rule or party ruin.

"Gentlemen of the South," exclaimed Douglas' spokesman, Pugh of Ohio, when the extremists tried to force their demand into the platform. "You mistake us—you mistake us—we will not do it." A majority of delegates stood firm against the Davis-Yancey doctrine. Thereupon the Alabama delegation rose in protest and walked out of the hall. The South Carolina delegation followed; others from the lower South fell into line. With the party split complete, the Charleston Convention adjourned without making any nominations. Its two fragments shortly organized as separate conventions, the Southern radicals nominating John C. Breckinridge of Kentucky, their opponents nominating Douglas. The significance of the split was greater than many realized at the time. Not merely had the Democrats made their defeat certain. One more of the great bonds holding North and South together had parted.

The Republican party went into the campaign with perfect unity. In an enthusiastic convention in Chicago it nominated its most popular Middle Western figure, Lincoln; and his disappointed rivals, Seward and Chase in the van, loyally rallied behind the rail splitter. Party spirit had been wrought up to a high pitch. A stern determination, an evangelistic ardor, animated the millions of voters who had proclaimed that they would allow slavery to spread no further. The party was successful, too, in enlisting such strong support from capitalist groups that it was far better provided with money than four years earlier. The brief, disastrous panic of 1857 had stimulated the demand in industrial communities for a protective tariff; it had increased the demand in commercial and financial circles for a better banking system. The Republican party promised to satisfy these yearnings. Simultaneously it appealed to land-hungry Northerners with a pledge that it would enact a law granting free homesteads to settlers. Economically, in short, it offered powerful attractions to important American groups. In Pennsylvania, which the Republicans had lost in 1856, the tariff plank helped mightily toward victory. In the old Northwest the internal-improvement program won thousands of votes. In the central West the homestead plan was equally potent.

On Election Day Lincoln polled 1,866,452 votes, Douglas polled 1,375,157, Breckinridge received 847,953, and John Bell of Tennessee, who had run on a platform of sectional conciliation, 590,631. Lincoln had a minority of the popular vote but in the electoral college a decisive majority. The popular vote was unquestionably for union and peace. Breckinridge, the only secession candidate, received less than one-fifth the total vote.

In the South, however, the extremists were in control. "The people are run mad," wrote the Unionist Alexander H. Stephens of Georgia. "They are wild with passion and frenzy." Already South Carolina had determined upon secession. Why? It seems probable that neither the South nor slavery stood in any real danger. During nearly his whole first term, Lincoln (if the Southern States remained in the Union) would face a hostile majority in Congress; The Supreme Court, too, was dominated by Southerners; his hands would be tied. For that matter, Lincoln had most explicitly denied any intention of molesting slavery where it stood. Slavery could not be abolished in the South save by constitutional amendment, and that would be impossible for decades to come. Yet the step was taken— taken though its sequel was certain. "Men will be cutting one another's throats in a little while," Stephens prophesied.

The step was taken, but there is no conclusive evidence that it was supported by the majority of the people outside of South Carolina. Unionist sentiment was strong throughout the South—and even in the Palmetto State—and so, too, was peace sentiment. In the election of 1860 voters from fourteen slave states had cast 124,000 more votes for the two compromise candidates, Douglas and Bell, than for the extremist Breckinridge. A careful analysis of the voting in some of the states of the deep South suggests that had the issue of secession been presented for a fair and open referendum, it would have been defeated. Even after secession and the outbreak of war there remained powerful groups in the South bitterly hostile to the Confederacy. Western Virginia seceded from the Old Dominion, conscription could not be enforced in western North Carolina, and it is said that some counties of eastern Tennessee contributed a larger proportion of their population as volunteers in the Union army than any counties in the North. Yet it must be remembered that revolution is usually the work of determined minorities and that secession assuredly had as wide popular support in 1860 as had the revolution against the rule of George III in 1776.

The lower South was actuated by a variety of motives: hatred of the North, pique over its defeat in the election, unwillingness to accept the verdict on the territories, a dream of brighter and better days under its own flag. South Carolina, leading the way on December 20, 1860, declared that the North had elected as President a man "whose opinions and purposes are hostile to slavery." Mississippi, following her, asserted that the Northern people "have assumed a revolutionary position toward the Southern States." But perhaps the chief reason was that the Southern extremists saw that it was now or never. Nullification had been stamped out by President Jackson. Secession by a single state was impossible. The North was growing steadily more powerful in relation to the South. If this crisis were permitted to pass without an attempt at establishing Southern independence, no such opportunity would recur. A Southern Confederacy might gain a strong place among the nations of the world and could soon expand southward around the Caribbean. Early in February delegates of seven seceding states met in congress at Montgomery, Alabama, formed the Confederate States of America, and elected Jefferson Davis its provisional President.

Four other states of the reluctant upper South, loyal to their section, were soon to follow. Last-minute attempts were made at compromise. But the most promising of these, John J. Crittenden's plan for returning to the Missouri Compromise line of 36° 30', foundered on the Republican refusal to let slavery enter any territory. At dawn on April 12, 1861, the Southern guns opened on Fort Sumter in Charleston Harbor.

Chapter Eleven

THE BROTHERS' WAR

Men and Resources

"I⊤ is enough to make the whole world start to see the awful amount of death and destruction that now stalks abroad. Daily for the past two months has the work progressed and I see no signs of a remission till one or both the armies are destroyed. . . . I begin to regard the death and mangling of a couple thousand men as a small affair, a kind of morning dash—and it may be well that we become so hardened." So wrote General William T. Sherman to his brother on June 30, 1864. He added: "The worst of the war is not yet begun." That sentence was true for Georgia, whose farms and towns he was about to lay waste in a broad swath of destruction all the way from the mountains to the sea. It was true for Virginia. It was almost true for Grant's and Lee's armies, their bloodiest fighting just under way. Yet the country had entered upon this conflict in a lighthearted spirit, Northerners shouting "On to Richmond!" and Southerners vaunting their chivalric superiority over the Yankee "scum," both sides dreaming that the conflict would be short and glorious.

The shock of conflict at Fort Sumter had at once united the North and also the South. A wave of fury tore Virginia from the Union and placed her in the Confederacy; the Old Dominion gave the South its capital, for Jefferson Davis and his government arrived in Richmond late in

June, 1861, and its ablest leader, for Robert E. Lee, hero of Cerro Gordo and Chapultepec in the Mexican War, former superintendent at West Point, and commander of the department of Texas, found the call of his state stronger than that of the nation. Tennessee swung into the Confederate roster. In the North the upper Mississippi Valley, declaring that it would never have "a line of customhouses" between it and the Gulf, took a vigorous stand with the Union. Far-off California did the same. The Border States of Maryland, Kentucky, and Missouri hesitated, for they were bitterly divided in sentiment. For a few days the secessionists controlled Baltimore and at one time seemed about to seize control of St. Louis. But in the end the three states of Francis Scott Key, Henry Clay, and Thomas Hart Benton stood by their old allegiance. North and South, party lines temporarily melted away. Douglas symbolically held Lincoln's hat when the new President stepped forward to deliver his first inaugural; Alexander H. Stephens, a lifelong Unionist, became Vice-President of the Confederacy.

Each side had certain advantages. The North was far stronger in population, industrial resources, and wealth. The census of 1860 showed that the twenty-three states under the Stars and Stripes (not counting West Virginia, soon organized out of the loyal counties of Virginia, or Kansas, soon admitted to the Union) had about twenty-two million people, as against eleven states and a little over nine million people under the Stars and Bars. And the Southern population included more than three and a half millions of Negroes. The Northern railway system comprised about twenty-two thousand miles, the Southern only nine thousand. The North held a tremendous advantage in its industrial development, for New York alone produced in 1860 a value of manufactured goods more than twice, and

THE INAUGURATION OF JEFFERSON DAVIS

Pennsylvania nearly twice, that of the whole Confederacy. In the last three years of the conflict the North made nearly all of its own war supplies, while the South had to depend on foreign guns, foreign drugs and surgical equipment, and to a great extent on foreign ammunition. The North kept control of the navy and, with it, the ocean. It had a more adaptable and variegated economy. It had the strength lent by immigration, which declined until Gettysburg and then rapidly swelled again. The South had in its favor the martial spirit of its people, the easy seizure of numerous forts and arsenals, the superior efficiency and organization of its agriculture, the fact that it was fighting on the defensive, and the ability of its armies to operate on inside lines. It had in its favor, above all, the fact that in order to achieve success it did not have to win the war in a military sense—did not have to invade and conquer the North. All that it needed to do was to fight long and hard enough to persuade the North that it could not itself be conquered. It could afford to lose battles and even campaigns; it could afford to suffer defeat after defeat. The Confederacy would win if it could convince Northern opinion that a Union victory would cost too much and that it was better, after all, to allow the erring sisters to depart.

Many believed that the South also possessed a great advantage in controlling the world's main cotton supply —that Britain, needing this cotton to keep her mills busy, would intervene on the Southern side. Time quickly showed that this was a miscalculation and that Britain needed Northern wheat no less than Southern cotton. A sublime defiance animated the South even in disaster, but it was matched by Northern determination. The Southern generals were on the whole quicker and abler than those of the North; but President Lincoln proved a far greater statesman than Jefferson Davis, who possessed intellectual distinction, dignity, and austere earnestness, but lacked breadth, and sometimes allowed temper, impatience, and personal prejudices to warp his judgment. All in all, the North was easily the stronger; and the South's great hope lay in the difficulty of subjugating a territory so huge, a population so large and irreconcilable as its own.

Those Northerners who believed the war would be short were taught their lesson by Bull Run. An army of about thirty thousand, hastily whipped into shape at Washington, was set in motion against a Confederate force of about the same size lying behind the deep-gullied Bull Run in northern Virginia. The Union forces on July 16 drove through the Confederate center, only to meet a smashing attack from the fresh Confederate right wing. All but the regulars stampeded in a wild flight back to Washington, choking the roads with men, guns, abandoned baggage, and Congressmen who had come in the hope of seeing a sort of picnic victory. Other Northern reverses followed in Missouri, and at Ball's Bluff on the Potomac, where Oliver Wendell Holmes, later of the Supreme Court, was wounded. Both sides girded themselves for a desperate struggle.

In the end the war dragged over four years, closing only when the South lay in utter exhaustion. Its cost in money, property loss, and lives was frightful. The North is estimated to have enlisted about two million men altogether, and when the last shot was fired had about a million in the field. The South is estimated to have enlisted between seven hundred thousand and a million men; no one will ever know the exact number. On the Union side about 360,000 men died in action, from wounds or disease; on the Confederate side the dead have been computed at 258,000. Great parts of the South were laid waste. The Shenandoah Valley was ravaged from end to end; Sherman destroyed fifty millions' worth of public buildings and hundreds of millions' worth of private property in Georgia; cities like Columbia, Richmond, and Atlanta were gutted by fire; railroads were torn up and factories smashed. With its old labor system destroyed and its physical property shattered, the South was economically prostrate. The scars of the conflict are still visible in that section. Though the North was enjoying a great industrial boom when the war closed, it too had suffered more than it at first realized.

The Campaigns

Four main fronts or theaters of action may be distinguished: the sea, the Mississippi Valley, Virginia and the Eastern-seaboard states, and the diplomatic front. The first may be briefly dismissed. At the beginning of the conflict practically the whole forty-ship navy was in Union hands, but was scattered and demoralized. An able head in Washington, Gideon Welles (best remembered now for his invaluable diary of the war), quickly reorganized and strengthened it. Lincoln proclaimed a blockade of the Southern coast, and although this was at first extremely weak, by 1863 it became highly effective. It prevented shipments of cotton to Europe and the importation of munitions, clothing, and medical supplies that the South sorely needed. Meanwhile, a brilliant naval commander, David G. Farragut, had emerged and conducted two remarkable operations. In one he took a Union fleet of wooden sloops into the mouth of the Mississippi, ran past two strong forts, and forced the surrender of New Orleans, the Confederacy's largest and wealthiest city. In another he forced his way past the fortified entrance of Mobile Bay, captured a Confederate ironclad, and sealed up the port. Ironclads were now beginning to supplant wooden ships. One of the anxious moments of the war occurred in March,

1862, when the new Confederate ironclad, *Merrimac,* issued from Norfolk, Virginia, destroyed two Union frigates in Hampton Roads at the mouth of the James River and seemed ready to attack Washington or New York. Fortunately, an armored Union vessel of curious design, "a cheesebox on a raft," the *Monitor,* which had been built in New York and hurried South, appeared in the nick of time, attacked the champion, and put a stop to its career. The Union navy gained another smart victory when a roving Confederate cruiser built in England, the *Alabama,* was sunk by the *Kearsarge* off Cherbourg. The navy served the Union well in blockading the South, in helping capture important coastal points, and in sinking or capturing Confederate commerce destroyers.

In the Mississippi Valley the Union forces won an almost uninterrupted series of victories. Ulysses S. Grant, an Illinoisan of dogged tenacity, unimaginative but with a clear grasp of the main principles of strategy, had been put in command of strong Western forces. He began with the breaking of a long Confederate line in Tennessee by capturing Forts Henry and Donelson on the Tennessee and Cumberland rivers, thus making it possible to occupy most of the western part of the state. The important city of Nashville had to be abandoned by the Confederates, and Union troops were able to advance to the southern boundary of Tennessee—that is, some two hundred miles into the heart of the Confederacy. Here the Southern troops concentrated under Albert Sidney Johnston and the dashing P. G. T. Beauregard. In April, 1862, they delivered a blow which came near routing Grant. By a swift attack they caught his army unprepared at Pittsburg Landing on the Tennessee River, its back to the swollen stream, its front unfortified. The sudden onslaught almost overwhelmed the Union forces. But just in time Grant was reinforced, while

Charles Hoffbauer

LEE AND HIS GENERALS, A MURAL IN BATTLE ABBEY, RICHMOND, VIRGINIA

the Confederates lost their brilliant General Johnston. The result was that the Confederates fell back to Corinth in Mississippi. Both sides had lost heavily in the battle of Shiloh—the Union forces 13,000 out of 63,000 men; but Lincoln said of Grant, "I can't spare this man—he fights."

In the spring of 1863 Grant's hard-bitten troops steadily but slowly advanced southward. Their great object was to gain complete control of the Mississippi, the lower reaches of which had been cleared of Confederates after Farragut's capture of New Orleans. For a time Grant was blocked at Vicksburg, where the Confederates had strongly fortified themselves on bluffs too high for a successful naval attack. But by an audacious movement he took his army below and around Vicksburg, conducted a six weeks' siege, and on July 4 captured the town together with the strongest Confederate army in the West. Now, as Lincoln remarked, the Father of Waters went again unvexed to the sea. The Confederacy was broken in two, and it became almost impossible to bring supplies from the rich Texas and Arkansas country east across the stream.

But in Virginia the Union troops had meanwhile met one defeat after another. The distance between Washington and Richmond, which the Confederates made their capital, is only a hundred miles, but the country is intersected by numerous streams which furnished strong defensive positions. Moreover, the Confederates had two generals, Robert E. Lee and Thomas J. ("Stonewall") Jackson, who in brilliant leadership far surpassed the early Union commanders. It is impossible to describe in detail the succession of bloody campaigns in which the Federal armies, trying to capture Richmond and destroy the Confederate forces, were again and again thrown back. George B. McClellan early in 1862 moved a finely trained arm of 100,000 men by sea to the peninsula between the York and

James rivers and, marching it against the much weaker army of Lee, fought the desperate Seven Days' Battles before Richmond. At one time his troops could hear the clocks striking in the steeples of the Confederate capital, but they finally retreated with heavy losses. The blundering John Pope failed in the second battle of Bull Run and was driven back toward Washington, while the North feared for its own safety. Another Union commander failed when, attempting to storm the heights behind the town of Fredericksburg, he was repulsed with terrible slaughter. Still another was beaten as ignominiously at the bloody battle of Chancellorsville; but there the Confederates lost Lee's right arm, the indomitable Jackson, whose bold raid in the Shenandoah Valley in 1862, defeating a whole series of Union forces and throwing panic into Washington, was perhaps the most thrilling exploit of the war. Up to the summer of 1863 the Confederates had all the best of it in the East.

Yet not one of these Confederate victories was decisive; the Union government simply mustered new armies and tried again. If the Union armies were unable to capture Richmond, the Confederates had no better success when they took the offensive. In August, 1862, Lee thought the time was ripe to strike into the North, but McClellan met him on the field of Antietam, in western Maryland, and fought him to a standstill. It was a drawn battle—but Lee withdrew, and Lincoln, desperately anxious for a victory, thought it enough of a success to justify the announcement of the Emancipation Proclamation. Again the following summer, after the crushing defeat of the Union troops at Chancellorsville, Lee struck northward and invaded Pennsylvania. His army almost reached the capital of the state, and Baltimore and Philadelphia were thrown into great alarm; but a stronger Union force intercepted his march at

Gettysburg. Here, in a three-day battle, the Confederates made a valiant effort to break the Union lines. Had they struck with smashing celerity, while the Union forces were concentrating, they might have won the contest. In the end they had to fight against a stronger army occupying better positions. Pickett's desperate charge on the final day, facing a terrific fire, was one of the most gallant efforts in the history of war. But it failed, and next day, as Lee's veterans, after losses which permanently crippled them, sullenly fell back to the Potomac, it was clear that the "high tide at Gettysburg" had been the high tide of all Confederate hopes.

Grant's army was then taking possession of Vicksburg. The blockade of the Southern coasts had become an iron cordon which few vessels pierced. The Confederacy, its factories running short of machinery and materials, its railroads falling into decay, was nearing the end of its resources. The Northern States, on the other hand, seemed more prosperous than ever, their mills and factories running full blast, their farms exporting bumper crops to Europe, their man power being restored by immigration.

In southeastern Tennessee the final phase of the Mississippi Valley campaigns also went decisively against the Confederates. Chattanooga, a busy railroad junction in this area, was only less vital to the Confederacy than Richmond and Vicksburg. Commanding railways that ran southwest, southeast, and east, and so placed that it blocked the path of Union armies southeastward around the Great Smoky Mountains, it was one of the portals to the lower South. A Union force under W. S. Rosecrans reached Chattanooga early in September, 1863, and found itself faced by a strong Confederate force under the second-rate Braxton Bragg. In a terrific battle at Chickamauga, Bragg almost won the day, but was finally held to a costly deadlock by General George

H. Thomas, a Virginian who had stood by the Union. The incompetent Rosecrans then allowed himself to be shut up in Chattanooga, and Grant had to be sent to the rescue. In November, ably supported by Sherman and Thomas, Grant fought and won the battle of Chattanooga, part of his force driving the Confederates from Missionary Ridge in an impetuous charge that could not be halted. The Union troops were thus placed in a position to begin that advance into Georgia which Sherman carried to so triumphant a conclusion. And though a Confederate army which remained under Hood in Tennessee fought a Union army to a sanguinary draw at Franklin, it was practically annihilated by Thomas at Nashville in December, 1864, in perhaps the most crushing single blow of the war.

It would have been far better for the South had it recognized its impending defeat and tried to make terms with the magnanimous Lincoln. But feeling had become too bitter to permit that. The Confederacy fought on until further resistance became almost impossible. It lost its last hope of French and British intervention in 1863. The Union government had great advantages on the diplomatic front, it used them skillfully, and after Gettysburg no European minister would bet on a losing cause. Moreover, in 1862 Lincoln had issued his Emancipation Proclamation, making the extirpation of slavery one of the main objects of the war; and this rallied the moral sense of the British masses to his side. The impoverished working people of Lancashire, deprived of cotton by the Union blockade, gave a memorable proof of their devotion to principle when they stood unshakably for the Union.

Early in 1864 Grant was brought east and made commander of all the Union armies. In battle after battle he relentlessly hammered at Lee, gradually wearing down the main Confederate force. Meanwhile General Sherman began in May, 1864 his campaign to subjugate Georgia. Occupying Atlanta early in September, he then moved onward to the sea, systematically destroying stores, railways, and other property on a sixty-mile front. Emerging at Savannah in December, he made that city a Christmas present to the nation. Then, turning northward, he captured Columbia and compelled the surrender of Charleston. And that autumn the dashing cavalry commander, Phil Sheridan, destroyed the agricultural resources of the Shenandoah Valley so completely that "a crow flying over it would have to carry his own rations." Finally, Lee had to abandon Richmond and on April 9, 1865, surrendered his army at Appomattox.

Internal Conflicts

Much might be said about the internal conflicts in both the North and South during these years of fearful exertion. On neither side did the government show high efficiency. The armies were filled by crude, blundering, inequitable systems. Conscription laws were passed, but were not fairly and democratically drawn; and in the North, where men were allowed to buy substitutes, they resulted in angry draft riots. Both sides were plagued by internal political squabbles. The Republican "radicals," led by Thaddeus Stevens of Pennsylvania, Ben Wade of Ohio, and Charles Sumner of Massachusetts, assailed Lincoln as too feeble in his conduct of the war, too slow to adopt emancipation as one of its objects, and too mild in his measures for reconstructing Louisiana and other conquered states. In the South such governors as Joseph E. Brown of Georgia and Zebulon Vance of North Carolina gravely impeded the Richmond authorities by their mulish insistence on state rights. On both sides, but particularly in the North, politics played an unhappy part in army appointments.

They pushed forward incompetents like Benjamin Butler and Ambrose Burnside, while brave and efficient leaders like Thomas were neglected. On both sides desertions became widespread and in the end gravely crippled the Confederate armies.

The North accused the South of terrible abuses at Libby Prison in Richmond, Andersonville in Georgia, and other prisons; but the Northern camps were bad enough. Favoritism, fraud, and corruption flourished in both sections. Washington became full of dishonest contractors, speculators, lobbyists, and other birds of prey, while some scheming Southerners made fortunes at the expense of their dying cause. The depreciation of paper money in the South carried prices to insane heights and ruined great numbers of hard-working people. In the North a pronounced inflation encouraged wild gambling and risky enterprises and helped to grow a crop of blatant millionaires. Altogether, the war had its very seamy side. But it also had its innumerable tales of heroism and devotion, of philanthropic effort and patriotic sacrifice.

Robert E. Lee; Abraham Lincoln

To the South war gave an immortal hero in Robert E. Lee, the knightliest of commanders. The brilliance of his leadership, the strenuosity of his service, the humanity he displayed throughout the conflict, and his magnanimity in accepting defeat and urging the Southern people to become loyal partners of their late enemies must always arouse admiration. His very faults were the defects of his virtues, for he was too courteous and considerate to make stubborn subordinates bend properly to his will. A better strategist than a tactician, he showed acuteness in divining the plans of his opponents, analytical keenness in using military intelligence, and sound judgment in estimating the power of

· THE CIVIL WAR ·

MAP SHOWING THE RECEDING LINES OF
CONFEDERATE POWER ··· BATTLEFIELDS,
AND UNION BLOCKADE OF THE SOUTH.

military units and positions. By virtue of his power of organization, his conscientious attention to details, his tender care for his men, his daring, and his fine presence, he inspired confidence and won the devotion of his troops. Like Washington, he had a self-control that he seldom lost, and then but briefly. This Christian gentleman was great in victory and defeat, in war and in peace. Surviving the conflict but five years, he devoted himself to the restoration of the South in economic, cultural, and political fields.

To the North the war gave a still greater hero in Abraham Lincoln. In its early months few perceived the true stature of this rough-looking Western lawyer, homely, awkward, and ill-schooled. His second Secretary of War, Edwin M. Stanton, for a time called him a gorilla—though he later declared that he was the greatest leader of men who ever lived; the hostile press spoke of him as an imbecile. Little by little the nation came to comprehend his deep sagacity, founded upon careful study and hard thinking; his intense love of truth, his inexhaustible patience, and his boundless generosity of spirit. If he seemed at moments to hesitate and vacillate, time always proved that he had known how to wait for the national advantage, how to combine strength with tact. Understanding the American people, he knew when to pause for public sentiment to crystallize and when to move forward boldly. He was the most honest of leaders and, though a skillful politician, never resorted to unfair measures. He constantly appealed to the intelligence, never the ignorance, of the electorate. He was so charitable in thought and deed that during all the agony of the conflict he never uttered a vindictive word against the Southern people. He was anxious above all to weld the country together as a union not of force, but of hearts; and even as the Union armies were winning their last victories, he proposed to pay the South handsomely for its slaves. His foreign policy showed dignity, integrity, and firmness. Though he had to use unprecedented powers, he believed fervently in democratic self-government and knew how to inspire the loyalty of his people, so that at the end he exercised the authority of a czar but commanded the complete faith of the masses. His eloquence grew with the need for it, and his Gettysburg Address, the Second Inaugural address, and some of his letters are among the finest treasures of English prose. His murder on April 14, 1865, less than a week after Appomattox, was a stunning stroke to the nation, a tragic misfortune to victor and vanquished. As James Russell Lowell wrote:

> Never before that startled April morning did such multitudes of men shed tears for the death of one they had never seen, as if with him a friendly presence had been taken from their lives, leaving them colder and darker. Never was funeral panegyric so eloquent as the silent look of sympathy which strangers exchanged when they met that day. Their common manhood had lost a kinsman.

The Heritage of the War

Under a new, untried, and unevenly equipped leader, Andrew Johnson, the nation had to face the trying problems of readjustment and reconstruction. They were not made easier by the widespread demand for vengeance which burst forth immediately after Lincoln's assassination. They were quickly complicated by selfish political and economic considerations—by the desire of the Republican party to exploit the situation in order to perpetuate its power, and by the wish of selfish business groups to use the situation to their own advantage. Manufacturers who wanted high tariffs, bondholders who wanted to be certain of interest payments in gold, railroad builders who wanted land grants, all rallied behind the Republican regime.

For the war left the country a mixed heritage of good and evil results. It had saved the Union and given it an "indestructible" character, but the Union that emerged from the fiery cauldron was not the Union of the Fathers. It had abolished slavery forever, but by violence, and without thought for the welfare of the freedmen or of the society in which they had to live and the economy which they had to share. It had struck down an aristocratic oligarchy in the South, but there was no other class ready to assume the responsibilities of government which that class had so largely monopolized, and the South was, for a generation, bereft of its natural leaders. Lincoln had pleaded for government of, by, and for the people, but no fair-minded observer could conclude that the war had advanced democracy in any direct or immediate sense.

The war left a hatred between North and South that lasted for decades—the hatred that Lincoln had hoped to sweep away. It made many people more intolerant, especially in political affairs. Republican demagogues in the North long waved the "bloody shirt" to catch votes; that is, they appealed to the prejudice against Southern Democrats. The opposing section, on the other hand, became a "solid South" under the Democratic banner. This intense partisanship was most unfortunate. Not until twenty years after the war ended did a Democrat enter the White House; not until nearly fifty years had elapsed did a man of Southern birth, Woodrow Wilson, become President. The war gave the North a body of veteran soldiers who held great voting power. They presently began to demand pensions from the government, and obsequious politicians ladled out the public money to them with disgusting carelessness. The conflict had an unhappy effect, too, on the social and moral fiber of the country. It brought into prominence a class of men who were eager for money and power, coarse in their tastes, and unscrupulous in their acts. The great mass of Americans, of course, remained hard working, conscientious, and patriotic. But a vulgar, brassy, greedy element was more conspicuous than ever before.

The Reconstruction of the South

Now that the South had been defeated, it had to be "reconstructed"; and this process occupied a dozen years, 1865–1877. Had Lincoln lived, he would have insisted that the Southern people be treated mildly and would probably have won a majority of Congress to his view. But Andrew Johnson, though right-minded on the subject, was rash, tactless, and ill-tempered. He quarreled with Congress over the scope of bills to aid the Negroes through a Freedmen's Bureau and to protect them by a Civil Rights Act—bills which unduly invaded the authority of the Southern States; and letting himself be outmaneuvered and discredited by the "die-hard" or radical leaders of that body, he totally lost control of the situation. Indeed, he almost lost his office. Congress enacted over his veto a law forbidding him to dismiss certain officeholders without its consent. He tried to test this law in the courts by dismissing his treacherous Secretary of War, Stanton. The radicals thereupon in February, 1868, impeached him for "high crimes and misdemeanors," tried him before the Senate, and came within one vote of ejecting him from the White House. Meanwhile, by winning the Congressional elections in 1866, the radicals had taken charge of reconstruction and compelled the South to submit to a program as humiliating as it was unwise.

The main features of this reconstruction program, harshly carried out by the vindictive Thaddeus Stevens of Pennsylvania, the fanatical Charles Sumner of Massachusetts, and other radical leaders, were three. First, the South was placed under military control, five districts being created under as many generals, well supported by troops. Second, the Southern whites were compelled to accept not only the Fourteenth Amendment, which made an elaborate attempt to assure the Negro of equal rights in everyday affairs, but the Fifteenth Amendment, which gave colored men (practically all illiterate and nearly all still densely ignorant) the ballot. Recent slaves, whose grandfathers had perhaps been African savages, who could not read a line of print, and who had spent their whole lives in the cotton field, were given a full voice in choosing public officers and making laws. Finally, a systematic use was made of these colored voters, of poor whites, and of fortune hunters or "carpet-baggers" who came in from the North, to set up new state governments in the South.

These Negro and carpetbagger governments were probably the worst that have ever been known in any English-speaking land. The blacks for a time controlled a number of state legislatures, elected men to Congress, and filled minor state offices; the carpetbaggers obtained most of the juicier plums. It is true that these reconstruction governments undertook some valuable work in building roads and bridges and passed good laws as to education and charities. But on the whole they were incompetent, wasteful, and corrupt. They squandered money in bucketfuls and laid taxes that the impoverished whites were utterly unable to bear. The South for a time was in despair.

But not for long. Little by little the self-respecting whites of the region gained the right of ruling themselves. In part they did this by violence and intimidation. They set up the Ku Klux Klan, which compelled many carpetbaggers

ULYSSES S. GRANT

to return to the North and frightened Negroes away from the voting places. In larger part they did it by the peaceful use of the old political machinery. Many blacks became tired of being the tools of crafty politicians from the North and quietly gave up voting; some even followed their former white leaders. State after state was reconquered by the Democratic party, until in 1876 only three—Louisiana, Florida, and South Carolina—remained in the hands of the "black-and-tan" Republicans. Even in these three the Negroes and carpetbaggers were then kept in power only by Federal garrisons. The election of 1876, one of the closest in American history and one of the most disorderly, made it plain that the South would know no peace until the troops were withdrawn. The next year, therefore, President Rutherford B. Hayes took them out. By this act the Republican leaders admitted the failure of their "radical" reconstruction policy. It had been adopted chiefly for two reasons: because the idealistic wing of the party wished to protect the Negro and because the materialistic wing hoped to hold the South for votes, offices, and power. Its result had been to retard and weaken the Negro and to commit the whole South to the Democratic party.

As we look back on the period of civil strife and turmoil between 1850 and 1877, it seems an almost unmixed tragedy. The country would have fared far more happily if, as Lincoln long hoped, the abolition of slavery could have taken place gradually and with due compensation to the slaveholders. That would have given time to educate the Negroes to their new place in society. It would have spared the nation the six hundred thousand vigorous young men who lost their lives in the conflict and the millions of children they would have brought into the world. It would have saved the South the stupendous ruin that cripples it to this day; it would have saved both sections the coarsening effects so clearly revealed in the "gilded age" of money-getting and vulgarity after the war.

Yet, even beyond the items already mentioned, the page shows credit entries. The storm unified the nation and knit it into one great whole as no slower process could have done. Socially and economically the South now became more closely akin to the North. The war did much to deepen and mature the national character; literature and education became in various ways more adult. And the conflict gave the country a set of memories, poignant and dramatic, to quicken its heart and lift its imagination. For centuries to come it would recall them with a thrill—the firing on Fort Sumter; the duel of the *Merrimac* and *Monitor;* the irresistible sweep of Stonewall Jackson through the Shenandoah, a trail of defeated Union armies behind him; the gunboats running the Mississippi below Vicksburg in a storm of shot and shell; the death grapple of Pickett's gray host with Hancock's blue line on Cemetery Ridge; the storming of the heights above Chattanooga by troops whom even Grant's order could not stop, a feat that surpassed Balaklava; the desperate valor of Hood's tattered veterans as they assaulted the Union ranks at Franklin, six thousand of them dead or wounded within two hours; the *Kearsarge* circling about the *Alabama* till she sank beneath the waves; Lee with his jeweled sword, Grant in his common private's dress, shaking hands at Appomattox; Lincoln walking through the fire-blackened streets of Richmond; the thousand-mile funeral given the remains of the martyred President; the grand review as the endless ranks of the Eastern and Western armies rolled up Pennsylvania Avenue in the closing scene of the war. It was an epic story, and it will be retold again and again.

Chapter Twelve

THE EMERGENCE OF MODERN AMERICA

The Impact of War

THE Civil War worked a revolution in American society and economy, North as well as South. Although the roots of modern America go deep into the prewar years, we can date its actual emergence from the war itself. That conflict gave an immense stimulus to industry, speeded up the exploitation of natural resources, the development of large-scale manufacturing, the rise of investment banking, the extension of foreign commerce, and brought to the fore a new generation of "captains of industry" and "masters of capital." It enormously accelerated the construction of the railway and telegraph network and ushered in the railroad age. It put a premium upon inventions and labor-saving devices and witnessed the large scale application of these to agriculture as well as to industry. It threw open vast new areas for farming and grazing, developed fresh markets for farm produce, and inaugurated both the agricultural revolution and the farm problem. It created conditions favorable to the growth of cities and offered work to the hundreds of thousands of immigrants who soon crowded into the New World. In the South, defeat largely destroyed the planter class, freed the Negro, revolutionized farm economy, brought a new middle class to the fore, and laid the foundations for that New South which was to emerge during the next generation. In the North it opened up new fields to investment and to speculation, created a host of war millionaires, and hastened the process of the concentration of control of resources, industry, and finance in the great urban centers, the subordination of the South and West to the Northeast, and the creation of new class divisions to take the place of the old.

In the generation after Appomattox the pattern of our present society and economy took shape. Growth—in area, numbers, wealth, power, social complexity, and economic maturity—was the one most arresting fact. The political divisions of the republic were drawn in their final form, a dozen new states were admitted to the Union, and an American empire was established. In a space of forty years population increased from thirty-one to seventy-six millions, fifteen million immigrants—an ever-increasing proportion of them from southern and eastern Europe—poured into the Promised Land, and great cities like New York, Chicago, Pittsburgh, Cleveland, and Detroit doubled and redoubled their size. In swift succession the Indians were harried out of their ancient haunts on the high plains and in the mountains and valleys beyond and herded into reservations, the mining and cattle kingdoms rose and fell, the West was peopled and farmed, and by the end of the century the frontier was no more. Vast new finds of iron ore, copper, and oil created scores of great industries, small business grew into big business, the corporation became the effective instrument of the new economy, the trust and the holding company its characteristic form of organization. Great banking houses, like that of the Morgans, moved quietly into a commanding position in the national economy. The railroad network was all but completed, mileage increasing from thirty to some two hundred thousand and giving the nation the greatest railroad system of any country in the world. Labor organizations, few and feeble before the war, increased in membership and established firmly their place in the economic order, and industrial conflicts, heretofore small and sporadic, became organized and threatening. The small republic became a world power, expanding into the Caribbean and the Pacific, while its industry, eager for markets, and its bankers, zealous for investments, developed new techniques of economic imperialism. No other generation in American history witnessed changes as swift or as revolutionary as those which transformed the rural republic of Lincoln and Lee into the urban industrial empire of McKinley and Roosevelt.

A new series of problems, complex and baffling, confronted an American people too inexperienced to understand their character, too busy to give them careful thought. The most urgent of these were the problems of the distribution of wealth, the control of vast and powerful aggregations of capital, the maintenance of political democracy under the impact of an undemocratic economy, large-scale unemployment and labor troubles, urban crowding and the assimilation of the foreign-born, the decline of farm income and the increase in farm tenancy, the conservation of natural resources rapidly being exhausted by reckless exploitation, the responsibilities of overseas rule and world politics, and the accommodation of political institutions, organized for the needs of a small rural republic, to the challenging demands of a great industrial nation.

The Transformation of the South

The impact of war and of defeat on the South was immediate and cataclysmic. Devastation without parallel in American history greeted the eyes of the veterans in gray as they trudged wearily home after Nashville and Appomattox. Large parts of Virginia and Tennessee had been ravaged by contending armies; Sherman had cut a fifty-mile swath through the heart of Georgia and South Carolina; Hunter and Sheridan had swept the rich valley of Virginia; vast areas of northern Alabama, Mississippi, and Arkansas lay in ruins. Proud cities like Richmond, Charleston, Columbia, and Atlanta had been gutted by fire or battered by bombardment. Bridges were down, roads neglected, hundreds of miles of railroad track torn up, rolling stock was destroyed, quays and docks were rotted. Normal economic life was almost paralyzed. Confederate money was worthless, and the only specie was that which had been hoarded or which the Union army brought into the conquered country. Banks had closed their doors, insurance companies were insolvent, industries and business ruined, and a large part of the cotton which had been stored in warehouses was put to the torch or confiscated by the military authorities.

Civil government had all but disappeared, and there was no effective authority to collect taxes, run the schools, maintain the roads, or enforce the laws against the marauders and guerrilla bands who harried the countryside. Churches had been burned and congregations dispersed; the endowments of colleges lost, their libraries and laboratories destroyed: the librarian of the University of Alabama managed to save just one book—the Koran—from the torch. Most public schools were closed, and education was at a standstill.

Even agriculture was in a desperate state—thousands of farms abandoned, fences down, ditches growing up in weeds, dams and levees broken, horses and cattle dead or stolen, plows rusting in the fields, the labor system utterly disorganized. The Carolina rice industry was permanently ruined, salt water inundating the fields; the sugar industry of Louisiana was destroyed. In 1870 Virginia had two million acres less in tobacco than in 1860; not again until

1879 did the South raise a cotton crop as large as that of the year of secession. During the winter of 1865 starvation was imminent throughout large sections of the South, and whites as well as blacks were supported by the Federal army or by the newly organized Freedmen's Bureau. As the Southern poet, Sidney Lanier, wrote, "Pretty much the whole of life has been merely not dying."

Reconstruction brought new woes and new burdens almost as heavy as those of war. The Confederate debt had been swept away and with it, of course, the investment which patriotic Southerners had made in their cause, but the South was expected to bear its share of the national debt as well as of the current expenses of the national government: in addition it was assessed a heavy excise tax on cotton. This was perhaps neither unjust nor exorbitant, but as much cannot be said for the debts and taxes of state and local governments. During the carpetbag regime, foisted upon the South by the radicals in Congress, millions of dollars were wasted in extravagances—like perfume and whisky and gold-plated cuspidors for legislators—millions were stolen outright, and additional millions insouciantly poured into dubious railroad and business ventures which rarely repaid ten cents on the dollar. Wealth had declined, in some sections, by more than one half, but taxes and debts mounted inexorably. Carpetbag and radical regimes increased the public debt of South Carolina from five to twenty-nine millions, that of Arkansas from three to fifteen, that of Louisiana from eleven to almost fifty. Taxes soared dizzily—eightfold in Louisiana, fourteenfold in Mississippi —until in sheer desperation hundreds of farmers abandoned their farms to the tax collector.

Yet with amazing vigor the defeated South turned to the task of physical reconstruction and to the rehabilitation of its agricultural economy and the restoration of the institutions of civilized society. "As ruin was never before so overwhelming," the Georgia editor, Henry Grady, later recalled, "never was restoration swifter." Richmond, Charleston, and Columbia rose from their ruins, and six months after the end of the war a visitor to Atlanta reported that:

> a new city is springing up with marvelous rapidity. The narrow and irregular streets are alive from morning to night with drays and carts and hand barrows and wagons, with hauling teams and shouting men, with loads of lumber and loads of brick and loads of sand, with piles of furniture and hundreds of packed boxes, with mortar makers and hod carriers, with carpenters and masons, with rubbish removers and housebuilders, with a never-ending throng of pushing and crowding and scrambling and eager and excited and enterprising men, all bent on building and trading and fortune-making.

Railroad tracks were relaid and new roads pushed into the Southwest, bridges rebuilt, dams and levees restored; ships once more put into the harbors of Norfolk and Charleston and Mobile; country merchants, small-scale traders, and, in time, banks and insurance companies opened their doors.

Somehow old factories were reopened, and capital was attracted to new industries—often at ruinous rates. Vast stands of white and yellow pine furnished the basis for a flourishing lumber industry. Union soldiers who had passed through Durham, North Carolina, and helped themselves to some of the tobacco made by Washington Duke wrote back for more, and the basis of the great North Carolina tobacco industry was established; by 1888 Durham had the largest tobacco factory in the world and was shipping ten million pounds of tobacco every year. Flour and grist mills sprang up to provide for local needs; the fertilizer industry, so essential to cotton growing, was re-established. Rich coal and iron deposits were uncovered in Tennessee and northern Alabama. Birmingham, which was a cotton field in 1870, became within two decades a city of fifty thousand, the center of a booming iron industry, served by six trunk-line railroads. By 1890 the South was producing one fifth of the pig iron of the entire nation. Other towns like Chattanooga, Durham, Winston-Salem, and Danville grew into thriving manufacturing cities.

A textile industry had flourished in the seaboard South ever since William Gregg had opened his cotton mills at Graniteville, South Carolina, in 1846. Like most other industries, however, it had been completely disorganized by the war. In the decade of the seventies it began once more to forge ahead, taking full advantage of the combination of cheap labor, proximity to water power, and easy access to raw materials. Scores of little factories, financed almost entirely by local capital, sprang up along the upcountry of the Carolinas and Georgia. By 1890 South Carolina had half a million spindles, and the whole South could boast almost four times that number; New England industrialists were already worried about competition from that section. And by 1890, too, the South had the beginnings of a labor problem which was to grow in seriousness with the passing years.

The Southern textile industry remained local and took on—largely from necessity—a curiously feudal character. Attracted by what seemed to be high wages and steady work, whole families moved in from the run-down farms to the near-by mill villages, bringing with them their labor habits and attitudes developed in farming. They took long hours for granted and they took for granted, too, that the whole family—women and children as well as men—would share the work. These mill villages, straggling on the edge of some town, were owned and controlled by the operators who had built the mills. Workers lived in company houses, went to company churches and schools, bought their food and clothing from company stores, were brought into the world by company doctors and buried by company preachers in a company cemetery. It was a new feudalism, and though it worked well enough in its early years, it was fraught with trouble for the future.

Yet notwithstanding the rise of the iron, lumber, tobacco, and textile industries, the South remained predominantly rural and agricultural; prior to 1900 it could not boast a single city, except New Orleans, with a population of one hundred thousand. Even its industries were closely connected with agriculture: tobacco and textile production were large, but the value actually added by manufacture was comparatively small. The vast majority of Southerners stayed on their farms, growing staple crops. But agriculture, too, had suffered disorganization during the war—a disorganization sharply accentuated by the destruction of slavery and of the labor system built upon it. It, too, had to go through a period of readjustment.

The great planters had been most impoverished by the war and reconstruction. With their capital in slaves swept away, their labor force disintegrated, taxes and overhead costs mounting, the majority of them were forced to break up their plantations or to let them go under the hammer to pay taxes and debts. The result was the most sweeping revolution in landholding in our history. With good land selling for three or four dollars an acre, thousands of small farmers enlarged their holdings, tens of thousands of poor whites, freedmen, landless mechanics, and shopkeepers were able to satisfy their earth hunger and become landowners. In 1860 there were some 33,000 farms in South Carolina; twenty years later the number had soared to 94,000. In

1860 there were fewer than 600 farms in Mississippi under ten acres in size; within a decade the number had increased to more than 11,000. Throughout the South, plantations of one thousand acres or more declined by over one half, and the average size of farms dropped from 335 to 153 acres in the space of twenty years. At the same time, new rich lands were being taken up in Arkansas and Texas, and soon Oklahoma was thrown open to settlement. King Cotton, who had, for a time, been toppled from his throne, re-established and expanded his empire.

With slavery gone it was imperative to work out a substitute labor system. Planters had no money with which to pay wages; Negroes no money with which to rent farms. Out of necessity, a third method emerged: countless autobiographies and memoirs tell us of its origin. When the war was over, planters called their former slaves about them, told them that they were now free, and asked them to stay on the old place and work. Wages were out of the question, but when the crop was in, the planter would divide up with his workers. This was the origin of the share-crop system. It became, in time, organized and regularized. Farmers furnished their tenants with a cabin, land, tools, fertilizer, and a mule and promised to keep them going until the crop was harvested. The share-cropper gave his labor and received, in return, one third of the crop. The system seemed to work well and was so convenient that it was soon extended to white tenants as well as to black.

Actually this share-crop system was an almost unmitigated evil. Small farmers, wholly dependent upon staple crops, usually fell into debt and became a species of chattel, mortgaged to the planters or merchants who carried them. Because they had no property to pledge as security for the supplies they received, they pledged their growing crop, and thus was evolved the demoralizing "crop-lien" system.

This system deprived the average tenant farmer of any genuine interest in his crop, encouraged slovenly and unscientific agriculture, played into the hands of planters or merchant creditors, and embittered the tenants. Because cotton was one crop that seemed a safe investment, creditors insisted that their tenants plant that to the exclusion of everything else, and thus prevented diversification and condemned the deep South to a ruinous one-crop economy. Within a generation the prospect of a wide distribution of land and the rise of a sturdy yeomanry had faded out; in some parts of the South seventy or eighty per cent of the farmers were tenants, and there was an average of one lien for every farm. The South of 1900 was less self-sufficient than the South of 1860, and in many sections farm wealth had actually declined over the years. Soon *Tobacco Road* was to take the place of *Uncle Tom's Cabin* as a representation of Southern life.

The Negroes, too, found that their status had changed legally rather than actually. Congress, which decreed their freedom, did nothing to provide them economic security, but wasted its efforts rather on the futile task of guaranteeing them political equality. For a year or two, the blacks were like refugees in a war-stricken land. Thousands of them took to the roads, wandering aimlessly from county to county: it is safe to say that more families were broken up by the first year of freedom than by any year of slavery. Thousands of them died of disease and starvation or were the victims of violence. Eventually, through the efforts of more responsible Southerners and with the co-operation of the Federal authorities, order was restored; when the Negroes found that they were not to get the "forty acres and a mule" which they fondly thought had been promised them, they returned to the one thing they knew—farming.

Some of the more enterprising made their way to the North or to the rising industrial towns of the South, but the vast majority of them became share-croppers, and as such they found that life went on for them much as it had before the war. They plowed the soil and cut cotton on white men's farms; they lived in the same ramshackle cabins, ate the same corn meal and collards and salt pork, wore the same tattered shirts and faded blue jeans, that they had always known. They did not try to vote or to send their children to the white folks' schools or to get "beyond themselves" socially.

The most encouraging development in the South of this postwar generation was the emergence of a sturdy middle class of independent small farmers, shopkeepers, businessmen, merchants, bankers, industrialists, and professional men. These were freed, now, from the incubus of slavery, and they freed themselves, in time, from the psychological incubus of "the lost cause." They were willing to forget the South of moonlight and gardenias and to recall Gettysburg and the Wilderness with pride rather than with bitterness. They set themselves energetically to integrate Southern with national economy and to rebuild their shattered social institutions. Colleges were reopened, Robert E. Lee setting an example to the whole South by taking the presidency of struggling little Washington College in Virginia. States democratized their educational systems, providing, on paper at least, for universal free public education in the elementary grades. Churches were re-established, and with the growth of Negro congregations soon boasted a larger membership than before the war. There were notable advances in social legislation, in provision for the poor and the infirm, and feeble gestures toward labor legislation. Economically, culturally, and politically the South knit itself once more into the national fabric.

The Revolution in the North

While the South was painfully rebuilding its economy and adjusting itself to new industrial and agricultural institutions, the North forged energetically ahead. Northern industry and finance, more fully than any other groups, harvested the fruits of victory. From its beginning the Republican party had been committed to high tariffs, internal improvements, railroad land grants, and free farms. Prior to Fort Sumter it was unable to translate any substantial part of this program into law. But after the secession of the Southern States there was no longer any effective opposition in the halls of Congress, and war furnished the occasion for a speedy enactment of the whole program. The Morrill tariff of 1861 sharply reversed the long downward trend of duties and established rates frankly protective; subsequent acts raised tariff walls still higher, and by the end of the war the average duties had been increased from eighteen to forty-seven per cent. Northern manufacturers were established in a position well-nigh impregnable; not until 1913 was an administration able to effect any substantial reduction in tariff rates. Further to encourage the business interests Congress shortly repealed the income tax and removed wartime taxes on coal, iron, and corporations. Under a series of railroad laws Congress subsidized the construction of transcontinental roads with loans of over sixty million dollars and outright gifts of over one hundred million acres of public lands—grants lavishly supplemented by state and local committees.

Favored by these auspices and stimulated by the insatiable needs of war and the equally insatiable needs of an expanding population, business and industry flourished as never before. "The truth is," wrote John Sherman to his brother, the General, "that the close of the war with our resources

unimpaired gives an elevation, a scope, to the ideas of leading capitalists far higher than anything ever undertaken in
this country before. They talk of millions as confidently as
formerly of thousands." Certainly there was scope if not
elevation to their ideas. Industry responded enthusiastically
to the myriad needs of the armed forces and to the even
greater demands of a war economy. Twenty thousand miles
of track were laid in a decade, most of it in the West, and
transcontinentals were pushed across the plains and the
mountains with dizzy speed. Telegraph lines were strung
from city to city and soon crossed the continent; cables
were laid across the Atlantic, and within a decade the telephone added a new means of lightning-quick communication. The McCormick harvester works at Chicago could
not keep up with the greedy demand for harvesting machines coming from the prairie lands of the Middle West;
factories at Akron and Canton, Ohio, turned out tens of
thousands of mowers; by the mid-seventies factories along
the Middle Border were sending out barbed-wire fencing
to the farms of the high plains. The McKay boot and shoe
industry, the great packing plants at Chicago and Cincinnati, the flour mills of the Twin Cities, the breweries of
Milwaukee and St. Louis, the iron and steel mills of the
Pittsburgh region, the oil refineries of Ohio and Pennsylvania, and a hundred others worked day and night to
meet the orders that poured in on them. The end of the
war saw no let-up in industrial activity. In the five years
after Appomattox almost every industrial record was shattered. More coal and iron ore, silver and copper, was
mined, more steel forged, more rails were laid, more lumber was sawed and more houses were built, more cotton
cloth was woven, more flour milled, more oil refined, than
in any previous five years in our history. In the decade from
1860 to 1870, the total number of manufacturing establish-

ments increased by eighty per cent and the value of manufactured products by one hundred per cent. The industrial revolution was an accomplished fact.

Bankers and investors profited along with the industrialists. By the National Banking Acts of 1863 and 1864 Congress swept away the independent banking system dear to Jacksonian democrats and substituted one more favorable to private bankers. To give a clear field to the notes of the national banks, state-bank notes were taxed out of existence. During the war the government had issued several hundred million dollars in paper money, and, secured only by the credit of the government, this rapidly depreciated in value. By its decision to halt further issues of these "greenbacks," call in a good part of them, and bring the value of the rest up to par, Congress endorsed a policy of deflation highly advantageous to the creditor and investor interests but fraught with hardship to the farming and laboring classes.

Speculation in greenbacks and in government bonds created many respectable fortunes. During the darkest period of the war, greenbacks had sold for as little as forty cents on the dollar, but they were still legal tender for the purchase of government bonds. When Congress pledged itself to the payment of both principal and interest on these bonds in gold, it was clear that those canny enough to have invested would realize a tidy profit—President Johnson estimated it at three to four hundred per cent! The fiscal policy of the government did more than anything else to accentuate class lines, for it meant that while soldiers were paid in greenbacks worth fifty or sixty cents, bondholders would be paid in dollars worth one hundred cents; while farmers borrowed dollars worth fifty or sixty cents, they would be called upon to pay back dollars worth one hundred cents. It meant that the whole nation could be called upon to pay a national debt which had appreciated to almost double its original cost.

But it was in railroads, mining, lumber, meat packing, iron and steel, oil, and similar investments closely tied up with the war or the opening up of the West that the greatest fortunes were made. Soon the names of railroad builders like Vanderbilt, Stanford, and Villard, of packers like Armour and Swift, of lumber kings like Weyerhaeusers, of iron masters like Andrew Carnegie and Abram Hewitt, of oil princes like John D. Rockefeller, were household words, supplanting the names of statesmen or of men of letters in popular esteem. The war redistributed national wealth with a lavish and careless hand, creating thousands of respectable and hundreds of disreputable fortunes. Money moved in and took over the governments, state and Federal; money greased the ways into social favor, and soon the Vanderbilts and Goulds were as acceptable as the old Knickerbocker families; money built the fine mansions that lined Fifth Avenue, New York, and Michigan Avenue, Chicago, financed colleges and universities, supported churches and missions, patronized orchestras and art museums. The concentration of wealth was apparent along geographical as well as along class lines: the three states of New York, Pennsylvania, and Massachusetts paid sixty per cent of the income tax of 1864.

The farmers, too, got something from the war and the postwar boom, though less than they thought. The Republican party had rallied support with the cry "vote yourself a farm" and, promptly after it took over the government, it re-enacted the Homestead Law that a Democratic President had earlier vetoed. By the terms of this act anyone might have 160 acres of public land by agreeing to cultivate it for five years. This enlightened legislation did enable several hundred thousand farmers to locate on the virgin soil of the West, and it thereby advanced economic democracy. Yet at the same time, larger areas were given to the railroads and other corporations or sold to land companies and speculators. Most of this, in turn, went eventually to farmers—but at a price. Another Congressional act, passed at the same time, granted several million acres of the public domain for the endowment and maintenance of agricultural and industrial colleges.

But agricultural expansion during and after the war was not dependent upon governmental subsidies or encouragement. The needs of the army, of the growing population of the cities, and of hungry millions abroad, all provided a stimulus to the growers of wheat and corn and to the dairy and cattlemen. Railways, pushing rapidly across the plains, gave access to unspoiled land, and the harvesters and plows and mowers and twine binders just then brought onto the market made it possible for one man—or boy—to do the work formerly performed by two. In the two decades after the election of Lincoln the production of corn, wheat, oats, and barley more than doubled, and so, too, did the number of cattle, sheep, and swine. As agriculture actually declined in New England and the South, most of this advance was in the Old Northwest and the trans-Mississippi West. During the war decade Missouri increased her population by over fifty per cent and emerged with almost two million people—the fifth state in the Union. Nebraska, admitted to statehood in 1867, counted almost half a million inhabitants by 1880. The Dakotas, where the Sioux ranged undisputed during the war, had a farming population of more than half a million fifteen years later. Wool production had moved from Vermont to Ohio, and soon the Mountain States of the West would take the lead; Iowa, Kansas, Nebraska, Minnesota, began to figure in the census as leading wheat and corn producers. The agricultural domain was moving irresistibly westward.

Yet, as if in anticipation of the future course of our economy, the farmers profited less by the boom years than did any other class except the workers, and they were the first to feel the impact of hard times. Overexpansion led to overproduction; the purchase of larger farms and of expensive agricultural implements with which to farm them meant a load of debt which could be carried only while high prices obtained. The farmers of the older-settled East felt keenly the competition from the new soil of the West; the farmers of the West, favored by rich soil, were far from markets and at the mercy of the railroads. As in ages past, the farmers toiled long hours under the hot sun, lived without the comforts of community life, and in the end had little to show for their labors.

Workingmen, alone of the major groups, failed to reap any material rewards from the war. Toiling ten or twelve hours a day in the coal pits and at the steel furnaces, working the looms and the shoe machines, building ships and laying tracks, they had contributed greatly to Union victory, and from their ranks, too, had come a large proportion of the men who did the actual fighting. Under the impact of war and of soaring prices some of the labor organizations shattered by the panic of 1857 were pieced together again. Labor had need of organization. Wages had gone up, to be sure, but prices had gone higher, and conservative estimates suggested that the majority of workingmen were worse off in 1865 than they had been in 1860. With the return to civilian life of over a million soldiers and the sharp upswing in immigration, competition for jobs became keen, and skilled craftsmen hastened to organize to protect their skills. The short-lived Knights of St. Crispin, a shoemakers' guild, was one such organization, and its early demise proved the futility of fighting against machinery and the factory system. More interesting were two larger and more amorphous combinations—the National Labor Union and the Knights of Labor, both dating from the sixties, both representing efforts to unite the most varied labor, farmer, and reform groups. Yet the vast majority of workingmen remained outside these organizations and suffered all the vicissitudes of a rapidly changing economic structure and, shortly, of panic and depression. The government, so zealous to legislate for business groups, did little for laboring men. In 1868, to be sure, it established an eight-hour day on public works, but this admirable example was not widely followed. And against this gesture may be set the act of 1864 legalizing the importation of contract labor. The act was shortly repealed, but the practice continued unabated for twenty years.

Politics

The most significant thing about the politics of the post-war years was their insignificance. Other administrations—those of Pierce and Buchanan, for example—had been dull and incompetent; it was reserved for the Grant administration to be incompetent and corrupt. Statesmanship, never more sorely needed than in the crisis of national reconstruction, gave way to politics, and politics were shot through and through with partisanship, privilege, and corruption.

The basic principle of reconstruction politics was the establishment in power of the Republican party. That party, it is well to remember, was relatively new and almost wholly sectional. During the war it had things all its own way and entrenched itself firmly in power. But with the end of the war and the return of some—and eventually of all—Southern States to the Union, the prospect of continued Republican control of all branches of the government was dimmed. For throughout this period the Democratic party remained numerous and strong, even in the North, while the war and especially reconstruction made the South solid for the Democracy. If Northern and Southern Democrats could be brought to agree on candidates and policies, there was every likelihood that they would sweep the Republicans out of office and recapture control of the government.

What was at stake was not only party supremacy, but also the maintenance of those policies to which the party was committed and which it had already so boldly advanced. What was at stake was the new tariff wall, the national banking system, the program of railroad subsidies, and—perhaps most important of all—the policy of currency deflation and of gold payment on government obligations. These economic questions were, of course, hopelessly tangled up with social ones—like the position of the Negro —and emotional ones—like rewarding those who had been loyal and punishing those who had been disloyal.

The grand strategy and the tactics which the Republicans had to adopt, then, were clear enough. To preserve and advance the economic policies already so auspiciously inaugurated required that the party be kept in office until those policies were so thoroughly established that they could not be reversed. Tentative steps had already been taken in the denial of suffrage and officeholding to large numbers of Confederate leaders and the exclusion from the halls of Congress of representatives from the more recalcitrant Southern States. But obviously this could not go on indefinitely. A far more promising, and more permanent, policy seemed to be to build up a Republican party in the South. The basis of such an organization would have to be those elements among the whites who had long opposed the ruling classes in the South—the poor and underprivileged who might welcome an opportunity to make their voices heard. But these were not sufficiently numerous to insure success. Numerical strength could be assured only by conferring the suffrage upon the Negro—and seeing to it that he voted right. This was arranged for, first by the reconstruction acts and then by constitutional amendments.

The program was neat enough, but it failed to work. Military reconstruction stiffened Southern opposition; even more important was the attempt to exploit the Negro politically. For Republicanism thereby became identified with the notion of racial equality—a notion intolerable to most Southerners at this time. So these shortsighted and ill-advised policies, instead of strengthening the Republican party in the South, weakened it. As soon as Federal military authority was withdrawn, the Republican organizations collapsed and Southern Democrats quickly found ways to withhold the vote from the Negro. Thereafter the Southern Democracy had things all its own way. From 1880 to 1928 no state of the Confederacy cast its electoral vote for a Republican presidential candidate.

Yet if the economic program of the Republican party was not to be permanently insured by military reconstruction or by the constitutional requirement of Negro suffrage, it was protected by another provision newly written into the Constitution. During the early stages of reconstruction, while the radicals were still quarreling with President Johnson, a joint committee of Congress had formulated an omnibus amendment designed to define citizenship, protect the civil rights of freedmen, disfranchise Confederate leaders, guarantee the Federal and invalidate the Confederate debt. This was the famous Fourteenth Amendment, the first article of which provided that

No State shall make or enforce any law which shall abridge the privileges or immunities of citizens of the

United States; nor shall any State deprive any person of life, liberty, or property, without due process of law; nor deny to any person within its jurisdiction the equal protection of the laws.

These memorable phrases did in time what Republican policies had failed to do: they threw constitutional sanctions around the property and the practices of great business corporations. For the courts, in due time, interpreted them to mean that no state might so legislate as to deprive corporations of property or of fair returns on that property. This interpretation, to be sure, was not fully developed until the decade of the nineties—just in time to meet and stem the rising tide of Populism.

The Grant administration concerned itself chiefly with the maintenance of reconstruction policies that would keep the South subordinate to the North and Democrats subordinate to Republicans. In this it was largely successful. It had behind it the immense prestige of victory and of Grant himself, and its tenure of power was prolonged by the persistent distrust of any party that was connected with slavery and secession, and strengthened by the cheerful support of the business interests which it had served. Yet these advantages were, in time, forfeited. Grant was a great soldier, but a sorry chief executive, and except in the realm of foreign affairs his administration presents a record of egregious failure. Young Henry Adams, viewing the course of American history from Washington to Grant, said that Grant made evolution ridiculous. But it was not his incompetence that disappointed friends and admirers, but his willing acquiescence in the exploitation of his office and his friendship for corrupt purposes.

Shortly after his accession to power, stories of corruption in high places became rife, and they were not without foundation. The Union Pacific, the nation's pride, had been financed by a group of crooked promoters who hired Congressmen to do their bidding; the Navy Department openly sold business to contractors; the Department of the Interior was a happy hunting ground for land thieves; the Indian Bureau sold post traderships to the highest bidders and neglected the welfare of its wards; the Treasury Department farmed out uncollected taxes to tax gatherers who made a good thing of it; the customhouses of New York and New Orleans were permeated with graft; a "whisky ring" in St. Louis defrauded the government of millions in excise taxes, and a gang of boodlers in the national capital vied with the carpetbag regimes of the South in extravagance and waste. "It looks," wrote one Republican Senator, "as if the Republican party were going to the dogs. . . . I believe it is today the most corrupt and debauched political party that ever existed."

This corruption, permeating the entire administration, seeping down into state and local politics, forfeited in time the confidence—though not the affection—of the people of the North. Grant had come to office with greater repute than any President since Jackson, and the Republican party with the greatest opportunity for constructive work of any party since 1789. Within four years the party was split, and a Liberal Republican organization, dedicated to reform and reconciliation, in the field. Even though the Democrats joined the Liberal Republicans, they were not strong enough to unseat Grant, but two years later the Democracy captured control of the lower House, and in 1876 its candidate polled a quarter million more votes than the Republican candidate for the presidency. The politics of acquisition was by no means ended, but not again for half a century was the nation to be shamed by corruption in the executive office and in the Congress.

Chapter Thirteen

THE RISE OF BIG BUSINESS

The Foundations of the Industrial Empire

JEFFERSON had dreamed of a great rural republic, filled
with an independent yeomanry, of a nation as free from
the degradation of great cities and the slavery of factories
or coal pits that he had seen in England as from the serf-
dom that had horrified him in France and Italy. "While
we have land to labor," he wrote, "let us never wish to
see our citizens occupied at the work bench, or twirling a
distaff." He had founded, so he believed, an agrarian
democracy and provided, through the Louisiana Purchase,
for its expansion. Here was land enough, he said, "for
the thousandth and thousandth generation." He had defeated Hamilton at the polls and confounded, so he thought,
the Hamiltonian plan to create a United States in the
image of contemporary England. The nation was to turn
westward, across the mountains and the prairies and the
plains, not eastward across the ocean; it was to be a farmers'
paradise, not a merchants', bankers', or industrialists' preserve. And as Jefferson's successors moved into the White
House and his followers took over the Congress, his dream
seemed well on the way to fulfillment. As the nation's
boundaries were pushed westward to the Pacific and southward to the Rio Grande, the agricultural domain expanded
far more rapidly than the industrial machine. Even in 1860
the nation was still overwhelmingly rural, and many ob-

servers viewed the Civil War not as a contest between a rising industrialism and an expanding agriculture but as a struggle between King Cotton and King Wheat.

Yet in the end it was Hamilton who won, at least on the economic front. It was his opinion on the bank that was accepted, his brand of mercantilism that was adopted, his *Report on Manufactures* that became the American gospel. A century after Hamilton fell on the dueling field of Weehawken, the United States was the greatest industrial nation in the world. It had uncovered more coal and iron ore, forged more steel, drilled and refined more oil, laid more tracks, built more factories, than any other nation on earth. A century after the Sage of Monticello went to his well-earned rest, the value of manufactured products was five times that of farm products, financial titans and industrial barons dictated policies in Washington, and the farmer seemed in danger of becoming a peasant.

This swift transformation of American economy was entirely natural, though it was assisted by governmental policies. The bases of American industrial development were six: raw materials vaster and more varied than vouchsafed to any other people except possibly the Russians; inventions and techniques for converting the raw materials into manufactured products; a transportation system of water and rail fully adequate to the demands of an expanding economy; a domestic market rapidly expanding with the increase in population and the growth of foreign markets; a labor supply constantly renewed through immigration; the absence of vexatious tariff barriers between states or sections, protection against foreign competition, and the maintenance of direct and indirect governmental subsidies. To these fundamental factors should perhaps be added the spirit of enterprise and the atmosphere of optimism which from its beginnings distinguished the nation.

The industrial revolution was based on coal, oil, iron, and eventually electricity. In the mountains of Pennsylvania and West Virginia, under the prairie grasses of Illinois, along the slopes of the Great Smokies, under millions of acres of Kansas, Colorado, and Texas, were inexhaustible quantities of anthracite and bituminous coal; New Mexico alone boasted enough to keep American factories going for a century. By 1910 the nation was mining five hundred million tons a year, but less than one per cent of its available reserves had been tapped. In the second great basic source of energy, oil, the United States was almost equally rich. In no year since 1900 has American production been less than the total production of the rest of the world, and the opening of fields in Texas, Oklahoma, Kansas, Illinois, and California has dispelled any fear of the early exhaustion of this essential resource. Iron ore, too, was abundant—all around the rim of Lake Superior, in the South where rose the Tennessee Coal and Iron, in the West where the Colorado Fuel and Iron grew powerful. Careful estimates after exploitation had been under way for half a century indicated that reserves would last at least two centuries more. And nature had given the United States greater potential water power than any other nation, a power fully adequate to the industrial needs of a population of more than three hundred millions.

A striking fact in the history of natural resources in the United States is that many of them were made available, on a large scale, only after 1850. Iron ore had been mined since the early colonial period, but it was the opening up of the northern Michigan and Lake Superior fields that gave the United States supremacy in iron and steel.

Colonel Drake struck oil in western Pennsylvania in 1859. Within five years annual production had increased to more than two million barrels, thousands of drills and hundreds of millions of dollars had been sunk, and the rush to the "oil regions" rivaled the gold rush to California a decade earlier. Copper had been mined in Michigan since the opening of that country, but it was not until the eighties that the rich veins of Montana and Arizona were exploited; soon after the Anaconda Mine was opened in 1882, the whole of Montana was a battlefield in the "war of the copper kings," contending not only for industrial monopoly, but for political control as well. The opening up of rich silver deposits in Colorado in 1859, in Nevada and Montana in the sixties, profoundly affected the economic structure and financial policy of the country. The lead mines of Missouri and of the Galena region of Illinois had been famous before the Civil War; but it was not until the seventies that the great increase in lead production made possible its widespread use for piping and printing. Portland cement came on the market in the 1870's; the electrolytic process made aluminum commercially available in 1887, and by 1900 production exceeded seven million pounds. When Henry Adams visited the World's Columbian Exposition in 1893, he saw the dynamo and concluded that its discovery was the most important event in modern history; by the turn of the century American engineers were harnessing it to great dams and preparing to substitute electricity for steam.

Americans probably patented more numerous and more ingenious inventions than any other people. Between 1860 and 1900 no fewer than 676,000 patents were granted by the United States Patent Office; since that time the number has reached almost astronomical figures. Important inventions dated back to the end of the eighteenth or the early years of the nineteenth century—Eli Whitney's cotton gin, Robert Fulton's steamboat, Elias Howe's sewing machine, Charles Goodrich's vulcanized rubber, the harvester invented almost simultaneously by Cyrus McCormick and Obed Hussey. But the large-scale production of new appliances awaited the development of the steel industry and the application of electricity to industry.

A brief enumeration of the most spectacular of the new inventions suggests their role in the making of modern America. Before the Mexican War, Samuel F. B. Morse, an American Leonardo who had turned from painting to science, had worked out the principles of electrical telegraphy and persuaded Congress to subsidize the stringing of wires from Washington to Baltimore; in 1856 the Western Union Company was organized to exploit the invention, and soon it and other companies were netting the continent with their poles and wires. Efforts to lay an Atlantic cable began in the middle fifties, but not until 1866 did the *Great Eastern* uncoil a permanently successful cable from Newfoundland to Ireland: the Associated Press promptly transmitted the entire speech of William of Prussia to his Parliament at a cost of almost six thousand dollars, so that Americans could appreciate the advantages of applied science! In 1876 a Scottish immigrant, Alexander Graham Bell, exhibited a telephone instrument, and within a few years a phone box was in every business office, and the streets of the great cities were all but darkened with overhead wires. A quarter of a century later, the American Telephone and Telegraph Company was incorporated with a capitalization of a quarter of a billion dollars.

Improvements in transportation kept pace with the expansion of the nation. The use of automatic block signals, the air brake, the car coupler, and, after 1900, of steel cars made railroad travel less perilous; the introduction of the

Pullman sleeping car made it more comfortable. Throughout the early eighties Americans were experimenting with electrical railways, and before the end of the decade perhaps a score of cities—among them Baltimore, Boston, and Richmond—had streetcars operated from overhead trolleys. The invention of the gasoline motorcar came in the nineties. Henry Ford, whose engineering skill and business acumen did so much to make it a universal necessity, recalled that at first

It was considered to be something of a nuisance, for it made a racket and scared horses. Also it blocked traffic. For if I stopped my machine anywhere in town a crowd was around it before I could start up again. If I left it alone, even for a minute, some inquisitive person was always trying to run it. Finally I had to carry a chain, and chain it to a lamp post whenever I left it anywhere.

This same decade witnessed S. P. Langley's bold experiments with the "flying machine" which, within the lifetime of those who derided it, was to alter the destinies of nations.

Invention quickened the tempo of business, introduced large numbers of women and "white-collar workers" into offices, and enlarged the importance of communication. The telephone speedily became an essential adjunct to every office and store. The typewriter, joint product of two Milwaukee inventors, Sholes and Glidden, was placed on the market in 1873, and the next year Mark Twain was hammering out a letter: "One may lean back in his chair and work it. It piles up an awful stack of words on one page. It don't muss things or scatter ink blots around." In time the machine became ubiquitous, and every business office had its quota of young lady typists. Adding machines and cash registers insured accuracy in accounting; address-ographs made it possible to bombard the public with un-solicited advertising and propaganda; the card catalogue helped make American libraries the best and most convenient in the world. The linotype composing machine, the Hoe rotary press, and the electrotype process worked a revolution in the printing of newspapers and books.

Electricity, so important to industry, transportation, and communication, intimately affected the social life of the nation. In 1878 a young Ohio engineer, Charles Brush, patented an arc lamp which was promptly adopted by a few enterprising cities for street lighting. More practical was the incandescent lamp which Thomas A. Edison had ready in time to illuminate his home when Garfield was elected President. The commercial possibilities of electric lighting were enormous. In 1882 Edison constructed a generating and distributing station in New York, and within a few years astute businessmen were obtaining exclusive franchises to furnish electricity to cities—and the power fight was in the making. In the nineties Edison experimented with a motion-picture machine; a decade later the commercial history of the movies began, and this powerful agency was launched upon a career of conquest which was to carry American speech, manners, and mores to the uttermost corners of the globe. Radio broadcasting, equally important in its social implications, came into effective use just after the First World War; two decades later every home had its radio set. The telephone, the electric lamp, the movies, the radio added immeasurably to the pleasure and scope of life and for better or worse did much to break down isolation and standardize social habits. Because their practical utilization required large investments of capital and large-scale organizations, they did much to accelerate the growth of big business.

Forty years after the completion of the first transcontinental line, the railroad network was substantially complete and was carrying a billion tons of freight every year; the merchant marine had recovered from the long depression sufficiently to make the American flag familiar once more on the seven seas; fifty million tons of ore and grain were passing through the Sault Sainte Marie Canal; and the Panama Canal was about to marry the Atlantic and Pacific. The looms of Europe clamored for American cotton and their operatives for American wheat and pork; in the half century after Appomattox the United States ran up a cumulative favorable balance of trade of more than two and a quarter billion dollars, and by 1910 her annual exports had passed the two-billion mark.

The supply of labor continued to fill the demand, and most of it was cheap. From the farms and the country villages, from the ranks of women and of children, from the teeming cities of Italy, Austria, and Poland, millions of workers poured into the industrial centers. In the thirty years after 1870 the total number of wage earners increased from twelve to twenty-nine millions, but those engaged in manufacturing from less than three to seven millions. More illuminating was the fact that the proportion of women in industry increased from one eighth to one fifth and that in the same period the number of child workers between the ages of ten and fifteen rose to one and three-quarter millions. An ever-greater number of immigrants were recruited from the poorer and less skilled peoples of southern and eastern Europe; the first decade of the new century brought in two millions of the unhappy peoples of the Dual Monarchy, another two millions from Italy, and a million and a half from Russia. Most of them were willing to work for whatever they could get; the average annual wage in manufacturing in 1909 was slightly over five hundred dollars!

One element in the pattern of rising industrialism remains to be considered: the role of government. Throughout the generation after the Civil War the business interests were in charge not only of the national, but also of state legislatures. The system of protective tariffs, established during the war as an emergency measure, was continued, and the iron, steel, copper, marble, woolgrowing, textile, and chinaware industries were particularly favored beneficiaries. The Congressional grant of subsidies to railroads was imitated by states and local communities, until altogether the railroads reaped a harvest of some three quarters of a billion dollars in land, stock, tax exemptions, and other gratuities. Government authorities took a complacent attitude toward land grabbing, and toward timber cutting, and cattle grazing on the public domain; numerous fortunes were founded on exploitation of the property of the nation. Congress showed little inclination to regulate private enterprise, and the courts gave substantial immunity to restrictive legislation coming from the states. Not until after the turn of the century was the philosophy of "rugged individualism" effectively challenged.

Iron and Steel

We may trace the interrelation of these factors in what proved to be the most important chapter in American industrial development, the story of iron and steel. Iron had been mined in America from the earliest colonial days. In 1619 John Berkeley built an iron forge on Falling Creek, Virginia; a century later William Byrd wrote a lively account of his *Progress to the Mines* of the West. In the Bay Colony an enterprising company obtained free land, tax exemption, and a monopoly for constructing a forge. Ethan Allen, leader of the Green Mountain Boys, built a blast furnace in the Litchfield Hills of Connecticut; forges in eastern Pennsylvania turned out cannon balls for Washington's hard-pushed continentals; and the Sterling Forge, near West Point, cast the greatest of the chains which were strung across the Hudson to bar the British fleet. The most important of the early ironworks were in the Ramapos of northern Jersey, the state where, in later years, Peter Cooper was to establish a great industry and Abram Hewitt was to introduce the open-hearth process of making steel. After 1800 flourishing ironworks sprang up west of the Alleghenies, at Pittsburgh, where there was a fortunate combination of ore, coal, limestone, and wood for charcoal; here forges were built in time to cast cannon balls for Commodore Perry and General Jackson.

Yet these early smelters and forges were small affairs. As late as 1850 the pig-iron production of the entire country was only one-half million tons a year and the manufacture of steel was negligible. Prospects for increased production were not encouraging, for the supply of iron ore was inadequate, and the cost of making steel prohibitive. Then came one of the most dramatic revolutions in the history of industry. In 1844 surveyors, running the boundary between Wisconsin and upper Michigan, noticed that their compasses swung crazily from side to side. They reported great outcroppings of black ore. For generations the Indians had told stories of a fabled mountain of iron; in 1845 a Chippewa chief with the name of Madjigijig guided a copper prospector to the Marquette range, overlooking Superior, and soon hundreds of frantic fortune hunters were pouring into the wilderness, staking out claims to copper and iron. Transporting the heavy ore by rail was difficult and expensive; a water route was essential.

Michigan proposed a canal around the rapids of the St. Marys River, connecting Huron and Superior, but even Henry Clay, father of the American system, ridiculed the idea. "It is a work beyond the remotest settlement of the United States, if not the moon," he said. Private enterprise and the driving energy of young Charles Harvey built the canal. It was open to ships in 1855 and before long floated more traffic than any other canal in the world. Docks were built at Marquette, Ashland, and Escanaba, and, after the opening of the Menominee range, crowding the western shore of Lake Michigan, and the wonderfully rich Gogebic range straddling the Michigan-Wisconsin boundary, fleets of mighty "red-bellies" carried millions of tons of ore to distant mills.

Before long, the deposits on the northern peninsula were to be dwarfed by those west of Lake Superior; the whole of that vast lake, indeed, was rimmed with iron. A surveyor stumbled on the Vermilion range in the 1870's; in 1884 Eastern capital had built a railroad connecting it with the Lakes, and in twenty-five years the Vermilion shipped out thirty million tons of ore. Meanwhile the five Merritt brothers of Duluth, imbued by a mystical belief in the existence of iron and their own destiny to find it, had been cruising the wilderness west of the lake. Seventy-five miles northwest of Duluth, on the watershed of the continent—the Mississippi running to the Gulf, the Rainy north to Hudson Bay, the St. Louis east to the Great Lakes —they found the Mesabi, "grandmother of them all," the most fabulously rich iron range in the world. This was in 1890, and two years later a rickety railroad pushed through timber and brush and swamp and carried out a million tons of ore. Within a decade the Mesabi had poured forty million tons into the giant converters of Pittsburgh and Chicago.

These iron-ore desposits of northern Minnesota had advantages possessed by no other deposits elsewhere in the world and were largely responsible for American supremacy in iron and steel production. They were practically inexhaustible. The iron ore lay not in rocky veins, deeply imbedded in the earth, but in loose deposits just below the surface; as one of the Merritt boys said, "if we had gotten mad and kicked the ground right where we stood we could have thrown up sixty-four per cent ore, if we had kicked hard enough to kick off the pine needles." The ore was unusually pure; it could be lifted out by great steam shovels; and it was sufficiently close to the Great Lakes for shipment to the industrial and coal areas at low cost.

But how transform the red ore into white steel? In the little town of Eddyville, Kentucky, some years before the Civil War an ironmaker, William Kelly, hit on the fantastic notion that he could turn iron into steel by blowing cold air through it, and proved that it wasn't fantastic at all. A little later the English engineer, Henry Bessemer, had the same idea. He not only proved it, but successfully applied it, and while Kelly got nothing but trouble for his invention, Bessemer ended up with a fortune, a "Sir" before his name, and a fame that ringed the world. The Kelly-Bessemer process as finally perfected was simplicity itself. The molten iron ore was poured into a pearlike container, through which cold air was forced. The oxygen of the air and the carbon and silicon of the iron waged a titanic battle with shrieks and roars, while the mouth of the converter belched fire like some fabulous dragon, its flames leaping forty or fifty feet into the air, and changing color from red to violet, from orange to white. In ten minutes the battle of the elements was over, the impurities of the iron ore had burned out, and the converter was tipped over to pour the flaming steel into molds. In time a new process for steelmaking, the open-hearth, supplanted the Bessemer, but for the critical last quarter of the century the Bessemer was supreme.

Iron ore, coal, and science made possible the steel industry; all that was needed to insure its success was enterprise, skill, and capital. The Indian Madjigijig who led white men to the Marquette, Harvey who built the Soo Canal, Lon Merritt who found the Mesabi, Kelly and Bessemer who invented the converter, had each contributed much; the spotlight was now to be focused on the greatest name in the history of the industry. Andrew Carnegie had come as a boy of twelve from Dunfermline, Scotland, his father, a master weaver, ruined by the advent of the factory system. There were relatives in Pittsburgh, and to that booming city at the juncture of the Allegheny and the Monongahela the family turned. Andrew got work as a bobbin boy, graduated to a steam boiler, to the telegraph office, and finally to the Pennsylvania Railroad. He was honest, clever, industrious, and wide-awake, and the charm of manner which never deserted him won the confidence and friendship of older men. Before he was thirty he had an income of forty or fifty thousand dollars a year from shrewd investments in oil and iron, express and sleeping-car companies. It is indicative of his vision and boldness that in 1865 he decided to abandon his other interests and concentrate on iron. Within a few years he had organized or bought into companies for making iron bridges, rails, and locomotives. When he was thirty he moved to New York and began to act as salesman for his many companies and as broker for numerous railroad and iron interests. He asserted later that he had sold thirty millions of American securities to London; he was to play a large part in making them good. Thus even before he was fairly launched in steel, he had been concerned with half a dozen industries destined to play major roles in American economic development: the telegraph, railroads, oil, Pullman cars, express companies, and iron.

Although Carnegie was slow to adopt the Bessemer process, when he did see it his conversion was complete; and the plant which he built in 1875 on Braddock's battlefield on the banks of the Monongahela was the greatest in the country. Within a year it was turning out more Bessemer steel than all the other American mills combined. Alert for every new improvement, quick to take advantage of hard times to buy up or to ruin his rivals, closely allied with the Pennsylvania and other railroads, aided by astute lieutenants like H. C. Frick and Charles Schwab, Carnegie was in a strategic position to assert his leadership in the steel industry. Year by year his empire grew—new mills, coke and coal properties, iron ore from Superior, a fleet of Great Lakes steamers, a port town on Lake Erie, and a connecting railroad. It was in effect a vertical trust. His iron and steel industry was intimately allied with a dozen others, it could command favorable terms from railroads and shipping lines, it had capital enough for expansion, the best workingmen, and the shrewdest managers. Nothing like it had ever been seen before in America, though the empire Rockefeller was building was to be just as mighty. Capitalized in 1878 at one and a quarter million dollars, its profits soon ran to two millions a year, then mounted to five millions. When in 1900 the business was recapitalized at 320 millions, it was turning out three million tons of steel a year with annual profits of forty million dollars.

One important element remained—labor. Again the experience of the iron industry, and of the Carnegie Company, is typical. The iron miners of the early years were recruited chiefly from Cornwall and Wales; then came Swedes and Finns, and after them a flood of Slavs and

Magyars. The same progression could be traced among those who fired the furnaces and lifted the fiery balls of molten steel into the molds. A survey of 1907 showed more than two thirds of the laborers in the Carnegie mills foreign-born and the vast majority of these from southern and eastern Europe. They were tough—and they needed to be, working twelve hours a day, seven days a week, in an inferno of heat and noise. Because there was a plentiful supply of unskilled workers, unions seldom made progress in the industry, and when they did they were put down savagely. Carnegie's labor policy was thoroughly bad.

In the rise of this industry, then, were all but one of the essential ingredients for world leadership: raw materials, transportation, science and invention, managerial skill and enterprise, cheap labor, and finally, with the growth of railroads and the use of structural steel for building, assured markets. The one additional element temporarily needed was protection against foreign competition. A tariff whose terms were dictated by the ironmasters took care of this; twenty-eight dollars a ton on steel rails was prohibitive, and even Carnegie came in time to admit that it might well be lowered.

These auspices presiding, American iron and steel forged ahead. By 1890 production surpassed that of Britain; by 1900 the United States was making more steel than Britain and Germany combined. By 1920 American blast furnaces were forging twenty-seven million tons of pig iron and forty-two million tons of steel, and the demands of the Second World War revealed that productive capacity could be stepped up, when necessary, to eighty-five million tons.

In one final respect, too, the history of the Carnegie Company illuminates the rise of big business in the United States. The enterprising Scotsman had long dominated the industry, but it was quite impossible for him to exercise a monopoly over the natural resources, transportation, and industrial plans involved in the making of steel. Rockefeller owned the most valuable of the Mesabi mines and a fleet of Great Lakes steamers; the Tennessee Coal and Iron ruled vast holdings in the South; new steel companies, like the Federal, the Pennsylvania, the American Steel and Wire, rose to challenge the pre-eminence of the Carnegie. Stung by competition, Carnegie threatened to acquire new mines, build a larger fleet of freighters, and embark upon the manufacture of tubes, barbed wire, tin plate, and a hundred other wares. A ruinous war loomed in the industry, and steel men turned, in dismay, to thoughts of combination. Carnegie preferred to sell out at his own price rather than fight; he was an old man, and he had long wanted to retire and give away his money. He listened willingly to the suggestion that he merge his holdings with a new organization which should embrace most of the important iron and steel properties in the nation. In 1901 the United States Steel Corporation was born, with a capitalization of $1,400,000,000—a sum larger than the total national wealth a century earlier. It was appropriate that the banking house of J. P. Morgan engineered the combine and that John D. Rockefeller realized perhaps the most generous profits in the deal.

Trusts and Monopolies

The organization of the United States Steel Corporation illustrated a process that had been under way for thirty years and that was to continue unabated until the present time. This was the combination of independent industrial enterprises into federated or centralized empires. The Carnegie Company, at the height of its power, had been merely one of some six hundred iron and steel establishments; the United States Steel Corporation was designed to absorb or eliminate most of these and to make two thirds of the steel products of the country. Within another generation two hundred giant corporations did half the corporate business of the nation, while three hundred thousand smaller ones did the other half.

The United States of Lincoln's day was a nation of small enterprises. A monopoly was practically unknown; the old Astor Fur Company and the newly organized Western Union were the nearest things to it since the weak royal monopolies of colonial days. Many communities, especially in the North, were substantially self-sufficient. Furniture came from the local cabinetmaker, shoes from the neighborhood shoemaker, meat from small butchers, carriages from community carriage makers. Manufacturing and mining were spread thin; more than two thousand factories made plows and cultivators and reapers; Pennsylvania alone had over two hundred oil refiners, and one hundred proprietors divided the wealth of the Comstock lode. Forty years later all this had changed. The International Harvester Company made almost all the farm implements; the Standard Oil had a practical monopoly of refining; and two or three Eastern corporations owned and mined the Comstock.

The change had begun during the Civil War and went on with revolutionary speed after the seventies. Astute businessmen realized that if they could bring competing firms into a single organization they could reduce costs and—what was more important—control prices. The primary instrument to achieve these ends was the corporation, then came the pool, and then the trust. The corporation was a device to create a fictitious person who could enjoy all the legal advantages but escape most of the moral responsibilities of a human being. It enjoyed a permanent life, the power to float issues of stocks and bonds, limited liability for debts, and, subject to charter restrictions, the right to do business everywhere in the nation. The trust was, in effect, a combination of corporations whereby the stockholders of each would place their stocks in the hands of trustees who would manage the business of all. In time the term "trust" came to mean any large business combination. The advantages of trusts, too, were obvious. They made possible large-scale combination, centralized control and administration, the elimination of less efficient units, the pooling of patents, and, by virtue of their capital resources, power to expand, to compete with foreign business companies, to drive hard bargains with labor, to exact favorable terms from railroads, and to exercise immense influence in politics, state and national.

Combination was a world-wide phenomenon, but it was more pronounced in the United States than anywhere else except perhaps Germany. That was in part because of the vast resources awaiting exploitation. But there were other reasons. The completion of the railroad system assured a national market for manufactured products. Patent laws gave a monopoly on crucially important processes. Generous land grants and a liberal interpretation of land laws played into the hands of companies big enough to undertake large-scale exploitation of timber, copper, or coal. The federal system enabled a company to incorporate in a state where laws were liberal and do business in other states, and the protective system prevented foreign competition.

It was the Standard Oil Company that led the way. While oil producers of western Pennsylvania were engaged in cutthroat competition, a silent, austere young businessman of Cleveland, Ohio, went quietly about buying up the local refineries and welding them into a single company. "The American Beauty rose," his son later said, "can be produced in its splendor and fragrance only by sacrificing the early buds which grow up around it." In 1872 Rockefeller took advantage of the organization of the short-lived South Improvement Company, and of favorable rebates from the New York Central and the Erie railroads, to obtain complete mastery of oil refining in Cleveland. That done, he moved on to take control of refining in New York, Philadelphia, and Pittsburgh. A superbly efficient marketing system was built up. Control of the pipe lines followed, and within a decade Rockefeller had a practical monopoly of the transportation and refining of petroleum. In 1882 the Standard Oil Company emerged as the first great trust; dissolved by the Ohio courts, it promptly reincorporated as a holding company under the more generous laws of New Jersey and proceeded unperturbed on its way. Before 1900 Rockefeller had brought order out of the chaos of the oil industry, eliminated most of his competitors, amassed a fabulous fortune, and created the greatest monopoly in the country.

Other trusts and monopolies followed rapidly; the cottonseed oil in 1884, the linseed oil in 1885, the lead trust and the whisky trust, and the sugar trust in 1887, the match trust in 1889, the tobacco trust in 1890, the rubber trust in 1892. Aggressive businessmen, following in the footsteps of Rockefeller and Carnegie, began to mark out princely domains for themselves. Four great packers, chief among them Philip D. Armour and Gustavus F. Swift, established a "beef trust." The Guggenheim interests got control of the copper deposits of Arizona and of Butte, Montana, where "the richest hill in the world" produced about two billion dollars' worth of copper in thirty years. The McCormicks established pre-eminence in the reaper business, and when their position was threatened formed a combine, the International Harvester Company, that all but monopolized the field. The Duke family built up a great tobacco trust. In silver, nickel, and zinc, in rubber, leather, and glass, in sugar, salt, and crackers, in cigars, whisky, and candy, in oil, gas, and electricity, the story was the same. A survey of 1904 showed that 319 industrial trusts, capitalized at over seven billion dollars, had swallowed up about 5300 previously independent concerns, and that 127 utilities (including railroads), capitalized at over thirteen billion dollars, had absorbed some 2400 smaller enterprises.

The life of the average man, especially if he was a city dweller, was profoundly changed by this development. Almost everything he ate and wore, the furnishings of his house, the tools he used, the transportation he employed, were made or controlled by trusts. When he sat down to breakfast he ate bacon packed by the beef trust, seasoned his eggs with salt made by the Michigan salt trust, sweetened his coffee with sugar refined by the American Sugar trust, lit his American Tobacco Company cigar with a Diamond Match Company match. Then he rode to work on a bicycle built by the bicycle trust or on a trolley car operating under a monopolistic franchise and running on steel rails made by United States Steel. Yet it is probable that his food was better, his transportation more efficient, than a generation earlier. What the average man noticed most was the effect of trusts on the business life of his community. Local industry dried up, factories went out of business or were absorbed, mortgages were placed with Eastern banks or insurance companies, and neighbors who worked not for themselves but for distant corporations were exposed to the vicissitudes of policy over which they had no control.

It was not only in manufacturing and mining that this process of combination and consolidation was under way. It was even more spectacular in the realms of transportation and communication. The Western Union, the earliest of the large combinations, was followed by the Bell Telephone System and eventually by the giant American Telephone and Telegraph. Gruff old Commodore Vanderbilt had early seen that efficient railroading required the unification of lines and in the sixties had knit some thirteen or fourteen separate railroads into a single line connecting New York City and Buffalo; during the next decade he acquired lines to Chicago and Detroit, and the New York Central system came into being. Other consolidations were already under way, and soon most of the railroads of the nation were organized into trunk lines and "systems," controlled by Vanderbilt, Gould, Harriman, Hill, and the bankers Morgan and Belmont. E. H. Harriman brought together the Illinois Central, the Union Pacific, the Southern Pacific, and half a dozen other lines and dreamed of creating a nation-wide consolidation. It was a banker, J. P. Morgan, who came closest to making that dream real.

The rise of the house of Morgan illustrates the final and perhaps most important development in the process of combination—the creation of the so-called "money trust." In 1864 Junius Spencer Morgan, who had long been engaged in selling American securities to English investors, placed his son J. Pierpont Morgan in charge of an American branch of the house. A few years later young Morgan went into partnership with the old banking house of Drexel, in Philadelphia, and in 1873 the firm of Drexel, Morgan and Company was strong enough to divide with Jay Cooke the refinancing of three quarters of a billion of the national debt. The spectacular failure of Jay Cooke that same year left the Morgan house in a strong position, and when, a few years later, it disposed of a vast quantity of New York Central stock abroad, its reputation was made. This tie-up with the New York Central pointed the way to the major financial activity of the house for the next twenty years.

All through the eighties Morgan reorganized and refinanced railroads, extending his influence more widely into this key field. The panic of 1893 threw half the mileage of the country into the hands of receivers, and railroad men everywhere turned to "Jupiter" Morgan to rescue them from their difficulties. In part because the business was highly lucrative, in part because it was essential to maintain the soundness of the securities which he had sold abroad, he responded. When the clouds of the panic finally blew away, the Morgan interests dominated a dozen major railroad lines—the New York Central, the Southern, the Chesapeake and Ohio, the Santa Fé, the Rock Island, and many others.

Meantime the Morgan interests had expanded into other fields, until by the first decade of the century there was scarcely a major business in which the house did not exercise a decisive influence. Morgan had financed the Federal Steel Company and put through the gigantic deal which resulted in United States Steel. He had brought together the warring manufacturers of agricultural implements and emerged with the International Harvester Company. He had organized American shipping in the ill-fated International Mercantile Marine and helped finance the General Electric, the American Telephone and Telegraph, the New York Rapid Transit Company, and a dozen other giant utilities. In 1912 a Congressional committee found that the banking houses dominated by Morgan, and the William Rockefeller interests, held 341 directorships in railroads, shipping, utilities, banks, express companies, coal, copper, iron, steel, and insurance, with aggregate resources of twenty-two billion dollars. "The great monopoly in this country," said Woodrow Wilson, "is the money monopoly."

What was the significance of the growth of combinations

and the rise of trusts? It created a system of absentee ownership more far-reaching than anything known heretofore to history—vast properties of coal, copper, iron, timber, railroads, owned and directed by New York corporations. It centered in the hands of a few men power over the fortunes of millions of people greater than that wielded by many monarchs. It concentrated economic control of the nation in a small section of the Northeast, creating a new sectionalism to take the place of the old. It separated ownership from management, lodging it in tens of thousands of stockholders who had little sense of responsibility and knew little about the financial or the labor policies of their companies. It created new aggregations of capital powerful enough to dictate policies to state and even to national legislatures and to influence foreign as well as domestic policies. It undoubtedly eliminated a great deal of cutthroat competition, achieved greater efficiency, released money for necessary improvements and for research, and made possible mass production and lower prices—but all at a heavy cost to society.

The Government Steps In

Andrew Carnegie called all this "triumphant democracy"; others were quite ready to admit that it was triumphant, but not at all sure that it was democracy. Indeed, as they looked about them and saw a large part of the natural resources, the industries, the railroads, and other utilities controlled for the benefit of a handful of men rather than of society, they began to doubt that democracy could endure. Exorbitant charges, discrimination, and wholesale land grabs by the railroads, the malpractices of Rockefeller and Carnegie in crushing competitors, the savage power with which many giant corporations beat down labor, the pocketing by the trusts of the savings that came from science and invention, the spectacle of corporation agents lobbying favorable laws through state legislatures and corporation lawyers finding loopholes in state tax or regulation laws, all aroused widespread alarm and bitterness.

Monopolies had long been illegal at common law, and many state constitutions contained clauses forbidding their existence. But these constitutional prohibitions were almost entirely ineffective. During the eighties many states wrote more stringent laws on their statute books, and some went as far as to dissolve trusts with a particularly malodorous record. But a trust dissolved in one state might incorporate in another, where laws were more lenient and enforcement was lax, and continue to do business at the same stand. Clearly this was a matter for Federal rather than state regulation.

As early as 1876 the millionaire philosopher, Peter Cooper, running for the presidency on the Greenback ticket, warned that "the danger to our free institutions now is only less than in the inception of the rebellion. . . . There is fast forming in this country an aristocracy of wealth, the worst form of aristocracy that can curse the prosperity of any country." With the return of prosperity in the late seventies agitation died down, but by the eighties the country was once more trust conscious. By 1884 there was an Anti-Monopoly party in the field, but in the excitement over the prospect of the return of the Democrats to power, it attracted few votes. Another four years, and the organization of half a dozen major trusts made the country alert to the danger. President Cleveland told Congress that "corporations, which should be carefully restrained creatures of the law and servants of the people, are fast becoming the people's masters," and both major parties went on record as opposed to monopolies in any form.

The first practical result of all this agitation was in the regulation of railroads. As early as the 1870's outraged farmers had clamored against the railroad monopoly, charging that it gouged them with excessive freight charges, gave poor service, and held millions of acres off the market for speculative purposes. At the behest of farm organizations like the Grange, Midwestern states placed on their statute books laws limiting the rates that the roads might charge, and outlawing such practices as rebates, special rates to favored shippers, charging more for a short than for a long haul over the same road, and free passes. This legislation was promptly challenged by the railroads on the ground that it deprived them of their property "without due process of law" and that it infringed upon Congressional control over interstate commerce.

In a series of remarkable decisions in 1876, notably Munn vs. Illinois, the courts sustained the state legislation on the ground that any property "affected with a public interest" or devoted to a public use is subject to regulation by government. But with respect to the problem of the encroachment of the state on the domain of Federal regulation the position of the court was ambiguous. Later decisions, however, made it clear that while states could regulate commerce entirely local in character, they could not touch it if it had in any way an interstate character. That was under the exclusive control of the national government. And as most commerce was interstate this put the issue squarely up to the Congress.

Congress responded with the Interstate Commerce Act of 1887. This act, designed as much to save the railroads from the evil results of rate wars and rebates as to protect the public, prohibited pooling, rebates, discrimination in rates or services, and required that all charges should be "just" and "reasonable." More important than these somewhat vague prohibitions and requirements was the provision for an Interstate Commerce Commission to supervise the administration of the act. This was the first of the many administrative boards which were to become so important as to constitute a fourth department of the government. The Interstate·Commerce Act was long ineffective, but new laws like the Elkins Act of 1903 and Hepburn Act of 1906, with a more rigid enforcement by the Commission and the courts, served in time to weed out the worst malpractices of the railroads and to establish effective control over rates and services.

The task of regulating railroads was relatively simple compared with that of regulating trusts. Perhaps the basic difficulty had its origin not in the vastness and complexity of business but in the confusion of the American mind. Americans feared big business, but they admired it, too. They wished to protect themselves against the dangers of monopoly, but also to enjoy the benefits of mass production and of the elimination of costly duplication. They believed in government regulation of business, but believed with equal fervor in the virtues of private enterprise and "rugged individualism." What they really wanted to do was to purify the trusts, not to smash them. As President Theodore Roosevelt said in one of his later trust messages:

> Our aim is not to do away with corporations; on the contrary these big aggregations are a necessary part of modern industrialism. . . . We are not attacking corporations, but endeavoring to do away with any evil in them.

His dilemma inspired a shrewd parody by the nation's jester, Finley Peter Dunne: "Th' thrusts are heejous monsthers built up by th' inlightened intherprise ov th' men that have done so much to advance progress in our beloved counthry. On wan hand I wud stamp them undher fut; on th' other hand, not so fast."

This, indeed, well represented the national attitude: not so fast. Certainly Congress did not go fast. As it became clear that the states could not singly cope with the trust problem, Congress was forced to take action. The Sherman Antitrust Act of 1890 outlawed all contracts, combinations, or conspiracies in restraint of trade, and all monopolies. It was widely supposed that this legislation would give the government a club over such giant corporations as the Standard Oil and combinations like the whisky and sugar trusts. But when the government tried, rather feebly, to break up certain monopolies, the courts sustained them, and they went merrily on their way. "What looks like a stone wall to a layman is a triumphal arch to a lawyer," said the irrepressible Dunne. So impressive was this defeat that the decade after the Sherman Act witnessed the formation of some of the largest and most notorious trusts. Only with respect to labor organizations and strikes did the law reveal unsuspected possibilities, for the courts held that in so far as labor unions restrained trade by strikes or other practices, they were violating the statute. The public bitterly realized that an act designed ostensibly to break up industrial monopolies was being used, instead, to smash strikes.

With the organization of United States Steel the storm of public disapproval broke. From the press and forum came torrents of criticism. Books like Ida Tarbell's *History of the Standard Oil Company* and Russell's *The Greatest Trust in the World* (the beef trust) and Lawson's *Frenzied Finance* (the copper trust) sold by the tens of thousands, while exposures of the iniquities of big business filled the new popular magazines like *McClure's, Everybody's,* and *Collier's* and pushed their way into the pages of the old respectable ones. So widespread and violent was this criticism that the first decade of the century has been called "the era of the muckrakers."

The demand for the more effective enforcement of the antitrust laws was irresistible, and Theodore Roosevelt responded with enthusiasm. "As far as the antitrust laws go," he said, "they will be enforced, and when suit is undertaken it will not be compromised except on the basis that the government wins." To the astonishment of Wall Street the President directed his Attorney General to break up a railroad combination engineered by the three greatest railroad overlords, Morgan, Harriman, and Hill—and was successful in the Northern Securities Company case. Action followed swiftly against the meat-packer trust, the tobacco trust, and the Standard Oil, and in each the government emerged victorious.

Yet these victories were more sensational than substantial. Dissolved, the constituent elements in the great monopolies found other ways to maintain a community of interest. Nor, aside from the creation of the Bureau of Corporations, effectively applying "pitiless publicity" to corporate malpractices, did Roosevelt do anything to strengthen the antitrust laws. Notwithstanding his success in the courts and his public denunciation of "malefactors of great wealth," the trusts were stronger when he went out of office than when he came in. Apparently Rockefeller was right when he said, "The combination is here to stay. Individualism has gone, never to return."

Chapter Fourteen

LABOR AND IMMIGRATION

The Laborer and His Hire

THE exploitation of the rich resources of the country, the mechanization of industry, the rise of monopolies, poured a steady stream of wealth into the hands of a small body of fortunate businessmen and a larger number of shrewd investors. But it profited little the workingmen upon whom the drudgery all fell. Labor was one of the basic factors in the growth of big business, but in the division of profits it was conspicuously left out. It was left out, too, when the social rewards were distributed: workingmen rarely lived on "the right side of the tracks," they were not asked to join the country clubs, and their leaders were ignored by the colleges and universities that every year bestowed honorary degrees on masters of capital. New sources of wealth should have meant its wider distribution, but that was long in coming; the application of labor-saving machinery should have meant shorter hours, but that, too, was long an unattained ideal; science should have insured the workingmen safer and pleasanter working conditions, but most of them continued to work in hot, noisy, ill-ventilated factories, or surrounded by dangers in mines and quarries, and the toll from industrial accidents and diseases mounted frightfully year by year. Crowded into the slums of the big cities, exposed to depression and unemployment, competing with hordes of unskilled hands from abroad or from the

South, the lot of the workers was far from enviable. Nor did they find it easy to improve their condition. Organization and strikes were regarded with suspicion, and in legislatures and Congress the toilers had few representatives.

Indeed, some of the developments which contributed most to the growth of industrial America were a positive disadvantage to labor. Two of these we can note briefly: the mechanization of industry and the rise of the corporation. Mechanization tended, on the whole, to lower the standards of labor. The skills which workingmen had painfully acquired ceased to have their old-time value, for the machine could do better, cheaper, and quicker most of the things the trained artisan had done. The creative instinct of craftsmanship was largely destroyed, and workingmen were reduced to a mere part of a mechanical process, automata performing every minute of the day some monotonous and deadening operation. As Upton Sinclair described it in *The Jungle:*

> Each one of the hundreds of parts of a mowing machine was made separately, and sometimes handled by hundreds of men. Where Jurgis worked there was a machine which cut and stamped a certain piece of steel about two square inches in size; the pieces came tumbling out upon a tray, and all that human hands had to do was to pile them in regular rows, and change the trays at intervals. This was done by a single boy, who stood with eyes and thoughts centred upon it, and fingers flying so fast that the sounds of the bits of steel striking upon each other was like the music of an express train as one hears it in a sleeping car at night. . . . Thirty thousand of these pieces he handled every day, nine or ten millions every year—how many in a lifetime it rested with the gods to say. Near by him sat men bending over whirling grindstones, put-

ting the finishing touches to the steel knives of the reaper; picking them out of a basket with the right hand, pressing first one side and then the other against the stone, and finally dropping them with the left hand into another basket. One of these men told Jurgis that he had sharpened three thousand pieces of steel a day for thirteen years.

Machinery had a tendency, too, to usurp the place of the worker in the economy of industry. It represented an enormous capital investment, it could work twenty-four hours a day seven days a week, and it came to determine working conditions; the fact that furnaces had to be kept going continuously was decisive in maintaining the twelve-hour day in the iron and steel industry for half a century. Machinery was in part responsible, finally, for a great deal of unemployment. It is probably true that in the end machines made more jobs than they eliminated, but it was not always the same people who got the new jobs, and there were usually agonizing periods of want before older men found new work. Large-scale unemployment is a product of the machine age.

The growth of the giant corporation as employer, too, often worked to the disadvantage of labor. Small-scale industry had close relations with its workingmen and with its community. Workers could bargain far more successfully with local employers than with some distant and impersonal organization. Theodore Roosevelt put this well:

. . . The old familiar relations between employer and employee were passing. A few generations before, the boss had known every man in his shop; he called his men Bill, Tom, Dick, John; he inquired after their wives and babies; he swapped jokes and stories and perhaps a bit of tobacco with them. In the small establishment there had been a friendly human relationship between employer and employee.

There was no such relation between the great railway magnates, who controlled the anthracite industry, and the one hundred and fifty thousand men who worked in their mines, or the half million women and children who were dependent upon these miners for their daily bread. . . . The great coal-mining and coal-carrying companies, which employed their tens of thousands, could easily dispense with the services of any particular miner. The miner, on the other hand, could not dispense with the companies. He needed a job; his wife and children would starve if he did not get one. What the miner had to sell—his labor—was a perishable commodity; the labor of today—if not sold—was lost forever.

And a New England mill owner, testifying before a Senate committee, succinctly remarked: "I never do my talking to the hands. I do all my talking with the overseers."

Several other factors, unique to the United States, conditioned the welfare of labor. The first of these was the passing of good cheap land a generation or so after the Civil War. It would perhaps be an exaggeration to say that the West had served as a "safety valve" for labor discontent or as a refuge for very many workingmen. But it is clear that for two or three generations the open land did drain off the surplus population of the countryside, the villages, and even the cities, and the immigrants from abroad. Had the five million immigrants who came over between 1850 and 1870 all stayed in the industrial cities of the East instead of swarming over the country, the position of labor would have been vastly worse than it actually was. With the rise in the cost of farming and the disappearance of good cheap land, surplus population did stay in the industrial areas.

Farming was no longer a practical alternative to the factory. Labor could no longer escape the problems of an industrialized society, but was forced to stand and face them.

A second factor, peculiar to the United States among industrial nations, was continuous and unrestricted immigration. In the forty years from 1870 to 1910 more than twenty million people poured into the country. Even subtracting the women and children—many of whom toiled— this meant that every year several hundred thousand recruits joined the ranks of labor, eager for work in the mills and the mines, at almost any wages and under almost any conditions. Nor was this the only competition that confronted Northern labor. From the South, after the turn of the century, came tens of thousands of sturdy Negroes ready to take their places beside the Poles, Italians, and Hungarians. Not every newcomer from abroad or from the South displaced a worker; in boom times there was work enough for all, and the newcomers as often pushed native labor to the top as out. Yet the general tendency of this mass movement was to drive down wages, depress standards, and disintegrate labor unions.

A third factor—again one unique to the United States— was the existence side by side of a national economy and a Federal political system. The problems of labor—in the coal industry, in textiles, in iron and steel mills—were much the same the nation over, but the power to deal with them was lodged, until very recent years, in the states alone. Competition was nation-wide, but the right to regulate wages and hours was only state-wide. Thus labor might win important concessions in the textile industry of New England or the garment shops of New York only to have them nullified by a shift of these industries to states where laws were less exacting. After the advent of the New Deal, to be sure, all this was changed. The Federal government found ways to establish national control over the whole field of industrial relations.

One final consideration merits attention: the deep suspicion which many Americans entertained toward labor unions, and their unwillingness to approach the problems of labor with the same sympathy with which they regarded the problems of industry. Lillian Wald, head of a famous New York settlement house, recalled that

> In my earlier years on the East Side labor unions were feared as Socialists were later, and as Communists are today. I remember telling at a dinner of comfortable people—bankers, industrialists, a lawyer or two—about one of these heroic labor leaders. Every knife and fork stopped when I mentioned casually that I knew and respected a "walking delegate." I went on to speak of a man who had organized the cloak makers in one of their early protests against the lot of the sweated workers. I still remember that faces sobered as I told about this leader and his struggle.

We have noted that the Sherman Antitrust Act was applied first and most effectively to labor: that was typical of the whole situation. Most Americans, until recent years, assumed that combination in business was good sense, but looked on combination of labor with disapproval; took for granted that business would participate in politics, but thought it un-American for labor to do so; approved government aid to industry, but insisted that government aid to labor was socialistic or a surrender to pressure groups; held that investors had a natural right to a fair return on their investments, but assumed that a workingman had no right to any return on his labor but what he could wrest from a reluctant employer, and that unemployment was an act of God. These attitudes changed as the nation became educated to the problems of modern industrialism, but they lingered long enough to place serious obstacles in the path of organized labor.

Yet we must not draw too somber a picture of the condition of labor during the industrial era. For the most part there was work enough for willing hands, and wages, though far from adequate, were high enough to keep a family in food, clothing, and shelter of a sort. There was no "laboring class" in the United States in the sense that there was in many European countries, while there was always the opportunity to shift from job to job, from one income group to another. An Englishman visiting the United States just after the Civil War commented perspicaciously on this:

> A workingman in this country is situated very differently from one of his own class at home; if he has the means he goes where he pleases without carrying a certificate of character in his pocket. Indeed it would be just as admissible in the social code for a man seeking work to demand a character of the "Boss" he may apply to, as that he should be asked for one. In these matters Jack is as good as his master. . . . This country has had the rare advantage of growing into national greatness without having had to pass through the ordeal of feudalism, or being trammeled in her progress by the tyrannical influence arising from pride of Caste.

This changed, to be sure: in time workingmen did have to carry certificates of character, and the use of the black list kept many an "agitator" from a job. But even a twentieth-century visitor could not discover distinct class lines in the United States. Free public education enabled the children of laborers to rise in business or the professions, and the ballot was a potential weapon whereby workingmen could, if properly aroused, compel legislators to pass friendly laws. Travelers talking with the foreign-born rarely found any who regretted coming to the New World or who cared to return to their old homes; and whatever the reasons, millions of poor continued to crowd into the United States.

In Union There Is Strength

The moral of the organization of business was not lost on labor. There had been labor unions, of a sort, ever since the early days of the republic, but these had been for the most part local and weak. During the fifties a number of strong craft unions were established—the Typographical is the oldest and most important—but these embraced only a minute percentage of the working class, and many of them petered out during reconstruction and the black depression that followed the panic of 1873.

During the postwar years three types of labor organizations emerged. The first was the industrial union, best represented by the Knights of Labor. The second was the craft union and the subsequent federation of craft unions into the American Federation of Labor. The third type was the radical socialist or revolutionary labor groups, numerically unimportant but persistent. At no time prior to the late 1930's did any or all of these organizations embrace a majority of American workingmen. Large segments of the working population—farm labor, migratory labor, domestic workers, white-collar workers—remained outside the circles of organization.

The most important and perhaps the most interesting of early labor organizations was the Noble Order of the Knights of Labor, founded in 1869 but dating its real history from 1879, when Terence Powderly became Grand Master. The most striking characteristics of the Knights were its democracy and its broad social and economic outlook. It was open to all workingmen—skilled and unskilled, farmers, mill hands, miners, and artisans; only gamblers, saloonkeepers, bankers, lawyers, and stockbrokers were excluded! Its purpose was "to secure to the toilers a proper share in the wealth that they create; more of the leisure that rightfully belongs to them; more societary advantages . . . all those rights and privileges necessary to make them capable of enjoying, appreciating, defending, and perpetuating . . . good government." These gleaming ends were to be realized not through strikes or violence, but by political agitation, education, and workers' co-operatives. The program of the Knights was radical but diffuse: an eight-hour day, the abolition of child labor, public ownership of utilities, income and inheritance taxes, and land reform. The combination of starry-eyed idealism with gentlemanly persuasion to effect radical economic changes was not effective, but when after 1885 the Knights resorted to strikes, they really got somewhere. Membership increased by leaps and bounds. Within a year they boasted seven hundred thousand members, and flushed with success they backed an ill-planned general strike for the eight-hour day. In Chicago the strike helped inspire a grand meeting at Haymarket Square, where some unknown anarchist threw a bomb which killed numerous policemen. Though the Knights were not responsible for the outrage, public opinion connected them with it. This, the failure of various strikes, and inherent weakness of organization sent the Order into a decline; when the Knights tied up with the Populist party, in 1892, the decline became a demise.

Meanwhile a new organization was rising to power: the American Federation of Labor. In 1863 a Dutch Jew, Solomon Gompers, decided to give up his London cigar-making shop and try his luck in America. He brought with him a thirteen-year-old son, Samuel, who promptly went to work rolling cigars. The next year the boy joined the Cigar-makers' Union; and from that time the life of Samuel Gompers was identified with union labor, and the history of union labor in the United States with Samuel Gompers. He had no formal education, but the cigar-making shop gave him a thorough training in labor history and economics. "The nature of our work," he later recalled,

> developed a camaraderie of the shop such as few workers enjoy. It was a world in itself—a cosmopolitan world. Shopmates came from everywhere—some had been nearly everywhere. . . . In the shop there was also reading. It was the custom of the cigar makers to chip in to create a fund for purchasing papers, magazines, and books. Then while the rest worked, one of our members would read to us for perhaps an hour at a time, sometimes longer. In order that the reader might not be the loser financially, each one of the other men in the shop gave him a definite number of cigars. I had a habit of saving any interesting magazine or newspaper articles to read to my shopmates. Others did the same. As my voice was strong and the men could hear me easily whenever I read, they always asked me to read more than my period. In fact these discussions in the shops were more like public debating societies or what we call these days "labor forums." This practice had a great deal to do with developing the interest of cigarmakers in leading economic questions.

Thus Gompers familiarized himself with the writings of the British reformers, and the German and Russian Socialists. There was practical education, too: by bitter experience with strikes, hard times, and the inadequacy of existing unions, Gompers learned the necessity of a practical, hardheaded labor policy. He saw the necessity of discipline, of building up large reserve funds with which to finance strikes and weather depressions, and of avoiding any commerce with politicians, radicals, or doctrinaires. In 1881 he brought together the representatives of various trade-unions in a Federation of Organized Trade and Labor Unions of the United States and Canada. Five years later this organization became the American Federation of Labor.

The A. F. of L. was closer to contemporaneous British labor organizations than to the American Knights of Labor. Unlike the Knights it was a craft union, limited in membership to the aristocracy of labor, and made up of a series of self-governing trade-unions, federated much as are the American states. Unlike the Knights, too, it was eminently practical and opportunistic in its policies. "We have no ultimate ends," said one of its spokesmen. "We are going on from day to day. We are fighting only for immediate objects." Those objects were for the most part higher wages and shorter hours, though such related matters as child labor, sanitation and health laws, the prohibition of contract and convict labor, and the exclusion of Chinese immigrants were not ignored. Throughout its long and successful history, however, the A. F. of L. was to be conservative, opportunistic, and somewhat exclusive. Eschewing politics, co-operating with capital whenever possible, supporting necessary strikes with the reserve funds built up by high dues, maintaining strict discipline, and gaining public confidence by its sober policies, the A. F. of L. weathered hostility, hard times, and rivals; and when Gompers accepted its presidency for the last time in 1924, he could take satisfaction in a membership of almost three million.

The third type of labor organization remained significantly weak. Socialism and Communism have long backgrounds in American history, but their earlier manifestations had been for the most part in such Utopian experiments as Brook Farm; perhaps the nearest thing to a socialistic order that America had known had been the Mormon commonwealth of Utah, and labor played little part in that. In the seventies a shadowy secret organization known as the Molly Maguires terrorized the anthracite fields of Pennsylvania, where working conditions were atrocious, until it was stamped out by force. In the seventies, too, German intellectuals, more familiar with the teachings of Karl Marx and Ferdinand Lassalle than with American labor, tried to establish an American Socialism, but with little success. The arrival of Johann Most in 1882 gave to the left-wing branch of labor a revolutionary slant. Most, who had been hunted out of Germany and of England, attempted to win American workers over to a policy of violence. The true solution for the labor problem, he held, was "the destruction of the existing class rule by . . . energetic, relentless, revolutionary, and international action," and he founded an American branch of the Black International. Aside from sporadic acts of violence, the Black International accomplished nothing but to discredit the labor movement as a whole.

In time the radical labor groups emancipated themselves from their foreign entanglements; the Industrial Workers of the World, formally organized in 1905, was thoroughly indigenous, though it borrowed something from the syndicalist teachings of Forel. Notwithstanding some successes in the lumber and mining camps of the West and in the textile centers of the East, the I.W.W. never had any real numerical strength, and its hostility to the First World War in 1917–1918 put it out of business, except in the lumber camps of the Northwest and among the migratory farm workers.

Labor Conflicts

The story of American labor is checkered with strikes and violence. From the beginning labor has had to fight for most of its gains: for the right to organize, to strike, to picket, for shorter hours and higher wages, for safe working conditions and accident compensation, for abolition of child labor, injunctions, yellow-dog contracts, the stretch-out system and the company-store racket, for immigration restriction and the closed shop. Mostly the fight has been waged in the industrial arena, sometimes in the domain of politics. And in this prolonged and bitter warfare labor has for the most part stood alone, while business has found powerful allies in public opinion, the police, and the courts. Confronted with such formidable opposition labor has lost or compromised more strikes than it has won, but its victories have been sufficiently numerous to justify the continued use of the strike as a weapon. Yet it must not be forgotten that the resort to force in industrial relations is as much a monument to the failure of reason as is the resort to force in international relations.

The strike was not at all uncommon in the early years of the republic, nor were the weapons later used to combat it unfamiliar. When the working girls in the textile mills of Lowell went on a strike in 1834 a newspaper reported that "they have committed some things which females ought not to have done, such as processions through the streets . . . and waving their handkerchiefs and scarfs, and one or two of them delivered public speeches." Public opinion was duly shocked at these improprieties, and the strike was broken. There was a wave of strikes in the fifties among textile workers, coal miners, iron molders, and others, but most of these, too, were defeated. The real period of violence was inaugurated with the "Great Strike" of 1877 and coincided with the rise of the Knights of Labor and the A. F. of L. and the growth of trusts and monopolies. From 1881 to 1905 there occurred no less than thirty-seven thousand strikes, some of them brief and local, some of them prolonged and nation-wide.

The most spectacular strikes of this period were the railroad strike of 1877, which first introduced large-scale industrial violence to Americans; the strike at the McCormick Harvester works in 1886, which culminated in the tragedy of the Haymarket riot; the Homestead strike of 1892, which was marked by a pitched battle on the banks of the Monongahela; the great Pullman strike of 1894, which tied up half the railroads of the nation; the terrible Cripple Creek war in the Colorado coal fields; and the anthracite-coal strike of 1902, which threatened to paralyze industry throughout the country and which was finally settled only by the intervention of President Theodore Roosevelt. It is neither possible nor profitable to trace their history in detail, but we may select one of them, the Pullman strike of 1894, as in many respects representative of them all.

It started in the "model" town of Pullman, Illinois, where workingmen lived in comfortable company houses (at rents one fourth higher than corresponding houses elsewhere), bought company gas and water, and traded at company stores—at a handsome profit to George Pullman and his stockholders. With the depression of the early nineties, wages were slashed in order to keep up generous dividend payments, and when representatives of the workers appealed to Pullman to arbitrate the wage question, they were summarily dismissed. The workers promptly laid down their tools. The newly organized American Railway Union, under the leadership of young Eugene V. Debs, made the cause of the Pullman workers its own, directing its members not to handle any Pullman cars. With this action, war between the railroads and the workers was on—and it covered half the nation. Within a few weeks transportation throughout much of the North and West was paralyzed, and a metropolitan daily, anticipating the method used to break the strike, announced that this was "a war against the government and against society." Alarmed at the apparent success of the strike, and determined to smash the nascent railway union before it could cause further trouble, an employers' organization, the General Managers' Association demanded that the Federal government intervene to maintain uninterrupted railroad service.

In this appeal the Association was successful. President Cleveland's Attorney General was Richard Olney, a former railroad attorney who was completely sympathetic to the operators' point of view. He responded to their demand with a sweeping injunction against all strike activities. Disorder promptly broke out, but whether by the strikers, *agents provocateurs,* or hoodlums has never been determined. Governor Altgeld of Illinois was ready to maintain order with state militia, but without giving him an opportunity to act President Cleveland ordered Federal troops to Chicago. The injunction broke the strike, and the soldiers almost broke the labor movement. Debs refused to obey the injunction and was jailed for contempt of court. Altgeld protested that the Constitution had been violated and the rights of the state invaded when Federal soldiers were thus sent into the state, but was rebuked by Cleveland and repudiated by the courts. Thus all along the line the railroads appeared victorious.

But subsequent investigations of Congressional committees and of students have sustained the strikers—and Altgeld—on almost every point. The industrial feudalism of the town of Pullman was condemned, the strikers were largely acquitted of responsibility for disorder, the General

Managers' Association was branded as arrogant and lawless, the policy of Olney improper, the use of the injunction of dubious legality, and the employment of Federal troops unnecessary and improper. This unhappy episode brought into sharp focus many of the forces that conditioned the position of labor all through these years: the insolence of a great corporation, the rôle of the sympathetic strike, the use of the Antitrust Act and of the injunction to curb labor, the hostility of the courts, and the tendency of government authorities to side with capital rather than with labor. It brought the labor question into politics as a major issue in the coming campaign and forfeited labor's confidence in President Cleveland. It strengthened the Socialist party and gave it a great leader, Eugene V. Debs, while it added to the ultimate fame of John Peter Altgeld —the "eagle forgotten" of Vachel Lindsay's poem:

> *A hundred white eagles have risen, the sons of your sons,*
> *The zeal in their wings is a zeal that your dreaming began,*
> *The valor that wore out your soul in the service of man.*

By 1900 labor had won most of its basic rights—the right to organize, to strike, to bargain collectively—and made some progress in its campaign for better working and living conditions. Yet it was clear that these gains were limited to a small segment of the working population and that they hardly touched the larger questions of security for the workers and the welfare of society as a whole. It was gradually becoming clear that the labor problem was not isolated from other social and economic problems and that society had a legitimate stake in the welfare and security of its workers. Where industry failed to pay a living wage, society had somehow to make up the difference. Where it failed to provide employment, society had to take care of the unemployed. Where it maimed workingmen or wore them out, prematurely, society had to support them. The labor of women and children was not merely an issue between them and their employers, for it involved the future of the race. It was a question, too, how long society could afford the luxury of industrial warfare, for whoever emerged victorious, society was always the loser.

Clearly these were matters calling for political action. No employers could hope to institute such far-reaching and expensive reforms as unemployment compensation or old-age pensions unless all his competitors were willing to take similar action, and such concerted benevolence was not to be expected. Nor could these matters be settled by collective bargaining, so long as the vast majority of workers remained unorganized. Only the government could effectively stop child labor, regulate labor conditions for women, require accident compensation, prohibit yellow-dog contracts and black lists, support the unemployed, the aged, and the derelicts of industry, inspect factories, improve housing, and do many other things to avert the evil consequences of unregulated modern industrialism. Nations like England, Germany, Denmark, Austria, and Australia had early seen this and taken appropriate action. But because in America the traditions of the frontier, plentiful opportunity, and rugged individualism lingered on, social legislation was delayed. When problems became sufficiently urgent the United States was to show that she could deal with them as swiftly; vigorous beginnings were made under Theodore Roosevelt and Woodrow Wilson, while in 1933–1940 the United States caught up with the older industrial nations in her labor and social legislation.

In the struggle for social reforms labor had powerful allies among the social workers, the Protestant clergy, the scholars and intellectuals. In any history of the war against industrial abuses and the slum the names of Jacob Riis, newspaper reporter extraordinary, Jane Addams of Chicago's Hull House, Washington Gladden, Unitarian clergyman, John R. Commons, professor at the University of Wisconsin, must loom large. They worked unceasingly to enlighten the public upon the social cost of child labor or the danger of the tenements and to stir sluggish legislatures into action. In some states the reformers were notably successful—Massachusetts, New York, Wisconsin, Oregon— but the problem was difficult. For where more advanced states set high standards they invited industry to move to backward states where no such limitations existed.

Yet there was real progress. By the First World War most states had—at least theoretically—prohibited the labor of small children; many had set an eight-hour limit to the labor of women, established systems of accident compensation, provided for careful inspection of factories and mines, prohibited the yellow-dog contract or the use of private detectives and private police in industrial disputes, and in other ways displayed social alertness. It is impossible to trace this legislation in detail, but it is well illustrated by the history of child-labor laws.

By 1900 child labor had become a public scandal. One and three-quarter million children between the ages of ten and fifteen were then gainfully employed. Many were working in factories and mines, others in canning establishments, beet fields, or cranberry bogs. One investigator found 556 children under twelve working in eight cotton mills; another found children six and seven years old canning vegetables at two o'clock in the morning. John Spargo, whose *Bitter Cry of the Children* shocked the nation, thus describes what he saw in the Pennsylvania and West Virginia coal mines early in the century:

Crouched over the chutes, the boys sit hour after hour, picking out the pieces of slate and other refuse from the coal as it rushes past the washers. From the cramped position they have to assume most of them become more or less deformed and bent-backed like old men. . . . The coal is hard and accidents to the hands, such as cut, broken, or crushed fingers, are common among the boys. Sometimes there is a worse accident; a terrified shriek is heard, and a boy is mangled and torn in the machinery or disappears in the chute to be picked out later, smothered and dead. Clouds of dust fill the breakers and are inhaled by the boys, laying the foundations for asthma and miners' consumption. I once stood in a breaker for half an hour and tried to do the work a twelve-year-old boy was doing day after day. . . . I could not do that work and live, but there were boys of ten and twelve years of age doing it for fifty and sixty cents a day. Some of them had never been inside of a school; few of them could read a child's primer.

There were state laws against these evils, to be sure, but they were often inadequate and easily evaded. Thus South Carolina finally worked up to a twelve-year limit for factory labor but permitted exceptions where this limit imposed a hardship upon families! And when Maryland required all persons under sixteen wanting to work to apply for a permit, applications were twice as numerous as the total number of persons under sixteen enumerated in the previous census! Legislation rarely affected anything but factory labor, leaving quite unprotected the hundreds of thousands of children working as messenger boys, boot-blacks, and hands in berry fields or canning establishments —which were not held to be factories. Not until 1909 did an American state—Delaware—provide that "no child under the age of fourteen shall be employed or suffered to work in any gainful occupation."

The inadequacy of state laws led to a demand for Congressional action. In 1916 Congress responded with a law forbidding the shipment in interstate commerce of the products of child labor. The problem seemed solved—but the courts blandly announced that this law was beyond the powers of Congress and therefore void. Three years later Congress tried again, this time by trying to tax out of existence the products of child labor. Once more the courts interposed their veto: Congress could not do indirectly what it might not do directly. To be sure, twenty years later the Supreme Court confessed that this was all a mistake, but the harm was done. All through the prosperous twenties child labor continued, and the census of 1930 showed more than two million boys and girls under eighteen gainfully employed. Then the New Deal cut across constitutional dialectic and practically ended the scandal.

Through these two methods—collective bargaining and legislation—labor vastly improved its position. Business, too, began to take a more enlightened view of the labor problem and to set its own house in order. No longer would any businessman say with the railroad manipulator, Jay Gould: "Labor is a commodity that will in the long run be governed absolutely by the law of supply and demand." The "law of supply and demand" had been amended on behalf of manufacturers, of bankers, and farmers; now it was amended on behalf of labor.

The Melting Pot

Most Americans have never properly appreciated the rôle of immigration in their history. They think of immigration as a "problem," and usually as one that has come to the fore only in the last half century or so. And when they think of immigrants, they conjure up a picture of olive-skinned Italians or bearded Jews or Polish peasant women with bright shawls coming down the gangplank onto Ellis Island. They do not think of the Pilgrim Fathers or of French Huguenots or of Scotch-Irish; they do not think, even, of poor black folk enduring the hell of the Middle Passage.

Yet all Americans, except Indians, are immigrants or the descendants of immigrants: the Colonial Dames and members of the Order of the Cincinnati as well as the Polish steel workers of Gary or the Negroes of Harlem. Immigrants came, to be sure, at different times, in different circumstances, from different parts of the globe. But all of them went through the same experience of being uprooted from their old homes and transplanted to a new one. All, even the ignorant and lowly, brought their strength, culture, and faith. All of them are ingredients in the giant melting pot of America.

We have already seen something of the various streams that went to make up the population of colonial America. All through the early years of the republic emigration from the Old World to the New continued, most of it voluntary. From 1820, when records were first kept, to the beginning of the Civil War, about five million newcomers from Ireland, England, and Germany threw in their lot with the Americans. Even the war did not seriously retard the stream of immigration, and after Appomattox it swelled to a torrent. The American population of 1870 was, consequently, a very heterogeneous one. Out of one thousand Americans, in that year, 435 were native-born whites of native parentage, 292 native-born whites of foreign or mixed parentage, 144 foreign-born whites, 127 Negroes; one Indian and one Chinaman rounded out the number. Between 1870 and 1920 almost twenty million more immigrants came to the United States. Yet the proportions of the foreign-born and native-born population remained substantially the same. Perhaps the most striking changes were the decline in the relative number of Negroes and the increase in the number of Mexicans.

But one very important fact about the changing character of the American population struck every observer. That was the sharp increase in the number of those whose homes or whose fathers' homes were in the nations of southern and eastern Europe. During the seventies and the eighties the majority of immigrants continued to come from those nations which had in the past furnished so many—Great Britain, Germany, and the Scandinavian countries. But even during these years there was a small stream of the "new" immigration. Enterprising steamship companies established direct connections with Naples, Danzig, Memel, Fiume, and Athens, and retained thousands of agents in Italy, Poland, and the Dual Monarchy to drum up steerage passengers. Enterprising corporations arranged to meet the immigrants at Ellis Island and take them to mining regions or factory towns. As the pressure of population became less acute in Great Britain, Germany, and Scandinavia, the trek to the New World slowed down. But the "new" immigration increased by leaps and bounds. The first decade of the new century, for example, brought only 340,000 immigrants from Ireland, and another 340,000 from Germany, but it brought over two million from Italy and another two million from the states of Austria-Hungary. Before the bars were finally put up, Italy had sent us more than four and a half millions of her sons and daughters, Austria-Hungary four millions, Russia and Poland three and a quarter millions.

To all of these newcomers—to those who fled religious persecution and sought freedom to worship as they would, to those who ran away from military service and from wars,

PERCENTAGE OF FOREIGN-BORN IN U.S. • 1920

0 – 1 %
1 – 5 %
5 – 10 %
10 – 15 %
15 – 20 %
20 – 29 %

to those who longed for a more democratic society, to those who hoped to escape grinding poverty and share in the fabulous riches of the New World—America was the Promised Land. All, whatever their reasons for taking the step, were caught up in the great adventure; all dreamed of a better life, and most of them helped build such a life for themselves and for their children. As President Wilson, who vetoed two bills designed to restrict immigration, wrote:

Has not every ship that has pointed her prow westward borne hither the hopes of generation after generation of the oppressed of other lands? How always have men's hearts beat as they saw the coast of America rise to their view! How it has always seemed to them that the dweller there would be at last rid of kings, of privileged classes, and of all those bonds which had kept men depressed and helpless, and would there realize the full fruition of his sense of honest manhood, would there be one of a great body of brothers, not seeking to defraud and deceive one another, but seeking to accomplish a general good!

Assuredly no commonly shared experience in modern history was more moving, more dramatic, than that first sight of the Statue of Liberty looming up on the horizon, in its arm the beacon flame of hope, on its base that inscription:

Give me your tired, your poor,
Your huddled masses yearning to breathe free,
The wretched refuse of your teeming shore,
Send these, the tempest-tost to me:
I lift my lamp beside the golden door.

The "old" immigration had spread out pretty evenly throughout the North and West, had gone, in about equal numbers, into farming and industry. But because it took money to start a farm, because the best land was gone, because there were jobs in the cities, and colonies of their own people and Catholic churches, the "new" immigrants congregated in the industrial centers of the East and Middle West. By 1900 two thirds of the foreign-born were living in towns and cities, and by 1920 this proportion had increased to three fourths. In New York City were hundreds of thousands of Italians, Poles, Russians, and Jews; Italians and French Canadians lived in large numbers in sedate Boston; Russians in Quaker Philadelphia; Russians and Poles in Cleveland; Scandinavians in St. Paul and Minneapolis; while Chicago presented as variegated a racial pattern as any other city on earth. In small industrial towns like Fall River, Scranton, or Hamtramck, the percentage of foreign-born was even higher than in the larger cities. What this meant was that newcomers from southern and eastern Europe were finding work in the mines, mills, and factories. As early as 1910, for example, three fourths of the coal miners of Pennsylvania were foreign-born, and of these the overwhelming majority were Italians, Poles, and Slovaks. In 1920 the foreign-born constituted one eighth of the total population, but one third of those employed in factories and more than one half of those working in mines.

What did the immigrants contribute? Most of all, themselves—their strength, their work, their faith. They owed much to their adopted country, but that country owed much to them. They did the hard, grueling work that had to be done if the resources of the nation were to be developed rapidly and cheaply. They broke the prairie sod; they laid the tracks of the transcontinentals; they dug the iron ore, coal, copper; they felled the lumber of the Northwest forests. But their contribution was not only that of unskilled labor. They gave richness and color to American life and in some fields added greatly to her cultural heritage. In music and arts they supplied a large part of the creative impulse. In 1930 there was not a major orchestra in the country whose leader bore an Anglo-Saxon name. Any list of distinguished contemporary painters would have to include Jonas Lie, Jerome Myers, Louis Eilshemius, Morris Kantor, Luigi Lucioni, Jon Corbino, and Yasuo Kuniyoshi, while a roll call of American sculptors reads like the football line-up of an urban university: MacMonnies, Saint-Gaudens, Zorach, Bitter, Epstein, Lachaise, Warnecke, Hoffman, Vonnoh, Borglum, and Niehaus. In business and politics, in science and education, the foreign-born and their children have left their imprint.

Yet immigration has created its problems, too. Labor felt it in the form of competition for jobs: as one labor leader said, "Our living is gauged by immigration; our wages are based on immigration; the condition of our family is gauged by immigration." City governments felt it in new problems of housing, sanitation, and police. The school system felt it in the problem of illiteracy and of social adjustment. Yet the assimilation of the foreign-born was not difficult, despite the fears of many representatives of "native stock" who trembled at "accents of menace alien to our air." The average immigrant was pathetically anxious to become an American. The experience which Mary Antin describes in her *Promised Land* was shared by hundreds of thousands of them:

> The apex of my civic pride and personal contentment was reached on the bright September morning when I entered the public school. That day I must always remember, even if I live to be so old that I cannot tell my name. To most people their first day at school is a memorable occasion. In my case the importance of the day was a hundred times magnified on account of the years I had waited, the road I had come, and the

conscious ambitions I entertained. . . . Father himself conducted us to school. He would not have delegated that mission to the President of the United States. He had waited the day with impatience equal to mine, and the visions he saw as he hurried us over the sun-flecked pavements transcended all my dreams. . . . At last the four of us stood around the teacher's desk; and my father, in his impossible English, gave us over in her charge, with some broken word of his hopes for us that his swelling heart could no longer contain.

It was the children of the immigrants, rather than the immigrants themselves, who raised problems of assimilation and adjustment. Many were truly uprooted and demoralized. At home they lived in one world, outside the home in another. They were still tied to the Old World, through their parents—and often through their Church— but this connection was derivative and unreal. With their different appearance and accent, they were not fully accepted by their American companions. Often they revolted against their old inheritance before they had learned to embrace the new. The public school was the great solvent, but sometimes the school accentuated differences instead of rubbing them out. The "second-generation" Americans presented more problems of social maladjustment, of violence and crime, than the first.

Around 1900 there developed a widespread feeling that it was time to call a halt on unrestricted immigration. Labor resented the competition; "old-stock" Americans feared that the racial strain was being debased by so many Slavic and Mediterranean newcomers; the average man thought that the United States had people and problems enough without inviting more. As early as 1882 Congress had stopped immigration from China, and that same year it had excluded those designated as "undesirable"—the sick, the mentally defective, the immoral, anarchists, and others. This may have had some qualitative but it had no quantitative effect; what was needed was a screen which would have both. The formula proposed was the literacy test. As illiteracy was almost nonexistent in the British Isles, Germany, and Scandinavia, while it was very high in Italy, Poland, Russia, and other states of southern and eastern Europe, this seemed to have the advantage of cutting down the total number of "new" immigrants without seriously affecting the "old" immigration.

Three Presidents—Cleveland, Taft, and Wilson—vetoed bills favoring a literacy requirement for admission to the United States, on the ground that this was a test not of ability but of opportunity. In 1917, however, Congress finally had its way. With the end of the World War and the prospect of large-scale emigration from the devastated nations of Europe, the problem appeared one of exclusion rather than mere restriction. In a series of laws, 1921, 1924, and 1929, Congress set a quantitative limit—eventually 150,000—upon those who might come from abroad. The restriction did not apply to immigration from Canada or Mexico or the states of South America, but a strict interpretation of the provisions forbidding the entry of any who might become public charges effectively cut down on immigration from these countries as well.

Thus, by 1930, an era in American history came to an end. The United States was still a melting pot and would so remain for generations to come. But it was no longer the Promised Land to the poor and oppressed of all nations.

Chapter Fifteen

THE WEST COMES OF AGE

Opening Up the Last West

WHILE the South was recovering from the agony of war and the chaos of reconstruction, while the North was gearing its economy to the factory and the machine, changes even more spectacular were taking place in the trans-Missouri West. In 1860 this region, comprising roughly half the total area of the United States, was for the most part a wilderness. The new state of California, to be sure, boasted a population of almost four hundred thousand; in the Willamette Valley were some fifty thousand Oregon pioneers; the Mormon commonwealth, clustered around the Great Salt Lake, numbered another forty thousand; while along the banks of the upper Rio Grande lived a straggling agglomeration of some ninety thousand Pueblo Indians, Mexicans, and white adventurers. The rest of this imperial expanse was the land of the Indians—the warlike Sioux and Blackfoot and Crow of the northern plains, the Ute and Cheyenne and Kiowa of the middle region, the cruel Comanche and Apache of the arid south—the numerous tribes whose names have sung themselves into American folklore. Mounted on fleet ponies, living off the vast herds of buffalo who provided everything from food to fuel, these roamed the plains, mountains, and deserts, undisturbed except by each other or by the mountain lions and coyotes.

Thirty years later all this was changed. The Indians had

been defeated and subjected to the dubious processes of civilization. The bellowing herds of buffalo had been wiped out. Miners had ranged over the whole of the mountain country, panning the clear streams whose very names are poetry—the San Joaquin, the Beaverhead, the Belle Fourche, the Bitter Root, the Sweetwater—tunneling into the earth, establishing feverish little communities in Nevada, Montana, Colorado, and even the Black Hills of Dakota. Railroads had pushed boldly across the unbroken prairie sod, found passes through the towering Rockies, and linked the Atlantic with the Pacific. Cattlemen, taking advantage of free grass, railroads, and new markets, had laid claim to a vast grassland kingdom stretching from the Panhandle of Texas to the upper Missouri, and sheepmen competed with them in the valleys and on the mountain slopes. Then farmers swarmed into the plains and the mountain valleys and closed the gap between the East and the West. By 1890 the frontier was gone, a solid band of states stretched across the continent, and five or six million men and women farmed where the antelope and prairie dog had played.

Why had the conquest of this immense region been so long delayed; why, when it came, did it proceed with such breathless speed? For two centuries Americans had pushed steadily westward from the Atlantic Coast—into the "Old West" of colonial days, across the Appalachians, down the Ohio, and into the Mississippi Valley. By 1850 the frontier of population had reached approximately the ninety-fifth meridian—and there, for the first time in our history, it stopped its progressive march. Instead of moving regularly forward, it leaped the plains and Rockies and established itself along the waters of the Pacific. The explanation lies in geography and climate. European peoples had come from countries of woods and rivers, and they found in the New

From "*Beyond the Mississippi,*" *Albert Richardson*

RAILS ACROSS THE CONTINENT

World woods and rivers and abundant rain for their crops. But the Great Plains confronted them, for the first time in two centuries of experience, with something new. This was the land of little water. Rainfall was scanty, and there were long periods of drought; the streams were shallow and uncertain, and there was little timber for houses or fences. It was no wonder that the early pioneers passed all this by and pushed out to the well-watered, well-timbered Pacific Coast.

Not until the farmer gained tools to adapt himself to a new environment could he hope to conquer the Great Plains. The adaptation came, in time. Railroads provided transportation; barbed wire was made available for fencing; deep-drilled wells and windmills supplied water; dry farming and irrigation solved, in part, the problem of farming where the rainfall was inadequate for the kind of cultivation to which the farmers had been accustomed. With these new tools the pioneer could live, raise crops, and plant permanent communities on the plains. Out of the experience came not only new ways of farming, but also new ways of living—new social and economic and cultural institutions.

The great trans-Missouri West, though largely unsettled, was not unknown. Intrepid pathfinders like Lewis and Clark and John C. Frémont had explored it; trappers and fur traders, working for the Northwest or the Astor fur companies, or on their own, had familiarized themselves with it; merchants and traders along the Santa Fé Trail had opened up the way to the Spanish Southwest; missionaries, Protestant and Catholic alike, had labored with the Indians; pioneers along the Oregon Trail, Saints on the Mormon Trail, fortune hunters on the California Trail, had blazed highways across it; the army had built forts to protect immigrants and traders; surveyors had mapped the country for railway routes; and even as the new era opened President Lincoln was signing a bill providing for the construction of the first transcontinental.

Ever since the forties, visionaries had dreamed of a railroad to span the continent, but not until the rush of population to California did the problem become urgent. After that there was acrimonious debate over its route. Southerners wanted a road that would link lower California and Texas with New Orleans or Memphis; Northerners plumped for a road that would tie the Northwest in with St. Louis or Chicago. Surveys were made, but the controversy was not settled until the withdrawal of the Confederate States gave the Northern advocates a free hand. The Pacific Railway Bill of 1862 incorporated two railroads—the Union Pacific and the Central Pacific. The Union Pacific was to build westward from Council Bluffs, Iowa, the Central Pacific eastward from California, until they met. To make possible so gigantic an undertaking the Federal government gave the two roads some twenty-four million acres of the public domain, and loans which came eventually to about sixty-five million dollars.

Spurred on by these endowments, and by additional gifts from state legislatures, the directors pushed energetically ahead with their plans. A Herculean task confronted them. Some 1700 miles of track had to be laid through a wilderness of prairie, mountain, and desert, inhabited only by hostile Indians. The engineering problem of the Central Pacific was particularly arduous. There was no labor available, and eventually some ten thousand coolies were imported from distant China. Every pound of iron rail, every car, every locomotive, every piece of machinery, had to be shipped around Cape Horn or over the Isthmus of Panama: at one time the company had fifty ships chartered just for this purpose. There were no roads over the Sierras, and thousands of tons of equipment, including massive locomotives, were hauled in giant sleds over the snowdrifts. Food, powder, supplies of all kinds, followed the same toilsome route. Roadways had to be blasted out of cliffs, bridges thrown over gorges, and in the space of sixty miles fifteen tunnels bored through the Sierras. When deep snows threatened to halt all construction, ingenious engineers constructed thirty-seven miles of snowsheds, and under these the work went on.

The engineering task of the Union Pacific was less difficult—in part, perhaps, because in General Grenville Dodge it had one of the greatest living engineers. His labor force was made up of Irish paddies and veterans from the Union and Confederate armies who were quick to exchange picks for rifles when Indians appeared. Under his driving leadership the road pushed out at the rate of two, three, even four miles a day, one construction gang laying ties, another swinging the rails into place and spiking them down. Dodge himself described the achievement with pride:

At one time we were using at least ten thousand animals, and most of the time from eight to ten thousand laborers. The bridge gangs always worked from five to twenty miles ahead of the track, and it was seldom that the track waited for a bridge. To supply one mile of track with material and supplies required about forty cars, as on the plains everything—rails, ties, bridging, fastenings, all railway supplies on the entire work —had to be transported from the Missouri River. Therefore, as we moved westward, every hundred miles added vastly to our transportation. Yet the work was so systematically planned and executed that I do not remember an instance in all the construction of the line of the work being delayed a single week for want of material. Our Indian troubles commenced in 1864 and lasted until the tracks joined at Promontory. We lost most of our men and stock while building from Fort Kearney to Bitter Creek. At that time every mile of road had to be surveyed, graded, tied, and bridged under military protection. The order to every surveying corps, grading, bridging and tie outfit, was never to run when attacked . . . and I do not know that the order was disobeyed in a single instance, nor did I ever hear that the Indians had driven a party permanently from its work.

On April 10, 1869, the two roads joined, at Promontory Point, Utah, and the whole nation joined in the celebration as the marriage was solemnized by the driving of golden and silver spikes. It was a great engineering feat, an epic story of tenacity, ingenuity, and courage. "When I think," wrote Robert Louis Stevenson,

how the railroad has been pushed through this unwatered wilderness and haunt of savage tribes . . . how at each stage of the construction, roaring, impromptu cities, full of gold and lust and death, sprang up and then died away again; how in these uncouth places pigtailed Chinese pirates worked side by side with border ruffians and broken men from Europe, talking together in mixed dialect, mostly oaths, gambling, drinking, quarreling, and murdering like wolves . . . and then when I go on to remember that all this epical turmoil was conducted by gentlemen in frock coats and with a view to nothing more extraordinary than a fortune and a subsequent visit to Paris, it seems to me as if this railway were the one typical achievement of the age in which we live. . . . If it be romance, if it be contrast, if it be heroism that we require, what was Troy town to this?

There were romance and heroism, to be sure, but there were "a fortune and a visit to Paris," too. Indeed the achievement which brought such pride brought at the same time a sense of shame. The directors of the Union Pacific, not content with government largess, organized a dummy construction company and voted that company fraudulent contracts that netted them profits running into millions of dollars. The "Big Four" of the Central Pacific—Huntington, Stanford, Crocker, and Hopkins—organized their own construction company and milked their road to the tune of more than sixty million dollars; each of them left over forty millions at his death. Both groups of directors engaged in wholesale bribery; both groups saddled their roads with such debts that the government had to whistle for its loans and the communities which they served had to pay exorbitant charges for a generation to come.

Meantime other transcontinentals were projected and four completed. Aided by a Congressional grant of forty million acres of public land, Jay Cooke inaugurated and Frederick Billings and Henry Villard completed the Northern Pacific, which, in 1883, linked Lake Superior with Puget Sound. Two other transcontinentals were scarcely less fortunate in land grants—the Santa Fé, which followed the old trail from Kansas into New Mexico and then struck across the desert to lower California; and the Southern Pacific, which ran from New Orleans to Los Angeles and San Francisco. These roads, as well as others which pushed their way into the West, received grants not only from the Federal government, but from states and counties as well. Only one of the transcontinentals was built without any government aid—the Great Northern. This road, the creation of the Canadian-born J. J. Hill, paralleled the Northern Pacific from St. Paul to Seattle. Financially it proved the soundest of them all, and in its economic and social policies the most beneficent.

The Mining and Cattle Kingdoms

It was the miners who established the first outposts of the Far West. The discovery of gold in California had transformed that commonwealth from a pastoral outpost of New Spain to a thriving American state and had opened up new and varied economic activities—farming, shipping, railroading, and manufacturing. That experience was to be repeated again and again in the history of the mining kingdom; in the rush to the Pike's Peak country in 1859, to Alder Gulch and Last Chance in Montana and the banks of the Sweetwater in Wyoming in the middle sixties, to the Black Hills of the Dakota country in the seventies. Everywhere the miners opened up the country, established political communities, and laid the foundations for more permanent settlements. As the gold and silver played out or fell into the hands of eastern corporations and the mining fever abated, the settlers would perceive the farming and stock-raising possibilities around them or find work on the railroads that were pushing in from the East and West. Some communities remained almost exclusively mining, but the real wealth of Montana and Colorado, Wyoming and Idaho, as of California, was in their grass and their soil. Even in mineral wealth the value of the precious metals which had first lured adventurers was shortly exceeded by that of the copper and coal and oil which was so abundant.

The decline of the mining kingdom was as swift as its rise, but it left an indelible impression on the American mind. The mining camps were wonderfully picturesque. A new strike would bring thousands of fortune hunters swarming to some wilderness outpost. Within a few days hundreds of tents and ramshackle huts would rise along the banks of some stream or straggle up the slope of the mountain where the wealth was hidden. Every other house might be a saloon or a dance hall, where bad liquor was dispensed at fifty cents a drink and hurdy-gurdy girls entertained the bewhiskered miners. Lawlessness was not as prevalent as the romantic writers have imagined, but there were few of the amenities of civilization, and the life of the camp was barbarizing. Yet in time, as the home, the school, the church, and the law moved in, the mining communities became orderly enough.

The mining kingdom did more than advertise the agricultural riches of the West, attract settlers, and furnish material to later novelists and moving-picture producers. It precipitated the Indian problem, brought in the railroads, poured a stream of riches into the coffers of Eastern investors, added some two billion dollars of precious metals to the nation's wealth, thus enabling it to redeem its greenbacks in specie, and introduced the "money question" into American politics.

Even while the miners were grubbing in the hills of Nevada and Montana, a new and more important chapter was being written in the history of the West. This was the rise of the cattle kingdom. The physical basis of the kingdom was the grasslands of the West, stretching unbroken from the Rio Grande to the northern frontier, from Kansas and Nebraska into the Rocky Mountain valleys. Here millions of buffaloes had roamed at will, but within two decades the buffalo was to become almost extinct and its place taken by even more millions of Texas longhorns and Wyoming and Montana steers.

For a century Spanish dons and missionaries had raised cattle in northern Mexico, along the Rio Grande, and in the valleys of southern California, but these were valuable only for local consumption and for their tallow and hides. With the coming of the railroads, the establishment of packing houses in St. Louis, Kansas City, Omaha, and Chicago, and the advent of the refrigerator car, it became profitable to improve the breed and drive the cattle north to markets. Beginning immediately after the Civil War, the long drive became an annual institution. Trails were pounded out by the hoofs of tens of thousands of cattle—the Chisholm, the Pecos, the Goodnight, the Bozeman—and roaring cattle towns like Abilene and Cheyenne sprang up at terminal points of the new railroads. Meanwhile cattlemen had found that they could winter the cattle on the rich grasses of the North, and the empire expanded into Colorado, Wyoming, and Montana. Texas had the most cattle, but Wyoming was the most typical cowmen's commonwealth. Here, for years, there was no interest to compete with the cattle interest, and the Wyoming Stock Growers' Association ruled unchallenged.

In the beginning almost anyone could start a herd, by picking up a few cows and calves and letting them graze on public lands. But within a short time the big cattlemen and cattle companies—many of them organized in the East or in Scotland—got control of the industry by helping themselves to the public grasslands or leasing lands from the Indian tribes and fencing in water holes and streams. One cattle company had fenced in one million acres of public land in Colorado; another had entirely surrounded Jones County in Texas; the Cheyenne had leased four million acres of their lands to one group of cattle companies, and the civilized tribes of the Indian Territory had surrendered six million acres to a single company. Cattle barons ruthlessly barred small competitors and waged relentless war on the sheepmen whose sheep cropped the grasses so close that they ruined the pasture.

The cattle kingdom, like the mining, had its romantic side, and the remembrance of this has persisted in the American consciousness. The lonely life on the plain, the roundup, the hieroglyphic brands, the long drive, the stampede, the war with cattle rustlers, the splendid horsemanship, the picturesque costume designed for usefulness, not effect—the wild life of the cow towns like Abilene and Cheyenne, all have found their way into American folklore and song. Children array themselves now in imitation cowboy suits, moving-picture *vaqueros* shoot down rustlers with unerring aim, and street urchins whistle versions of the *Texas Lullaby:*

> *It's a whoop and a yea, get along my little dogies,*
> *For camp is far away.*
> *It's a whoop and a yea and a-driving the dogies.*
> *For Wyoming may be your new home.*

The Coming of the Farmers

Cattle and sheep raising were natural to the High Plains, and many cattlemen were convinced that it would be a mistake for the farmers to attempt to establish themselves in this country. Early in the century Zebulon Pike had reported that "on the rivers Kansas, Platte, Arkansas, and their various branches, it appears to me to be only possible to introduce a limited population . . . the inhabitants would find it most to their advantage to pay attention to the multiplication of cattle, horses, sheep, and goats," and half a century later a United States Senator, opposing the admission of Kansas to the Union, declared that "after we pass the Missouri River, except on a few streams, there is no territory fit for settlement or habitation." These generalizations have proved erroneous, yet subsequent events have revealed that in large sections of the arid West, farming is unprofitable. The cattlemen, in any event, were sure that

they held a title deed from Nature herself to all the grasslands of the West. By fair means or foul they flouted the
land laws, fenced in vast areas, monopolized watercourses,
and tried to stem the advance of the farmer.

But it was a losing fight. Cattlemen might scare off
individual "nesters" but they could not permanently defy
the Federal government, and when Presidents Arthur and
Cleveland ordered the barbed-wire fences cut and the
grasslands thrown open to homesteaders, the game was up.
During the seventies and eighties the railroads had opened
up access to the whole of the plains country and engaged in
large-scale colonizing activities. The Northern Pacific, with
forty million acres to dispose of, flooded Europe with ad-
vertisements describing the almost tropical richness of the
Western soil (hence Jay Cooke's "Banana Belt"), and
Cooke's successor, Villard, had at one time over eight hundred agents abroad drumming up land sales. The Santa Fé
brought in thousands of Russian Mennonites; the Southern
Pacific attracted Germans and Scandinavians; Hill built up
his empire by lending money to impecunious farmers, sub-
sidizing scientific farming, building churches and schools.
Indian resistance was broken, and the remnants of defeated
tribes were harried out of the land or herded into reservations. Factories dotting the edge of the plains region turned
out the millions of miles of barbed wire and the thousands
of windmills and drills which made farming in the arid
land possible. Eight million immigrants poured into the
country, population increased by twenty-two million; the
pressure on the older-settled regions was heightened while
the domestic market for farm produce expanded.

These auspices presiding, the decades of the seventies and
the eighties witnessed a veritable stampede into the plains
country. Hamlin Garland remembered that when he went
to stake out a claim in Dakota:

CHIEF R.R. SYSTEMS 1910

×××× HARRIMAN   +++++ HILL
○○○○○ GOULD   ◇◇◇◇ VANDERBILT
═══ MORGAN   SANTA FE
PENNSYLVANIA

Trains swarming with immigrants from every country of the world were haltingly creeping out upon the
level lands. Norwegians, Swedes, Danes, Scotchmen,
Englishmen, and Russians all mingled in this flood
of land-seekers rolling toward the sundown plain,
where a fat-soiled valley had been set aside by good
Uncle Sam for the enrichment of every man. . . . The
street swarmed with boomers. All talk was of lots, of
land. Hour by hour as the sun sank, prospectors returned to the hotel from their trips into the unclaimed
territory, hungry and tired but jubilant.

Similar scenes were enacted all along the plains. In two
decades Minnesota increased her population threefold, Kansas fourfold, Nebraska eightfold, while Dakota jumped
from fourteen thousand to half a million, and imperial
Texas, with two and a quarter million inhabitants, was
toppling ancient Massachusetts out of sixth place in the
population lists. Altogether during this twenty-year period
the population of the predominantly farming states of
Minnesota, Kansas, Nebraska, the Dakotas, Colorado, and
Montana increased from one million to about five millions
—a rate of increase eight times that of the country as a
whole. As the French traveler, De Tocqueville, had said
half a century earlier, "This gradual and continuous progress of the European race onward toward the Rocky
Mountains had the solemnity of a providential event. It is
like a deluge of men, rising unabatedly, and driven daily
onward by the hand of God."

By the close of the eighties the tidal wave of migration
onto the plains had spent its force and in some places begun
to ebb. Hard times and drought drove many ambitious
farmers out of the arid lands of western Kansas and Nebraska and the Dakotas and back to the East. The rate of
population increase slowed up perceptibly: Nebraska, for

example, gained only four thousand inhabitants during the nineties, Kansas only forty thousand—whereas elsewhere the additions were scarcely greater than could be accounted for by the natural increase of a fertile population.

Yet the most spectacular chapter in the history of the opening of the West was still to be written. For half a century pioneers had gazed hungrily at the rich land between Texas and Kansas, given over as a permanent reservation to the Five Civilized Indian Tribes. By the mid-eighties pressure for the rich bottom lands of the Arkansas, the Canadian, the Red, and the Washita and for the rolling prairie land between them was so strong that the government could no longer resist it. Indian rights were purchased, and in April, 1889, the territory was thrown open to settlement. The rush into the new country was frantic. A newspaper correspondent who witnessed it wrote:

When the word was given to advance at the north line, the boomers started forward at various rates of speed. All who desired to locate anywhere near the track in the north end of the Territory found themselves forestalled. Some turned back in disgust, and others pushed farther on into the interior. . . . What happened when the train began to slacken beggars all description. Boys, middle-aged men, and old fellows threw themselves off the platform and commenced a wild rush. They fell upon each other, scrambled to their feet, and made off, some carrying their grips and others dropping everything in the eagerness of the chase. . . . All roads seemed to lead to the land office at which a line over one hundred yards long was already formed. For a second the runners paused. Then they commenced a wild tear out east, and each man, as he found an unclaimed lot, proceeded to stake it out and hold it down. . . . There was a considerable interval before another train arrived, but the third and fourth came in close together, each discharging its cargo of passengers to add to the astounding crush. Altogether ten trains got in before three o'clock, and making allowance for those who went on to Oklahoma City, there must have been at least six thousand people in Guthrie three hours after the Territory was legally opened for settlement.

A few years later there was a similar rush when the Cherokee Strip of northern Oklahoma was thrown open to settlement. By 1900 this new territory had a population of almost eight hundred thousand.

The mining kingdom and the cattle kingdom had disappeared; now the frontier, too, was gone. There were still mines in the West, to be sure, but they were well-regulated businesses, owned and operated by Eastern corporations. Millions of cattle still ranged over the grasslands from Texas and New Mexico to Montana and the Dakotas, but the open range was gone and cattle raising was just one of a number of economic interests. There was still land in the West, too, but it was for the most part in the mountains or in country so arid that only irrigation could make farming profitable. More and more, in its economic structure, the West was assimilated to the rest of the country.

Politically, too, that assimilation proceeded apace. Nevada had been admitted to statehood as early as 1864—chiefly because Lincoln thought that he might need her electoral votes. Nebraska achieved statehood in 1867, and Colorado came in as the Centennial State in 1876. Then there was a long delay, while the last West filled up and political parties jockeyed for control of the new territories. At last, in 1889–1890, the bars were let down and an Omnibus Bill admitted six Western states—the two Dakotas, Wyoming, Montana, Idaho, and Washington. Utah, long populous enough for statehood but regarded with suspicion because of Mormon control, came in a few years later; Oklahoma in 1907, and the two Southwestern states of Arizona and New Mexico in 1912. Thus the political boundaries of the nation were drawn in their permanent pattern, and the process so auspiciously inaugurated with the Northwest Ordinance of 1787 was brought to completion.

In their political organization the Western commonwealths resembled the Eastern. The familiar form of government—a tripartite division of powers, a bicameral legislature, the town and county system of local administration—was everywhere adopted. In some respects, however, the new state constitutions did differ from the older ones. They were far more detailed, more carefully drawn, and on the whole more liberal. Most of them provided for some form of woman suffrage, prohibited trusts and monopolies, regulated railways, and established progressive labor standards. Yet neither the philosophy that inspired them nor the energy that animated them was fundamentally different from that common to the whole of the United States.

Life on the Last Frontier

The frontier had always spelled hardship and danger, and the last frontier was no exception. For the men and women who left the towns or the wooded farms of the East to try their luck on the High Plains, life was always hard and often bitterly disappointing. The work was harder, the rewards more meager, than on the farms of the Ohio or Mississippi valleys. For some the limitless prairie, stretching out to the farthest horizon, the great billowing clouds, the gorgeous sunsets, had their own beauty, but for most the plains seemed drab and monotonous. In the summer the burning sun beat down remorselessly on the plowmen or the harvesters, and the dry, hot winds sweeping up from the south made even the nights all but unbearable. The winter descended swiftly and with cruel cold, temperatures dropping to twenty and thirty below zero; blinding blizzards sometimes raged for days on end, leaving the carcasses of thousands of cattle strewn over the prairie, killing or maiming men and women unfortunate enough to be caught in them; sometimes men got lost fumbling their way from their house to their barn.

The men had their work and their ambitions; the drudgery and loneliness bore hardest on the women. Many of them, reared in comfort back East, made their first homes in dugouts or sod cabins, dark and badly ventilated, the windows and doors covered with blankets or hides, every rain making puddles on the bare floor. The rude frame houses that succeeded these primitive structures were more comfortable but scarcely less ugly. Set out on a treeless prairie, small, hastily built, painted a dull leaden gray, they were hot in summer, cold in winter, cheerless all the time. The trees and bushes and flowers that had been part of even the poorer farms of the East were missing, though in time some were planted and—when water was available—tended. There was little water to spare for gardening, however, little to spare even for house cleaning and washing. In times of drought, when the corn dried up and the vines withered and the wells gave out and the south wind blew a flinty dust into every corner and crevice of the house and the temperature stayed up in the nineties day and night, even the most courageous lost heart. Stuart Henry remembered the effect of the drought of '74 in Kansas:

One knew how the women slouched around red-hot cookstoves three times a day for the regular if skimpy meals. Some strength must be kept up, some flesh must be kept on bones. Even wives who had had a little

pardonable vanity left quit trying to save their com-
plexions. They let their tresses go dry and stick out
any way. Hair got crinkly, few bothering much about
brushes and combs. Hollow-eyed, fagged out, the fair
sex came to care little how they looked, what they
wore. . . . Men swore, and played poker no more.
Fathers dreaded to face their children, who grew rag-
geder. As for their dirtiness, who, you might ask,
hardly dared spare water to wash them? Husbands
hated to go home to meals, for they must meet the
appeals of their wives to climb on wagons and strike
out for back home.

Almost worse than the heat and dirt and drudgery were
the loneliness and isolation. Cut off from the pleasures of
social intercourse, the consolations of the church, the help
of doctors, many a frontier wife—like Beret in Ole Röl-
vaag's great *Giants in the Earth*—became unbalanced. Children were born with the aid of kindly neighbors—or
often without any aid; infant mortality, as the pathetic
little cemeteries bore witness, was cruelly high. Sickness
was always dreaded, for medical aid was hard to come by
and costly. The ague, transmitted by the mosquitoes which
bred in swamps and stagnant pools, was all but universal;
polluted water caused typhoid; cholera, pneumonia, and
measles were common, while accidents took a heavy toll.
Harassed country doctors performed heroic operations,
often without anesthetics and with the crudest of surgical
instruments. Everett Dick tells of one young doctor who
performed his first appendectomy without anesthetic, and
by the light of a kerosene lamp; when the lamp broke the
operation was continued in the flickering light of a smoking
flame.

Life in the towns offered more variety and sociability,
but it too was drab and isolated. The typical plains town

of this period was a small and tentative affair, its inhabitants dreaming of a magnificent future but ready to pack up and move to a more promising location at a moment's notice. Picture a narrow muddy street, with wooden sidewalks ending abruptly at the edge of the prairie, lined on either side with a row of ramshackle frame houses, their gray paint blistered by the sun. The most prominent structures are the saloons, the general store, the livery stable, the hotel, and the station where everyday the townsfolk gather to await the train that brings in the newspapers and magazines, the mail-order catalogues, the letters from friends and family back East, the occasional drummer or loan agent or grain buyer. At one end of the street is a church—usually Methodist or Baptist or Presbyterian— where once a month a hard-pressed and poorly paid clergyman dispenses hell-fire and brimstone. Across from it, set back in a square ill-kempt yard, is the grammar school, a rude two-roomed affair, with wooden benches for the scholars, a chair and a desk for the teacher—some young lad back from a year at the normal school or some spinster or widow lady in need of a job. A few of the more progressive townsfolk have planted trees, and here and there a row of sunflowers or hollyhocks or a morning-glory vine shows where some housewife has made a brave attempt to create beauty. Children, clad in calico or denim, play in the back yards or gaze in fascination at the work of the blacksmith; bewhiskered men, in the ubiquitous overalls, lounge in the general store or at the livery stable, talking over the prospect for crops or the price of corn or chewing the cud of politics.

There is little crime or vice, but a good deal of drunkenness and—on Saturday night, when the farm boys come in after a week of labor—numerous brawls. Occasionally there is a big gathering, on the Fourth of July or at a

EMIGRANTS TO THE WEST

Grange picnic, when all the townsfolk and the farmers from far around hitch up their horses and buggies and ride out to the banks of the nearest river for a prolonged celebration. Everett Dick describes such a Fourth of July celebration at Blue Springs, Nebraska:

A committee of three was appointed to catch catfish . . . by the Fourth these men had over a thousand pounds of large catfish penned up in the mouth of a nearby creek. . . . Another committee of three built a brush canopy and secured boards at a sawmill for a forty foot table and a dance platform. A large pile of logs was gathered from the timber for fuel. The promotors sent to Brownsville, forty miles away, for a two hundred and fifty pound hog which furnished an abundance of lard to fry the fish. A corn crusher was improvised of sheet iron. There was much good cornbread even though the meal was not grated fine nor bolted. There was a sumptuous repast of catfish and corn dodger with a little white bread which a few had brought for dessert. On the afternoon of the third people began to come. By the next day there were one hundred and fifty people. They came walking, riding in ox wagons, and any way they could get there. The ladies were dressed in sunbonnets and plain dresses. There was but one silk dress in the whole crowd; some of the men were barefoot. The flag was run to the top of a pole seventy feet high; the Declaration of Independence was read; and after a sumptuous meal had been served, the fiddles, brought from over an area of eighty miles, were tuned up and the dance began. This lasted until broad daylight of the fifth, when the settlers wended their way back to their lonely homes, thinking of this bright event, an oasis in the desert of dreary frontier life.

Some of these little towns flourished. Streets and sidewalks were paved, brick and stone replaced the wooden structures, a new hotel, an opera house, banks and stores, a high school, all testified to prosperity and civic pride. Others languished and died; in Kansas alone two thousand geographical names have disappeared from the map. The success or failure of a frontier town was determined pretty much by the railroad—and by politics; and the county-seat wars of the plains country were notorious. As the *New York Tribune* described it:

The existence of the western Kansas court house is at best transitory and uncertain. The golden morning sunlight floods it in Pottawatomie City, but its lengthening evening shadow falls across the streets of Little Paradise Valley. One day the stray swine of Occidental City seek its hospitable shade, the next some predatory calf in Big Stranger bunts open the back door and eats a deed and two mortgages while the register is taking a nap. Today we mark it in Grand Junction with a new front door painted yellow, and the gable end blown off by the last tornado, but tonight a band of determined men will come from Rattle Snake Crossing and haul it away with a yoke of oxen, with the mayor and city council of Rattle Snake pushing on the end of the court house. The Kansas court house is the Wandering Jew among public institutions.

This last frontier, like earlier frontiers, was thoroughly democratic. Most of the new communities adopted some form of woman suffrage—Wyoming had led the way as early as 1869. Some of the new constitutions provided for the initiative, and the referendum on public questions, and most officials—even judges—were chosen by popular election. Democracy was most apparent, however, in social rather than in political relationships. Anyone who dressed better than his neighbors, who put on airs, who flaunted domestic help, was looked upon with suspicion. The banker, the storekeeper, the lawyer, the farmer, and the liveryman sat together in their shirt sleeves in the town square and occupied the same benches in church, and all children went to public schools and the more ambitious of the young men and women to near-by denominational colleges or to the normal schools and state universities that were early provided by every Western commonwealth. Many races mingled in these frontier communities—British, Germans, Norwegians, Bohemians, a sprinkling of Jews, along with native Americans from bordering states; and there was universal toleration for differences of race, language, and creed. In many respects this last frontier was the most democratic and the most American of all frontiers.

Chapter Sixteen

THE FARMER AND HIS PROBLEMS

The Agricultural Revolution

THE industrial revolution has long been considered the basic fact of modern history. The revolution in agriculture, however, was just as important. The triumphs of the iron-makers, the railroad builders, the engineers, the captains of industry, and the masters of finance have excited the imagination of two generations of Americans, but the triumphs of the farmers and the "hunger fighters," if less spectacular, have been no less remarkable. Of course the two revolutions—the industrial and the agricultural—were interdependent. Without machinery and railroads, the agricultural revolution could not have taken place; without the flood of grain flowing into the warehouses of the great cities, the industrial revolution would not have been possible. For centuries men had struggled to raise enough food for their sustenance, and the growth of population itself had been controlled by the amount of food available. For centuries the specter of famine had been a familiar one, and famine itself had exacted its toll of millions of lives: it was one of the Four Horsemen of the Apocalypse and perhaps the most dreaded. The nineteenth century freed most of mankind from the haunting fear of inadequate food, and for that emancipation American farms were largely responsible.

In the forty years from 1860 to 1900 the farm acreage of the United States doubled, and the acreage of land actually under cultivation trebled. In other words, twice as much land was brought under cultivation in this one generation as in the previous two hundred years of our history. Production more than kept pace with this increase in acreage. The two million farms of 1860 produced something under 200 million bushels of wheat, a little less than one billion bushels of corn, and about four million bales of cotton; the six million farms of 1900 raised over 655 million bushels of wheat, well over two and one-half billion bushels of corn, and almost ten million bales of cotton. In this same period the population of the nation more than doubled—and most of the increase went to the cities—but the American farmer grew enough grain and cotton and raised enough beef and pork and clipped enough wool not only to supply American workers but to send ever-increasing surpluses to feed and clothe Europeans.

Two basic factors largely explain this extraordinary achievement. The first was the expanse of the agricultural domain into the West; the second the application of machinery and science to the processes of farming. With the first we are already somewhat familiar. The new West of the plains and the mountain valleys was predominantly a farming region, and within a miraculously short time it took the lead in the agricultural production of the whole country. The wheat belt moved westward from the states along the Ohio River to the Missouri Valley. Illinois, Indiana, Wisconsin, Ohio, Virginia, and Pennsylvania were the leading wheat-producing states in 1860; by 1900 only Ohio still lingered uncertainly among the six leaders, and a decade later it too had disappeared from the list. The shift in corn production was not quite so striking, but here, too, the movement was from the Ohio to the Mississippi Valley. The story of cotton is much the same: by the turn of the century Texas was far in the lead among the states, and not far from half the total cotton crop was raised west of the Mississippi. And during these same years the armies of cattle and sheep moved irresistibly onto the grazing lands of the plains and the mountains.

This westward movement of farming spelled hardship, of course, for the farmers of the East and the seaboard South. Unable to compete with the rich virgin soil of the West, burdened with higher taxes and investment charges, farming in these regions entered upon a decline from which it has never entirely recovered. Much of tidewater Virginia was given over to broom sedge and became that Barren Ground which Ellen Glasgow has described in her novel; large areas in Pennsylvania and New York reverted to wilderness or to a playground for vacationers. Hundreds of thousands of acres of New England were abandoned to brush and forest: in the half century after the Civil War, farm land under cultivation in this section declined by almost fifty per cent. A traveler through New England wrote:

> Midway between Williamstown [Massachusetts] and Brattleboro [Vermont] I saw on the summit of a hill against the evening sky what seemed a large cathedral. Driving thither, I found a huge old-time two story church, a large academy, a village with a broad street, perhaps 150 feet in width. I drove on and found that the church was abandoned, the academy dismantled, the village deserted. The farmer who owned the farm on the north of the village lived on one side of the broad street, and he who owned the farm on the south lived on the other, and they were the only two inhabitants. All of the others had gone—to the manufacturing villages, to the great cities, to the West. Here had been industry, education, religion, comfort and con-

tentment, but there remained only a dreary solitude of forsaken homes.

Territorial expansion alone could not account for the sharp upswing in farm production, which was out of proportion to the increase in land under cultivation or of men engaged in farming. The explanation lies rather in the increased efficiency of farming. It was a curious fact that the mechanization of agriculture lagged considerably behind the mechanization of industry. The factory hand and the miner of 1800 were using tools unknown to their fathers and grandfathers, but the farmer of 1800 tilled the soil much as had his ancestors a thousand years earlier. His plow was a crude wooden or iron contrivance pulled by a single horse or ox; he sowed wheat and planted corn and potatoes by hand; he weeded with a hoe, harvested his grain with sickle or scythe, flailed it on the floor of his barn, shucked and shelled his corn by hand. It was as much as a family could manage to farm eight or ten acres, even when the womenfolk and the children turned in to help.

The first important American invention—Eli Whitney's cotton gin—profoundly affected agriculture and worked a revolution in the whole economy of the South. Yet the cotton gin had to do with the processing rather than the growing of cotton. Actually, except for such operations as plowing, cultivating, and spraying, cotton has remained relatively immune to machinery. Other crops were more fortunate, but for most of them, the application of machinery was long delayed. Yet there was incessant experimentation. The story of the plow is typical. The first patent for a plow was taken out in 1797, and since that time some twelve thousand more have been issued. The initial problem was to find a plow that could cut and turn the soil cleanly, without becoming clogged with earth or breaking against roots and stones. Jefferson experimented, and his mold-board, designed to cut resistance to a minimum, won the gold medal of the Royal Agricultural Society of Paris. In 1837, John Deere, on the prairie of Illinois, faced his wooden plows with steel sufficiently tough to break the virgin sod, and soon his products were in wide demand. The Oliver chilled plow, which came on the market in the late sixties, combined a smooth steel surface with a tough iron base and seemed to answer all the needs of the prairie farmers. Thereafter improvements were legion, and in 1900 the Department of Agriculture reported that

> we have sulky plows, gang plows, plows combined with harrow cultivators and with seed drills, sidehill plows, vineyard plows, beet plows, subsoil plows, doubleland-side plows, and lastly, what has been the aim, and seems to be the end, of plow invention, we have the steam gang plow combined with a seeder and a harrow, which has reduced the time required for human labor (in plowing, sowing, and harrowing) to produce a bushel of wheat, on an average from 32.8 minutes in 1830 to 2.2 minutes at the present time.

The story of the reaper is even more significant. The farmer of 1800, using a hand sickle, could hope to cut half an acre of wheat a day if he worked hard enough; with the cradle, thirty years later, he might cut two acres a day. But with such primitive tools he could not grow grain on a large scale, and he could not have invaded the plains country of the West. Early in the 1830's two farmers were experimenting with a mechanical reaper, Obed Hussey and Cyrus McCormick; and by 1840 both were performing the miracle of cutting five or six acres of wheat a day with their curious machines. Hussey moved to Baltimore to make and market his reaper; McCormick, more farsighted, headed west to the young prairie town of Chicago. Here, in 1847, he established his reaper factory and began turning out machines. By the Civil War the McCormick works had sold a quarter of a million reapers, and by supplying a machine that would release men for the army, this transplanted Virginian had done as much to insure Union victory as had any general.

Every year witnessed some improvement in the reaper. The backbreaking task of gathering up the grain and binding it into sheaves was eliminated by a moving platform upon which the grain was deposited into the hands of men who stood on a footboard and bound it up. Then in 1872 came an automatic wire binder and a few years later the Appleby twine binder. Meanwhile threshing machines had been perfected, and in the sixties and seventies these giant monsters, each with its thrashing gang, moved from farm to farm along the Middle Border. Herbert Quick describes the scene on an Iowa farm:

All rules were suspended during thrashing time. The morning when the McConkeys began thrashing, the house was aroused and alive at three o'clock, electrified by the arrival of the machine, which had run late the evening before at a neighbor's and was pulled in before dawn. . . . The great red machine stood between the high, hive-shaped stacks. The ten horses were standing hitched to the five long wooden sweeps of the horse-power. The driver stood on the board platform in the center with his long whip in his hand. The pitchers had climbed the stacks with their forks, the handles polished by long contact with hard hands, their three tines inserted into the top sheaves of the stack. . . . A deep growl, like that of a bulldog magnified fifty diameters, filled the air, and as the cylinder gathered speed it rose from a bass to a baritone, and then to a tenor of a volume which sang over four square miles of haze-obscured prairie. The feeder looked up at the pitchers, saw the man who pitched to the machine, with his next bundle ready to fall on the table, saw Frank with his band-cutter's knife ready to slice softly through the band of it, and then, he moved the first two sheaves gently over between the open lips, deftly twitched their butts upward, and the great operation was on.

In the eighties came the revolutionary reaper-thresher, or combine, which reaped, threshed, cleaned, and bagged the grain all in a single continuous operation. Drawn by twenty or forty horses—later by a steam or gasoline tractor—it could harvest seventy or eighty acres in a single day.

In every department of agriculture, with the notable exception of cotton picking, machinery came to the aid of the farmer. Mechanical corn planters, corn cutters, huskers, and shellers, the de Laval cream separator, the manure spreader, the potato planter, the hay drier, the poultry incubator, the fertilizer, and a hundred other inventions immensely lightened the labor of the "man with a hoe" and increased his efficiency. With the combines four men could do the work formerly done by three hundred—and do it better. The cornhusker replaced eight men with one, the corn sheller fifty; the time required to harvest a ton of hay was reduced by four fifths. And the twentieth-century application of steam, gasoline, and electricity to farming released millions of acres formerly devoted to pasturage and still further cut down human labor and increased agricultural efficiency.

It was the Middle West and the Far West that absorbed most of the new harvesters and threshers and tractors as fast as they could be manufactured. In the East, farms were too small, agriculture too diversified, to justify investment in expensive machinery; in the South, cotton and tobacco did not yield to mechanized cultivation and labor was cheap. The value of farm machinery increased from a quarter of a billion dollars in 1860 to three and a half billions in 1920, but most of this increase came in the region west of the Mississippi. The farmers of Iowa alone, in 1920, had a larger investment in machinery than did the farmers of all New England and the Middle Atlantic states combined; the average value of machinery on a South Dakota farm was $1500; on each of the farms of the cotton belt, $215.

The mechanization of farming made it possible for the farmer to feed a growing number of city dwellers and to send abroad a surplus which in turn helped finance industrial and railroad expansion. For the farmers themselves it was not an unmixed blessing. It involved many of them in expenditures heavier than they could afford, forced them to expand their operations to justify those investments, and to concentrate on staple crops. It gave the large farmers a distinct advantage over their small competitors and hastened, at once, the development of "bonanza" farming and of tenancy. The small self-sufficient farm of the fifties, with its fields of wheat, corn, and oats, its vegetable patch, its henhouse and pigpen, its eight or ten cows pasturing in the meadow, gave way to the large wheat or cotton holdings of the twentieth century, dependent even for food supplies on the grocery store.

Scarcely less important than machinery was science. From the beginning American agriculture was extensive rather than intensive, for it seemed easier to take up new land than to preserve the old. Yet the rapid exhaustion of the soil of the tidewater South frightened the planters, and Washington and Jefferson were merely the most prominent of the many Southerners who attempted to meet this crisis by introducing new plants, rotating crops, and improving their livestock. "The greatest service which can be rendered to any country is to add a useful plant to its culture," wrote Jefferson. But these early reforms were largely in vain, for the opening up of the vast trans-Appalachian lands and the invention of the cotton gin made it more profitable for farmers to move on to fertile lands than to attempt to restore the fertility of old soil by more careful husbandry. The "mining" of new land, perhaps an inevitable part of the frontier economy, was to be repeated again and again on successful frontiers.

The Federal government made its first appropriation specifically for agriculture in 1839; but the real beginning of government interest dates from the passage of the Morrill Land-Grant College Act of 1862. This provided an endowment for agricultural and industrial colleges out of the public domain: for each Congressman that it sent to Washington a state was entitled to thirty thousand acres of land. Under this act, state after state established agricultural colleges independently or in connection with a state university, and these eventually pushed research in scientific farming. Equally important was the Hatch Act of 1887, appropriating generous funds for the creation of agricultural experiment stations throughout the Union. At the same time direct appropriations for the research activities of the Department of Agriculture mounted into the millions of dollars. By 1930 some seven or eight thousand scientists were working for these various governmental agencies on a bewildering variety of research projects, and contributions of the most far-reaching importance were coming from their experimental farms and laboratories.

Typical of these "hunger fighters" was Mark Alfred Carleton, who brought the great Kubanka and Kharkov wheats to western America. Farming and teaching in Kansas, Carleton saw, year after year, how the drought and the black rust killed off all but the hardiest wheat that the plains farmers could grow. But he saw, too, that the Russian Mennonites, whom the Santa Fé Railroad had brought in to settle on its lands, had better luck with their wheat, and he discovered that they grew it from seed which they had brought all the way from their homelands. All wheat was, after all, an importation; and Carleton was convinced that the secret of hardy, drought- and rust-resisting grain was to be found somewhere in the Ukraine or the steppes of Eurasia.

In 1898, with the blessing of the Department of Agriculture, he headed for this Promised Land. Finally, in the Turgai steppes, just west of the Ural River—where climate and topography were strikingly like that of western Kansas —he found what he was looking for: the Kubanka wheat. On the plains it grew more bushels to the acre than the Fife and Blue Stem and proved miraculously immune to the black rust. But it was in the region from Minnesota north to the Saskatchewan that the Kubanka scored its greatest triumphs; curiously enough, it did not take to the southern plains. So once more Carleton betook himself to Russia, and in the Ukraine, near that Kharkov where forty years later Germans and Russians were to slaughter each other by the thousand, he found the Kharkov wheat. By 1914 half the winter wheat of the country was of the Kubanka or Kharkov varieties.

Other hunger fighters made scarcely less important contributions. Marion Dorset conquered the dread hog cholera and George Mohler the mysterious hoof-and-mouth disease which had worked such havoc with cattle. From North Africa J. H. Watkins brought back the Kaffir corn, and from Turkestan Niels Hansen imported the yellow-flowered alfalfa. Luther Burbank, in his California laboratories, produced scores of new fruits and vegetables, and David R. Coker, on his South Carolina experimental farm, proved that long-staple cotton could grow in the piedmont and upland country. At the University of Wisconsin Stephen Babcock invented a milk test for determining the butter-fat content of milk. The Negro scientist, George Washington Carver, working at the Tuskegee Institute, found hundreds of new uses for familiar products like the peanut, the sweet potato, and the soybean. And Seaman Knapp rescued the rice industry from its postwar decline by introducing new varieties from the Orient and inaugurated a far-flung system of demonstration farms which pointed the way to improved agricultural methods throughout the South.

Hard Times on the Farm

With every year the American farmer tilled the soil more efficiently and raised larger crops. Industrious, intelligent, blessed with rich land, ingenious machinery, and ready markets, he should have been prosperous and happy. But his lot was hard and grew steadily harder. At the close of the most wonderful century of agricultural expansion in all history the farmers, instead of being the "chosen people of God"—as Jefferson phrased it—had become a major economic problem. What is the explanation of this paradox?

The farm problem is complex, presenting itself to the Southern planter, the grain grower, the corn and hog farmer, the cattleman, the dairyman, and the orchardist in very different guises. It appeared at one time as a railroad problem, at another as a money question, and at still another as a question of land policy; it involved sectional interests, party programs, and international relations. Yet basic to almost every aspect of the farm problem were certain unchanging factors. Chief among them were the exhaustion of the soil, the vagaries of nature, overproduction of staple crops, decline in self-sufficiency, and lack of adequate legislative protection and aid.

The soil of the South had long been exhausted by tobacco and cotton culture and by the use of ignorant farm labor. In the older parts of that section millions of acres reverted to scrub, while water running down undammed gullies washed away millions of tons of rich topsoil every year. Something of the cumulative impoverishment of the Southern soil is suggested by the fact that the South uses seventy per cent of all the fertilizer sold in this country and that the expenditures of South Carolina farmers for fertilizer come to one fourth the value of their cotton crop. In the West, too, erosion and wind storms ravaged the land. Much of the High Plains was unsuitable for farming or even for the kind of grazing that was practiced there, and where the land was overfarmed or overgrazed the "dust bowl" spread.

Recurring droughts, too, spelled disaster to the plains farmers. Over a period of sixteen months, in 1859–1860, not one good rain brought relief to the farmers of Kansas and Nebraska, and the ruined pioneers who had come out with such high hopes had to be rescued by Eastern charity. That experience, though rarely in so drastic a form, was to be common enough on the plains, and sometimes the drought lasted for several years.

Scarcely less menacing were the insect pests and plant diseases. Of the insects the boll weevil was undoubtedly the worst. This scourge, crossing the Rio Grande from Texas in 1892, thereafter progressed at about fifty miles a year until it had infested the whole cotton kingdom. The farmers of Enterprise, Alabama, erected a monument to it for its success in forcing diversification of crops, but during the years of its worst ravages it cut cotton production over wide areas by more than fifty per cent. There was more truth than poetry in the *Ballet of de Boll Weevil*:

> *Boll weevil say to de preacher:*
> *"Bettah close up dem church doors,*
> *When I get through wid de farmer,*
> *Can't pay de preacher no mo'*
> *I have a home, I have a home."*

> *Boll weevil say to de farmer:*
> *"You can ride in dat Fohd machine.*
> *But w'en I get through wid yo' cotton,*
> *Can't buy no gasoline,*
> *Won't have no home, won't have no home."*

All efforts to eradicate the weevil have been in vain, and only by early planting and the lavish use of poison can the cotton farmers hold it in check.

The insect pests of the plains were legion, but the most terrifying was doubtless the grasshopper. It was in 1874 that the plains farmers had their first experience with the grasshopper plague—an experience that was to be repeated again and again. Stuart Henry described how the 'hoppers

> ate up every bit of green vegetation from the Rocky Mountains to and beyond the Missouri River. I recall that when coming home late one afternoon for supper I stepped back surprised to see what became known as the Rocky Mountain locusts covering the side of the house. Already inside, they feasted on the curtains. Clouds of them promptly settled down on the whole country—everywhere, unavoidable. People set about killing them to save gardens, but this soon proved ridiculous. Specially contrived machines, pushed by horses, scooped up the hoppers in grainfields by the barrelful to burn them. This, too, was nonsensical. Vast hordes, myriads. In a week grain fields, gardens,

shrubs, vines, had been eaten down to the ground or
to the bark. Nothing could be done. You sat by and
saw everything go.

The chinch bug, corn borer, and alfalfa weevil were almost
equally destructive.

The farmer was selling in a world market—in competition with the farmers of Russia, the Argentine, Canada,
Australia—and buying in a protected market. The price
he got for wheat, or cotton, or beef was determined in
Liverpool; the price he paid for his harvester, his fertilizer,
his barbed wire, his shoes and clothes, his lumber and furniture, was fixed by trusts operating behind a protective
tariff. His costs were going inexorably up—the cost of what
he used on the farm, the cost of freight, the cost of the
money he borrowed, the cost of government. Fresh land
and machinery enabled him to produce more every year,
but his income was not going up appreciably. In the years
of greatest agricultural expansion, 1870–1890, the value of
American farm products increased only half a billion dollars; in this same period the value of manufactures increased
by six billion dollars. Prices of most farm products moved
irregularly downward. Wheat that brought a dollar a bushel
throughout the seventies fell to fifty cents in the mid-
nineties. Cotton declined from seventeen cents a pound in
1873 to nine cents twenty years later, and then tumbled to
six. Substantially the same story could be told for corn,
oats, barley, tobacco, and other farm produce: the average
value per acre of ten leading crops was fourteen dollars in
the early seventies, nine dollars in the early nineties.

Perhaps the most serious of all the economic handicaps
under which the farmer labored was the rising cost of
money. When he went to the local banker or mortgage
agent to borrow money he found that he was expected to
pay from eight to twenty per cent on his loan. The situa-

tion came home to him in an even more injurious fashion in declining prices. If we think in terms of the cost of the dollar rather than the cost of farm commodities we can more readily understand this. In 1870 the farmer could buy a dollar with a bushel of wheat, two bushels of corn, or ten pounds of cotton. By 1890 it took two bushels of wheat, four bushels of corn, or fifteen pounds of cotton to buy a dollar. The farmer who borrowed a thousand dollars in 1870 could repay his loan with a thousand bushels of wheat; if he let the mortgage run to 1890 it cost him two thousand bushels of wheat to get rid of it.

In the face of these adverse conditions it is not surprising that the mortgage indebtedness of the American farmer increased by leaps and bounds. By 1890 over ninety thousand farms in Illinois were mortgaged, one hundred thousand in Nebraska, and still more in Kansas. Most of these mortgages were held in the East; inhabitants of New Hampshire alone had some twenty-five million dollars in Western mortgages. Tenancy, too, was on the upgrade. The average for the whole country was twenty-eight per cent, but in the South and the West the proportion was appreciably higher.

These were the chief ingredients of the farm problem. The failure of the farmer to use the government as an instrument to protect his interests was as much a consequence as a cause of his malaise. Although farmers constituted half the population of the nation, they rarely sent one of their number to Congress or even to the state legislatures, and when in the early nineties farmers like Senator Peffer and Congressman Simpson did get to Washington they were looked upon as curiosities. Men who wrote the national laws were much more zealous to serve the interests of manufacturers, bankers, and railroad men than to take care of the farmers, and legislation reflected this zeal. The protective tariff may have helped business, but it made the farmer pay more for almost everything that he bought. The banking and currency legislation written into the statute books was a boon to bankers and investors, but a terrible burden to farmers. Laws designed to regulate trusts and railroads were so written or interpreted that they caused little inconvenience to those interests, and when agrarian states tried their hand at stricter laws, courts threw them out. Even legislation designed ostensibly to assist the farmer, such as the Homestead Act, proved disappointing; up to 1890 more land had been sold directly or through railroads and speculators than had gone to homesteaders.

Thirty years after Appomattox, then, the American farmer had expanded his domain over the whole continent and, with the latest machinery and the help of science, increased his production to the point where he was ready to feed the Western world. And he was on the road to peasantry.

The Farmers Organize

Business, banking, even labor, were organizing; it was high time for the farmer to follow their example. Yet nothing was more difficult. The farming interest consisted of millions of units, each operating separately, each in a sense competing; the farmer was naturally an individualist who did not take kindly to outside control; and neither the soil nor the weather could be effectively regulated. In the end, control of farm production did not come until the Federal government took charge. Meanwhile, if the farmer expected to save himself from exploitation by railroads, trusts, mortgage companies, and middlemen, he had to take action.

The first nation-wide farmer organization was the Grange, or Patrons of Husbandry. In 1866 a government clerk, Oliver Kelley, made a long trip through the war-ravaged South, and what he saw persuaded him that the poverty, backwardness, and isolation of the farmer could be ameliorated only by common action. With a few friends he organized the Patrons of Husbandry, a social and educational order designed "to develop a higher and better manhood and womanhood among ourselves. To enhance the comforts and attractions of our homes and strengthen our attachments to our pursuits. . . . To make our farms self-sustaining." A few Granges, as the local branches were called, were set up in New York and Pennsylvania, but as long as the order remained in the East it made little progress. In 1869 its headquarters were moved out to the Middle West, and during the hard times of the early seventies it spread like wildfire. By 1873 there were Granges in almost every state, and membership had reached three quarters of a million. Its greatest strength was in the Middle West, but it flourished in the South, too, and along the Pacific Coast.

Kelley's idea was that the Grange should be chiefly a social organization. Women were admitted as well as men; an elaborate ritual was copied in part from the Masonic; there were to be monthly meetings devoted to education, patriotic celebrations, and festivities. The great object was to break down the isolation of the farmer, introduce color and interest into his life, bring about an interchange of views, and build up a solidarity of interest. In all this the Grange was highly successful. Grange papers found a wide circulation, Grange libraries distributed farm publications, Grange lecturers addressed meetings in country schoolhouses, and Grange picnics became an established institution. Hamlin Garland, recalling one of these picnics, wrote:

It was grand, it was inspiring—to us, to see those long lines of carriages winding down the lanes, joining one to another at the cross-roads, till at last all the granges from the northern end of the county were united in one mighty column advancing on the picnic ground, where orators awaited our approach with calm dignity and high resolution. Nothing more picturesque, more delightful, more helpful, has ever risen out of American rural life.

But it was inevitable that when farmers came together, even for fun, they should talk business and politics. Talk led to action, and soon many of the state Granges set up co-operative marketing organizations, stores, loan agencies, and even factories. These were not always well run and they encountered from the beginning fierce opposition from established business. Yet they saved their members a good deal of money: the Iowa Grange, for example, shipped five million bushels of grain to Chicago at savings of from ten to forty per cent and by co-operative buying saved its members one hundred dollars on each reaper that they bought. To meet this kind of competition, and to serve directly the needs of the Grangers, the mail-order house of Montgomery Ward was established.

Of course the Grangers went into politics, too, notwithstanding the prohibition against political discussion or action in their Constitution. In a number of Midwestern states they elected their members to the legislature and pushed through so-called "Granger laws" regulating railroads and warehouses. But nowhere did the Grangers organize as a political party, nor did they build up anything like the later "farm bloc" in Congress.

With the failure of many of their business enterprises and the frustration of their legislation, and with the return of relative prosperity in the late seventies, the Grange petered out. It was later revived, but as a purely social and educational organization. Meantime some of the discontented farmers drifted into the Greenback party—an ill-assorted conglomeration of farmers, laborers, and doctrinaire reformers—which in 1880 chose as its presidential candidate an old Granger leader, James B. Weaver of Iowa.

The real successors to the Grange, however, were the Farmers' Alliances, the most interesting farm organizations in American history. The Alliances had their origin in the depression of the late eighties and the early nineties. Times were harder than ever before. Drought descended on the stricken plains, and went on, year after year; the share-crop and crop-lien systems plunged the South into misery; wheat fell to fifty cents a bushel, cotton to six cents a pound; it was cheaper to burn corn for fuel than to ship it to market. And in Washington purblind Congressmen, sensitive only to the demands of big business, fastened upon the country in 1890 the McKinley tariff, the highest it had ever known, maintained a cruelly inflexible banking and credit system, and voted away hundreds of millions in pensions and "pork-barrel" legislation. Stimulated by governmental injustice, the Alliance movement spread like an epidemic, and by 1890 the various Alliances had not far from two million members.

The Northwestern and the Southern Alliance were in many respects like the earlier Grange. They undertook elaborate educational programs, circulated books like Henry George's *Progress and Poverty* and Edward Bellamy's *Looking Backward,* published Alliance newspapers—Kansas alone had over a hundred—sent out lecturers to advise farmers on the latest developments in scientific agriculture and to agitate for remedial legislation, and established farmers' institutes and study clubs. They embarked, too, upon far-reaching economic programs. The Texas Alliance sponsored co-operative buying, marketing, and warehousing; in the Dakotas the Alliance underwrote crop insurance; in Illinois it organized a series of farmers' exchanges. Some of these undertakings were successful and saved farmers millions of dollars in profits and middlemen's charges; others, confronted with the implacable hostility of the banks and the railroads, failed.

And before long the Alliances gave birth to a crusading political party. From the beginning they had called for a program of political reform: government ownership of railroads, cheap money, the abolition of national banks, prohibition of alien landownership, reduction of the tariff, and the creation of a "subtreasury" scheme to provide easy credit to farmers. This last was particularly interesting. It called for the construction by the Federal government of warehouses in every agricultural county, where farmers might store their produce, receiving in exchange certificates worth eighty per cent of the market value of the produce. This scheme would give the farmer credit at a very low rate of interest, enable him to hold his crops off the market until the price was advantageous, and inflate the currency—thus enhancing the value of the crop. When first advanced, it was denounced as a harebrained and socialistic device; within a generation it was adopted, in all essentials, by the Federal government.

Between 1890 and 1892 the Alliance was metamorphosed into the Populist party—the most colorful of American political parties. The rank and file of the party was recruited from the farmers of the South and the West, but it embraced many other minority groups—the remnants of the Knights of Labor, of the Greenback and Union Labor parties, advocates of woman suffrage, Socialists, single-taxers, silverites, and professional reformers. Its strength was concentrated on the Middle Border, and from that region, too, came its leaders. Chief among these was the Minnesota Irishman, Ignatius Donnelly, farmer, orator, agitator, discoverer of the lost continent of Atlantis, champion of the Baconian theory, author of the popular novel *Caesar's Column,* who for twenty years had troubled the waters of American politics. From Kansas, the hotbed of Populism, came Senator William Peffer, whose long flowing beard reminded observers of a Hebrew prophet and whom young Theodore Roosevelt denounced as "a well-meaning, pinheaded, anarchistic crank." And from Kansas, too, came the greatest of the women revivalists—Mary Ellen Lease, who eloquently implored the plains farmers to "raise less corn and more hell." Down in Georgia the cadaverous, redheaded Tom Watson, "sage of Hickory Hill" and self-appointed successor to Thomas Jefferson, rallied the tenant farmers and the mill hands to the Populist standard and sent shivers running up and down the spines of all the Southern Bourbons. And in Nebraska a young Democrat named William Jennings Bryan was urging his party to fuse with the new Populist organization.

Never before in American politics had there been anything like the Populist revolt which swept the prairies and the cotton lands in the early nineties. "It was a religious revival, a crusade, a Pentecost of politics, in which a tongue of flame sat upon every man, and each spake as the spirit gave him utterance," wrote one witness; it was "a fanaticism like the Crusades," another recalled. After a hard day in the fields, farmers hitched up their buggies and with their wives and children jogged off to the Grange or the schoolhouse and applauded the impassioned oratory of their grass-roots leaders. "Wall Street owns the country," declaimed Mary Lease. "It is no longer a government of the people, by the people, for the people, but a government of Wall Street, by Wall Street, and for Wall Street. Our laws are the output of a system that clothes rascals in robes and honesty in rags." And outraged farmers voted new declarations of independence. "The history of the United States," read one of them, "for the past twenty-eight years is a history of repeated injuries, tyranny, and usurpation, unparalleled in the history of the world, and all laws enacted having a direct object; viz., to establish a moneyed aristocracy on the ruins of a once free America."

The elections of 1890 swept the new party into power in a dozen Southern and Western states and sent a score of homespun Senators and Representatives to startle the staid halls of Congress. Flushed with this success, the party planned even greater triumphs. On Independence Day of 1892 a thousand enthusiastic and sweating delegates met at Omaha to select a presidential candidate and endorse Ignatius Donnelly's perfervid preamble to a boldly progressive platform:

> We meet in the midst of a nation brought to the verge of moral, political, and material ruin. Corruption dominates the ballot-box, the legislatures, the Congress, and touches even the ermine of the bench. . . . The newspapers are largely subsidized or muzzled; public opinion silenced; business prostrated; our homes covered with mortgages; labor impoverished; and the land concentrating in the hands of capitalists. . . . The fruits of the toil of millions are boldly stolen to build up colossal fortunes for a few . . . and the possessors of these, in turn, despise the republic and endanger liberty. From the same prolific womb of governmental injustice we breed the two great classes—tramps and millionaires.

The Populists polled over a million votes. But it was Grover Cleveland who went to the White House, not James B. Weaver, who had led so many lost causes. The winds of revolt blew in from the sun-baked cotton fields of the South and the hot, dusty prairies of the West, but the old parties went their accustomed way. Nothing less than an earthquake could shake them out of their smug apathy. That earthquake was not long in coming.

1896

Times were bad, in 1892, and they grew steadily worse. No sooner had portly Grover Cleveland taken the oath of office for the second time than a major panic burst upon the country. Business houses crashed, banks closed their doors, railroads went into the hands of receivers, factories shut down, trade languished, creditors foreclosed their mortgages. In the cities long lines of unemployed waited outside soup kitchens, and in the country the army of tramps added thousands of recruits. This was worse even than the panic of 1873, more widespread and more devastating in its effects.

In the face of this disaster the government followed the traditional policy of noninterference in economic disturbances. Cleveland was an able leader, honest, courageous, and well intentioned, a fine exponent of Manchester liberalism in fighting corruption and special privilege. In his first term (1885–1889) he had made an admirable record. But he was wedded to the prevalent philosophy of *laissez faire*. His program was still one of tariff reduction and administrative reform, and he rejected most suggestions of remedial economic legislation. He believed that the storm had to blow itself out; that the depression could best be cured by automatic forces. For two years matters grew steadily worse. The year 1894 witnessed the great Pullman strike, the march of Coxey's army of the unemployed on Washington, and a further collapse of farm prices. From the cotton, corn, and wheat fields came a ground swell of revolt. The Southern and Western wing of the Democracy threatened to bolt the old party, and when in 1894 Cleveland barred the road to an inflationary measure, the old war horse from Missouri, Richard Bland, announced that "we have come to the parting of the ways." That fall a host of discontented Democrats joined hands with the Populists, who rolled up a vote of almost a million and a half.

Many anticipated a repetition of the 1854–1856 crisis, when the decrepit Whig organization had disintegrated and the vigorous young Republican party had taken over. But the astute leaders of the Western Democracy were not yet ready to give up, while in the South Democracy had become so completely identified with white supremacy that no third party stood a chance. Instead of going over to the Populists, the radical leaders of the Southern and Western Democracy therefore moved to capture the party organization. "Then," as Bryan later described it,

> began the struggle. With a zeal approaching the zeal which inspired the Crusaders, who followed Peter the Hermit, our silver Democrats went forth from victory unto victory. . . . In this contest brother has been arrayed against brother, father against son. . . . Old leaders have been cast aside when they have refused to give expression to the sentiments of those whom they would lead, and new leaders have sprung up to give direction to this cause of truth.

The agrarian Democrats elected to make their fight on the money question. This has often been considered a mistake, yet it is doubtful whether any other issue could have appealed to so many voters or have lent itself so readily to dramatization. The money question of that time was complex, yet it will not be too misleading to suggest that it boiled down to the question of inflation versus deflation. For years, while the population and the business of the nation grew, the government had been following a policy of contracting the currency. In the year 1873, just before the production of the silver mines of the West began to threaten to depreciate the value of money, Congress by a purely routine measure demonetized silver—that is, refused to purchase or to coin any more of it. Then in 1878 and again in 1890 the government was forced into such extensive purchases of silver that the maintenance of a gold basis for the currency of the United States became seriously endangered. A succession of Presidents, backed by all the conservative forces of the nation, were resolved to uphold this standard. Cleveland in especial waged a titanic—and successful—battle for it. It was this money policy, so many farmers were convinced, that was chiefly responsible for low prices. Restore silver, coin all that was mined, open the mints to all the precious metal in the world, and the value of money would fall back to normal, prices would soar, prosperity would return. So argued the Silverites.

The conservative hard-money men remained convinced that such a policy would be financially disastrous. Inflation, once begun, could not be stopped, and the government itself would be forced into bankruptcy. Only the gold standard offered stability. More than this, they talked themselves into believing that the gold standard was not only sound finance but sound morals, and they most unjustly denounced the silver dollar as a "dishonest" dollar. It was an old quarrel—this controversy over cheap money—and an ever-new one.

On strategic grounds much was to be said for making the fight on the issue of free silver. Silver-mine owners, facing bankruptcy, could be counted on to help finance a campaign. The silver interest was all-powerful in half a dozen sparsely populated Western states which were normally Republican and which commanded a disproportionate vote in the electoral college; if these could be swung into the

Democratic column they might turn the election. Easy money would appeal to the vast debtor class throughout the country and to some workingmen as well as to farmers. Silver, finally, had an emotional quality that would be easily exploited. Gold was the rich man's money; silver the poor man's friend. Gold was the money of Wall Street and of Lombard Street; silver of the prairies and the little towns.

But it was not enough to have an issue; the silverites had to have a candidate. "All the silverites need," wrote the New York *World,* "is a Moses. They have the principle, they have the grit, they have the brass bands and the buttons and the flags, they have the howl and the hustle, they have the votes, and they have the leaders so-called. But they are wandering in the wilderness like a lot of lost sheep because no one with the courage, the audacity, the magnetism, and the wisdom to be a real leader has yet appeared among them."

In William Jennings Bryan of Nebraska they found their Moses. A delegate to the tumultuous Chicago convention of 1896, he was slated to speak on the money question. And as he climbed to the platform, that sweltering night of June 8, he was stepping forth to immortality:

> We do not come as aggressors. Our war is not a war of conquest; we are fighting in the defense of our homes, our families, and posterity. We have petitioned, and our petitions have been scorned; we have entreated, and our entreaties have been disregarded; we have begged, and they have mocked when our calamity came. We beg no longer; we entreat no more; we petition no more. We defy them! . . .

So spoke "the boy orator of the Platte," and every sentence evoked a frezy of applause. And when he delivered his famous peroration, the hall shook with such a Niagara of noise as had never before been heard at any American gathering:

> If they dare to come out in the open field and defend the gold standard as a good thing, we will fight them to the uttermost. Having behind us the producing masses of the nation and the world, supported by the commercial interests, the laboring interests, and the toilers everywhere, we will answer their demand for a gold standard by saying to them: You shall not press down upon the brow of labor this crown of thorns, you shall not crucify mankind upon a cross of gold.

Bryan might have been nominated even without this speech, for he had made a careful preconvention campaign and was in many respects a logical candidate. After the speech his nomination was a foregone conclusion. The victory of the silver wing of the Democracy was complete. They wrote the platform, they named the candidate, and they forced the Populists to come over to them.

With this campaign the engaging figure of Bryan steps into the national arena, and off and on for two decades he held the spotlight. He was in some respects the most remarkable political leader since Henry Clay. Magnificent in appearance, with coal-black hair, black flashing eyes, and a voice of mellifluous beauty, quick-witted, intelligent, fearless, he captured the imagination, the worshipful devotion, of millions of plain people. They recognized in him one of their own and gave him the elder Pitt's title of "The Great Commoner." He had grown up on a farm, attended a country college, moved to the plains country, and there practiced law and politics; he was a devout Presbyterian, and his political speeches were studded with apt quotations from the Scriptures; he was a plain democrat, unspoiled by success, sincerely devoted to the public interest as he saw it, and convinced that the voice of the people was the voice of God. Though his limitations were many, for he was not widely nor deeply read, and was far from being an original or profound thinker, he was a highly representative American.

The campaign of 1896 was more bitterly fought than any since Jackson's day. Bryan's task seemed at first insurmountable. His party was split wide open, its titular chieftain, Cleveland, in opposition and most of its Eastern leaders flocking into the Republican camp. The Democrats, too, were unjustly blamed for the three-year depression. Ranged against Bryan were almost all the forces of respectability: business, the universities, the press, the money power. Mark Hanna, boss of the Republican party, drummed up a campaign fund which has been estimated at from three to seven million dollars; against this the Democrats could match less than half a million. In only one respect did the Democrats have a clear advantage—in Bryan himself. Crisscrossing the country from New England to the West, riding hot, dusty day coaches, speaking eight and ten times a day, appealing to laborers and farmers, to liberals and progressives, he made the most spectacular campaign in American history.

In a coat like a deacon, in a black Stetson hat
He scourged the elephant plutocrats
With barbed wire from the Platte. . . .
Prairie avenger, mountain lion,
Bryan, Bryan, Bryan, Bryan,
Gigantic troubadour, speaking like a siege gun,
Smashing Plymouth Rock with his boulders from the
    West.

It was magnificent, but it was not enough. In the

end William McKinley won by more than half a million votes. The West and the South, the combination which had swept Jefferson into power and supported Jackson and Douglas, had failed. For that matter, McKinley and the Republicans carried such Middle Western states as Illinois, Iowa, and Wisconsin, and such Far Western states as California and Oregon. But Bryan's campaign was to become legendary—and the ideas of the Populists and agrarian Democrats were ultimately, without a single important exception, to be written into legislation. They were to change the course of American history.

Chapter Seventeen

THE AGE OF REFORM

The Challenge to Democracy

WHEN Bryan came to write the history of the campaign of 1896 he called it *The First Battle*. The title was an inspiration. For that battle, though it ended in defeat for the forces of agrarian democracy, was the beginning of the progressive campaign. Before the war was over, the armies of farmers and workingmen swept over state after state in one victorious campaign after another, carried the bastions of reaction by storm, planted their banner triumphantly atop the White House, and restored the national government to its traditional democratic course.

For this was the Progressive Era—these two decades between Bryan's first battle and Woodrow Wilson's second. It was marked by revolt and reform in almost every department of American life. Old political leaders were ousted and new ones enlisted; political machinery was overhauled and modernized; political practices were subjected to critical scrutiny, and those which failed to square with the ideals of democracy were rejected. Economic institutions and practices—private property, the corporation, the trust, great fortunes—were called before the bar of reason and asked to justify themselves or to change their ways. Social relationships were reconsidered—the impact of the city, immigration, inequalities in wealth, the growth of classes, all came in for critical attention. Almost every notable figure in this period, whether in politics, philosophy, scholarship, or literature, derives his fame in part, from his connection with the reform movement: Weaver, Bryan, La Follette, Roosevelt, and Wilson in the political arena; William James, Josiah Royce, and John Dewey in philosophy; Thorstein Veblen, Richard Ely, and Frederick J. Turner in scholarship; William Dean Howells, Frank Norris, Hamlin Garland, and Theodore Dreiser in literature. The heroes of the day were all reformers. Courageously, defiantly, they manned the battlements of democracy and even sallied out to make new conquests. Not since the forties had there been such a ferment in the intellectual world; not since then had reform been so firmly in the saddle.

And what was it all about, this fine frenzy of reform? What was it that so troubled the waters of American life? We have already seen something of the problems of the farmer and of the workingman. But these, distressing though they were, were symptoms rather than causes. The problem was not economic merely, nor was it confined to these two great interests of agriculture and labor. It affected every aspect of American society.

The fact is that the promise of American life was not being fulfilled. Here in this New World was to have been created a society where freedom and equality were assured to all, a state where liberty was everywhere protected. This was, to be sure, a dream, but it was not a pipe dream, nor were the creators of the American republic visionaries who took refuge in the opium of false hopes. Never before in history had nature vouchsafed to men so rich an opportunity, never before had there been sounder reason to suppose that men might create for themselves an earthly Eden. In the beginning the American people were indeed, in the words of Turgot, "the hope of the human race."

This hope had not been fulfilled. Americans were better

off than their contemporaries overseas, but they were worse off than they should be. The material achievements of the nation were impressive, but the social and cultural achievements disappointing. As President Wilson said in his First Inaugural address:

> The evil has come with the good, and much fine gold has been corroded. With riches has come inexcusable waste. We have squandered a great part of what we might have used, and have not stopped to conserve the exceeding bounty of nature . . . scorning to be careful, shamefully prodigal as well as admirably efficient. We have been proud of our industrial achievements, but we have not hitherto stopped thoughtfully enough to count the human cost, the cost of lives snuffed out, of energies overtaxed and broken, the fearful physical and spiritual cost to the men and women and children upon whom the dead weight and burden of it all has fallen pitilessly the years through. . . . With the great Government went many deep secret things which we too long delayed to look into and scrutinize with candid, fearless eyes. The great Government we loved has too often been made use of for private and selfish purposes, and those who used it had forgotten the people.

This was not because wicked men had done evil things; it was not because powerful men had rejected democracy and set out to destroy it; it was not because tyranny or despotism had been established in the place of liberty. No, the causes were more subtle than that. The basic difficulty was one common to the whole Western world. Science and machinery had outrun social science and political machinery. The practices and principles inherited from an eighteenth-century rural republic were no longer adequate to the exigencies of a twentieth-century urban state. This was true in the political realm, where the fear of government persisted into the period when only government could adequately control the forces that machinery had let loose on society. It was true in the moral realm, where old notions of personal responsibility were rendered irrelevant by the rise of the impersonal corporation. It was true in the social realm, where the habits of rural life in a homogeneous society were no longer applicable to the exigencies of urban life in a highly heterogeneous society.

Growth itself had created a host of problems. The farm domain grew beyond the bounds which nature had fixed; immigrants poured in faster than they could be absorbed; cities grew so fast that they could not house or adequately govern their teeming populations; factory production increased beyond practicable consumption; business became so big that nobody could fully understand it or manage it; a few men became so rich that they did not know what to do with their money—and society had not learned how to relieve them of their burden.

These were the fundamental difficulties, but few men were perspicacious enough to appreciate them. What the reformers saw, rather, was poverty, injustice, and corruption; what they saw was the land question, the labor question, the woman question, the money question. So they girded themselves to battle with the slums; they cleaned up politics; they busted trusts and fought "malefactors of great wealth"; they waged war on the "demon rum," on child labor, on sweatshop labor; they led crusades for the Indian, for the Negro, for the "little brown brothers" of our new island possessions; they devised new machinery for government—the initiative, the referendum, woman suffrage, primary elections, corrupt-practices acts, and the merit system; they saved the forests and the water resources, and beautified the cities. Hundreds of societies to do good sprang up and flourished. The presses groaned with books exposing the iniquities of the present order and presenting blueprints for a better one. Magazine editors struck pay dirt with articles exposing everything everywhere. Novelists turned from romance and local color to problem novels and moral sermons; poets forgot their "triolets, villanelles, rondels, rondeaus" and discovered "the man with the hoe"; scholars emerged from their ivory towers to grapple with social problems; preachers rediscovered the social gospel and troubled respectable parishioners with a literal reading of the New Testament.

All this was thoroughly in the American tradition. It was in protest and revolt against conditions in old England that the Pilgrims and the Puritans had come to New England; colonial leaders in turn—Roger Williams, Nathaniel Bacon, Jacob Leisler—had revolted against tyranny or intolerance when established here; the nation had been born from a revolution, and its national heroes—Jefferson, Franklin, Sam Adams, Thomas Paine—were rebels, not only against the mother country, but also against the ruling classes at home; the great writers and preachers and philosophers of New England in the forties and fifties—Emerson and Whittier, Garrison and Parker—enlisted in the fight for equality and liberty. To inquire, to challenge, to protest, to prove all things and hold fast that which was good, was native to the American character.

Neither the philosophy nor the methods of the new progressive revolt differed from those of the earlier reform movements. The philosophy asserted complete faith in democracy: all the ailments that afflicted society could be ascribed to a want of democracy, and all could be cured by more democracy. Thus the confidence in such measures as woman suffrage, the initiative and referendum, and popular election of Senators. The methods were largely political and sought to function through the established parties rather than to found new ones: because of the inertia and conservatism of the large parties this proved a definite drag on the movement.

Two main currents of reform merged during these years. One had its origin in the agrarian West, concerned itself largely with economic issues, and revealed occasional flashes of real radicalism. The philosophers of this Western protest were Henry George, author of *Progress and Poverty,* and Edward Bellamy, whose *Looking Backward* envisioned a Utopian economy; its political spokesmen were Altgeld and Donnelly, Bryan and La Follette. The other current was Eastern, and even English, in origin and addressed itself to problems such as tariff reform, the merit system, and anti-imperialism. Its intellectual spokesmen were E. L. Godkin, editor of the powerful New York *Nation,* George William Curtis, and President Charles W. Eliot of Harvard University; its political representatives were Carl Schurz, Abram S. Hewitt, Grover Cleveland, and Woodrow Wilson.

The Crusade for Social Justice

In 1890 a Danish immigrant, Jacob Riis, working as a reporter for the New York *Sun,* brought out his book *How the Other Half Lives.* It was an unvarnished account of conditions in the teeming slums of New York, and it pictured the overcrowding, the dirt, disease, crime, vice, and misery of the "other half" who had fallen behind in the march of democracy. Soon newspapermen in other cities were making similar reports, and the nation awoke to a realization that the challenge of the city was no less urgent than the challenge of the farm.

The city, as Lord Bryce observed in his *American Commonwealth,* was the one conspicuous failure of American democracy. Here the extremes of wealth and poverty were most flagrant, slums crowding the marble palaces of the rich, beggars haunting the doorways of luxurious restaurants. Here corruption was most unashamed, "rings" and "halls" fattening on the public treasury, selling public franchises, exploiting crime and vice. Here the saloon and the house of ill-fame were protected and encouraged by the politicians and the interests who profited by them, while criminal gangs like the Whyos of Mulberry Bend, New York, or the Lake Shore Push of Cleveland went their predatory ways undisturbed by police interference. Here sweatshops testified to the exploitation of women, newsboys and bootblacks to the failure to take care of the children. Here the problems of public health, housing, education, and government were most acute.

It was the housing problem that first commanded the attention of reformers, for this was one that concerned not only the wretched slum dwellers, but all of the inhabitants of the cities. In the decades after the Civil War the population of cities had grown far more rapidly than housing facilities, and the result had been the development of tenements—rickety wooden structures, five or six stories high, dark, ill-ventilated, and filthy, breeders of disease and nurseries of vice. In New York City alone, in 1890, probably half a million persons lived in these "slums"—where the death rate was four times that of the more fortunate parts of the city. One typical block on the lower East Side contained 2781 persons—but not a single bathtub. Of the 1588 rooms, one third were without light or ventilation and another third gave upon "twilight air shafts." Let Riis describe one of these slums of lower Manhattan:

Suppose we look into one, No.——Cherry Street. Be a little careful, please! The hall is dark, and you might stumble over the children pitching pennies back there.

Not that it would hurt them; kicks and cuffs are their daily diet. They have little else. Here where the hall turns and dives into utter darkness is a step, and another, another. A flight of stairs. You can feel your way if you cannot see it. Close? Yes. What would you have? All the fresh air that ever enters these stairs comes from the hall door that is forever slamming and from the windows of dark bedrooms that in turn receive from the stairs their sole supply of the elements. . . . That was a woman filling her pail by the hydrant you just bumped against. The sinks are in the hallway, that all the tenants may have access—and all be poisoned alike by their summer stenches. Hear the pump squeak? It is the lullaby of tenement house babes. In summer, when a thousand thirsty throats pant for a cooling drink in this block, it is worked in vain. . . . Here is a door. Listen! That short, hacking cough, that tiny, helpless wail—what do they mean? They mean that the soiled bow of white you saw on the door downstairs will have another story to tell . . . before the day is at an end. The child is dying with measles. With half a chance it might have lived, but it had none. That dark bedroom killed it.

The "battle with the slum" was really a long campaign, waged on many fronts. Pleading the hazards from fire and epidemics, reformers like Richard Watson Gilder persuaded reluctant legislators to outlaw the worst of the tenements and require proper ventilation and sanitation in the others. Indomitable social workers like Jane Addams and Lillian Wald, inspired by the example of Toynbee Hall in London, established settlement houses in the heart of the slums of the great cities. Some of these, like Hull House in Chicago and the Henry Street Settlement in New York, became world famous; before the end of the decade almost a hundred of them had been founded and had undertaken a large and varied program of relief, education, and public health. To take children off the streets and away from gangs and give them a better chance at health and decency, playgrounds were built in the most crowded sections of cities, fresh-air funds provided vacations to the country, milk depots distributed free milk to those unable to buy it, day nurseries relieved working mothers of anxiety for their children, Visiting Nurses' Associations gave free medical and nursing care, and organizations like the Young Men's Christian Association and the Boy Scouts provided healthy and normal outlets for youthful energies.

One of the most urgent problems that engaged the attention of reformers was that of crime, and particularly of mounting juvenile delinquency: the decade of the eighties had witnessed a fifty per cent increase in the number of prison inmates, and child offenders constituted one fifth of these. The United States had a long and honorable record of interest in penal and prison reform, but notwithstanding the efforts of enlightened critics like Edward Livingston, Dorothea Dix, and Frederick Wines, the penal code of many states remained barbarous, and prison conditions in some states reminded visitors forcibly of the "Black Hole of Calcutta." The old notion of punishing offenders rather than reforming them died hard, and so, too, did police brutality, the third degree, and the practice of applying one law to the rich and the powerful, another to the poor and the friendless. Altgeld of Illinois who had pardoned the Haymarket "anarchists," had argued that society rather than individuals was guilty when crimes were committed, and had worked heroically for the reform of the penal code of the state. One of his disciples, Mayor "Golden Rule" Jones of Toledo, took the same attitude—and found opportunity to dramatize it.

He was always going down to the city prisons or to the workhouses [wrote Brand Whitlock] and talking to the poor devils there quite as if he were one of them. . . . And he was working all the time to get them out of prison, and finally he and I entered into a little compact by which he paid the expenses incident to their trials . . . if I would look after their cases. . . . For instance, if some poor girl were arrested and a jury trial were demanded for her and her case were given all the care and attention it would have received had she been some wealthy person, the police, when they found they could not convict, were apt to be a little more careful of the liberties of individuals; they began to have a little regard for human rights and for human life.

But such measures, of course, were palliatives rather than reforms. More important was the adoption, by the turn of the century, of the indeterminate sentence and the probationary system. Inspired by the example of Thomas Mott Osborne, some of the worst prisons were cleaned up and a determined attack was launched upon the chain gang and the system of leasing convict labor, widely prevalent through the South. Special courts were set up, too, for child offenders. Judge Ben Lindsey, who for a quarter of a century presided over the Juvenile Court of Denver, Colorado, attracted nation-wide attention by the success with which he cut down juvenile delinquency. Of his experiences here Judge Lindsey wrote:

I had begun merely with a sympathy for children and a conviction that our laws against crime were as inapplicable to children as they would be to idiots. I soon realized that not only our laws but our whole system of criminal procedure was wrong. It was based upon fear, and fear, with children, is the father of lies. . . . I learned that instead of fear we must use sympathy, but without cant, without hypocrisy, and without sentimentality. We must first convince the boy that we were his friends, but the determined enemies of his misdeeds; that we wished to help him to do right, but could do nothing for him if he persisted in doing wrong.

One obvious cause of crime and poverty—so it was thought—was the saloon, and these years witnessed a concerted attack upon the "demon rum" that ended, finally, in national prohibition. The origins of the temperance movement go back to the early years of the republic, and before the Civil War thousands of men had "signed the pledge" of total abstinence and several New England states had experimented with legal prohibition. The postwar years, however, brought an increase in the consumption of beer and of hard liquor, and, in the cities, of saloons; by 1900, places like New York, Buffalo, and San Francisco confessed one saloon to every two hundred inhabitants. Some of these were merely "the poor man's club," but many of them were run with a total disregard of temperance or even decency in drinking. Sunday closing laws were ignored, high license fees evaded, and the liquor interest entered everywhere into a corrupt alliance with the worst elements in politics.

To meet these conditions a Prohibition party entered the field as early as 1869, but was ineffectual. Far more effective were such organizations as the Women's Christian Temperance Union, the Anti-Saloon League, and the evangelical churches. These were not satisfied with political agitation, but carried on a ceaseless propaganda, in the press, the church, the lecture hall, and the school. The militant leader of the prohibition forces was, for many years, Frances Willard, who carried the war into the enemy's country by leading temperance ladies into saloons, where they would sing psalms and fall to their knees in prayer.

By the end of the century these methods had dried up seven states, all of them rural, and had introduced "local option" to a great many more. During the early years of the new century the prohibition movement made great headway, and by the time of the World War two thirds of the population lived under dry laws. Only the cities were recalcitrant. Whether the drys could ever have carried these battlements in normal times is uncertain, but the World War played into their hands. At the beginning of the war Congress, for reasons of economy, efficiency, and morality, prohibited the manufacture or sale of intoxicating liquors, and before this law expired prohibition was written into the Federal Constitution. There it remained for more than a decade, a "noble experiment" that failed. In 1933 it was repealed, and the problem returned to the states.

The States Point the Way

The history of all these reform movements pointed one unmistakable moral: private individuals and organizations could accomplish little except through legislative channels. Discouraged by her experiences with private charity, Josephine Shaw Lowell, founder of New York's Charity Organization Society, and active in many good works, decided to withdraw from them all. "I think," she explained,

> there is far more important work to be done for working people. Five hundred thousand wage earners in this city, 200,000 of them women and 75,000 of these working under dreadful conditions or for starvation wages. That is more vital than the 25,000 dependents. . . . If the working people had all they ought to have, we should not have the paupers and the criminals. It

is better to save them before they go under than to spend your life fishing them out when they're half drowned, and taking care of them afterwards.

Charity was obviously a mere palliative, and even the humanitarians who distrusted political action usually ended up in the legislative chambers, hat in hand, asking for aid. Slum clearance, prison reform, the salvation of children, prohibition—all required legislative action. And if anything more fundamental were to be obtained, it must be through the agency of the state.

The first great battles of the reform movement were fought out in the states, and these continued to be the battlegrounds of reform even after many issues had been transferred to the national arena. Under the American constitutional system, it cannot be too often repeated, the states were presumed to have jurisdiction over almost all matters of a social character. The hours and wages of labor, the conditions of factory work, the welfare of women and children, prisons, reform schools and charitable institutions, education, the suffrage, municipal government— all of these things were matters of state, not Federal, concern. The New Deal, to be sure, changed all this, but it took a national catastrophe to justify and a bold administration to attempt that change, and it was effected only over the determined opposition of the Supreme Court.

The states, then, were the laboratories of reform. It was here that most of the subsequent national reforms were first tested; it was here that they justified themselves on principle and proved their inadequacy in practice. The states, too, were the training schools for the reformers who later performed on the national stage. Theodore Roosevelt went to school in New York City and at Albany before he moved on to Washington; La Follette learned the economics of railway and trust regulation in Wisconsin before he tried to apply them to the nation; Wilson made his reputation as a liberal as governor of New Jersey before he justified it as President of the United States; Albert B. Cummins, George Norris, and Franklin D. Roosevelt—all served an apprenticeship in their states.

What was the nature of the reforms carried out by the states? Many of them had to do with the democratization of political machinery: the initiative and referendum, the secret ballot, the direct primary, and direct election of Senators, corrupt-practices acts, provision for municipal home rule, and woman suffrage. Others were directed toward economic objectives: railway and trust regulation, public-utility commissions, tax reforms, regulation of hours and conditions of labor, workmen's compensation, and prohibition of the labor of children. Still others had broad social connotations: educational reforms, public-health programs, the conservation of natural resources.

The immediate problem was to get control of the governments. It is a nice question whether the state or municipal governments were more corrupt. Everywhere the field for corruption was vast and inviting, and the rewards were almost limitless. State legislatures and city councils had in their control the granting of valuable public-utility franchises, the fixing of railroad and utility rates, the control of insurance practices, the assessment and collection of taxes, the award of juicy highway-construction contracts, the power to protect or destroy the saloon. Hundreds of millions of dollars were involved, and business was prepared to pay well for favors, exemptions, or protection. Payment was not always in the form of outright bribery; it might take the form of political advancement, or contributions to political campaigns, or lucrative legal business to attorneys who saw the light. Whatever form it took, it was usually effective, as reformers learned to their dismay.

A grand jury investigating conditions in Missouri at the turn of the century concluded that "for twelve years . . . corruption has been the usual and accepted thing in state legislation, and that, too, without interference or hindrance." The verdict might have been applied with equal truth, at one time or another, to almost every state in the Union. From New Hampshire to California, from New Mexico to Montana, legislators were up for auction. Everywhere the great corporations had their lobbyists who engaged in shameless bribery or, where that failed, in blackmail. In the Yankee state of New Hampshire, as Winston Churchill tells in his *Coniston* and *Mr. Crewe's Career,* the railroads ruled supreme; the *Octopus* of Frank Norris' powerful novel of California was the Southern Pacific. The "copper kings" corrupted Montana; railroads and insurance companies bought up the New York assembly; the Standard Oil was accused of having refined everything in Pennsylvania but the legislature. Even in a small frontier commonwealth like New Mexico, an unholy alliance of two or three railroads, coal- and copper-mining companies, timber and land speculators, and the great ranchmen, completely dominated the state. Coal companies seized millions of acres of the most valuable mineral lands, lumber companies looted the national forests, ranchmen grazed thousands of cattle and sheep on the public domain, railroads and mines defeated labor laws, and all escaped taxation. To achieve these glittering ends the corporations worked through as precious a gang of blackguards as ever strutted on a political stage.

It would be repetitious and confusing to attempt to rehearse the war on corruption or trace the coming of political reforms in the various states. The history of one commonwealth will illustrate—though somewhat optimistically—what was happening widely throughout the Union. Wisconsin, in the 1880's, was a flourishing and enlightened state, but her government was run by a triumvirate of bosses—Boss Keyes, the millionaire lumberman, Philetus Sawyer, and the railroad attorney, John Spooner,—who dominated state politics through the caucus and convention system. The whole state, according to Frederic C. Howe,

> was a feudatory of the railway, lumber, and franchise interests, which, with the machine of federal office-holders, nominated and elected governors, United States senators and congressmen who, in turn, made use of their power to enrich their creators. Federal and state patronage was used for the same ends. The biennial session of the legislature was a carnival for the benefit of the few. Politics was a privileged trade, into which ambitious men entered only when approved by the state machine. Few believed any other methods were possible, and no one challenged the rule of the oligarchy which distributed elective as well as appointive offices for the maintenance of its political and industrial power. There was no organized protest. The press was indifferent or controlled. The great fortunes of the state had been made from timber taken from government lands, from railroad and franchise corporation promotion and from building contracts identified with these interests.

Stirred by the currents of reform sweeping across the prairie states in the eighties, young Robert M. La Follette, fresh from the state university, decided to take a hand. Without machine support, he fought his way into Congress and in four successive terms justified the confidence which the common people had come to cherish for him. Defeated in the Democratic landslide of 1890, La Follette turned to state politics. The people were with him, but the machine would have none of him, and on three successive occasions boss-ridden conventions turned him down for more complaisant candidates. From this experience La Follette learned the necessity of abolishing the caucus and convention system and putting in the direct primary.

Finally in 1900 "Fighting Bob" forced his nomination upon a reluctant convention and was swept triumphantly into the governorship. For the next quarter of a century—with a brief war interlude—he and his followers dominated the state, making it the most democratic, the most progressive, and the best governed in the Union. The "Wisconsin Idea" as formulated and applied by La Follette in the first ten or twelve years of the century was not mere windy doctrine, but a practical and coherent program. It enlarged democracy through the direct primary, the initiative and referendum, the recall of all but judicial officials, the prohibition of corrupt election practices, publicity for and limitation on campaign expenditures, municipal home rule, civil-service reform, and the creation of bureaus of experts to advise on administration. To protect the citizens of the state against exploitation by corporations, La Follette set up commissions to regulate railway and other public-utility charges, forced the railroads and the great timber companies to pay their just share of taxes and to cough up back taxes which they had evaded, and provided for a state income tax and state insurance on savings-bank deposits. To safeguard labor there were workmen's compensation laws, the prohibition of child labor, and the limitation on the hours of labor for women. Agriculture was encouraged by the reduction in railroad rates, by a far-reaching conservation and water-power program, and by vigorous support to the experiment stations and demonstration farms connected with the state university.

Nothing was more interesting than the manner in which La Follette made the university the nerve center of the state. President Van Hise, himself a scientist of note, brought to the school on the shores of Lake Mendota one of the most distinguished faculties to be found in any institution of higher learning in the world. Even more important, he brought the notion that it was the function of the university to serve the people of the state. Its economists served on railway and tax commissions; its political scientists drafted legislative bills; its historians cultivated local history; its engineers planned road-building programs, its school of agriculture taught animal husbandry to practical farmers, carried on investigations which saved the farmers of the state—and of the nation—hundreds of millions of dollars, and was chiefly instrumental in making Wisconsin the Denmark of the New World.

Here was an experiment in practical progressivism which excited the interest of the whole nation. La Follette proved that reform did not need to be doctrinaire and that scholars and scientists could make contributions to practical politics. He showed how a state could regulate public utilities without incurring the charge of socialism and how such regulation could be profitable for the utilities as well as for the public. He revealed the possibilities of a state as a laboratory for political experiments and pointed the way not only for other states but for the nation.

Theodore Roosevelt and the Square Deal

Admirable as was the achievement of states like Wisconsin, it was clear that most of the problems to which reformers addressed themselves could not be solved in the insulated compartments of the Federal system. Only if reforms were projected on a national scale could they be effective, and only the national government was powerful enough to insure their success. Congress had indeed already enacted some legislation of a mildly progressive nature—the Pendleton Civil Service Act of 1883, the Interstate Commerce Act of 1887, the Antitrust Act of 1890, the Erdman Act for the arbitration of labor disputes on railways in 1898. But these and similar laws were largely ineffective for two reasons: they did not go far enough and they were not rigorously enforced. They were, in short, gestures, sops thrown out by a reluctant Congress to appease public opinion.

For a generation the Federal government had been chiefly in the hands of Republican leaders who, acquiescent in the *laissez faire* philosophy of the period, were indifferent to most of the newer social and economic demands. Without exception they were friendly to big business, while they catered to Civil War veterans with generous pension legislation. Pressure groups and special interests held a sway that was seldom broken. The Republican Presidents in succession—Grant, Hayes, Garfield, Arthur, Harrison, McKinley—were estimable men but lacking in vision and constructive energy. The one Democratic President, Cleveland, had more strength of character and a clearer program. He reformed the Federal departments, reclaimed vast areas of public land from corporation control, fought pension grabs and other special legislation, invigorated the civil service, and even forced through Congress a reduction of the tariff with an income-tax law attached—a law which was promptly annulled by the Supreme Court. But Cleveland's tenure was broken and troubled. In the great industrial states and to some extent in Washington, the real control was exercised by men like Platt of New York, Quay of Pennsylvania, and Hanna of Ohio, who made no pretense to statesmanship or to anything except serving their corporation masters and rewarding their party henchmen.

Most Congressmen were party hacks; they filled the *Congressional Record* with their oratory and, arrayed in frock coats and high hats, decorated many a platform, but the average American would find it difficult to recall a single law which they passed that made any marked difference in the course of the nation's history.

The agrarian forces under Weaver and then Bryan genuinely frightened the Old Guard of both parties, and the ground swell of revolt in many states indicated that reforms could not be too long delayed. Then came the Spanish War, and reform was, for the time, forgotten. The campaign of 1900 was waged on the somewhat unrealistic issue of imperialism, and McKinley, who had managed to be on both sides of the question, was triumphantly re-elected, and "The Great Commoner" for the second time repudiated. With prosperity at full tide, it looked as if the country were in for another long experience with the philosophy of standpat.

Then, on September 6, 1901, McKinley was shot by an anarchist, and with his death, a week later, the whole outlook of American politics was changed. For in young Theodore Roosevelt, so dramatically elevated to the presidency, the country found a leader of remarkable stimulation and power, and the progressive movement a national leader. Roosevelt had been born to wealth, reared among moneyed Easterners, and educated at Harvard. Yet he was thoroughly democratic and passionately interested in reform. He was, at the same time, a political realist, an ardent nationalist, and a faithful Republican. After Jefferson he was the most versatile of American Presidents, though entirely without Jefferson's intellectual depth or subtlety and equally without his philosophical idealism and his vision. He had ranched, hunted big game, written numerous books, served in the New York State legisla-

Harper's Weekly

THEODORE ROOSEVELT IN ACTION

ture, administered the New York City police, helped manage the Federal civil service, directed the navy, fought in Cuba, and made a first-rate governor. He read omnivorously, was interested in everybody, and had opinions on everything. He had a knack of coining memorable phrases, and his earnestness made him an effective preacher of civic righteousness. Like Andrew Jackson, he had a genius for winning the confidence of the plain man and making all his battles seem dramatic. Like Jackson, too, he believed that the President was closer to the people than the Congress and that executive leadership was essential for getting things done. But unlike Jackson he had no suspicion of the expert in civil service. Within a year he had shown that he understood the great changes sweeping over America and meant to deal with them in a statesmanlike way. He was not a radical, but an enlightened conservative; he did not want to revolutionize the existing economic system, but to save it by weeding out the abuses that had crept into it. He was determined to prove that the government was supreme over business and to give the plain man more of a "square deal."

In these undertakings Roosevelt made use of the public sentiment generated by the Populist movement, by the progressive impulse flooding in from states and cities, and by a valiant band of "muckrakers" whose books and magazine articles exposed graft and corruption, the malpractices of business, the social evil, the suppression of racial minorities, and a host of other evils that afflicted American life. The muckrakers were not only themselves an instrument of reform, but their astonishing popularity was a symptom that the public was ripe for their message.

"The great development of industrialism," said Roosevelt, "means that there must be an increase in the supervision exercised by the Government over business enterprise." In his enforcement of the antitrust laws Roosevelt early furnished an example of such "increase in supervision," but the trusts were by no means the only interests that felt his "big stick." The extension of government supervision over the railroads constituted one of the notable achievements of the Roosevelt administration. Roosevelt himself called railroad regulation the "paramount issue" and by incessant pressure succeeded in forcing through two major regulatory bills. The Elkins Act of 1903 made published rates the standard of lawfulness and shippers equally liable with railroads for rebates, and under its provisions the government successfully prosecuted the great Chicago packing houses and the Standard Oil Company. Even more important was the Hepburn Act of 1906, which gave the Interstate Commerce Commission real authority in rate regulation, extended the jurisdiction of the Commission to storage and terminal facilities, sleeping cars, express companies, and pipe lines, and forced the roads to surrender their interlocking interests in steamship lines and coal companies. By the end of the Roosevelt administration rebates had practically disappeared and railroad rates had ceased to be a pressing problem.

The use of the "big stick" in the affairs of labor was dramatic rather than significant. Under presidential prodding Congress pushed through a Workmen's Compensation Act for government employees, child-labor laws for the District of Columbia, and safety-appliance legislation for railroads, while the President himself saw to it that the eight-hour day on government work, which had been something of a mockery, was enforced. More spectacular was Roosevelt's intervention in the great anthracite coal strike of 1902. After a long struggle the United Mine Workers, under the leadership of the youthful John Mitchell, had succeeded in winning important concessions;

when the mine operators abrogated these, the miners struck. The operators were led by a representative of the paleolithic age of American industry, George Baer, who announced that "the rights and interests of the laboring man will be protected and cared for, not by the labor agitators, but by the Christian men whom God in His infinite wisdom has given control of the property interests of the country." When they refused to arbitrate it looked as if the country would face winter without fuel. At this juncture Roosevelt stepped in with a threat that he would take over the mines and run them with soldiers unless the operators came to terms. The threat was effective, and the miners won increased wages and shorter hours.

Of more permanent interest to the average American was the pure-food and drug legislation placed on the statute books in 1906. For years meat packers and food and drug manufacturers had been selling adulterated foods and dangerous drugs and patent medicines to the public. Popular indignation was aroused by a series of exposures by Dr. Harvey Wiley, chief chemist of the Department of Agriculture, and by Upton Sinclair's shocking revelation of conditions in the Chicago stockyards, *The Jungle*. Congress responded with a Meat Inspection Act and a Pure Food and Drugs Act which went far to eliminate the worst abuses.

But easily the most important of Roosevelt's achievements on the domestic front was in the conservation of natural resources. The country had long been deluded by the concept of infinity with respect to its forests and its soil; at the end of the century it awoke to a realization that three quarters of the forests were gone, much of the mineral wealth had been wasted, water power was being exploited for private profit, and the soil was being washed away by floods or blown away by dust storms. Roosevelt's love of nature and his familiarity with the West gave him a personal interest in conservation. In his first message to Congress he announced that "the forest and water problems are perhaps the most vital internal problems of the United States" and he recommended a far-reaching program of conservation and reclamation. Taking advantage of the Forest Reserve Act of 1891, Roosevelt set aside some 150 million acres of land as a forest reserve and withdrew from public entry another 85 million acres in Alaska and the Northwest, pending study of their forest and mineral wealth. At the same time he placed forest conservation under the control of the vigorous and enlightened Gifford Pinchot. A Reclamation Act of 1902 provided for large-scale irrigation projects at the expense of and under the supervision of the Federal government, and under the terms of this act work was soon under way on the great Roosevelt Dam in Arizona, the Arrowrock Dam in Idaho, and the Elephant Butte Dam on the Rio Grande. All this was, to be sure, only a beginning, but the precedents established and the public interest aroused made possible the far more elaborate program of the Franklin Roosevelt administration.

By 1908 Roosevelt had served one term as successor to McKinley, one in his own right. He was at the height of his popularity and could doubtless have had another term for the asking. But he hesitated to challenge the third-term tradition and chose, instead, to pick a successor to carry out "my policies." His choice fell on the learned and able William Howard Taft, and that choice was ratified first by the Republican nominating convention and then, after a dull contest with Bryan, by popular election.

Taft had been judge of the circuit court, Governor General of the Philippines, and Secretary of War. In all these administrative posts he had acquitted himself well, but in none had he revealed any political talent or any trace of liberalism. He was genuinely anxious to continue the Rooseveltian program, and his accomplishments were not negligible. He stepped up the prosecution of trusts; strengthened the Interstate Commerce Commission; established a postal-savings bank and a parcel-post system; expanded the merit system in the civil service; and sponsored the enactment of two amendments to the Federal Constitution—one providing direct election of Senators, another authorizing an income tax. Yet against these progressive achievements must be set policies and gestures unmistakably reactionary. The most notorious of these was the acceptance of a tariff whose protective schedules outraged liberal opinion, the dismissal of Pinchot as head of the Forestry Service, the opposition to the entry of Arizona into the Union because of her liberal Constitution, and the growing reliance on the ultraconservative wing of the party.

By 1910 Taft had succeeded in splitting his party wide open, and a landslide swept the Democrats back into control of the Congress. Roosevelt, anxious to give his successor a free hand, had gone off to Africa to hunt lions; now a popular ditty voiced the hope of his followers:

> *Teddy, come home and blow your horn,*
> *The sheep's in the meadow, the cow's in the corn.*
> *The boy you left to tend the sheep*
> *Is under the haystack fast asleep.*

Roosevelt did come back, after a triumphal tour of Europe, and liberal Republicans like La Follette and Pinchot hurried to pour their indignation into his attentive ear. Roosevelt was not yet ready to act, but La Follette was, and in 1911 he began his campaign to win the Republican nomination. That campaign evoked such widespread support that

Roosevelt decided to cash in on it; early in 1912 he announced that "my hat is in the ring." There followed a spirited campaign between Roosevelt and Taft, in which the former won all the popular support and the latter most of the delegates. At the Chicago convention the party steam roller flattened out T. R.'s vociferous supporters and gave the nomination to Taft. Roosevelt denounced the action as "naked theft" and promised to make a fight on an independent ticket. A few weeks later twenty thousand of his hysterical followers met at Chicago and, singing

Follow! follow!
We will follow Roosevelt
Anywhere, everywhere,
We will follow on . . .

organized the Progressive party and named their beloved leader its candidate.

The Democrats watched all this with unrestrained enthusiasm. For many years they had wandered with Bryan in the political wilderness; now they caught a glimpse of the Promised Land. Competition for the presidential nomination was keen. The conservatives rallied behind an old war horse, Champ Clark of Missouri, Speaker of the House; the liberals shouted and voted for a newcomer, Woodrow Wilson, Governor of New Jersey. In the end it was Bryan who dictated the choice, poor Bryan who had never been able to win the presidency himself but who now, at the most dramatic moment of his career, named Woodrow Wilson the next President of the United States.

Chapter Eighteen

THE RISE TO WORLD POWER

New Forces and Horizons

WHEN we consider American political history in the generation after the Civil War we meet a spate of dramatic occurrences: reconstruction, the Granger movement, the felling of the spoils system, tariff battles, the Populist upsurge, the rise of progressivism. When we consider industrial history we encounter an equally crowded era: the building of imperial railroad systems, the growth of trusts, the birth of huge new industries, the feats of captains like Rockefeller, Carnegie, Morgan, and Hill. By contrast foreign relations offer a thin chronicle. Only two or three striking episodes give color to the years between the French evacuation of Mexico under American pressure in 1867 and the sinking of the *Maine* off Havana in 1898. "What have we got to do with abroad?" a parochial-minded Congressman of this period is supposed to have ejaculated. Preoccupied with domestic problems, most citizens took only an intermittent interest in foreign affairs.

Yet the field was more important than it seemed, for inexorably certain facts of direct concern to every American were emerging. The United States was becoming a true world power, with a heavy interest in the peace, order, and prosperity of the more and more interdependent family of nations. It was also becoming aware of a special relation-

413

ship with Great Britain. Because the Monroe Doctrine, commercial expansion, and, after 1899, the Open Door in the Orient demanded an ocean dominated by freedom-loving powers, because of natural business ties with its best customer, and because of a common interest in the promotion of democracy, the United States moved toward closer association with the British Empire. At the same time, the United States assumed a more sternly protective attitude toward Latin America. With manufactured goods as well as raw materials demanding outlets, it gave more attention to the development of overseas markets. Partly for commercial and strategic reasons, partly from idealistic motives, partly from pride of power, it swung to an exuberant expansion overseas.

Long before the Spanish-American War the United States had begun to show consciousness of its position as a true world power. Under Presidents Arthur and Cleveland it began building a strong modern navy. By 1890 the "white squadron" was an object of keen national pride. The total exports of the United States by 1880 exceeded $835,000,000 and twenty years later were roughly $1,400,000,000. No nation could ship so much outside its borders without taking a lively interest in foreign affairs. For a time after the Civil War the old fever for expansion had seemed almost completely gone. After the purchase of Alaska in 1867 most citizens felt that the American flag waved over enough territory, and Grant's effort to annex Santo Domingo was overwhelmingly defeated in the Senate. But gradually expansionist sentiment again rose. When Germany tried to lay greedy hands on Samoa, the United States stood firm with Great Britain in asserting its rights there. A three-power protectorate was set up, and in a division at the end of the century the United States took all the islands but the two largest, receiving the long-coveted harbor of Pago Pago. In Hawaii, where Americans had obtained control of the sugar-growing industry, the United States obtained in 1887 the exclusive right to use the priceless Pearl Harbor as a naval station. Six years later an effort to effect the annexation of Hawaii was on the verge of success when Cleveland's reaccession to power halted it—for he rightly thought that the methods used were improper. But thereafter the Hawaiian Islands were controlled by resident Americans until in 1898 they definitely passed under the American banner. Meanwhile, in 1889 the United States brought delegates from nearly a score of southern republics to the first Pan-American Conference in Washington. American influence was reaching farther and farther from home.

In the thirty years after the Civil War most of the international controversies of the United States were naturally with the only other major power in the Western Hemisphere, Great Britain. Some of them were grave. But the significant fact is that they were all settled by arbitration or adjudication, and in such a way as to improve Anglo-American feeling.

The whole list of friendly settlements is impressive. Strong antagonism to Britain had been aroused in the North during the Civil War. Much of it was unfounded; the British recognition of Confederate belligerency was quite correct, the British navy pursued a policy which on the whole favored the North, and the British masses even in the hard-hit cotton-spinning districts of Lancashire stood with Lincoln. But Tory unfriendliness and the ravages of British-built or -equipped cruisers under the Confederate flag were angrily remembered. For a time, as leaders like the fanatical Charles Sumner pressed exaggerated claims for damages, a clash seemed possible. Fortunately, the United States had one of the sagest of all its Secretaries of

State in Hamilton Fish. Under his leadership, a plan was worked out for submitting the American claims for damages wrought by the *Alabama* and other cruisers to arbitration. The first great international tribunal of modern times met at Geneva; it closed the whole controversy by awarding the United States $15,500,000; and the British promptly paid this moderate sum. At the same time a minor boundary dispute between the United States and Canada, involving a few islands on the Northwest coast, was arbitrated; a few years later a dispute over fishery rights in the North Atlantic was adjusted by a joint commission. In the late 1880's a new controversy arose over the question whether Canadians had a right to share in the capture of Alaskan fur seals in the Bering Sea. The State Department bumptiously insisted that these waters were a mare clausum under exclusive American jurisdiction. Once more the quarrel was submitted to an international board of arbiters, which decided in favor of the British.

Most telling of all was the amicable settlement of the Venezuelan boundary dispute which flared up so dramatically and dangerously in the closing days of 1895. This dispute came to a head with startling suddenness. On December 16, 1895, few men in America or Britain dreamed of any serious friction between the two nations. On December 17, the public of both countries was thunderstruck by the news that President Cleveland had sent Congress a message which contained an implied threat of war against Britain. How came such a message to be possible?

There had long been an unsettled boundary between British Guiana and Venezuela. Repeatedly the United States had proffered its good offices to bring about a decision. But the Venezuelan pretensions were absurdly exaggerated; and the British refused to arbitrate the claims except west of the so-called Schomburgk line, surveyed half a century earlier. Many Americans suspected the British of land-grabbing designs at the expense of a weak nation. Finally, in the summer of 1895 the State Department sent London what Cleveland called a "twenty-inch gun note," which in effect accused Great Britain of violating the Monroe Doctrine and asked for a categorical answer on arbitration. "Today the United States is practically sovereign on this continent," asserted the note. When the long-delayed British answer came, it denied that the disputed frontier had anything to do with the Monroe Doctrine, pointed out certain historical errors in the American note, and once more refused arbitration. Cleveland was "mad clear through." He at once sent Congress a message declaring that an investigating commission should be hurried to Venezuela to determine the true boundary line, and when it had finished, the United States "must resist by every means in its power" any encroachments on land assigned to Venezuela.

For a time many feared the worst; jingo elements in America had a field day. But the ultimate results of the episode proved happy. The British people and government showed remarkable restraint, while the Kaiser's telegram to the Boer leader Kruger came early in 1896 to divert their attention to other topics. Powerful American newspapers, led by the New York *World*, condemned Cleveland's rash act. Commercial and religious bodies rose in opposition. Professional circles were grieved and resentful. Multitudes on both sides of the Atlantic declared that war was unthinkable. Messages of friendship and confidence were exchanged. Some 1300 British authors appealed for American amity; more than 350 members of Parliament asked for the arbitration of all disputes. In the end, Britain and Venezuela, using the good offices of the United States, agreed to an arbitration which excepted those areas held by either nation for fifty years or more. The whole affair cleared the air between England and America, increased their mutual respect, and showed how powerful were the attachments which operated beneath the surface of politics.

It was well that this was so. The foreign policy of the United States was more and more clearly in the grip of powerful new forces. The republic was about to play a role on a larger stage, and Anglo-American antagonism had to be discarded for Anglo-American harmony.

The Spanish-American War

The last decade of the nineteenth century found imperialist sentiment running high in most great nations. The partitioning of Africa was being concluded; China seemed about to be torn in pieces for the benefit of the powers. Some of the roots of imperialism were economic, for growing populations and expanding industrial systems demanded new markets. Some were political, for rival nations sought strength in overseas dependencies. Some were naval; Alfred T. Mahan's books had emphasized the value of chains of naval bases. Some were religious and ethical, for evangelical churchmen felt it a Christian duty to spread light in dark places, while reformers talked of the white man's mission of uplifting backward peoples. Still other roots were purely emotional; sensational newspapers whipped up a taste for adventure in foreign spheres. In the United States the panic of 1893 and the re-election of the anti-imperialist Cleveland had done something to check the spirit of jingoism and expansionism. By 1897, with the depression wearing away and Cleveland discredited, this spirit was resurgent. It found its opportunity when a bloody rebellion in Cuba gained impressive headway.

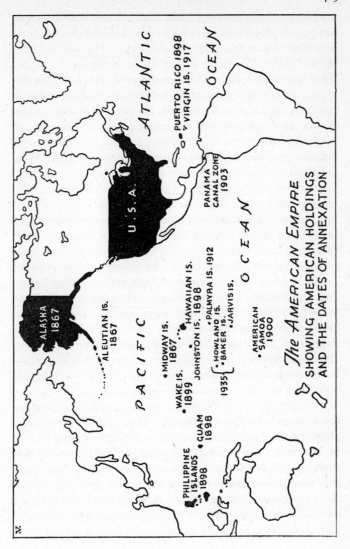

The AMERICAN EMPIRE
SHOWING AMERICAN HOLDINGS
AND THE DATES OF ANNEXATION

ATLANTIC OCEAN

PUERTO RICO 1898
VIRGIN IS. 1917

U.S.A.

PANAMA CANAL ZONE 1903

ALASKA 1867

ALEUTIAN IS. 1867

PACIFIC OCEAN

MIDWAY IS. 1867
HAWAIIAN IS.
JOHNSTON IS. 1898
PALMYRA IS. 1912
HOWLAND IS.
BAKER IS.
JARVIS IS.
1935

WAKE IS. 1899

GUAM 1898

PHILIPPINE ISLANDS 1898

AMERICAN SAMOA 1900

The Spanish government in Cuba had long been corrupt, tyrannical, and cruel. Year after year it had drained the island of at least two fifths of its annual income, diminishing its productive capacity and impoverishing the people. The Spaniards practically monopolized the government, paying themselves outrageous salaries and maintaining a system of continuous thefts. Almost intolerable levies were placed upon industry and commerce. Abusive excise taxes burdened agriculture and mining, while the tariff gave Spanish manufacturers and traders a monopoly which they exploited by charging ruinous prices for goods. Life and property were unsafe. Any Cuban might be summarily arrested and "shot while trying to escape." The courts were tools of the Spanish rulers, and a lawsuit was usually another name for robbery. The press was muzzled. The Church, which was in the hands of Spanish prelates, was corrupt, inefficient, and out of sympathy with the plain people. Its reactionary hierarchy kept such a strangulating grip upon education that illiteracy was general. A heavy standing army had to be supported by the people. Revolt lay always just underneath the surface; and when a heavy depression, accentuated by an American tariff upon sugar, fell upon the island, the suffering masses could no longer be restrained. The patriot José Martí raised his flag in 1895, and soon the whole country was aflame.

Although both the Cleveland and McKinley administrations made an earnest effort to keep neutral, it became clear that if the war were prolonged America would have to intervene. The economic effects on the United States were serious; about fifty million dollars of American capital was invested in Cuba, while trade with the island before the revolt had amounted to $100,000,000 a year. Diplomatic troubles with Spain became irritating. When Cuban revolutionists used the United States as a base for military expeditions, Madrid complained. But the situation was hard to meet, and the ineffectiveness of the Spanish blockade was an important factor. American citizens in Cuba suffered losses of property, liberty, and even life, and Washington offered vigorous remonstrances over their treatment. Above all, American feeling was deeply stirred by the savagery with which the war was being waged on both sides and by the brutality of Spanish policy. After the able but ruthless Valeriano Weyler was sent out to crush the revolt, the struggle became one of the most horrible in history. Both sides laid waste the country and massacred their prisoners. Wanton outrages were committed upon helpless noncombatants. In the fall of 1896 Weyler turned certain towns and cities into concentration areas, driving women, children, and old men within stockaded quarters where they perished like flies. By the end of 1897 more than half of the 101,000 people of Havana Province who had been placed in concentration areas were dead; and the American consul general reported that, in the island as a whole, 400,000 inoffensive women and children had been beggared and reduced to the condition of wild animals—buried by the hundred daily from starvation and fever.

The Spanish government poured troops into Cuba until by the beginning of 1898 it had 200,000 men there. Its Foreign Office attempted to organize a league of European powers to prevent the United States from interfering; cold-shouldered by Russia and actively opposed by Great Britain, it received some encouragement from Germany, Austria-Hungary, and France. But by 1898 the sands were running out. Congress was growing clamorous for decisive action. Public sentiment, responsive in part to the naked facts of the situation, in part to the clamor of a sensational press led by William Randolph Hearst's New York *Journal,* was ready for war. President McKinley and the group of big-business Senators who were his closest advisers wished to avoid a conflict. But political considerations and a belief in the right of the popular will to rule placed limits upon McKinley's resistance to pressure. The stupid Spanish minister in Washington, Dupuy de Lome, did not help matters when in February he let the Hearst press get hold of a letter in which he called McKinley "a would-be politician," a "bidder for the admiration of the crowd" and a man guilty of bad faith with Spain. A week later the battleship *Maine* was blown up in Havana harbor with a loss of 260 lives. Whether this was the work of irresponsible Spaniards, or of Cubans acting as *provocateurs,* it rendered war almost unavoidable. The Spanish government made hasty last-minute concessions. Properly seized upon, they might have resulted in the peaceful liberation of Cuba. But McKinley believed it too late for further delay, and on April 11 sent Congress a war message. It was unquestionably a popular step.

No other American conflict ever brought such quick returns in a certain kind of glory as the Spanish-American War. Fighting began on May 1, 1898, and was all over in ten weeks. Not a single reverse of any importance occurred. On May Day Dewey steamed into the unmined waters of Manila Bay at dawn, approached the Spanish fleet—which he outranged—until the distance was perfect, remarked, "You may fire when you are ready, Gridley," and put the enemy out of action without losing a man. The event was fitly celebrated by the Kansas versifier who wrote:

> *Oh, dewy was the morning,*
> *Upon the first of May,*
> *And Dewey was the admiral,*
> *Down in Manila Bay.*
> *And dewy were the Spaniards' eyes,*

Them orbs of black and blue,
And dew we feel discouraged?
I dew not think we dew!

Troops equivalent to a single army corps were landed near Santiago, Cuba, won a rapid series of engagements, and brought the port under fire. Admiral Cervera's fleet of four armored cruisers plunged out of Santiago Bay and a few hours later was a row of smashed hulks along the coast—with but one American seaman killed. General Miles's army landed on Puerto Rico and marched through it as if on a holiday parade. Mr. Dooley wrote of the conquest of the island as "Gineral Miles's Gran' Picnic and Moonlight Excursion in Puerto Rico."

The American people accepted the war with a light-hearted patriotism. Every band played Sousa's new air, *The Stars and Stripes Forever,* and every piano strummed the ragtime march, *There'll Be a Hot Time in the Old Town Tonight.* Party lines were forgotten as Bryan served as colonel of a Nebraska regiment. The last vestiges of sectional antagonism between North and South melted away in the fire of national feeling; and Joe Wheeler, the famous Confederate cavalry leader, fighting before Santiago, exclaimed that a single battle for the Union flag was worth fifteen years of life. From Boston to San Francisco whistles blew and flags waved on the hot July day when word came that Santiago had fallen. Newspapers rushed their correspondents to Cuba and the Philippines to see the fun, and these writers trumpeted the renown of a dozen new national heroes. There were "Fighting Bob" Evans of the *Iowa,* who took Cervera on board after his defeat; Captain Philip of the *Texas,* who as a Spanish vessel sank said, "Don't cheer, boys; the poor fellows are dying"; Lieutenant Victor Blue, who plunged into the Cuban jungle to gain information on Spanish forces;

and Captain R. P. Hobson, who sank the collier *Merrimac* in a vain effort to plug the mouth of Santiago Bay. Above all other heroes loomed George Dewey, to whom the nation gave a home in Washington, and Theodore Roosevelt, leader of the Rough Riders, whose war record helped him to a more famous Washington house. It seemed an ideal war. Its casualty lists were short, it cost no great debt, it raised American prestige abroad, and the nation emerged with its pockets full of booty.

Yet when scrutinized closely it had less creditable sides. Its glory was won at the expense of a helpless foe, for enemy resistance was pitiable. The Spanish navy was so ill-equipped and demoralized that although American marksmanship was atrocious, it hardly inflicted a scratch on American ships. The 200,000 troops in Cuba were so handicapped by bad leadership and wretched transport that only 12,000 could be placed in Santiago when American forces approached that city. Our victories were attributable in part to dash and courage, but in still larger part to Spanish weakness. And the background of these victories was a record of bureaucratic corruption, inefficiency, and bungling which seemed to reflective citizens highly discreditable. The War Department was so badly mismanaged that its head was shortly forced out of the McKinley administration, giving place to a leader who put it and the army on a high plane of efficiency—Elihu Root. The army death rate from disease was a grave reflection not only upon its medical branch, but upon American sanitation and health services in general. Naval gunnery had to be taken sharply in hand. The paralyzing grip of politics upon the war services in Washington was once more demonstrated. Altogether, Theodore Roosevelt was right in calling the conflict the War of America the Unready. The army was soon raised to a strength of 100,000, a permanent General

Staff was created, the navy was rapidly enlarged, and professional services in both branches were strengthened. By taking the lessons of the war to heart, the United States was helped to prepare adequately for the terrible ordeal of 1917–1918.

Peace with Spain was rapidly arranged by a meeting of commissioners in Paris. Only two points of controversy arose. The Spanish representative tried to insist that Cuba should assume responsibility for debts which Spain had contracted upon a pledge of the island revenues; and they demanded that Spain should keep all or a part of the Philippines. But on both points the American delegation stood firm. Cuba was reborn a debt-free republic. The entire Philippine archipelago was ceded to the United States, and with it Puerto Rico. By this acquisition of overseas territories, peopled by stocks alien in language, culture, and political tradition, America seemed to enter upon a new path. Vehement objections were raised by the anti-imperialists, led by Bryan, Carl Schurz, E. L. Godkin, Mark Twain, and Senator George Frisbie Hoar. But that the treaty met general approval was shown by the election of 1900, which returned McKinley to power by increased majorities. Time was to prove that the overseas responsibilities which the United States assumed were in part merely temporary and that at heart the nation remained nonimperialistic. As the years passed, it chose to reduce its overseas holdings, not to enlarge them.

Nevertheless, the Spanish-American War did mark an important turning point in American history. At last the nation recognized itself as a world power; less and less it felt isolated and self-centered, more and more it played a leading role in broad international arrangements. It consciously became one of the tutors of backward peoples. Under such proconsuls as General Leonard Wood, huge tasks of reorganization, reform, and development were undertaken in the Philippines, Cuba, Puerto Rico, and a little later in Panama. With races like the Igorot and Moros we took up the training of what Kipling called "new-caught, sullen peoples, half-devil and half-child." The conquest of yellow fever as a result of experiments in Cuba by Dr. Walter Reed and others of the army medical staff was a triumph alone worth the whole cost of the war. For centuries "yellow jack" had destroyed life throughout all tropical areas, and it had been a standing menace to our Southern ports. Until the Spanish conflict the United States had tacitly depended on the British navy for maintenance of the Monroe Doctrine; thereafter it insisted on a navy able to maintain the Doctrine unaided. The war, and particularly the sixty-eight-day voyage of the battleship *Oregon* from the Pacific Coast round the Horn to Cuban waters, brought home to everybody the necessity for an isthmian canal. Finally, the struggle did something to increase Anglo-American friendship and to chill German-American relations, for the British celebrated the American victories almost as their own, while a German squadron which kept a jealous watch at Manila had given Dewey anxiety and irritation.

The Open Door: Rooseveltian Diplomacy

The first postwar token of a new attitude in world affairs was the enunciation of the Open Door principle. China, defeated by the Japanese in 1894–1895, had become the prey of European powers, which descended upon her to seize economic privileges and territorial concessions. Russia took practical possession of northern Manchuria; Germany leased the port of Kiaochow, gaining economic control of Shantung Province; France obtained various favors. Both the United States and Great Britain watched this looting with alarm. They valued Chinese trade and feared the erection of high commercial barriers. Just before the Spanish-American War began, the British suggested joint Anglo-American action to preserve free commercial opportunities in China, but the State Department was chilly. Then in 1899 Washington swung to a different position. Manufacturing and trading interests exerted pressure for a firmer policy in the Orient and recalled that the Bureau of Foreign Commerce had termed China "one of the most promising" spots for "an American invasion of the markets of the world." Missionary interests lent their voice. A timely book by Lord Charles Beresford on *The Breakup of China* aroused much feeling. Various men were at work behind the scenes; and finally in September, John Hay, Secretary of State, asked nations with spheres of interest in China to promise that they would not levy special tariffs, harbor dues, or railway charges within these spheres. Though most of the answers contained some qualifications, Hay early in 1900 announced the "final and definitive" assent of the powers.

After Theodore Roosevelt in 1901 succeeded to the presidency, with first Hay and then Root as Secretary of State, American foreign policy fell into two main sections. One part of it centered about the new insular possessions and the Panama gateway and was primarily a consequence of the Spanish-American War and the resultant emergence of the United States to a position where it felt more vulnerable in both the Atlantic and Pacific. The other part of it represented certain personal adventures of Roosevelt in world diplomacy and signalized the arrival of the United States at the position of a world power. These adventures, of which Roosevelt's use of his good offices in 1905 to end the Russo-Japanese War and his participation in the Algeciras Conference of 1906 were the chief, need be given little attention. Both were spectacular, and from Roosevelt's point of view both were successful. Neither was really necessary; Russia and Japan might have settled their quarrel at some different place than Portsmouth, New Hampshire, and Henry White need not have been sent to support France in her historic duel with Germany over North African ports and privileges. It was Roosevelt's foreign policies affecting the Philippines, the Caribbean islands, and Panama which were genuinely important to Americans.

And, we may add, his policies respecting Anglo-American relations; for though men did not suspect it, in two titanic wars the hopes of democracy, nay of civilization itself, were soon to rest upon the collaboration of two great English-speaking powers. The United States, a somewhat shivering newcomer in the bleak arena of world affairs, saw clearly enough that the support of the British navy was highly desirable. Great Britain, for her part, was faced on every hand by the menace of German might. In international trade, German competition; in Africa, German demands for a share; in Asia, German hostility to the Open Door; in Europe, Germany's Triple Alliance and German naval ambitions. It is by no means certain that Germany was without territorial ambitions in the West Indies or Latin America—some of her leaders would have liked a naval base there. For evident reasons the United States and Britain found themselves more and more clearly in accord in the Far East, the Caribbean, and on the maritime highways, where they maintained what was later called "the Atlantic system."

As it became plain that the United States was determined to construct an isthmian canal, the British government made generous concessions to help clear the way. The old Clayton-Bulwer Treaty (1850) had provided that the two nations should possess equal privileges in any canal and that neither should fortify it. Negotiations between Secretary Hay and the British ambassador in Washington resulted in the Hay-Pauncefote Treaty, duly ratified in 1901. Providing that the United States might "construct, maintain, and control" the canal (though no discrimination in rates was to be permitted), it represented a surrender by the British of all their old treaty rights. No *quid pro quo* was asked, and the gesture was duly appreciated by Americans. A little later Great Britain took a course upon the Venezuelan debt question which again pleased Washington. Three powers, Britain, Italy, and Germany, had claims against the disreputable government of President Castro. In the fall of 1902, failing to get payment in any other way, they agreed upon a line of "co-operative coercion." Germany, Britain, and Italy blockaded the Venezuelan coast, seized some gunboats, and bombarded two forts. The United States was willing to see Venezuela spanked good and hard, but nothing more. When Great Britain perceived that her course was irritating American opinion, she receded. A debate was arranged in the House of Commons to denounce joint action with Germany, and the ministry declared it wished to avoid any use of force. The American people contrasted the British attitude favorably with the tactics of the Germans; and later Roosevelt told a dramatic story (inaccurate, but perhaps not wholly unfounded) of how he had got Dewey and the fleet ready for action to persuade the Kaiser to back down.

Early in the century the British government, again, helped settle the Canadian-Alaskan boundary in a fashion which gratified Americans as much as it irritated Canadians. Under the old Anglo-Russian Treaty of 1825, the boundary of the Alaskan panhandle was to follow "the summits of the mountains situated parallel to the coast" in such a fashion as to leave Russia a coastal strip thirty miles wide. The United States inherited this strip. The question was whether it ran in a jagged line around the heads of the deep inlets on the coast or cut in a straight line across their heads. The Canadians hoped to be given harbors at some of these heads. After much discussion the matter was referred to a panel of jurists representing Britain, Canada, and the United States. Roosevelt, intent upon winning, waved the big stick. But this was not really necessary; right was with the Americans, and the British jurist Lord Alverstone consistently voted with them. Finally, when in 1906 the British navy was redistributed in three main fleets, Mediterranean, Channel, and Eastern Atlantic, the squadron long based on Bermuda to cover the West Indies was recalled. German threats had forced this move, but the United States, with its now powerful navy, appreciated having a free hand in the Caribbean.

It did so in part because the Panama Canal was then under way. "I took Panama," Roosevelt told a Western audience in 1912. "It was the only way the canal could be constructed." The first half of the statement is almost literally true. By a law enacted in 1902, Congress authorized the President to buy up the rights of the old French canal-digging company in Panama, to obtain from Colombia perpetual control of a strip of land in that state from the Atlantic to the Pacific, and to begin digging the great ditch. Negotiations were opened with Colombia. But that republic, knowing that Panama was one of its greatest assets, was unwilling to part with it for a mess of pottage. A treaty drawn up in Washington for American control of a six-mile strip was defeated by the Senate in Bogotá. Such defeats had been common enough in the United States, where the American Senate had made mincemeat of more than one important compact. But Roosevelt denounced it as an outrage, characterizing the Colombian politicians as greedy and corrupt. He was determined to have the canal site before the Congress met again in December, for he feared that if he did not, some of his plans might be upset. Two other powerful elements wanted immediate action. One was the French company, which had a stake of forty millions in an early sale. The other was the people of Panama, who feared that if the United States did not soon begin the canal there it would be constructed in Nicaragua instead. The result was that the idea of a revolution in Panama occurred to a great many persons at once. The *Review of Reviews,* edited by a close friend of Roosevelt, blossomed out with an article, "What If Panama Should Revolt?" Talk of an outbreak filled the air in Washington, and cruisers were dispatched to the Panama coast. French agents were busy on the isthmus. On November 3, 1903, immediately after the arrival of the warship *Nashville* at Colón, the State Department sent a cable to American consuls on the scene:

"Uprising on Isthmus reported. Keep Department promptly and fully informed. Loomis, acting."

The consul at Panama, who was no fool, wired back: "No uprising yet. Reported will be in night. Situation critical." And an hour or two later he reported:

"Uprising occurred tonight, 6, no bloodshed. Army and navy officers taken prisoners. Government will be organized tonight."

American marines were landed and stopped Colombian troops from dealing with the revolt. A minister from Panama was promptly received in Washington, and with extraordinary speed the little new republic signed a treaty giving the United States the coveted strip for ten millions down and a reasonable annual rental. Roosevelt later remarked: "If I had followed traditional conservative methods I should have submitted a dignified state paper of probably two hundred pages to Congress and the debate would be going on yet. But I took the Canal Zone and let Congress debate, and while the debate goes on the canal does also." Quite true. Within a decade, thanks to the engineering genius of Colonel George W. Goethals and the sanitary genius of William C. Gorgas, the canal was ready for operation. But Roosevelt's rough course had shocked and alarmed public sentiment throughout Latin America.

Theodore Roosevelt was actuated by a genuine desire for better relations with the Latin republics, but both his policies and their results were very mixed. When the third Pan-American Conference was arranged at Rio Janeiro, he sent Secretary Root for a good-will tour of South America. He made it clear that he wanted to befriend Latin America. He treated the Monroe Doctrine as a vital protection to the southern republics. But he added to this Doctrine a famous corollary which deeply disturbed many of them. Pointing out that since the United States would not permit European powers to take rough action with unruly little nations which defaulted their debts, seized alien property, or maltreated alien residents, he declared that this placed an unescapable responsibility on American shoulders. Uncle Sam himself would have to see that such republics behaved. He illustrated this principle in his treatment of Santo Domingo. When that nation was threatened in 1904 with intervention, he induced it to let him establish an American financial receivership. This set a precedent for the erection of a number of virtual protectorates in the Caribbean area. The policy made for peace and order, but it inspired fears in Latin America that the United States was embarking on a predatory course.

In the Pacific, also, Roosevelt followed a course which had mixed results. Japanese-American relations were beginning to become a source of anxiety. The President intervened in a controversy between Japan and the city of San Francisco, which was giving discriminatory treatment to Japanese in the schools. By his best endeavors he smoothed the ruffled feelings of the Japanese, obtained a "gentlemen's agreement" to prevent immigration of Japanese laborers, and induced the San Francisco authorities to follow a more politic course. But because he thought that a warning was proper, he sent the fleet on a tour of the world in which it stopped at Japanese ports, receiving there a courteous welcome. This was in the spirit of one of his most-quoted utterances: "Speak softly, and carry a big stick."

As the years passed it became more and more clear that the United States was not only a world power, but one of the three or four greatest of world powers. It took a prominent part in both of the Hague Conferences for the promotion of world peace. It gave moral support all over the globe to democratic principles and freedom of commercial intercourse. Despite Roosevelt's occasional untactfulness and Taft's "dollar diplomacy"—that is, the promotion of American trade and investments by diplomatic means—it made progress in winning the confidence of Latin America. Despite occasional pinpricks, it steadily grew closer to Britain and the great British Commonwealth overseas. When the First World War began, it was in a measure still isolated. It was not so much isolated but that it was quickly drawn into that terrible maelstrom.

Chapter Nineteen

WOODROW WILSON AND THE
WORLD WAR

Woodrow Wilson

WOODROW WILSON was in many respects the most remarkable figure in American politics since Jefferson. A scholar and an intellectual, unaccustomed to the hurly-burly of public life, he was nevertheless astute, hardheaded, and resourceful. A visionary and an idealist, he was at the same time the most thoroughly realistic and adroit political leader since Lincoln. He was a moralist in politics and in international affairs, and in him the spirit of his Covenanter ancestors was reborn. With an old-fashioned courtliness went a hot-tempered belligerence, with passionate devotion to principle a ruthlessness in maintaining it. His speeches had none of the homely quality of Bryan's or the forthright vigor of Roosevelt's, but they had a soaring eloquence and a poetic beauty unmatched since Lincoln. He was a student of politics, had written several capital books on government, and had his own well-matured notions of the nature of the presidential office, of the party system, and of the place of the United States in the world of nations, and he was prepared to put these notions into effect. "Clean, strong, high-minded, and cold-blooded," as Secretary Lane observed, he was also intellectually arrogant, brittle, and, when crossed, petulant. Impersonal in his relations, he attracted men to him as to an abstract principle, and he never permitted personal affection to interfere with his policies or forgave a friend who failed to measure up to his high standards.

Most of Wilson's life had been spent in academic cloisters, as professor of politics and president of Princeton University. In 1910 the Democratic bosses of New Jersey put him forward as gubernatorial window dressing, and he took over the whole political shop. Within two years he had driven the bosses from the political temples and transformed New Jersey from one of the rotten boroughs of American politics into a model commonwealth, and in the process he had perfected many of the techniques he was later to use with such skill—the audacious boldness, the disarming candor, the insistence upon his own position as party leader, the appeal over the heads of politicians to the people themselves, and the strategy of swift and relentless attack. It was Wilson's spectacular achievement in New Jersey that made him a national figure, brought him the support of men like Bryan, and gave him the presidential nomination; it was his own transparent sincerity and his matchless campaign eloquence that carried him to victory over Roosevelt.

Wilson's inaugural address was at once a challenge and a promise. "No one can mistake," he said,

the purpose for which the nation now seeks to use the Democratic party. It seeks to use it to interpret a change in its own plans and point of view. Some old things with which we had grown familiar, and which had begun to creep into the very habit of our thought and of our lives, have altered their aspect as we have latterly looked critically upon them, with fresh, awakened eyes. . . . Some new things, as we look frankly upon them willing to comprehend their real character, have come to assume the aspect of things long believed

in and familiar, stuff of our own convictions. We have
been refreshed by a new insight into our own life.

Then followed a program of constructive reform to achieve
the New Freedom, a program at once bold and com-
prehensive. "We have itemized," said Wilson, "the things
that ought to be altered," and he mentioned "a tariff
which makes the government a facile instrument in the
hands of private interests," a banking and currency system
perfectly adapted to "concentrating cash and restricting
credits," an industrial system which "restricts the liberties
and limits the opportunities of labor," an agricultural economy inefficient and neglected, and the exploitation of natural resources for private gain. On its positive side the
government was to be "put at the service of humanity"—in
safeguarding the health and the welfare of women and
children and of the underprivileged.

These reforms were to be achieved deliberately and efficiently. Yet the process of reform was "no cool process of
mere science."

The nation has been deeply stirred, stirred by a solemn
passion, stirred by the knowledge of wrong, of ideals
lost, of government too often debauched and made an
instrument of evil. The feelings with which we face
this new age of right and opportunity sweep across our
heartstrings like some air out of God's own presence
where justice and mercy are reconciled and the judge
and the brother are one. We know our task to be no
mere task of politics, but a task which shall search us
through and through, whether we be able to understand our time and the need of our people, whether we
be indeed their spokesmen and interpreters, whether
we have the pure heart to comprehend and the rectified
will to choose our high course of action.

The New Freedom in Action

These were lofty ideals, eloquently phrased; could this college professor, so miraculously elevated to the presidency, translate them into law? He quickly showed that he meant business. Congress was called into special session, and when it convened, Wilson, reviving an almost forgotten custom, addressed it in person. "The tariff duties must be altered," he said. "We must abolish everything that bears even the semblance of privilege." This was a dangerous issue. There had been no real break in the protective system since the Civil War; Cleveland had obtained only minor concessions from the protectionists, and the astute Roosevelt had avoided the issue altogether. Underwood of Alabama and Hull of Tennessee had their bill all ready, however, and under executive prodding the House passed it promptly enough. But when the Senate took it up, the lobbyists swarmed over the capital like harpies, and observers predicted a repetition of the 1894 fiasco. Then in a public letter Wilson lashed out at the lobby. "It is of serious interest to the country," he said, "that the people at large should have no lobby . . . while great bodies of astute men seek to create an artificial opinion and to overcome the interests of the public for their private profit." The reprimand was effective, and six months after he took office Wilson had the satisfaction of signing a tariff bill which faithfully reflected platform promises and campaign pledges by effecting the first genuine downward revision in over fifty years.

The country sat up and took notice: here was an executive who meant what he said and did what he proposed. Wilson did not give his party pause; even while Congress was wrestling with the tariff schedules, he reminded it of his inaugural promise to reform "a banking and currency system based upon the necessity of the government to sell its bonds fifty years ago and perfectly adapted to concentrating cash and restricting credits." This issue, like the tariff, was packed with political dynamite. The nation had long suffered from an inflexible credit and currency system; almost everyone agreed on the diagnosis, but few on the cure. During the Roosevelt administration there had been stopgap legislation permitting the national banks to issue emergency currency, and a Monetary Commission had submitted an elaborate series of reports on the banking practices of other nations. But a thorough overhauling of the banking system was long overdue. The bankers rallied to write a law which would continue them in control; Bryan, who had long argued that the money question was the paramount issue, was determined that the government should control credit. Wilson, who knew little about the technical aspects of banking but who had not studied in vain the history of the first and second Banks of the United States and the later experiment of the independent-treasury system, sided with Bryan. "Control," he said, "must be public, not private, must be vested in the government itself, so that the banks may be the instruments, not the masters of business and of individual enterprise and initiative." The Federal Reserve Act which emerged from prolonged debate fulfilled these requirements. It decentralized the banking system, affording better banking facilities to the neglected South and West, and it provided in Federal reserve notes an elastic currency under government control. The Federal Reserve System came just in the nick of time; without it, the government could scarcely have weathered the crisis of the World War.

A third major legislative achievement of the new administration was in the control of trusts. The Sherman Act had been more effective against labor than against great industrial combinations, and recent investigations had revealed

WOODROW WILSON

that the movement toward concentration of control in industry, transportation, and banking was going on apace. "A private monopoly," Bryan had written into the Democratic platform, "is indefensible and intolerable," and as soon as tariff and banking legislation was out of the way, Wilson moved to implement this plank. The Clayton Antitrust Act of 1914 carefully defined a number of malpractices, prohibited discriminations in price which might tend to create monopolies, forbade the tying together of large corporations by "interlocking directorates," and made corporation directors personally liable for infractions of the antitrust laws. At the same time a Federal Trade Commission was set up to investigate business operations, hear complaints of unfair methods, and stop harmful practices by issuing "cease and desist" orders.

The farmers and labor were not forgotten. A Federal Farm Loan Act made credit available to farmers at low rates of interest, and a Warehouse Act, authorizing loans on the security of staple crops, gave substantial effect to the old subtreasury scheme of the Populists. One provision of the Clayton Antitrust Act specifically exempted labor from its provisions and prohibited the use of the injunction in labor disputes—a prohibition which failed to win judicial approval. Two acts designed to end child labor in industry got through Congress, only to be nullified by the courts. The La Follette Seamen's Act of 1915 emancipated the hard-driven common seamen from the tyranny under which they had long suffered, and the Adamson Act of the following year established an eight-hour day for railroad labor.

Thus in three years Wilson had pushed through more and more important legislation than any President since Lincoln. He had revealed unsuspected possibilities of executive leadership of Congress and presidential leadership of party. He had proved that democracy could function, swiftly and effectively, in a crisis.

A Democratic Foreign Policy

Wilson's foreign policy departed as sharply from that of his predecessor as did his domestic. Roosevelt had cheerfully wielded the "big stick" in foreign affairs, Taft had encouraged what came to be known as "dollar diplomacy." These policies had unquestionably brought the United States a greater measure of influence in world affairs, but at the cost of antagonizing the nations of Latin America and of imperiling our own welfare by involving us in fortuitous diplomatic and business adventures in which we had no genuine interest. One of Wilson's first official acts was to withdraw official approval from a proposed bankers' loan to China because he "did not approve the conditions of the loan or the implications of responsibility." That same week he announced his purpose "to cultivate the friendship and deserve the confidence" of the Latin American republics, and a short time later, in his Mobile address, elaborated that announcement with a specific repudiation of dollar diplomacy and a promise that the United States would never again seek territory by conquest. Circumstances were to involve the United States in the affairs of several of the Caribbean and Central American republics, but throughout his administration Wilson steadfastly refused to make intervention an excuse for exploitation.

The difficulties of the Wilsonian policy were amply illustrated by relations with Mexico. For thirty-five years that unhappy land had groaned under the tyrannical rule of Porfirio Diaz, who reduced his own people to peonage while he sold out his country to foreign mining and business interests. In 1911 the middle classes and peons rose in revolt, drove Diaz out, and placed a liberal, Francisco Madero, in the presidency. It looked like the dawn of a new day for Mexico, but within two years a counterrevolutionary movement under the leadership of Victoriano Huerta overthrew and assassinated Madero. The foreign oil, railroad, mining, and land-owning interests, who saw a return of the fat days of Diaz, were jubilant, and most of the great powers hastened to recognize the new President. But not Wilson. He felt that to recognize Huerta would be to condone murder, and he was unmoved by the importunities of American businessmen who were interested only in their own profits. "We hold," he said, anticipating the position he was to take later in a greater crisis, "that just government rests always upon the consent of the governed, and that there can be no freedom without order based upon law and upon public conscience and approval." This policy of basing recognition upon moral considerations was criticized then and later as a departure from correct practice and the dictates of expediency. As the German Emperor remarked, "Morality is all right, but what about dividends?" But Wilson realized, as did Franklin D. Roosevelt a generation later, how fatal were the consequences that might follow an acquiescence in lawlessness or a recognition of the fruits of violence.

Wilson not only refused recognition to the bloody-handed Huerta; he brought Britain around to support his policy—a support won through timely concessions on the Panama Canal tolls question. Relations with Mexico, however, rapidly worsened, and when Huerta arrested some American sailors at Tampico, Wilson promptly landed marines at Vera Cruz. War appeared inevitable, but Wilson had no intention of permitting the situation to get out of hand, and by drawing a distinction between the Mexican people—whom he wished to befriend—and the Mexican government—which he was determined to destroy—suc-

ceeded in restraining the war clamor at home while maneu-
vering Huerta into an untenable position. Then he seized
the opportunity of the Mexican crisis to dramatize his policy
of treating the Latin American republics as equals by in-
voking the aid of Argentina, Brazil, and Chile in settling
the dispute. When these sided with the United States,
Huerta was forced to flee the country, and Carranza, leader
of the Constitutionalists, came into power. Even after that,
difficulties continued, and when the Mexican bandit chief,
Pancho Villa, raided Columbus, New Mexico, Wilson sent
an expeditionary force under General Pershing to punish
him. Carranza resented the invasion, and American chau-
vinists clamored for war, but peace was maintained and
Mexico allowed to work out her own salvation. The policy
of "watchful waiting," denounced as pusillanimous, had
succeeded in its dual object of aiding Mexico and gaining
the confidence of the Latin American republics.

In two other fields the Wilson administration revealed
its interest in the maintenance of peace and the sanctity of
treaty agreements. Bryan, who now presided over the State
Department, had long been convinced that all international
disputes were susceptible to arbitration, and with Wilson's
blessing he drew up and negotiated "cooling-off" treaties
with foreign nations. These provided for arbitration and
conciliation of all issues—not excepting those involving
national honor—and for the suspension of all war preparation for a "cooling-off" period of one year. Thirty such
treaties were negotiated, twenty-two went into effect; Germany conspicuously refused to accept one. And in 1915,
when Japan, already headlong on that policy of ruthlessness
which was eventually to lead to war with the United States,
presented her infamous "twenty-one demands" to China,
the State Department protested that these constituted a flagrant violation of the Open Door and of international law.

The United States, wrote Bryan, would refuse to recognize any impairment of American rights or of the territorial and political sovereignty of China.

The World War and Neutrality

But it was Europe that presented the most serious threat to American peace. On June 28, a Serbian patriot fired a shot whose echoes reverberated around the world; within five weeks all Europe was locked in the greatest war of modern times. The American reaction was one of incredulity and bewilderment. When President Wilson formally proclaimed American neutrality, he spoke for a unanimous nation; even when he counseled neutrality in thought as well as in action he expressed the attitude of the majority of Americans.

Yet Americans could no more be indifferent to the struggle of 1914 than they could to the struggle of 1939, and neutrality, whether of mind or of governmental policy, proved in the end impossible. American feeling was from the beginning violently enlisted. The great majority of the people hoped that Britain and France and Belgium would win. A hundred ties of culture, tradition, common institutions, and common outlook existed with the British people; memory of French aid in the Revolution and admiration for the gallant resistance of the French and Belgian peoples were only less potent. Comparatively small elements, chiefly German-Americans who responded to the call of blood, and Irish-Americans who had an inherited hatred of Britain, sympathized with the Central Powers. German policy in the Pacific, in China, in the Caribbean, the ruthless acts of German militarists and the arrogance of German intellectuals and statesmen, had alienated Americans long before the war, and the unprovoked invasion of Belgium confirmed their worst suspicions of Germany. It was clear, too,

that the Germans stood for absolutist ideas in government
and society, and that if they dominated Europe they would
be certain to come into conflict, sooner or later, with democratic America.

These two considerations—sympathy for the Allies, fear
of the consequences of German victory—were in the end
decisive in controlling American policy. Economic considerations re-enforced sentimental and political ones. The
American people loaned large sums of money to Britain
and France. American industry rapidly geared itself to
Anglo-French war needs, supplying enormous quantities of
guns, shells, high explosives, and other materials, and reap-
ing heavy profits. American banks acted as purchasing
agents for the Allies, floated Allied loans, and established
Allied credits in the United States. American agriculture,
recovering from a sharp prewar depression, found ready
and profitable markets for cotton, wheat, and pork in England and France. Trade with the Central Powers, meantime, was negligible, and the British blockade effectively
controlled trade with neutrals as well.

Yet it was not these economic considerations that persuaded Wilson and the American people of the necessity of
war, but rather the German policy of "frightfulness." Submarines were used to sink merchant ships, and they could
not save the lives of crew or passengers. When the British
vessel *Lusitania* was sent to the bottom in 1915 with the loss
of more than eleven hundred lives, 128 of them American,
a wave of horror and anger swept the country. Germany
promised to mend her ways, and Wilson kept the nation at
peace, but those who believed that America should prepare
for war increased in numbers and determination. Meantime, Wilson himself had come to see that the only way to
keep the United States out of the war was to bring the war
itself to an end. All through 1916 he worked heroically to

persuade the belligerents to state their war aims and to pave
the way for the organization of the postwar world.

In the presidential elections of 1916 Wilson was successful, largely because he had "kept us out of war." Yet he had
given no commitments for the future, no promise to buy
"peace at any price." Indeed, as early as January, 1916, he
had warned the American people in words that the war
lords of Germany would have done well to heed:

> I know that you are depending upon me to keep this
> nation out of the war. So far I have done so and I
> pledge you my word that, God helping me, I will—
> if it is possible. But you have laid another duty upon
> me. You have bidden me see to it that nothing stains
> or impairs the honor of the United States, and that is
> a matter not within my control; that depends upon
> what others do, not upon what the government of the
> United States does. Therefore there may at any moment
> come a time when I cannot preserve both the honor
> and the peace of the United States. Do not exact of me
> an impossible and contradictory thing.

Early in 1917 the Germans, sure that they could starve
England out in six months and that American help could
not become effective in that time, announced the reopening
of unrestricted submarine warfare. Within a few weeks
eight American vessels were sent to the bottom, and the
nation was aroused by the revelation of a plot to involve
the United States in a war with Mexico and Japan. The
preservation of both honor and peace had become "an impossible and contradictory thing" and on April 2, Wilson
appeared before the Congress and asked for a declaration
of a state of war:

> It is a fearful thing to lead this great peaceful people
> into war, into the most terrible and disastrous of all

wars, civilization itself seeming to be in the balance. But the right is more precious than peace, and we shall fight for the things which we have always carried nearest our hearts,—for democracy, for the right of those who submit to authority to have a voice in their own Governments, for the rights and liberties of small nations, for a universal dominion of right by such a concert of free peoples as shall bring peace and safety to all nations, and make the world itself at last free. To such a task we can dedicate our lives and our fortunes, everything that we are and everything that we have, with the pride of those who know that the day has come when America is privileged to spend her blood and her might for the principles that gave her birth and happiness and the peace which she has treasured. God helping her, she can do no other.

On Good Friday, April 6, 1917, the United States went to war.

War

Now that war had come, the overwhelming majority of Americans supported the government in its determination to achieve a complete victory. Wilson's policy of waiting until the country was united on the necessity of war was justified. Disloyal groups were fewer and weaker than in the Civil War, and nowhere were they able seriously to interfere with the war effort.

"Force, force to the uttermost, force without stint or limit," President Wilson had promised, and the nation hastened to fulfill this promise. Never before had the government revealed greater intelligence or efficiency in war, never before had the American people more effectively displayed that energy, resourcefulness, and inventive genius for which it was famous. Wilson proved one of the greatest of war Presidents, controlling every aspect of the war effort, maintaining morale at home and abroad, never losing sight of the ultimate objectives for which the nation was fighting. He was ably assisted by his War Secretary, Newton D. Baker, his Secretary of the Treasury, McAdoo, and by Bernard Baruch, chairman of the War Industries Board. The government had to take steps far more drastic than any contemplated in any previous war, and it did so with dispatch and energy. It became dictator over industry, labor, and agriculture. It took over the railroads and the telegraph lines. Food was needed, and farm production was increased by one fourth; fuel was needed, and coal production was raised by two fifths. By loans and taxes the government raised some thirty-six billion dollars, lending ten to its Allies and spending the rest on its own war effort. Above all, the government concentrated on winning the battle of the Atlantic—which, in the spring and summer of 1917, appeared all but lost. By seizing interned German ships, commandeering neutral and taking over private shipping, and launching a colossal shipbuilding program—more than three million tons in a single year—the battle was won.

Conscription had been voted early, and before the war was over, the registration of some twenty-five million men suggested something of the immense man-power resources of this Western democracy. But could the United States train and equip an army and ship it to France in time to stem the tide of German advance? That was the great question of 1917 and 1918.

The first American contingent landed in France in June, 1917—hurried over for its effect on morale rather than for military purposes. On July 4, the little army paraded down the Champs Élysées, the red, white, and blue fluttering in the breeze. Brand Whitlock described the scene:

I heard the band; it was playing *Marching Through Georgia*. I could not withstand that! And so downstairs, and out into the Rue de Rivoli bareheaded. There was the crowd sweeping along the street below the great iron fence of the Tuileries, from curb to curb, with no order, men, women, children, trotting along, hot, excited, trying to keep up with the slender column of our. khaki-clad regulars, who marched briskly along. French soldiers in their light blue trotted beside them, as closely as they could get, looking at them with almost childish interest and wonder, as boys trot hurrying beside a circus parade. Our soldiers were covered with flowers—and always the steady roar of the crowd and now and then cries of *Vive l'Amérique*.

But this was merely a token force; the real American army was still in the training camps back in the United States.

It was desperately needed, for in 1917 the war had taken a turn for the worse. In October the Italian army was smashed at Caporetto, and the Allies had to hurry reinforcements to stem the Austrian advance. A month later the Russians, already torn by revolution, caved in and sued for peace. Forty new German divisions, drawn from the Russian and Balkan fronts, were hurried to the West. By the spring of 1918 the Germans had clear numerical superiority in the West and girded themselves for the knockout blow against the decimated and weary armies of Britain and France. In March, 1918, came the first major offensive; within a week the Germans had smashed through the British Fifth Army, capturing ninety thousand prisoners and immense stores. In April came another great drive, and General Haig issued his memorable appeal: "With our backs to the wall, and believing in the justice of our cause, each one of us must fight on to the end." A third offensive was launched in June, and, with the Germans on the right

DANIEL WEBSTER

From a Portrait by J. Ames

bank of the Marne, the Allies placed Marshal Foch in supreme command and advised President Wilson that "there is great danger of the war being lost unless the numerical inferiority of the Allies can be remedied as rapidly as possible by the advent of American troops."

Already the race with time had begun. The United States government girded itself for a Herculean effort. Shipping was given priority over everything, and one massive convoy after another sailed from American ports, laden with khaki-clad doughboys. In March, 80,000 were shipped overseas; in April, 118,000; in May, almost 250,000. By October the American army in France numbered over one and three-quarter million soldiers.

They came just in the nick of time. First at Mondidier and Cantigny and then at Belleau Wood, they proved their mettle, and the German Command, which had discounted American help, reluctantly admitted that "the American soldier proves himself brave, strong, and skillful. Casualties do not daunt him." But the great crisis was still ahead. At midnight of July 14, the Germans launched their long-awaited offensive on the Marne, designed to crack the last Allied line and open the path to Paris, only fifty miles away. They thundered across the Marne, everywhere successful except where they ran into fresh American divisions. "Right here on the Marne," wrote the German Chief of Staff, Walther Reinhardt, "we well-nigh reached the objectives prescribed for our shock divisions. . . . Especially all divisions of the Seventh Army achieved brilliant initial successes, with the exception of the one division on our right wing. This encountered American units. Here only did the Seventh Army . . . confront serious difficulties. It met with the unexpectedly stubborn and active resistance of fresh American troops. While the rest of the divisions . . . succeeded in gaining ground and tremendous booty it proved impossible for us to move the right apex of our line, to the south of the Marne, into a position advantageous for the development of the ensuing fight. The check we thus received was one result of the stupendous fighting between our 10th Division of infantry and American troops." And he added ruefully, "The Americans appear inexhaustible." By the eighteenth the German attack was played out, and Foch called upon the Americans to counterattack. This they did, and with spectacular success. "The tide of war," wrote General Pershing, "was definitely turned in favor of the Allies." And from the German Chancellor Hertling came confirmation of this. "At the beginning of July, 1918," he later wrote, "I was convinced . . . that before the first of September our adversaries would send us peace proposals. . . . That was on the 15th. On the 18th even the most optimistic among us knew that all was lost. The history of the world was played out in three days."

In September came the attack on the Saint-Mihiel salient. "The rapidity with which our divisions advanced overwhelmed the enemy," wrote General Pershing. Casualties reached seven thousand, but the Americans wiped out the salient and captured sixteen thousand prisoners to boot. And the next month an American army of over a million took a leading part in the vast Meuse-Argonne offensive, which, in the end, cracked the vaunted Hindenburg line and shattered German morale.

Meantime Wilson, by an eloquent definition of the war aims of the democracies, was doing scarcely less than the armed forces to insure victory. From the beginning he had tried to sow dissension in Germany by insisting that our fight was not with the German people but with their tyrannous and autocratic government. He had insisted, too, that the peace terms ought not to include annexation of unwilling peoples or money payments of a punitive nature.

And in a message to Congress of January, 1918, he had submitted the famous Fourteen Points as the basis for a just peace. These were: open covenants openly arrived at; freedom of the seas in peace and in war; the removal of economic barriers between nations; the reduction of armaments; an impartial adjustment of colonial claims; cooperation with Russia in the establishment of her own national policy with institutions of her own choosing; a readjustment of the boundaries of Europe with due attention to the principle of the self-determination of peoples; and the establishment of a "general association of nations" to afford "mutual guarantees of political independence and territorial integrity."

With their armies beaten back and their allies on the verge of collapse, and with fresh American troops pouring up to the front in ever-increasing numbers, the German government saw that only an immediate peace could prevent the invasion of German soil. It turned therefore to Wilson and appealed to him to negotiate on the basis of the Fourteen Points. While diplomatic fencing was still under way, mutiny and revolution at home made further German resistance impossible. The Kaiser abdicated and fled, and on November 11 the war came to an end.

The League and Isolationism

Thus far Wilson had proved a leader of consummate skill. But as the war ended he made a succession of missteps. He appealed to the people to elect a Democratic Congress, and in resentment at this partisan act they chose Republican majorities in both chambers. He decided to go to the Peace Conference in person, thus offending many Americans who believed that the President should never leave national soil, and in doing so he ultimately lowered his prestige in Europe. He failed to place any prominent

Republican—or indeed any man of first-rate ability—on his Peace Commission. And while he committed these errors of judgment, war weariness, a renewed suspicion of Europe, a sense of disillusionment, and party bitterness were engulfing the country. As he sailed for France, ex-President Roosevelt, bitter and defiant, warned "our Allies and our enemies" that "Mr. Wilson has no authority whatever to speak for the American people at this time. . . . His Fourteen Points and his four supplementary points and all his utterances every which way have ceased to have any shadow of right to be accepted as expressive of the will of the American people."

The treaty makers—Wilson, Lloyd George, Clemenceau, Orlando, and a host of lesser statesmen—met at Paris in an atmosphere of hatred, greed, and fear—hatred of the enemy, greed for colonies and reparations, fear of Bolshevism. The peace that was concluded was a dictated, not a negotiated, peace. The Treaty of Versailles fastened war guilt upon Germany, wrested from her all of her colonial possessions, provided for territorial readjustments on all of her borders, and imposed upon her heavy indemnities. Other treaties created or recognized new states which had come into existence in accordance with the Wilsonian principle of self-determination—Czechoslovakia, Yugoslavia, Poland, Finland, among others. In accepting these terms Wilson was forced to compromise on some of his Fourteen Points; he was willing to do this only because he was firmly convinced that all errors would be rectified through the machinery of the League of Nations.

For Wilson had succeeded, against the most formidable opposition, in sewing the League of Nations into the treaty arrangements. The idea of an association of nations was not a new one, and many persons from many lands had contributed to the clarification of that idea. But the League of

Nations that was ultimately established was Wilson's creation. Its function was "to promote international co-operation and to achieve international peace and security." Membership was open to all nations; control was to be lodged in an upper Council consisting of the Great Powers and in an Assembly in which all members were represented. The members of the League pledged themselves to "respect and preserve as against external aggression the territorial integrity and existing political independence" of all members— the famous Article Ten—to submit all disputes to arbitration, and to employ military and economic sanctions against nations resorting to war in disregard of the League. In addition, provision was made for disarmament, the government of mandated colonies, and the creation of a Permanent Court of International Justice and an International Labor Bureau.

When Wilson returned to the United States with the Versailles Treaty and the League, he found opposition widespread and fierce. Many Republican leaders—like the embittered and intensely partisan Senator Lodge—saw in the issue an opportunity to defeat the Democrats and humiliate Wilson. Personal dislike of the President swayed a number. German-Americans, Italian-Americans, and Irish-Americans all found reasons for denouncing the terms of peace. To some vengeful people the treaty seemed too easy upon Germany; to many liberals it seemed too harsh. A substantial number of conservative Americans feared entanglement in European quarrels and recalled that for more than a century the nation had in general kept aloof from Old World affairs.

Yet there is evidence that a majority of the people—or certainly a majority of the best-educated groups—approved the League, and at no time did the treaty lack a majority in the Senate. Even the two thirds necessary for ratification might have been obtained had Wilson been willing to compromise on Article Ten. But this he was unwilling to do. "Article Ten," he told a Senate Committee, "seems to me to constitute the very backbone of the whole covenant. Without it the League would hardly be more than an influential debating society." But the Republican opposition was unconvinced, and Wilson took the issue to the people, who had so often in the past understood him and sustained him against the politicians. As he crusaded through the West his health gave way, and on September 25 he suffered a paralytic stroke from which he never recovered. The great cause that he espoused was lost. In March, 1920, the Senate, by its final vote rejecting the treaty and the League Covenant, condemned the United States for years to come to a sterile and unheroic isolationism.

The election of 1920 swept the Republicans back into power by an unprecedented majority, and they hastened to make isolation a party principle. Broken in health but not in spirit, Wilson retired to watch, with profound disillusionment, that breakdown of collective security he had predicted. He had lived, like that James Petigru whose epitaph he so admired,

> Unawed by opinion
> Unseduced by flattery
> Undismayed by disaster

and like him

> He confronted life with antique courage,
> And Death with Christian hope.

Not until a Second World War, even greater than the first, had shaken the very foundations of the firmament were men to recognize the validity of the principles for which he had fought so gallantly.

Chapter Twenty

FROM WAR TO WAR

Normalcy and Isolation

THE defeat of Wilson, the repudiation of the New Freedom and of internationalism, set the stage for the appearance of isolation and *laissez faire,* and these two forces dominated it for the next decade. The Republican party, to be sure, had not taken a clear stand on the League, but sought refuge, rather, in a masterly obfuscation of that issue. But the decisive majority which the party commanded in the 1920 elections convinced most leaders—and certainly the weak-willed President Harding—that the isolationists spoke for the people, and placed men like Johnson, Borah, and Lodge in positions of strategic strength while it tended to discredit such international-minded Republicans as Hughes, Root, Taft, and Butler. Once in power the Republicans hastened to give official status to isolationism.

This was something new, both in the history of the Republican party and of the nation. Never before had the United States so cavalierly betrayed the hopes of mankind: the traditional American policy had been rather one of fulfillment of the promise of world leadership. Nor had the Republican party ever before committed itself to isolation. Grant and Seward had urged expansion into the Caribbean and the Pacific; Blaine had espoused Pan-Americanism; McKinley had led the nation to war on behalf of the Cubans and acquired new colonies in the Pacific; Theodore

Roosevelt had claimed for the nation a dominant position in world power politics. The Republican tradition was one of imperialism and internationalism.

But now the party stood committed to a narrow nationalism and an evasion of responsibility comparable to that which afflicted Britain in the middle of the nineteenth century. Yet real isolation was impossible, and the United States could not remain aloof from affairs elsewhere in the world. Actually, during these years of Republican rule, the government took an active part in bringing about the solution of some of the more vexatious problems that disturbed international relations. President Harding sponsored a conference on naval disarmament—with some success. His successor, Coolidge, obtained the support of sixty-two nations to the Pact of Paris, outlawing war as an instrument of international relations. The Young Plan and the Dawes Plan for the settlement of reparations had their origins here, and President Hoover took the lead in proposing a moratorium on war-debt payments. All of the Republican Presidents urged American membership in the World Court—though in vain—and all of them made tentative gestures toward co-operation with some of the work of the League of Nations.

But these gestures toward disarmament and peace were more than counterbalanced by American aloofness from the real work of the League and by the steady growth of economic nationalism. It was, indeed, in the economic realm that isolationism had most serious consequences. Fearful of foreign competition, eager for foreign markets, and infected with the notion of economic autarchy, the nation embarked upon a neomercantilistic policy fraught with danger not only to itself but also to the whole world.

As early as 1920, a Republican Congress rushed through an emergency tariff bill designed to raise a wall of protection against foreign products. In his veto message President Wilson urged common sense on this matter. "If there ever was a time when America had anything to fear from foreign competition," he said, "that time has passed. If we wish to have Europe settle her debts—governmental or commercial—we must be prepared to buy from her. Clearly this is no time for the erection of high trade barriers." But this sage advice the Republicans chose to ignore, and no sooner were they in complete control of the government than they enacted the Fordney-McCumber tariff, raising duties to unprecedented heights and effectively preventing European nations from selling us their goods. Eight years later the still recalcitrant Republican majority pushed through the Smoot-Hawley tariff, highest in American history, and, over the protest of almost every respectable economist in the country, Hoover signed it. These tariffs not only closed the American market to the products of European farms and factories but led to retaliatory tariffs which closed European markets to American goods.

But this was only one aspect of the economic question. The war and postwar years witnessed the transformation of the United States from a debtor to a creditor nation. During the period of war and reconstruction, the government had lent some ten billion dollars to Allied and associated nations; in the twenties, private investors poured an additional ten or twelve billions into the investment markets of Europe, Asia, and Latin America. How were these debts to be serviced and, ultimately, repaid if the United States would not permit debtors to sell to us? To this pertinent question the Republican statesmen had no ready answer.

Throughout the twenties, Republican policy was conditioned by these two contradictory considerations. Toward foreign indebtedness the administration adopted an attitude of adamantine stubbornness. There were, to be sure, generous concessions on interest, but on the matter of the repayment of principle the government was firm; as President Coolidge remarked, "They hired the money, didn't they?" But as long as American tariff walls were unbreached, repayment was all but impossible. Indeed, the only way Germany was able to continue reparation payments and other countries to buy American goods was by further lending.

In the domestic arena, the Harding administration inaugurated the reign of "normalcy"—and Harding's idea of normalcy was a return to the good old days of Mark Hanna and McKinley. This was not, as is sometimes supposed, pure *laissez faire,* but rather a felicitous combination of two policies—one, freedom of private enterprise from governmental restraint, and the other, generous subsidies to private enterprise. Government withdrew from business, but business moved in and took over government.

On the positive side the record is impressive. The tariffs of 1922 and 1930 constituted a practical guarantee against foreign competition. The Department of Commerce, under the indefatigable Herbert Hoover, engaged actively in opening up new markets abroad and justified the boast that it was "the world's most formidable engine of foreign-trade conquest." In the domestic field the Department co-operated actively in the organization of some two hundred trade associations and cartels much like those later organized under the National Recovery Administration. "We are passing," said Hoover sententiously, "from a period of extreme individualistic action into a period of associated activities." Generous subsidies were voted to the merchant marine and to aviation companies carrying United States mail. The taxation policy adopted by the millionaire Secretary of the Treasury, Andrew Mellon, shifted a substantial part of the tax burden from the shoulders of the rich to those of the middle classes and the poor.

At the same time traditional *laissez faire* was honored no less faithfully. The railroads, which the government had operated with striking success during the war, were returned to private owners, and on generous terms. A large part of the war-built merchant marine was turned over, at ridiculously low prices, to private companies. The Sherman and Clayton Antitrust Acts were practically suspended, both executive and judiciary taking the position that they were not called upon "to repeal economic laws." The most characteristic expression of *laissez faire* came in connection with proposals for government construction and operation of hydroelectric plants. In 1916 President Wilson had authorized, as a wartime measure, the construction of dams at Muscle Shoals, on the Tennessee River, to furnish power for nitrate plants. After the war the disposition of these plants and dams became a matter of prolonged and bitter controversy. Conservatives contended that they should be turned back to private owners; progressives, under the leadership of the courageous Senator Norris of Nebraska, insisted that they be continued under government ownership and operation. In 1928 a bill calling for government operation passed the Congress, only to be vetoed by President Coolidge. A similar measure passed in 1931 was defeated by President Hoover, whose veto message perfectly expressed that philosophy of "rugged individualism" to which he and his party subscribed:

> I am firmly opposed to the government entering into any business the major purpose of which is deliberate competition with our citizens. . . . For the Federal government deliberately to go out to build up and expand an occasion to the major purpose of a power and manufacturing business is to break down the initiative

and enterprise of the American people; it is destructive of equality of opportunity of our people; it is the negation of the ideals upon which our civilization has been based. . . . I hesitate to contemplate the future of our institutions, of our country, if the preoccupation of its officials is to be no longer the promotion of justice and equal opportunity but is devoted to barter in the markets. That is not liberalism, it is degeneration.

This concern for equality of opportunity would have come with better grace had the Coolidge and Hoover administrations at any time revealed any genuine interest in the welfare of labor and farmer groups. But these administrations were interested only in the "businessman," and their conception of business was a narrow one. Neither the farmers nor the workingmen shared the piping prosperity of the twenties. There was a brief but sharp break in farm prices in 1921; by the mid-twenties a gradual decline set in and continued without interruption until the operation of the New Deal reforms became effective. Between 1920 and 1932 farm income declined from fifteen and one-half to five and one-half billion dollars. Some eight hundred million bushels of wheat, in 1920, brought about one and one-half billion dollars; a slightly smaller crop in 1932 brought less than three hundred million dollars. Thirteen million bales of cotton, in 1920, were sold for just over one billion dollars; the same cotton crop, twelve years later, sold for less than half a billion dollars. The same story could be told for most other crops. The result was to be seen in the mounting figures of farm tenancy and mortgage foreclosures. By 1930 forty-two per cent of the farms of the country were operated by tenants, and the total mortgage indebtedness had risen to over nine billion dollars, while in the five years between 1927 and 1932 not less than one tenth of the farm property of the nation was foreclosed at auction.

Yet in the face of this situation the Coolidge and Hoover administrations, so eager to place the government at the disposal of business, evinced an attitude of indifference and even of hostility to the farming interests. The Republican solution to the farm problem was a tariff on agricultural products; since the United States exported rather than imported farm produce, the solution was irrelevant, to say the least. Concrete proposals looking to governmental subsidies and crop control that had the support of farmer organizations were rejected by presidential vetoes.

Politically this era of "normalcy" was one of dullness and incompetence, unrelieved except by the spectacular scandals of the Harding and the internecine party battles of the Hoover administrations. Never before had the government of the United States been more unashamedly the instrument of privileged groups; never before had statesmanship given way so unreservedly to politics. Warren G. Harding, an amiable but weak Senator from Ohio, was nominated to the presidency because no one knew anything against him, and elected because the country was weary of Wilsonian idealism. In the two and a half years of his tenure of office his easygoing acquiescence in the exploitation of government by big business and his tolerance of gross corruption amply justified the expectations of those who looked for an end to idealism. Calvin Coolidge who succeeded him was a thoroughly mediocre politician, dour and unimaginative, thrifty of words and of ideas, devoted to the maintenance of the *status quo,* and morbidly suspicious of liberalism in any form. Herbert Hoover, who came to the presidency in 1929, was a man of far-greater ability, with a reputation as an efficient executive, an international-minded statesman, and a great humanitarian; in four years he managed to lose all three reputations and to make more and more serious errors of judgment than any President since Grant.

Society in the Postwar Years

These three Presidents, each so different in personality and character, represented well enough the dominant forces in American society during the postwar years. The idealism of the Wilson era was in the past; the Rooseveltian passion for humanitarian reform was in the future. The decade of the twenties was dull, bourgeois, and ruthless. "The business of America is business," said President Coolidge succinctly, and the observation was apt if not profound. Wearied by idealism and disillusioned about the war and its aftermath, Americans dedicated themselves with unashamed enthusiasm to making and spending money. Never before, not even in the McKinley era, had American society been so materialistic, never before so completely dominated by the ideals of the market place or the techniques of machinery. It was an age of bigness and of efficiency, and popular admiration went out to these things: the engineer, the stockbroker, the salesman, the advertiser, and the moving-picture star were the popular heroes. The nation grew in population by seventeen million and grew in wealth even more spectacularly; if the wealth was crazily distributed, there seemed enough to go around and men talked glibly about the "new era" with a chicken in every pot and two cars in every garage. Cities were bigger, buildings taller, roads longer, fortunes greater, automobiles faster, colleges larger, night clubs gayer, crimes more numerous, corporations more powerful, than ever before in history, and the soaring statistics gave to most Americans a sense of satisfaction if not of security.

It was an era of conformity and of intolerance with nonconformity, and the literary figure accepted by most Americans as most representative was George Babbitt, who believed everything that he heard and read. It is a striking fact that the public did not react violently to the shocking scandals of the Harding administration or penalize the party responsible for them; it visited its displeasure rather upon those who exposed these scandals or who criticized the "American" way of life. The seeds of intolerance had been planted during the war; after the war they sprouted in strange and terrifying form. Nationalism was chauvinistic; isolationism took on moral and intellectual as well as political character. There was widespread hostility to foreigners and to foreign ideas. Aliens suspected of radical notions were rounded up and deported by the thousands; legislatures were "purged" of socialists; and states tried to enforce loyalty to political and economic institutions by law. The Ku Klux Klan, which boasted a membership of millions, dedicated itself to that notion of Aryan supremacy which European dictators were to take up a decade later, and its hooded Klansmen · intimidated Catholics, Negroes, and Jews. Religious fundamentalism took the form of legislative prohibition of the teaching of evolution; censorship laws emasculated moving pictures, plays, and books. Hostility was directed against the critics of American business practices, embracing, indiscriminately, labor leaders, liberal economists, socialists, pacifists, or "agitators" of any stripe who dared to question the ethics of business or refused to bow down to the idols of the market place. In two notorious cases—that of Mooney and Billings in California and of Sacco and Vanzetti in Massachusetts—there was a tragic miscarriage of justice; in both cases the victims were punished more for their radicalism than for any crimes proved against them.

Yet it is easy to exaggerate both the extent and the depth of this intolerance. It is well to remember that it was inspired by a misguided zeal for democracy rather than by hostility to democracy. And throughout the entire period the current of dissent and protest ran strong and deep. No intolerance went unrebuked; no victim of injustice was too humble to raise up men to champion his cause. Perhaps the most interesting thing about the Mooney-Billings and Sacco-Vanzetti cases is the fact that they inspired eloquent and courageous protests—successfully in the one case, unsuccessfully in the other. Liberal magazines like *The Nation* and *The New Republic* commanded a substantial circulation and a wide influence; poets and novelists who preached the gospel of revolt enjoyed wide popularity; the colleges and universities remained centers of freedom of thought and inquiry, and scholars pursued everywhere their search for truth, untrammeled by government restrictions or popular hostility. And throughout all these years the courts stood stanchly for the protection of personal liberties and the guarantees of the bills of rights. This was the era not only of Harding, Coolidge, and Hoover, but also of Brandeis, Cardozo, and Holmes.

The most important factors conditioning social development during this generation were the growth of cities and the acceleration of technological changes. By 1930 over half the population of the country lived in towns and cities, and a substantial part of it in the great metropolitan areas. The cities were the centers of industry and business, of government, of entertainment, of education, of literature and the arts. Urban ideas and ways of life spread out over the countryside. Under the impact of the movies, the radio, the automobile, syndicated newspaper features, national advertising, and a host of other influences, provincialism gave way to standardization. Even in humor, perhaps the most characteristic form of national expression, the tall story of the frontier gave way to the sophisticated anecdote or cartoon purveyed by *The New Yorker*.

Of the many forces making for standardization, the automobile, the moving picture, and the radio were easily the most important. They were, indeed, the most important factors in the social life of this decade. Of the three, the automobile was the oldest and, in some respects, the most significant. Henry Ford had built a "gasoline buggy" back in the mid-nineties, but it was not until the second decade of the new century that Ford's famous Model T and other cheap cars came on the roads by the hundreds of thousands. In 1920 there were some nine million automobiles in use; ten years later the number had increased threefold. The automobile broke down isolation, sped up life, discovered new ways to spend leisure, gave a new freedom to youth, created vast new industries, gave work to millions of men, stimulated a nation-wide road-building program, provided serious competition to the railroads, and exacted an annual toll of life and limb as high as that of the Civil War. Within a few years the automobile ceased to be a luxury and became a necessity, perhaps *the* necessity. When the depression came, the car was always the last thing to go, and tire and gasoline rationing did more to bring the Second World War home to the average American than almost anything else.

The movies and the radio, both relatively new, were scarcely less important than the automobile. Moving pictures date from the early years of the century, but they did not become a big-time business until the First World War or attain their immense influence until the advent of "talkies" in 1927. By the end of the decade, between eighty and one hundred million persons went to the movies every week—and a very large proportion of these were children. It was from the movies that the rising generation got many of its ideas about life, usually romantic and often highly misleading. To many the moving pictures offered an escape from drab reality into the never-never world of romance, where wickedness was always punished and virtue always rewarded, where all women were beautiful and all men handsome and acrobatic, where riches brought happiness and poverty contentment, and where all stories had a happy ending. Directly and indirectly the movies exercised an incalculable influence. They set the styles in dress and coiffures, in furniture and interior decoration, they originated popular songs, they taught manners, inculcated morals, and created popular heroes and heroines. Their influence spread throughout the world, and they proved perhaps the most powerful instrument of American imperialism. To rapt moviegoers of the British Isles, of Russia, of Malaya, of the Argentine, they carried a picture —often a caricature—of American life.

The radio was equally influential as an instrument for entertainment, education, and standardization. Radio developed rapidly during the First World War, and the first commercial broadcasting station began business in 1920. Within a decade almost every family in the nation was able to tune in on Amos 'n' Andy or Charlie McCarthy, on news broadcasts, or on music. The radio, like the movies, was a big business, and like the movies, too, it was geared to mass consumption and had to fit its programs to popular interest: a study of radio programs would reveal more, perhaps, about the popular mind than would any other study. In two fields the radio aimed at something more than popular entertainment. It undertook educational programs— rather feebly, to be sure—and it broadcast news and political campaigns. It is interesting to note that the radio remained, with very few exceptions, a private enterprise, supported not by taxes but by advertisers who bought time and accompanied programs with tributes to the virtues of the products which they sold. Whether Americans paid too high a price for freedom from government control of the radio is a matter about which opinions differed.

The Great Depression

Herbert Hoover assumed office under auspices more favorable than those which had attended any other President since Taft. To all appearances the country had never been more prosperous or society more healthy. Stocks soared to dizzy heights, and every month hundreds of millions of dollars in new securities were snapped up by avid investors who hoped to share in the wonderful new game of making something out of nothing. Factories could not turn out automobiles, refrigerators, radios, vacuum cleaners, and oil burners fast enough to keep up with the insatiable demand for new gadgets; railroads groaned with their burdens; hundreds of thousands of new houses, in fantastic colonial, Tudor, Gothic, Spanish, pueblo, and modernistic styles, sprang up in the suburbs of great cities or in the new industrial towns of the South and the West. Colleges and moving-picture theaters were jammed; furnishing men with sporting goods and women with cosmetics became a big business; while advertising rose from the level of a business to the higher levels of a science and an art. Every day some new and marvelous technological improvement or scientific advance gave assurance of still better times ahead. It was the New Era, and if the farmers and the unskilled workers did not share in its benefits, all that would come later. And it was appropriate that the New Era was to be ushered in by a man who had made his reputation as an engineer, had proved himself a great humanitarian, and had revealed his understanding of the business civilization by his yeoman work as Secretary of Commerce. "We in America," Hoover had boasted, "are nearer to the final triumph over poverty than ever before in the history of any land," and almost everyone expected that Hoover himself would celebrate that "final triumph."

Then, with dramatic and outrageous abruptness, came the crash of October, 1929. On the twenty-first of that month came the first break; on the twenty-fourth over twelve million shares changed hands in a delirium of selling; on the twenty-ninth came catastrophe. Sound stocks like the American Telephone and Telegraph, General Electric, and General Motors lost from one hundred to two hundred points in a single week. By the end of the month stockholders had suffered a paper loss of over fifteen billion dollars; by the end of the year the shrinkage in securities of all kinds had reached the fantastic sum of forty billion dollars. Millions of investors lost their life savings. But the spiral of depression did not stop here. Business houses closed their doors, factories shut down, banks crashed, and millions of unemployed walked the streets in a vain search for work. Hundreds of thousands of families lost their homes; tax collections dropped to the point where cities and counties were unable to pay schoolteachers; construction work all but ceased; foreign trade, already badly hit, declined to an unprecedented low.

What were the causes of this panic and the long depression that followed? It is neither very satisfying nor very illuminating to say that depression is a normal part of the business cycle, though where government does not step in to control the excesses of individualistic enterprise that is correct enough. In the case of the 1929 panic there were certain factors that led, clearly enough, to the collapse. In the first place, the productive capacity of the nation was greater than its capacity to consume. This was largely because too large a part of national income was going to a small percentage of the population who promptly turned it back into savings or investment, and not enough of the income to the labor, farmer, and white-collar classes upon whose continued ability to buy the whole business system rested. In the second place, the tariff and war-debt policies of the government had pretty effectually cut down the foreign market for American goods, and with the world-wide depression of the early thirties that market collapsed. In the third place, easy credit policies had led to an inordinate expansion of credit, a vast extension of installment buying, and unrestrained speculation. Government and private debts totaled between one hundred and one hundred and fifty billion dollars, and speculation had pushed stock and property beyond their true value. Finally, the persistent agricultural depression, the continuous industrial unemployment, and the uninterrupted tendency toward concentration of wealth and power in a few giant corporations produced a national economy fundamentally unhealthy.

Whatever the explanations, it was soon clear that the nation was in the grip of the most ruinous depression in its history. The panic of 1837 had lasted three or four years; that of 1873 had dragged on for five years; the dreadful depression of 1893 came to an end in the spring of 1897; while the panics of 1904, 1907, and 1921 were short-lived affairs. But the great depression of 1929 lasted almost a full decade. It was unprecedented in length and in the wholesale poverty and tragedy which it inflicted upon society. And in another respect, too, it differed from earlier depressions: it was clearly the product of abundance, not of want. More completely than any other depression it was a monument to the breakdown of the system of distribution of wealth and of goods.

Since the depression arose not out of natural causes but out of artificial ones, it called insistently for aggressive governmental action. But this was not forthcoming. The Great

Engineer had no solution; his was a prosperity, not a depression, government. He did not entirely repudiate the obligation of the government to act, but he did hold that relief was exclusively the concern of private charity and of local governments. "As a nation," he said, "we must prevent hunger and cold to those of our people who are in honest difficulties," but he stubbornly rejected every specific proposal of direct relief to the unemployed or the starving. He adopted from the first the policy of minimizing the extent of the depression and, when that was no longer possible, embraced the theory that prosperity was "just around the corner." While Great Britain and her Dominions—as well as many other nations—confronted with substantially similar problems—were embarking upon elaborate programs of direct relief, firm control of banking practices, currency and credit, drastic income taxes, agricultural subsidies and crop control, large-scale public works and slum clearance, and far-reaching economic planning, the Hoover administration contented itself with measures designed to ease rural credits and to make money available to railroads, banks, and large corporations.

These measures were obviously inadequate, and the situation went steadily from bad to worse. By 1932 the number of unemployed had mounted to over twelve million; over five thousand banks had closed their doors; commercial failures totaled thirty-two thousand; farm prices had fallen to the lowest point in history; the middle class was in danger of being wiped out; national income had declined from over eighty billion in 1929 to forty billion. The whole economy of the nation seemed to be disintegrating, and the people were in an ugly mood.

Americans are not prone to violence or to revolution, and in this crisis they turned hopefully to a different leadership. A group of Republican Progressives, led by Senators Norris,

La Follette, Costigan, and Cutting, had challenged Hoover's policies, but they were not strong enough to wrest control of the party from the Old Guard. Of necessity the country looked to the Democrats for salvation. In 1930 the Democrats swept the Congressional elections, and in 1932 they prepared to take over the presidency. The Republican Old Guard, which had learned nothing from the depression, defiantly renominated President Hoover, who appealed once again to "rugged individualism" for a solution to the national crisis. The Democrats presented the brilliant and magnetic Franklin D. Roosevelt, who as Governor of the Empire State had revealed himself a resourceful, courageous, and humane leader, and who promised the nation a "new deal." In the November elections Roosevelt rode triumphantly into the White House on the crest of a popular majority of seven million votes.

Franklin D. Roosevelt and the New Deal

One of the most heartening things about American democracy is that it has always managed to find great leaders in time of crisis. Sometimes, as in the case of Washington, the choice has been reasoned and deliberate; at other times, as in the cases of Lincoln and Theodore Roosevelt and Wilson, it has been largely fortuitous. It cannot be said that Franklin Roosevelt was an unknown quantity when first elected to the presidency; it can be asserted that few of those who so hopefully voted for him realized that in Roosevelt they had a leader who as spokesman for democracy and nationalism was the peer of Lincoln, as a leader toward a better world order the peer of Wilson.

Roosevelt had made his reputation as an efficient and socially minded Governor of New York, but behind that lay a long apprenticeship in politics. A man of wealth and of distinguished family, a graduate of Groton School and of

Harvard, Roosevelt had early decided to follow the example of his kinsman in the White House, by taking an active interest in politics. His early ventures were distinguished by two qualities which characterized his later: devotion to progressive principles and a talent for commanding the confidence of people from all walks of life. He had served in the New York State Assembly, been Assistant Secretary of the Navy under Wilson, and run for the vice-presidency in 1920. Then, at the very threshold of a brilliant career, he was stricken with infantile paralysis. Slowly he fought his way back to health, and during the years of retirement from active politics he studied American political history and built up through correspondence and personal contacts a wide and devoted following. In 1928 he ran way ahead of his ticket in capturing the governorship of New York State and two years later was triumphantly re-elected by an even larger majority. With this background and experience, Roosevelt was probably the best-informed Democratic leader in the country in 1932,

But the new President had other qualities besides experience and knowledge. He had an instinctive faith in the common people as profound as Bryan's, a rationalized faith in democracy as profound as Wilson's. He was politically astute, understood the art of leadership, had a talent for apt phrases, and the best radio voice in America. Opportunistic as to means, he was tenaciously consistent as to ends; compromised on nonessentials but rarely on essentials; knew that politics was an art as well as a science; was not deluded by the notion that society could be remade by blueprints or that statecraft could be watered down to a kind of scientific management or engineering project. He was a student of history, government, and political theory, knew the American past, understood the world in which he lived, and had given thought to the organization of the world of tomorrow. He trusted politicians but did not distrust experts; was sensitive to public opinion but did not hesitate to mold it or fear to challenge it. He had broad interests, indefatigable energy, and an infectious buoyancy which he communicated to those about him and, eventually, to the whole people. Unassuming in manner and simple in address, he was indubitably a great gentleman.

Roosevelt's inaugural address was a promise of what was to come, as significant, though not as eloquent, as Wilson's First Inaugural. The nation, he asserted, was fundamentally sound; "plenty is at our doorstep, but a generous use of it languishes in the very sight of plenty." The fault was in the "money-changers" and "self-seekers"; these had been driven from the temples, and the task ahead was one of restoration. To that task the President dedicated himself: to the relief of poverty and want, the restoration of the balance between agriculture and industry, the supervision of banking practices, the readjustment of international economic relationships, the inauguration of the policy of the good neighbor, and the assumption of the international responsibilities proper for a great power. "I am prepared," he said boldly, "to recommend the measures that a stricken nation in the midst of a stricken world may require. These measures . . . I shall seek within my constitutional authority, to bring to speedy adoption." And if Congress should fail to respond, "I shall ask the Congress for the one remaining instrument to meet the crisis—broad executive power to wage a war against the emergency as great as the power that would be given me if we were in fact invaded by a foreign foe." And he concluded:

We face the arduous days that lie before us in the warm courage of national unity, with the clear consciousness of seeking old and precious moral values; with the clean satisfaction that comes from the stern performance of duty by old and young alike. We aim at the assurance of a rounded and permanent national life. We do not distrust the future of essential democracy.

This inaugural address served formal notice on the nation that there was to be a New Deal. That New Deal was long overdue. For over a decade, now, politicians had played with marked cards, and business had gathered in almost all the chips. Roosevelt proposed to restore the rules of the democratic game. To many contemporaries the New Deal seemed like revolution. Actually it was profoundly conservative—conservative in the same sense that Jeffersonian and Wilsonian democracy had been conservative. It aimed to protect, against violence from the left or from the right, the essentials of American democracy—the balance of interests under the Constitution, security for property and for men, and liberty.

In philosophy the New Deal was democratic, in method evolutionary. Because for fifteen years legislative reforms had been dammed up, they now burst upon the country with what seemed like violence, but when the waters subsided it was clear that they ran in familiar channels. The conservation policy of the New Deal had been inaugurated by Theodore Roosevelt; railroad and trust regulation went back to the eighties; banking and currency reforms had been advocated by Bryan and partially achieved by Wilson; the farm-relief program borrowed much from the Populists, labor legislation from the practices of such states as Wisconsin and Oregon. Even judicial reform, which caused such a mighty stir, had been anticipated by Lincoln and Theodore Roosevelt. And in the realm of international relations the policies of the New Deal were clearly continuations of the traditional policies of strengthening national security, maintaining freedom of the seas, supporting law and peace, and championing democracy in the Western world.

The New Deal in Action

When Franklin Roosevelt assumed office on March 4, 1933, the depression was at its lowest ebb and the economic system of the country on the verge of complete collapse. Roosevelt met the crisis with boldness and vigor, and before his first term had ended he had forced through a more varied and more important body of legislation than had any of his predecessors. The New Deal that the Roosevelt administration gave the country was made up in part of measures for recovery and relief, in part of measures for reform; many, to be sure, partook of both purposes, and it is not always possible to determine where recovery left off and reform began. In the realm of relief the government assisted hard-pressed business by Federal loans that soon aggregated billions of dollars. It set on foot a broad and generous program of spending on public works and loans for housing, roads, bridges, and local improvements, in order to stimulate business and provide employment. It set up elaborate systems of unemployment relief and, by 1940, had spent some sixteen billion dollars on direct relief and an additional seven billion on various public works. It inaugurated a far-reaching program for the conservation of natural resources, one of the chief instruments of which was the Civilian Conservation Corps, which gave work to some three million young men. It came to the aid of the railroads, brought about consolidation of facilities, and financed long overdue improvements. It brought order into the chaos of the coal and the oil industries. Through Federal sponsorship of writers' projects, theaters, concerts, and the decoration of public buildings, it gave aid to distressed writers, artists, and musicians, thus greatly enriching the cultural life of the nation. Many of the long-range reforms in the realms of agriculture and industry were designed likewise for relief.

Looking in the direction of permanent reform was much of the banking, water-power, farm, labor, social-security, and political legislation. The New Deal closed the banks and reopened them under stricter supervision and with government guarantees of bank deposits. It abandoned the gold standard and devalued the dollar in order to achieve a mild controlled inflation and thus raise commodity prices. It set up careful control of the selling of stocks and bonds and other securities, and broke up the great holding companies which had obtained control of a large part of the business of supplying the country with electric light and which had often been manipulated for the benefit of a few insiders. It formulated codes of fair practices for business, designed to end wasteful competition. It raised taxes on the income of the rich and of corporations, plugged up loopholes in the tax laws, and cleared up much of the confusion that had long obtained with respect to the taxation policies of state and Federal governments. It erected the Tennessee Valley Authority to develop the resources of one of the great interior basins of the country through the use of government-owned hydroelectric dams and through a broad program of economic and agricultural rehabilitation; this highly successful venture was followed by similar, though less ambitious, ones in the Far West.

Four large fields of New Deal reform merit particular attention: agriculture, labor, social security, and administration. In agriculture the objects were to raise commodity prices to the pre-World War level, to reduce farm production to a point where it would eliminate ruinous surpluses, to encourage the maintenance of soil fertility, to make credit more easily available to farmers, to rescue tenant farmers and those on marginal lands, and to open up new markets abroad and at home for farm products. All of these objectives were in considerable part achieved. An Agricultural Adjustment Act, looking to the voluntary reduction of production of certain staples in return for governmental subsidies, was passed in 1933. It was voided three years later by the Supreme Court, whereupon the Congress passed a second and better farm-relief act. This provided that the government would make money payments to farmers who would devote part of their land to "soil-conserving" crops. By 1940 nearly six million farmers had joined in this program and were receiving subsidies that averaged more than a hundred dollars for each farmer. The new act likewise provided commodity loans on surplus crops, storage facilities to ensure an "ever-normal granary," and insurance for wheat. The resultant decrease in the production of staple crops plus the devaluation of the dollar and the opening up of new markets succeeded in raising the prices of agricultural commodities: by 1939 farm income was more than double what it had been in 1932. A Farm Credit Administration made credit available at almost nominal rates of interest; a Farm Security Administration undertook to finance farm ownership for tenant farmers and the rehabilitation of marginal farmers.

In the field of labor the New Deal enacted a whole series of epoch-making laws. The National Recovery Act of 1933 attempted to spread work, shorten hours, raise wages, and end child labor, guaranteed the right of collective bargaining, and outlawed yellow-dog contracts. It was voided by the Supreme Court in 1935, but its labor provisions were improved upon in two great basic laws: the Wagner Act of 1935 and the Fair Labor Standards Act of 1938. The Wagner Act guaranteed to workers the right to set up and bargain through unions of their own choice, forbade employers to discriminate against any member of a union, and set up a Labor Relations Board to adjudicate all labor disputes. The law aroused violent controversy, but gave labor a squarer deal than it had ever before enjoyed. Under its auspices the old A. F. of L. was revitalized, and a new and vigorous labor organization came into being—the Congress for Industrial Organization. This C.I.O. revived the industrial unionism of the old Knights of Labor and succeeded in organizing the steel, textile, automobile, and other industries heretofore all but invulnerable to unionization. The Fair Labor Standards Act was designed to put "a ceiling over hours and a floor under wages." It fixed forty hours as the normal working week and forty cents an hour as the normal minimum wage, and it outlawed child labor in industrial plants.

Of fundamental importance, too, was legislation to give security to the unemployed, the aged, and the disabled. Up to this time these matters had been left to the states. Some states had enacted effective unemployment insurance and old-age-pension schemes, but it was clear that the states singly were unable to handle the problem, which was, after all, national in dimensions. At the insistence of the President, Congress, in 1935, enacted a series of Social Security Acts providing pensions for the aged, unemployment insurance, benefit payments to the blind, to dependent mothers, and to crippled children, and appropriations to public-health work. These programs were to be financed partly by employers, partly by workers; to be operated by the states and supervised by the Federal government. Notwithstanding widespread initial opposition, the social-security program soon commanded all but universal support, and in subsequent years its provisions were made more generous and its scope was enlarged.

Finally, the Roosevelt administration inaugurated important and far-reaching reforms in administration. The executive department of the government, which had grown in a helter-skelter fashion and which was inefficient and extravagant, was reorganized and reformed. The Hatch Act, perhaps the most important civil-service reform measure since the original act of 1883, prohibited "pernicious political activities" on the part of governmental employees and struck at the corruption and extravagance of political parties. And in 1937 the President, deeply concerned by an unprecedented series of Supreme Court decisions nullifying most of the New Deal measures, proposed a plan to "reform" the Court. The method was to bring about the retirement of aged justices and infuse new blood into the Court; the purpose to persuade the Court to return to the great tradition of Marshall and Story and Holmes—the tradition that interpreted the Constitution as a flexible instrument of government rather than as a barrier to government. Roosevelt's specific proposal was defeated, but his purpose was achieved. The Court, frightened perhaps by criticism and sobered by a realization of its own inadequacy and incompetence, took a more enlightened view of the legislation enacted by the other equal and independent branches of the government, and reversed most of its earlier paralyzing decisions. Not the least of Roosevelt's achievements was this of educating the nation to the real character of the American constitutional system and persuading the Court to accommodate itself to American democracy.

The Shadow of War

Roosevelt's domestic program, like Wilson's, was rudely interrupted by the clamor of foreign affairs, and before his second term was well under way it was clear that international problems would have to take precedence over domestic. Beginning in the twenties and continuing unabated into the thirties the system of collective security which Wilson had so hopefully projected disintegrated. For this breakdown the United States must bear some responsibility. The policy of isolation which she had so confidently embraced deprived the League of the moral and practical support of the greatest and most independent of world powers; tariff policies contributed to world economic collapse; withdrawal from the Far East appeared to invite a continuation of Japanese aggression; and agitation for disarmament discouraged a realistic attitude toward the problems of naval and military preparedness among the democracies.

The roots of the Second World War go deep down into the decade of the twenties. Japan felt that the League of Nations had slammed shut the door to further expansion and resented the power of Britain and the United States in the Orient. Italy was discontented with the fruits of her belated participation on the side of the Allies, and her new swashbuckling leader, Benito Mussolini, hungered and thirsted after glory. Germany was resentful of defeat and restless under the restrictions of the Versailles Treaty. Economic depression, the pressure of growing populations, social confusion and demoralization, all prepared the way for new leaders impatient with the slow processes of peaceful readjustment and for new philosophies which challenged the assumptions and conclusions of the old. Japan, to be sure, had little need for a new philosophy; she needed only weapons with which to implement the old. Italy turned to Fascism. Germany, after a decade of confusion, permitted a fanatical Austrian veteran of the first war, Adolf Hitler, to organize a revolutionary National Socialist party and seize the reins of government. By the early thirties all three nations had organized totalitarian governments and all three were prepared to repudiate not only the

Versailles and subsequent treaties, but the whole structure of international law and order.

Thereafter events moved with breath-taking speed. Each of the totalitarian powers, in turn, seized the aggressive. Each built up its military machine, threatened its weaker neighbors, embarked upon imperialistic ventures. Most of these ventures were rationalized on plausible grounds and carried through in a manner that greatly enhanced the prestige of the aggressors but did not challenge too sharply the opposition of the democratic powers. Japan, in 1931, invaded Manchuria and set up the puppet state of Manchukuo, from which vantage point she flanked Siberian Russia to the north, China to the south. Italy, which had already consolidated her position in the Dodecanese, seized Fiume, and enlarged her boundaries in Libya, inaugurated the revival of the Roman Empire by warring on Ethiopia and in 1935–1936 reduced that backward but valuable country to subjection. Germany repudiated the Versailles Treaty, reoccupied the Rhineland, and boldly undertook large-scale rearmament. The League protested, diplomats deplored, and democratic leaders declaimed, but no nation or group of nations interposed an effective barrier to totalitarian ambitions.

Most Americans watched these developments with indifference—indifference tinged, to be sure, with disapproval. This was, they felt sure, just another chapter in the age-old story of rival imperialisms. No more than most Englishmen did they understand the revolutionary nature of the forces now unleashed in the world. They did not realize that they were confronted here with a menace more dangerous, more explosive, than any before in modern history. They congratulated themselves, rather, that they were safely out of it all, protected by two great oceans, self-sufficient, rich, and powerful.

It was indeed difficult for most Americans to understand the real nature of the threat that hung over them and over the whole world. It was no mere military threat. The United States had met military threats before and emerged triumphant. It was a new thing, new and incomprehensible. Americans are an easygoing people, have never known defeat or demoralization; the notion of evil, as Santayana has observed, is foreign to the American mind. They could not believe that a new philosophy had emerged which repudiated and warred on their way of life and their system of values.

The core of the American, and of the English, philosophy of government is the individual. The individual is the source of government. He has rights and liberties in society: the right to worship as he will, to speak and to write, to go about his own business, choose his own work, marry whom he will, rear his family as he will, undisturbed by the state. No matter how socialized our thinking, our administration, or our business has become, it is still true that the ultimate objective of our government and of our economy is the creation and protection of the free man.

To this philosophy totalitarianism, as practiced by Italy, Germany, and Japan, opposed one diametrically different. Totalitarian philosophy subordinated the individual to the state or to the race. In the Fascist and Nazi systems the individual was relatively unimportant, his liberties, his rights, his property, his ambitions and hopes, his social and family relationships, insignificant.

This profound difference in the attitude toward the relation between individual and state affected the whole system of values to which democrats and Fascists subscribed. Democracy appeals to reason, Fascism to authority; democracy depends upon co-operation, Fascism upon obedience; democracy has faith in education and in the ultimate triumph of truth; Fascism perverts education to propaganda and truth to national or party purposes; democracy exalts tolerance, Fascism exploits intolerance; democracy practices fair play, Fascism treachery and terror. The ends, too, are profoundly different. The end of democracy is the free man in a free society, the well-being and happiness of the individual. The end of Fascism is the power, wealth, glory of the state or of the party or of the master race.

As the real nature of totalitarianism became clear, Americans grew increasingly apprehensive, and as Germany, Italy, and Japan renewed their aggressions, striking down one smaller nation after another, apprehension turned to indignation. In 1936–1938 came the martyrdom of Spain, where the armies and planes of Mussolini and Hitler aided the Nationalists in overthrowing the Republican regime, while the democracies stood by, paralyzed with indecision. Even as the victorious foreign legions were battering at the gates of Madrid, Japan precipitated the "China incident" which was to drag out for many years until it merged into a general world war. In 1938 came Hitler's violent incorporation of Austria into the Reich, and the Greater Germany was under way. Czechoslovakia was next, and before the democracies had recovered from the shock of the Austrian annexation, Hitler was demanding the cession of the Sudeten region of the little democracy which Britain and the United States had helped create. Frightened, the leaders of Britain and France appealed for an arbitration of the issue. When arbitration was rejected, Mr. Chamberlain flew to Munich and there surrendered Czechoslovakia to the German war lords. "It is peace in our time," said Chamberlain on his return, but Winston Churchill said, "Britain and France had to choose between war and dishonor. They chose dishonor. They will have war."

The American reaction to all this was not one which future generations will recall with pride. Disillusioned with the results of the last war, fearful of involvement in a new one, confident that any decision as to war or peace lay entirely in their own hands, they adopted a policy of peace at any price. They hastily abandoned many of those rights which their fathers and forefathers had twice fought to preserve, and announced to the world that in no circumstances could any belligerent, victim or aggressor, look to them for aid. All this was embodied in the neutrality legislation of 1935–1937 which prohibited trade with or credit to any belligerent.

President Roosevelt had from the first disapproved of this legislation, and so too had his Secretary of State, Cordell Hull. Roosevelt now set himself to instill in the American people a realization of the nature of the thing that was abroad in the world, and to arm America, morally and materially, to meet and overcome it. Speaking at Chicago in 1937 he called for a moral quarantine against aggressor nations, only to be met with the charge that he was playing politics. He denounced Japanese aggression in China, built up friendly relations with Latin American countries and with Canada, and urged upon Congress the imperative necessity of larger appropriations for arms. "Peace by fear," he warned the dictators, "has no higher or more enduring quality than peace by the sword," and he refused to confess fear or to be intimidated by force. As the totalitarian policy became more aggressive, the American spirit hardened against it.

War

Britain too, humiliated by Munich and outraged by the subsequent destruction of Czechoslovakia, was feverishly rearming, for it was clear, at last, that the policy of appeasement was bankrupt. But Hitler did not choose to wait until Britain and the United States had achieved military equality with Germany. All through the spring and summer of 1939 he thundered against Poland, demanding the cession of Danzig and the Polish Corridor; his position was immeasureably strengthened when, in midsummer, he concluded an alliance with the most powerful of Continental nations, Russia. Then, even while negotiations with Poland were still under way, Hitler struck. On September 1, his armies rolled across the frontier while his planes rained death and destruction upon Polish cities. Two days later Britain and France, faithful to their commitments, declared war upon Germany.

In two weeks Germany had overrun Poland, Russia advancing from the east to complete the conquest of the hapless nation. Then ensued a long stalemate, which many Americans fatuously characterized as a "phony" war. By spring Hitler was ready for the second round. Without warning, his armies moved into Denmark and on to Norway. The British attempt to rush aid to the sturdy Norse ended in failure, and within little more than a month the resources of all Scandinavia were in German control. On May 10 Germany turned westward and struck at neutral Holland and Belgium and at France. The *Blitzkrieg* lasted a little over a month, and when it was over Holland had been conquered, the Belgian army had surrendered, and France itself had fallen, while a British Expeditionary Force, hastily rushed across the Channel, was rescued only by a miracle of energy and heroism.

Britain stood alone. But it was no longer the Britain of Munich or Britain of the futile Norwegian campaign. It was a Britain that remembered that for a thousand years no invader had ruled her soil. "Come three corners of the world in arms, and we shall shock them," Shakespeare had boasted, and the proud boast was echoed now by Winston

Churchill, the great leader into whose hands had been entrusted the destiny of the nation and of the cause of freedom:

> We shall prove ourselves once again able to defend our island home, to ride out the storm of war, and to outlive the menace of tyranny, if necessary for years, if necessary alone. . . . Even though large tracts of Europe and many old and famous states have fallen or may fall into the grip of the Gestapo and all the odious apparatus of Nazi rule, we shall not flag or fail, we shall go on to the end, we shall fight in France, we shall fight on the seas and oceans, we shall fight with growing confidence and growing strength in the air, we shall defend our island, whatever the cost may be, we shall fight on the beaches, we shall fight on the landing grounds, we shall fight in the fields and in the streets, we shall fight in the hills; we shall never surrender, and even if, which I do not for a moment believe, this island or a large part of it were subjugated and starving, then our Empire beyond the seas, armed and guarded by the British fleet, would carry on the struggle, until, in God's good time, the New World, with all its power and might, steps forth to the rescue and liberation of the Old.

"In God's good time"—but when would it be? The attack on Poland had precipitated the greatest debate since slavery days, carried on not only in the halls of Congress, but in every newspaper, in every public hall, in every home in the land. Roosevelt moved energetically for the repeal of the neutrality legislation and, after prolonged discussion, he was able to wrest from a reluctant Congress the "cash-and-carry" legislation which did, at least, make American resources available to the fighting democracies. The fall of France convinced most Americans at last of the might of

Photo Wide World Photos Inc.

THE ATLANTIC CHARTER

PRESIDENT ROOSEVELT AND PRIME MINISTER CHURCHILL
CONFERRING ON BOARD SHIP

the German military machine, and the air attack upon Britain that summer and fall brought home to them the realization that if Britain fell America would stand alone against the most formidable military coalition in history.

Confronted with this possibility, Congress voted astronomical sums for rearmament, an agreement was reached with the Latin American republics extending collective protection to the possessions of the democratic nations in the New World, the United States and Canada set up a joint Board of Defense, and peacetime conscription with military training for almost a million men was inaugurated. More important even than these moves was the dramatic agreement between Roosevelt and Churchill whereby, in return for fifty overage destroyers, Britain leased to the United States a series of naval bases extending from Newfoundland to British Guiana. It was, said Roosevelt, the most important step in our national defense since the Louisiana Purchase, and Churchill added that "these two great organizations of the English-speaking democracies, the British Empire and the United States, will have to be somewhat mixed up together in some of their affairs for mutual and general advantage." It was a prophetic observation.

Roosevelt had mapped out the course which the nation would follow: would he be able to hold it to that course? In the summer of 1940 the American people were called upon to choose a President who would guide them through the dangerous years ahead. The Democrats, boldly abandoning the antithird-term tradition, once more named Franklin Roosevelt their candidate. The Republicans, meeting in an atmosphere of confusion, selected a newcomer to politics, Wendell Willkie of Indiana and New York. The Democratic party and its leader had committed themselves irrevocably to the policy of aid to Britain—a policy which might well lead to war. Would the Republican party and

The UNITED STATES IN

SHOWING LEND-LEASE BASES,
STRATEGIC POINTS ON THE

THE SECOND WORLD WAR

MILITARY OUTPOSTS AND
WORLD-WIDE SUPPLY LINES

the new, inexperienced candidate espouse the opposite policy? Willkie attacked the New Deal on its domestic side, but resolutely refused to play politics with the issue of aid to Britain. Indeed, on this crucial issue he ranged himself on the side of the President, supported conscription, applauded the destroyer deal, and promised, if elected, that there would be no turning back on the road which the President had marked out and the Congress followed. It was a great and statesmanlike decision and it revealed that in Wendell Willkie the Republican party had at last found a leader of courage, wisdom, and vision.

In the November elections Roosevelt was re-elected and, confident now of popular support, pushed vigorously ahead with his policies. When the Congress met in January he presented it with a proposal designed to circumvent the remaining limitations of the neutrality legislation—the lend-lease bill. This measure provided that the United States might lend or lease any defense articles or facilities to any nation whose defense was vital to that of the United States. After protracted debate the measure was passed, and under its wise provisions a stream of planes, tanks, raw materials, foodstuffs, and other articles began to flow across to Britain and her allies. This measure was clearly unneutral, but the United States, committed now to the defeat of Germany, was not to be stayed by the niceties of international law. Other equally unneutral acts followed— the seizure of Axis shipping, the freezing of Axis funds, the transfer of tankers to Britain, the occupation of Greenland and, later, of Iceland, the extension of lend-lease to the new ally, Russia, and—eventually, after a series of U-boat attacks on American shipping—the presidential order to "shoot on sight" any enemy submarines.

Scarcely less important than these material contributions to the cause of the fighting democracies was the formulation of democratic war aims. On August 14 Roosevelt and Churchill met in mid-Atlantic and there drew up the Atlantic Charter, containing certain principles upon which they based "their hopes for a better future for the world." These principles were: no territorial aggrandizement; no territorial changes that do not accord with the wishes of the people involved; the right of all people to choose their own form of government; the enjoyment by all states of access to trade and raw materials; economic collaboration between nations; freedom of the seas; and the abandonment of the use of force as an instrument of international relations. Here were Wilson's Fourteen Points in new, and simpler, dress.

It seemed as if the United States might drift into war with Germany, but it seemed, too, as if that drift might be a prolonged one. The United States had made its decision, but was not yet bold enough to submit it to the fortunes of war. Meantime tension mounted in the Far East. Japan had already formally joined the Axis and now, taking advantage of British and American involvement in the European war, was pushing boldly ahead with her "New Order"—an order in which the Nipponese were to rule the entire Orient and the Pacific as well. A policy of appeasement having proved futile, both Britain and the United States adopted toward Japan a more resolute attitude. This was equally futile. The Japanese war lords were in control now, they had tasted victory, they were confident of greater victories ahead. In November, while the Russians were battling heroically before Moscow and Leningrad and the British fighting the battle of the Atlantic, Japan poured troops into French Indo-China and prepared air bases along the border of Thailand. On December 6 the situation was so critical that President Roosevelt addressed a personal appeal to the Emperor of Japan to join in arriving at a solution which would maintain the peace.

It is improbable that the Emperor ever received this message. For Japan was ready now for the most desperate throw of the dice in modern history. On Sunday, December 7, she struck with devastating ferocity at American outposts in Hawaii, Guam, Midway, Wake, and the Philippines. War had come.

Eighty years ago the poet of democracy, Walt Whitman, had written:

> *Long, too long America,*
> *Traveling roads all even and peaceful you learn'd from*
> *joys and prosperity only,*
> *But now, ah now, to learn from crises of anguish, ad-*
> *vancing, grappling with direst fate and recoiling now,*
> *And not to conceive and show to the world what your*
> *children en-masse really are.*

In that great Civil War of which Whitman wrote, America had shown to the world what her children really were. She had seemed then, in Lincoln's stately phrase, "the last best hope of earth." Now once more she was vouchsafed the opportunity to show to the world what her children really were, once more the opportunity to fulfill her destiny as the "best hope of earth," to vindicate her title to a nation of freemen.

INDEX

493